Dispossession without Development

Land Grabs in Neoliberal India

MICHAEL LEVIEN

OXFORD
UNIVERSITY PRESS

OXFORD
UNIVERSITY PRESS

Oxford University Press is a department of the University of Oxford. It furthers the University's objective of excellence in research, scholarship, and education by publishing worldwide. Oxford is a registered trade mark of Oxford University Press in the UK and certain other countries.

Published in the United States of America by Oxford University Press
198 Madison Avenue, New York, NY 10016, United States of America.

Library of Congress Cataloging-in-Publication Data
Names: Levien, Michael, author.
Title: Dispossession without development : land grabs in neoliberal India / Michael Levien.
Description: New York City : Oxford University Press, [2018] | Includes bibliographical references.
Identifiers: LCCN 2017036637 (print) | LCCN 2017050010 (ebook) |
ISBN 9780190859176 (updf) | ISBN 9780190859183 (epub) |
ISBN 9780190859152 (hbk) | ISBN 9780190859169 (pbk)
Subjects: LCSH: Land reform—India. | Economic development—India.
Classification: LCC HD1333.I4 (ebook) | LCC HD1333.I4 L48 2018 (print) |
DDC 333.3/154—dc23
LC record available at https://lccn.loc.gov/2017036637

Dispossession without Development

MODERN SOUTH ASIA

The Other One Percent
Sanjoy Chakravorty, Devesh Kapur, and Nirvikar Singh

Social Justice through Inclusion
Francesca R. Jensenius

The Man Who Remade India
Vinay Sitapati

To Ismay Lirette and the memory of Druis Lirette (Mamaw and Papaw)

Between the simple backward look and the simple progressive thrust there is room for long argument but none for enlightenment. We must begin differently: not in the idealization of one order or another but in the history to which they are only partial and misleading responses.

—Raymond Williams, *The Country and the City* (1985: 37)

CONTENTS

PREFACE: FROM NARMADA TO RAJPURA

In August 2004, I watched the monsoon rains gather behind the newly raised Sardar Sarovar Dam in central India and flood hundreds of families from their homes. Although India was already over a decade into economic liberalization, large public-sector dams were still the most potent symbols of what was often called "development-induced displacement." Since Independence in 1947, the Indian state had uprooted tens of millions of people from their land for projects of economic modernization. Large dams were the single largest cause. The victims were disproportionately indigenous groups living in remote river valleys that made for ideal dam sites. And they were almost always brutally impoverished by their dispossession. India's postcolonial leaders were, nevertheless, fairly successful in legitimizing this large-scale dispossession as the inevitable and necessary cost of development; over three decades elapsed before popular struggles began to seriously challenge this practice.

From the 1980s onward, the Narmada Bachao Andolan (NBA), the people's movement against large dams in the Narmada Valley, helped pioneer anti-dispossession politics in India. Its innovative tactics, like refusing to vacate flooding villages, and its defiant slogans—such as "no one will be moved, the dam will not be built" and "we want development not destruction"—inspired anti-dispossession movements across India and the world. Nevertheless, these movements—along with those opposing other public-sector projects—faced an uphill battle. Tarnished as "anti-development" and even "anti-national," they were ignored by political parties and rarely succeeded in preventing dispossession. Witnessing the devastation of villages that had fought the Indian state for two decades also made me wonder whether dispossession was, indeed, unstoppable.

I was astonished, then, when just a few years later farmer protests were stopping dozens of mega-projects and "land grabs" were at the center of Indian politics. Just as India's heated economic boom was hitting its peak during the mid-2000s, a new constellation of land struggles emerged. In contrast to the anti-dam struggles, many were located in the plains rather than forests and river valleys; and their targets now included large private investments: hi-tech parks, real estate colonies, privatized infrastructure, and factories for multinational corporations. Above all, the Indian government's post-2000 strategy of promoting privately developed Special Economic Zones (SEZs) proved to be explosive. Attempts by state governments to transfer large chunks of rural land to private developers for hundreds of SEZs unleashed widespread and militant farmer protest across the country.

On March 14, 2007, India's simmering land conflicts burst into the national spotlight. In an orchestrated early morning attack, police and party cadre of West Bengal's Left Front government—led by the Communist Party of India (Marxist)—massacred fourteen farmers and raped and assaulted many more in a collection of villages called Nandigram. The mostly Muslim and lower-caste Hindu paddy farmers of Nandigram had been refusing to relinquish their land for a private SEZ promoted by the Salim Group of Indonesia. The ensuing uproar shook the West Bengal government, which came under attack by the media, civil society organizations, and opposition parties at the state and national levels. On the defensive, the Left Front not only abandoned the project but suffered grave political damage, which contributed to its subsequent defeat in the 2009 local elections and, after thirty-four years of continuous rule, its ultimate ousting from state power in 2011 (Bag 2011). The national government, for its part, felt compelled to issue a temporary moratorium on land acquisition for SEZs, to reduce their maximum size, and to introduce amendments to India's Land Acquisition Act (LAA) that would provide greater compensation to farmers.

Meanwhile, so-called "land wars" appeared to be springing up everywhere, thrusting the names of previously obscure villages into the popular lexicon. The most astonishing feature of these conflicts was that farmers were winning many of them. Militant farmer resistance in peri-urban Mumbai and Gurgaon forced India's largest private company, Reliance Industries, to abandon its two proposed mega-SEZs. In coastal Odisha, several villages of forest cultivators held up India's largest proposed Foreign Direct Investment to date—a twelve-million-ton steel plant and captive port of South Korea's Pohang Steel Company (POSCO)—with bamboo barricades and human chains. In Singur, West Bengal, farmers thwarted the car factory that was to build Tata Motors' much-hyped "Nano." In Western Uttar Pradesh, farmers engaged in a gun battle over land acquisition for the privately built Yamuna Expressway, which included upscale real estate development and a Formula 1 racetrack. SEZs were facing stiff opposition near Mangalore, Hyderabad, Pune, Chandigarh, and coastal Andhra Pradesh. A statewide opposition movement led to the cancelation of all proposed SEZs in Goa (Da Silva 2014; Sampat 2015). Even in Gujarat, often heralded as a pro-business state that could get the job done for industry, SEZs were facing resistance and substantial delays (Asher 2014; Arora 2009; *DNA* 2010). Beneath the more visible conflicts, government agencies were besieged by prosaic legal challenges to almost every project they undertook. On top of this, India was facing a growing Maoist insurgency that controlled large swaths of mineral-rich territory from Andhra Pradesh to Nepal, and that, by the government's own assessment, was being fueled by land dispossession for private mining and industry (Government of India 2008: 50). The international press took notice of India's land acquisition woes, offering headlines such as: "India Grapples with How to Convert Its Farmland into Factories" (Sengupta 2008); "India's Biggest Industrial Barrier? Farmers" (Chopra 2008); "India's Divisive Economic Zones" (*BBC* 2008); and "In India, Fresh Clashes over Rural Land as Farmers Stand Up to Government" (Denyer 2011).

By the end of the 2000s, this widespread opposition to land dispossession was taking its economic toll. The vast majority of approved SEZs had yet to be built (PWC-Assocham 2009). Delays plagued roads, power plants, and other infrastructure projects. As India's growth slackened in the aftermath of the global financial crisis, Prime Minister Manmohan Singh argued that the timely completion of infrastructure projects was a top priority, and the government's annual economic survey proclaimed "the urgent need to streamline land acquisition and environmental clearance" (*Economic Times* 2011). But doing so was no easy matter; as the pro-liberalization prime minister recognized, land acquisition had become "a very sensitive issue" (*DNA* 2011). As farmers made it increasingly difficult for the state to transfer land to private industry, private industry protested that farmers were becoming the largest obstacle to India's emergence as a "world class" economic power. Having committed itself to private sector–led growth, the Indian government was thus faced with a problem: how, under the auspices of an electoral democracy, could it acquire large amounts of land from farmers for large private corporations? Land dispossession was no longer a marginal issue taken up by isolated social movements but was at the center of Indian politics. And it has remained there as a new BJP government has struggled to aggressively promote private sector growth while avoiding the electoral wrath of farmers.

India's "land wars" were, for me, an indication that something very significant had changed in the relationship between land dispossession and capitalism in post-liberalization India. This book is an effort to understand that change. Modernization theorists and Marxists alike had long seen the disappearance of the peasantry as inevitable and progressive: the former as a necessary cost of development and the latter as a stage in the transition to capitalism and, ultimately, socialism. India's farmers, however, appeared to be calling the "inevitability" of their dispossession into question. Were they merely "backward-looking" saboteurs of economic progress? Or did anti-dispossession movements represent a radical defense of rural communities against the predations of state and capital? Fierce debates were occurring in the Indian public sphere over these questions. But these debates remained largely speculative and trapped in the binary framework that pits modernization against peasant romanticism. Although a raft of studies existed on the effects of large dams and public-sector infrastructure on displaced populations, there were as yet no studies of these new SEZs that could help us to answer the question: How had dispossession and its consequences changed in post-liberalization India? Answering this required, I concluded, studying an already dispossessed village. I thus decided to go in the opposite direction of the cameras and activists: to where opposition had not emerged or succeeded. Rather than a stalled SEZ, I began to search for a functioning one.

My search eventually led me to a village in Northwest India that I call Rajpura. Located 25 km from Jaipur, the state capital of Rajasthan, Rajpura is a large multi-caste village whose economy was, until 2005, largely based on dryland agriculture and animal husbandry. In that year, Rajpura became one of nine villages to have its farmland and grazing commons—3,000 acres in all—dispossessed for the Mahindra World City (MWC). One of the first private SEZs established in North India, the MWC was marketed as the largest Information Technology SEZ in India and one of the largest private investments in Rajasthan's history. When I arrived in 2009—and as "land wars" continued to sink SEZs across India—the MWC was up and running, with campuses for Infosys and Deutsche Bank already operational. The Indian media heralded it as a rare case of SEZ "success" that had given a "fair deal" to farmers (*NDTV* 2008). I set out to examine the nature of this success.

Interviewing government officials and company executives proved fairly easy, but it took over a month of persistent inquiries before a sociology graduate student at Rajasthan University, named Omprakash Choudhary, provided me with an entrée to the village. Omprakash's distant relative by marriage was a sharply dressed young man named Rajesh Choudhary whose family still owned a significant amount of land in Rajpura. Rajesh agreed to drive me there and provide introductions.

The first leg from Jaipur was a smooth ride along National Highway 8, which had just been widened to six lanes as part of India's "Golden Quadrilateral" highway modernization project. Peri-urban sprawl eventually gave way to tan-orange fields of millet stubble, broken periodically by clusters of metal-shuttered concrete shops. At the 20-km mark, a blue sign pointed left for the Mahindra World City. The rutted country road, which still provided the only access to the SEZ, passed two villages with a few more small shops and concrete houses than one might expect. Most notable were the omnipresent signs of a recent land boom. Faded advertisements for property dealers were plastered on brick walls, telephone poles, and concrete buildings. At the intersection with a half-constructed radial road, we passed the ornate entrance to an upscale residential colony that, I learned, was a joint venture between a large Delhi-based real estate firm and Dubai-based Emaar, builder of the Burj Khalifa, the world's tallest building. Inside a vaguely Mediterranean entryway, goats grazed on a vacant expanse of land. A few kilometers later, sleek office buildings for Infosys and Deutche Bank rose like Oz above the arid Rajasthan countryside. A sign welcomed us to the Mahindra World City; a ten-foot boundary wall, barbed wire fencing, and a guarded checkpoint sent a more ambiguous message. We continued past the SEZ and into Rajpura.

Our first stop was the house of Lalaram Choudhary in a small *dhani* (hamlet) outside the main village. Lalaram was from the same agriculturally dominant Jat caste as Rajesh and had clearly been doing well since the SEZ's arrival. His home was strikingly built of concrete and marble, with an incongruous tinted glass door typical of city shops. An SUV was parked inside his walled compound. Sitting on plastic chairs, Lalaram explained that half of his 16 *bighas* (4 hectares) of land had been expropriated by the government for the SEZ. Under the Rajasthan government's compensation policy, he was allotted small residential and commercial plots adjacent to the SEZ that were one-fourth the size of his previous land. This policy, I had learned in Jaipur, was the Rajasthan government's way of making land acquisition more attractive to farmers. Instead of the usual fixed—and invariably low—cash compensation, it gave farmers a stake in subsequent land appreciation. Lalaram considered this a good deal because land values had already greatly multiplied, and he predicted that they would increase more as the SEZ developed. Agriculture was, anyway, "weak" and "not very profitable" due to lack of water. Lalaram's only criticism was that the SEZ was not providing local people with employment. Still, he felt it was "good for the village." "There will be a benefit," he predicted. "I have no complaints."

I left Lalaram's house puzzled. If he had not yet sold his compensation plots, was unemployed, and agriculture was unprofitable, how, I asked my companions, did he acquire the big house and SUV? With a chuckle, Rajesh and Omprakash explained that Lalaram was a land broker (*dalal* in Hindi). When the SEZ unleashed a land boom in the surrounding villages, many farmers like Lalaram became property brokers, facilitating land sales between fellow villagers and outsider investors for commission. "Everyone [here] is a broker," joked Omprakash. By "everyone," I thought Omprakash was just exaggerating the number of farmers-turned-brokers in the village. Later, I realized he may have been referring to himself and Rajesh. Rajesh's family had sold some of their land in Rajpura and he and his younger brother had entered the real estate business. Omprakash, son of a mid-level officer in the Rajasthan police, was looking for more lucrative opportunities than a sociology PhD, which he considered a "time pass." I had entered the village, I belatedly realized, through the very social networks that enabled better-off farmers like Lalaram to profit massively from the SEZ-induced real estate boom.

Despite having entered Rajpura through its contented brokers, I quickly met extremely disgruntled farmers. Sitting with a mixed-caste group of villagers on stools in a motorcycle repair shop as Rajesh saw to business, I explained that I wanted to study what changes had occurred in the village because of the SEZ, and what "benefits" and "losses" they had experienced. They immediately made it clear that they had received no benefit from the SEZ, "only loss and more loss." The government (*sarkaar*) had not only taken all of their farmland but had enclosed their 1,000-acre grazing land and transferred it to Mahindra, depriving them of fodder and forcing them to sell their profitable milk-producing livestock. On top of this, the SEZ was not providing local people with jobs, leaving them unemployed. It was only "outsiders," brokers, and the village *sarpanch* (elected headman), they insisted, who had received any benefit.

These early interviews in Rajpura pointed toward deep divisions and complex inequalities that would take time to unravel. Most immediately, these divisions shaped my attempt to find housing. After two more day trips, I managed to secure a room to rent. This also came through the local elite who, as I would observe, were very good at capturing anything of value that entered the village: whether land values, development funds, or a sociologist. Hanuman Choudhary, another Jat broker from Rajpura, put me in touch with a political and business acquaintance in the nearby village of Shivpura who had a room to spare. Eager for any foothold in the village, I accepted sight unseen and arrived several weeks later at the expansive compound of Bansilal Sharma.

Bansilal, I learned upon arrival, was the former Brahmin *sarpanch* of Shivpura, was well-established in the Congress Party, and had a prospering dairy business in Jaipur. Smaller and relatively tranquil compared to Rajpura with its bustling market, Shivpura was a predominantly Brahmin village. I had a room to myself in Bansilal's joint-family compound, and the food was excellent: twice a day Bansilal's sister- and daughter-in-law served me meals—which I ate alone—consisting of several *sabzis* (vegetable dishes), curd, buttermilk, and *rotis* (flatbread) slathered with homemade *ghee* (clarified butter). Bansilal, along with most of his brothers, sons, and nephews, left early in the morning to attend to business or studies in Jaipur, and I spent the days making conversation at *chai* stalls and walking through the village, which was bordered on one side by the SEZ and two others by hardly built upscale residential colonies. Most of the village's Brahmins were shrewdly maximizing their real estate gains and many had become brokers. But the young men milling about the village, some with BAs, were very disgruntled about their inability to find good jobs.

While materially comfortable, a *sarpanch's* house in a Brahmin village was sociologically unsatisfactory. After a month of gathering valuable data on how the SEZ was experienced by the relatively well-heeled upper castes, I extracted myself from Bansilal with the help of Aseem Sharma, the headmaster of the private "English Medium" primary school in Shivpura. Although Aseem could not understand why I would want to live in less comfortable circumstances, he put me in touch with the father of three of his Dalit pupils from Rajpura.

Lada and Mahesh Bunkar and their three young children lived in one of two caste-segregated alleys (*mohallas*) occupied by the Balai subcaste. Rajpura's various caste *mohallas* spread outward in a roughly discernible hierarchy from the old sandstone fort of the Rajput *thakur*—Rajpura's ruler-landlord until India's Independence in 1947. While many Jat and Brahmin families lived near their farmland in small outlying *dhanis*, the nuclear village was densely settled by the various "service castes." The Balais were historically an "untouchable" caste but ranked slightly above the village's two other main Dalit subcastes—the Regars who lived on the far West side of the village, and the Sangats (sweepers) who lived on the far East. Before the SEZ's arrival, Balais were mostly small cultivators and laborers. Mahesh and Lada's *mohalla* of twenty-two families from two lineages was nestled behind the fort, facing the stone latrines built into its back wall.

A storage room in Mahesh and Lada's house became my home for the remainder of my fieldwork. Constructed with compensation money only a few years before, the house was concrete but already showing signs of wear; peeling plaster, malfunctioning circuits, broken ceiling fans, and mildewing walls. In much more straitened circumstances than Bansilal, Lada and Mahesh had both gained and lost from the SEZ, which, as subsequent chapters will show, launched them on a very precarious and ambivalent trajectory. While their gains included a concrete (*pukka*) house, TV, refrigerator, and motorcycle, they had very little income and were falling back into debt. Their loss of farmland and livestock was visible in their poor diet of dry *roti* (flatbread) and watery *sabzi* (vegetable dish), which lacked the milk, buttermilk, curd, and clarified butter that were in such abundance at Bansilal's. They rarely ate *daal* (lentils), except when I bought it, and the lack of protein was visible in the undernourishment of their children. We did eat together, and in Lada and Mahesh's family I found a home of sorts—one not uncomplicated by our vastly different resources and the role my rent played in their struggle to make ends meet.

With the Balai *mohalla* as my base, I set out to untangle the complex story of how Rajpura's various inhabitants were navigating post-SEZ life. In following their lives over the next thirteen months—and several revisits over the following years—disparate stories began to slowly form a coherent pattern. This pattern of change was strange, seemed without precedent in the annals of village studies, and did not fit well with existing theories of dispossession. It was driven, I came to see, from the interaction of a radically new regime of dispossession and the specific inequalities of a non-idyllic rural order.

ACKNOWLEDGMENTS

In "Rajpura," I watched the melancholy and often tragic aftermath of dispossession play out in the lives of many people. My responsibility to protect their anonymity prevents me from mentioning their real names here. But their stories make this book, and I am deeply grateful for their time and the countless cups of *chai* and *chaach* they forced upon me. My deepest gratitude goes to "Lada" and "Mahesh" and their three children. I hope that some of my predictions are wrong, and that life in Rajpura takes a turn for the better, particularly for the proletarianized and excluded.

My first tutorial in the politics of dispossession took place in the very different context of the Narmada Valley, where I learned a great deal from the many people who had been struggling there for twenty-five years. Although the dam was built, the repercussions of that struggle continue to reverberate. I am one of many to have taken inspiration from it.

A number of other villages across India allowed me to learn about their struggles for shorter periods of time. I thank the people in Jagatsinghpur, Odisha; Polepally, Telengana; Tada, Andhra Pradesh; Nandigram and Singur, West Bengal; Kerim, Goa; Sadhopur and Dadri, Uttar Pradesh; Gorai and Karla, Maharashtra; and in the villages surrounding the Mangalore SEZ in Karnataka for taking the time to speak with me. Amita Bag, Vidya Dinker, Sampat Kale, Ulka Mahajan, Prashant Paikray, Sudhir Patnaik, Prafulla Samantray, Sujatha Surepally, and Usha Seethalakshmi provided much appreciated insight on these struggles. The "People's Audits of SEZs," organized by Preeti Sampat, were both important and informative. I also thank the many government officials, corporate executives, and industry representatives who took the time to speak with me, even though some may not agree with the book's conclusions.

In Rajasthan, the Mazdoor Kisan Shakti Sangathan (MKSS), including Nikhil Dey, Mukesh Goswami, Aruna Roy, and Shankar Singh, not only shared their considerable insight into rural Rajasthan but provided inspiration among depressing circumstances. In Jaipur, I am also grateful to the Institute of Development Studies for several good discussions and occasional use of their library; and the teachers at the American Institute of Indian Studies for helping to improve my Hindi.

This project was funded by an International Dissertation Research Fellowship from the Social Science Research Council, a Simpson Memorial Research Fellowship from the Institute of International Studies at U.C. Berkeley, a Leo Lowenthal Fellowship from the Department of Sociology at U.C. Berkeley, a dissertation fellowship from the Northern California Association of Phi Beta Kappa, and a small grant from the Land Deal Politics Initiative. The Institute of Economic Growth in Delhi generously offered me affiliation during my fieldwork and invited me back for a productive visiting professorship in the summer of 2014.

My interest in dispossession became a sociology of dispossession at Berkeley, where I had the great privilege of learning the vocation from Michael Burawoy. Above all, I am deeply grateful for his unreasonable generosity, penetrating criticism, and unfaltering faith in this project. Raka Ray has been an all-around exceptional mentor since I first walked into her office. Peter Evans' seminars and expansive intellect greatly advanced my thinking about development. Michael Watts has been a unique guide to the study of dispossession and agrarian change; many of the ideas in this book were first developed in his "Primitive Accumulation" seminar. Gill Hart has been an extremely generous and insightful interlocutor. Usha Jain was a tough and venerable Hindi teacher. My friends and fellow graduate students at Berkeley provided the rich intellectual milieu in which this project could grow, and made it all very fun. Abigail Andrews, Ariel Aron, Dan Buch, Ryan Calder, Jennifer Carlson, Jia-Ching Chen, Julia Chuang, Fidan Elcioglu, Eli Friedman, Asher Ghertner, Daniel Immerwahr, Zach Levenson, Marcel Paret, Fareen Parvez, and Alina Polyakova deserve special mention.

Amita Baviskar provided invaluable advice throughout every stage of this project, and graciously sponsored my affiliation with the Institute of Economic Growth. In the great intellectual hub of Delhi, I have benefited from numerous conversations with Susana Barria, Amit Bhaduri, Benny Kuruvilla, V.R. Lenin, Harsh Mander, Diya Mehra, Arup Mitra, Shekhar Singh, and Aseem Srivastava. Satendra Kumar has, in particular, been a good friend and an inspiring intellectual comrade. I have also learned much about dispossession from many individuals involved in the National Alliance of People's Movements. In particular, I wish to thank Mukta Srivastava for being a friend and mentor for almost fifteen years.

A number of people heroically commented upon this entire manuscript: Samantha Agarwal, Joel Andreas, Abigail Andrews, Nina Aron, Amita Baviskar, Michael Burawoy, Phil Campanile, Jia-Ching Chen, Brett Christophers, Madeleine Fairbairn, Patrick Heller, Ho-fung Hung, Suchi Pande, Marcel Paret, Fareen Parvez, Raka Ray, and Beverly Silver. Graduate students in seminars at the

Institute of Social Studies in The Hague and the geography department at Penn State also provided valuable feedback on the entire book. A number of individuals provided great comments on one or several chapters: Yousuf Al-Bulushi, Rina Agarwala, Rishi Awatramani, Fred Block, Ryan Calder, Alvin Camba, Sam Chambers, Yige Dong, Kathy Edin, Eli Friedman, Asher Ghertner, Michael Goldman, Manu Goswami, Meredith Grief, Jane Guyer, Eric Harms, Gill Hart, Conrad Jacober, Peter Jacobs, Sahan Karatasli, Satendra Kumar, Zach Levenson, Smitha Radhakrishnan, Poulami Roychowdhury, Paromita Sanyal, Erica Schoenberger, Llerena Searle, Sonal Sharma, Nikita Sud, Rajesh Veeraraghavan, Gowri Vijayakumar, and Carole Yerochewski. The book also benefited from feedback and advice in various contexts from: Shapan Adnan, Sarah Benabou, Henry Bernstein, Jun Borras, Neil Brenner, Sharad Chari, Andy Cherlin, Rohit De, Madhumita Dutta, Charles Geisler, Bret Gustafson, Aaron Jakes, Sunila Kale, Jens Lerche, William Martin, Matthew McCartney, Partha Mukhopadhyay, Dann Naseemullah, Jonathan Parry, Jon Pattenden, Nancy Peluso, Shahra Razavi, Tom Rosin, Srirupa Roy, Susanne and Lloyd Rudolph, Preeti Sampat, Mindi Schneider, Ian Scoones, James Scott, K. Sivaramakrishnan, Vikram Thakur, Anand Vaidya, Ajay Verghese, Namita Wahi, Ben White, and Wendy Wolford. Several chapters received exceptional commentary at the Yale Agrarian Studies Colloquium, the Harvard Urban Theory Lab, South Asia seminars at Oxford and NYU, and the SOAS Agrarian Change seminar. The book was expertly shepharded to print by David McBride at Oxford University Press; series editors Ashutosh Varshney and Pradeep Chibber; and the book's two anonymous reviewers. None of the aforementioned should be associated with the book's argument.

The sociology department at Johns Hopkins University has been the ideal intellectual environment in which to complete this project. The faculty and graduate students in the Program on Global Social Change have been a great source of stimulation and support, and they organized a very productive and exhausting book workshop in March 2017. Samantha Agarwal, Shozab Raza, Shereen Shafi, and Smriti Upadhyay contributed superb secondary research assistance. Jessie Albee, Linda Burkhardt, and Terri Thomas helped me get this book done while enlivening Mergenthaler Hall.

I owe much to my parents, Merril and David Levien, my siblings Bill and Rach, my grandparents, my aunts and uncles, and the entire family "down the bayou." I am also grateful to the late Chuck Matthei for his friendship and mentorship in the political economy of land. Phil Campanile has been my closest friend and intellectual companion for fifteen years. I have developed many of the ideas in this book in conversation with him; and he thoroughly read and commented upon every page, twice. Suchi Pande entered my life at the most disheartening moment of fieldwork, and has heartened it since. Her contributions to this book cannot be briefly summarized.

MAP

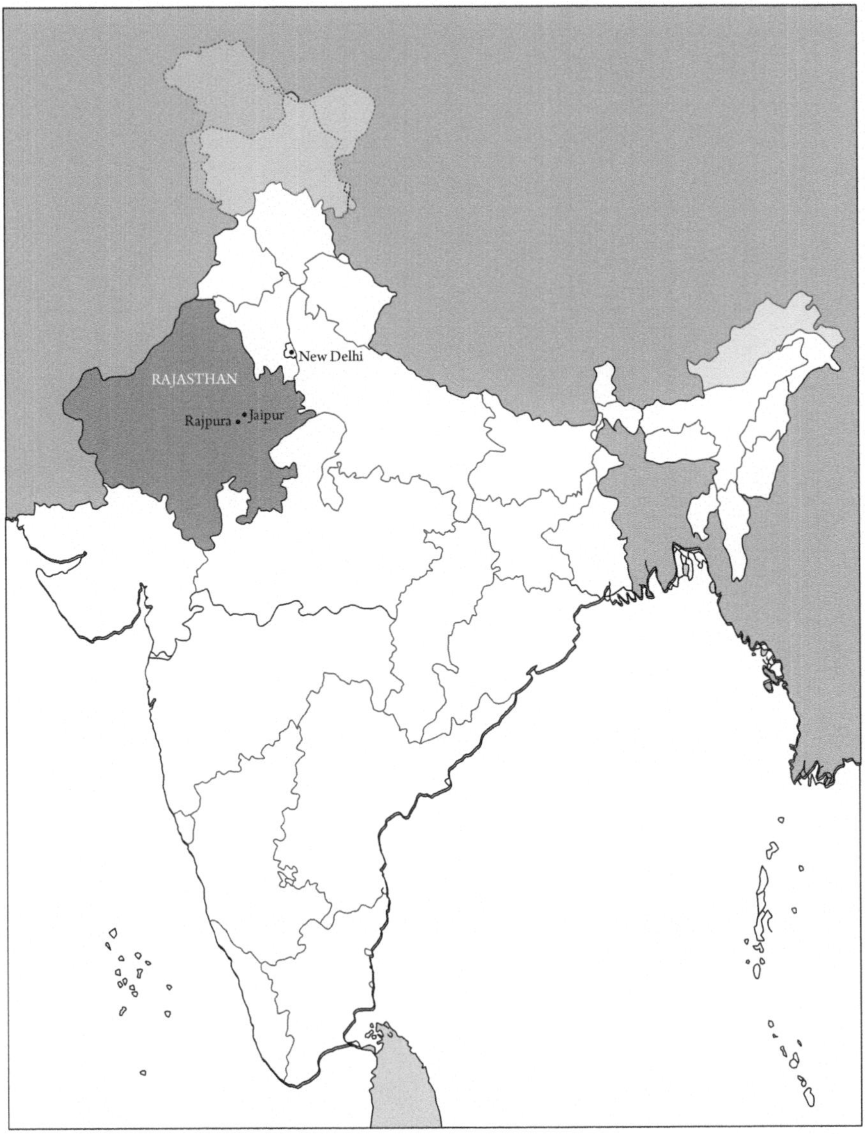

Map of India showing field site

DRAMATIS PERSONAE

In Alphabetical Order by First Name

Aseem Sharma: Brahmin principal of private school in Shivpura; connected me to Lada and Mahesh.

Asim Hussein: Vegetable vendor, truck owner, advocate for youth.

Balu Singh Gujjar: Cuckolded *chaiwala* in village market; quasi-legal owner of his plot thanks to Laduram Meena.

Bansilal Sharma: Former *sarpanch* (elected headman) of Shivpura, broker, and owner of prosperous dairy business; my initial landlord.

Banvarilal Sharma: Muckraking Brahmin politician and Ayurvedic doctor, the first to challenge *thakur* Jagat Singh's power as *sarpanch* in the 1970s.

Bhagwan Gujjar: Newlywed security guard from camel-rearing family.

Cheetur Jogi: Construction laborer in Mahindra World City who led failed sit-in against contractor.

Goverdhan and Rada Saini and six sons: The lone standouts against land acquisition, clashed with police and JDA officials and obstructed State Bank of India headquarters with legal case.

Hariram Sharma: Priest and resident of seldom-visited village temple. Has not received compensation for farmland because ostensibly "temple land."

Jagat Singh: The last *thakur* (feudal lord) of Rajpura and *sarpanch* for many decades thereafter.

Kailash Sharma: Young Shivpura *chaiwala*; family excluded from compensation because of ambiguous title.

Kamla Devi Nayak: Proletarianized ex-farmer, laborer on NREGA, and outspoken about domestic abuse. Mother of Sherpal, aspiring computer technician working as security guard in Bagaru.

Kanaram Choudhary: Broker, owner of JCB machine, insistent that "everyone" has benefited from SEZ.

Kanaram Regar: Successful Dalit vegetable vendor and wholesaler after shrewdly timed sale of compensation plots.

Lada Bunkar: My host-landlord, occasional construction and NREGA laborer, astute social critic, wife of Mahesh.

Laduram Meena: Rajpura's *sarpanch* when the Mahindra World City arrived, big land broker, businessman, and dollar millionaire.

Lalsingh Choudhary: Former Jat milk-middleman of Neempura, now broker, real estate speculator, and cold drinks store proprietor.

Mahesh Bunkar: My host-landlord, struggling petty rentier and vegetable vendor, husband of Lada.

Mahinder Singh: Grandson and heir of the last *thakur*, former Mumbai investment banker, real estate mogul, and acting village *sarpanch*.

Mohan Nayak: Proprietor of "sex hotel" on the 250 Foot Road.

Prakash Bunkar: Semiproletarian worker in Sanganer's block print mills, then struggling driver, life (perhaps) soon to change due to unsold compensation plot.

Puneeta Sharma: Daughter-in-law of Bansilal Sharma, critical of enclosure of grazing land and now confined to the house.

Pushpa Bunkar: Neighbor to Lada and Mahesh, hoped to use self-help group to finance daughter's wedding.

Rajesh Bunkar: Lada's cousin, small-time broker who enlists Mahesh into one deal before falling out.

Ram Kishore Prajapat: Potter, tenant in Rajpura, absentee landlord elsewhere, laborer, and owner of empty tobacco kiosk.

Ranjan Gujjar: *Chai* stall proprietor on corner of Laduram Meena's future marriage garden.

Sanjay Bunkar: Dalit owner of tire-puncture stall, driver for private college, and aspiring hotelier.

Santosh Balai: Dalit proprietor of pirate DVD store, laborer, and small-time broker.

Shiv Choudhary: Wealthy Jat farmer, land broker, partner and backer of Laduram Meena.

READER'S NOTE

All translations of Hindi conversations are my own. Where conveying the original Hindi seemed important, I have provided transliteration in parentheses or footnotes. In some cases I have opted for the more common rendering over the phonetically accurate. While most residents of "Rajpura" spoke Hindi, their first language was a dialect of Rajasthani that they called Marwari. I occasionally relied on Hindi speakers to translate for the relatively few who spoke only Marwari (and who tended to understand Hindi but reply in Marwari); unless very simple, I do not rely on these double translations for direct quotes.

The names of all villages and individuals have been changed.

Where I have converted Indian Rupees to U.S. Dollars I have used an exchange rate of Rs 50 to $1 (the actual exchange rate varied from approximately Rs 44 to Rs 63 during the course of research).

It will be useful to keep the following terms in mind:

> *Bigha*: a unit of agriculture land equal to one-quarter of a hectare
> *Lakh:* 100,000
> *Crore:* 10,000,000

ABBREVIATIONS

ABD	Accumulation by Dispossession
APL	Above Poverty Line
ASSOCHAM	Associated Chambers of Commerce and Industry
BJP	Bharatiya Janata Party
BPL	Below Poverty Line
BPO	Business Process Outsourcing
CII	Confederation of Indian Industries
CPM	Communist Party of India (Marxist)
CSR	Corporate Social Responsibility
DDA	Delhi Development Authority
DTA	Domestic Tariff Area
EPZ	Export Processing Zone
FICCI	Federation of Indian Chambers of Commerce and Industry
GNIDA	Greater Noida Industrial Development Authority
HSA	Hindu Succession Act
IT	Information Technology
ITES	Information Technology Enabled Services
JDA	Jaipur Development Authority
LAA	Land Acquisition Act
LARRA	short for Right to Fair Compensation and Transparency in Land Acquisition, Rehabilitation and Resettlement Act
MLA	Member of Legislative Assembly
MWC	Mahindra World City
NASSCHOM	National Association of Software and Services Companies
NBA	Narmada Bachao Andolan (Save the Narmada Movement)
NREGA	short for Mahatma Gandhi National Rural Employment Guarantee Act
NRI	Non-Resident Indian

OBC	Other Backward Classes
PAP/F	Project Affected Person/Family
PDS	Public Distribution System
PPP	Public-Private Partnership
PSU	Public Sector Undertaking
R&R	Resettlement and Rehabilitation
RIICO	Rajasthan State Industrial Development and Investment Corporation
SC	Scheduled Caste
SEZ	Special Economic Zone
SBI	State Bank of India
ST	Scheduled Tribe
STPI	Software Technology Parks of India
TBI	Technology Business Incubator
TMC	short for All India Trinamool Congress
UPA	United Progressive Alliance

Dispossession without Development

1

Introduction

Land dispossession is an old phenomenon receiving new attention. The practice of states forcibly taking land from rural populations for economic purposes has a long and variegated history (cf. Reynolds 2010), but it takes on particular importance in the history of capitalism. Indeed, some trace the origins of capitalism itself to the dispossession of the English peasantry (Marx 1977; Dobb 1947; Brenner 1977). Since then, land dispossession has shown no signs of stopping. Rural land dispossession was an integral component of both extractive and settler colonialisms across Asia, Africa, and the Americas from the 15th to the 20th century. Although it has received much less attention, postcolonial states in those same regions dispossessed tens of millions of people for state-led development projects such as large dams, mines, and industry. Only in the 21st century, however, has land dispossession—increasingly referred to as "land grabbing"—captured global political and scholarly attention. Whether for industry, urbanization, agricultural plantations, or extractive industries, land dispossession is now an unprecedentedly explosive political issue in many parts of Asia,[1] Africa,[2] and Latin America.[3] Land grabs have, in recent years, instigated mass protests and armed insurrections; been repressed through severe human rights violations; become the object of UN resolutions, transnational campaigns, and legislative debates; and brought down governments on the left and right. Land grabs are now featured in *New York Times* articles, *BBC* documentaries, popular books, and scholarly conferences. No longer the sole concern of social and environmental activists, land dispossession is now a contentious public issue in many parts of the world.

India is arguably the global epicenter of land grab protests. Land dispossession is far from new on the subcontinent, having occurred on a large scale under both British colonialism and post-independence state-led developmentalism. And beginning in the late 1970s, India's vibrant non-party "people's movements" pioneered resistance to what was often called "development-induced displacement," taking large dams as their main target. Yet these movements were relatively few in number, politically marginalized, and, despite tremendous efforts, rarely successful in stopping their dispossession. In the mid-2000s, however, just as India's economy launched into an extraordinary boom, farmer[4] protests against land dispossession—for real estate, infrastructure, factories, and, most controversially, Special Economic Zones (SEZs)—rapidly multiplied across the countryside. These seemingly ubiquitous protests were popularly dubbed "land wars" (*NDTV* 2011).

In the late 2000s, these so-called land wars—or, more accurately, farmer protests over land dispossession—shot to the center of national attention in the wake of violent clashes between farmers and police. As Figure 1.1 indicates, "land acquisition"—as state-orchestrated land dispossession is often called in India—had by the late 2000s exploded into the national media limelight. No longer the sole concern of social movement activists, land dispossession was now being taken up by opposition parties and was even a salient issue in state elections. Most surprisingly, many of these farmer uprisings quickly succeeded in stopping or stalling high-profile investments, including many of India's proposed SEZs and its largest proposed Foreign Direct Investment to date. By the end of the decade, resistance to land dispossession was posing a significant obstacle to accumulation: by one estimate, in 2011 capital investments worth 3% of India's GDP were stalled due to land acquisition problems (CMIE 2012). Stalled investments were being singled out—rightly or wrongly—as a cause of India's decelerating growth and had become a key object of concern for both state and capital. Overcoming these "road blocks" was the goal of amendments to India's Land Acquisition Act (LAA), which had served as the chief instrument of dispossessing land for the previous 120 years, and was a top priority of the Bharatiya

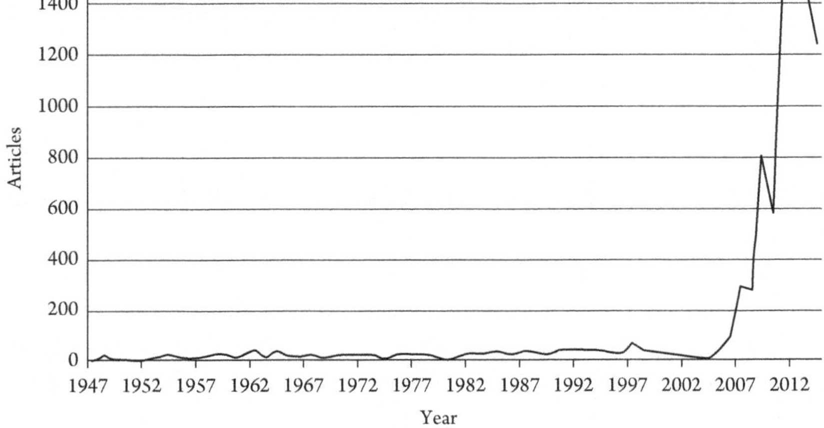

Figure 1.1 *Times of India* articles mentioning "land acquisition." Source: *Times of India* Historical Archive.

Janata Party (BJP) government when it assumed power in 2014. A contradiction had emerged between the land requirements of post-liberalization Indian capitalism and the political strength of farmers in India's democracy.[5]

This contradiction was as much a surprise for social scientists as it was for India's political leaders. Having largely ignored the role of land dispossession in capitalist development for decades, social scientists faced a burning global issue with old conceptual tools. As a consequence, much of the ensuing debate remained stuck within the polarized terms of a much older one: dispossession is either a necessary and inevitable cost of progress, or it is the predation of idyllic peasant communities by state and capital. The first position has been by far the most influential. It rests on the assumption that "peasants" are doomed to extinction by virtue of their social and economic backwardness—"a class," as Barrington Moore (1966: 505) famously put it, "over whom the wave of progress is about to roll." Shared by neoclassical economists, many Marxists, and political regimes of all stripes, this assumption is deeply rooted in the common sense of modernity. Those who harbor doubts are typically seen as fuzzy-headed romantics with a distorted sentimentalism for rural societies. And, indeed, critics of land dispossession have often been guilty of rural romanticism, seeing homogenous and sustainable "peasant communities" where there are, in actuality, stark inequalities, deep poverty, and political domination. This binary—dispossession as progress versus dispossession as predation—is unhelpful and even obstructive to social scientific analysis. Neither position can help us understand the specific causes, consequences, and politics of dispossession in the contemporary world.

First, this is because the causes of dispossession change over time and vary across context. The forms of dispossession faced by rural populations of the Global South today are *not* the same as those faced by European peasants three hundred years ago, or even the same as those faced by fellow citizens twenty years ago. Focusing on postcolonial India, this book shows that the driving causes of land dispossession changed dramatically in the early 1990s when India transitioned from state-managed capitalism to neoliberalism. Having dispossessed land almost exclusively for large public-sector industrial and infrastructure projects in the forty years after Independence, Indian states began to dispossess land on behalf of large private corporations for increasingly rent-heavy and non-labor-absorbing purposes, including upscale residential and commercial real estate. They became what I call *land broker states*. While these land broker states continued to *justify* dispossession as necessary for "development," such justifications obscure the changing forms of dispossession in post-liberalization India and beg the question of whether they are, in fact, "developmental." The contribution of dispossession to "development"—that inescapable but ultimately political term—is always a matter of perspective; and from any perspective, it is a variable, not a constant.

The second problem is that it is not empirically defensible to see the rural villagers targeted by dispossession in India today—and I suspect much of the world—as either doomed to extinction by their economic backwardness *or* as sustainable peasant communities. Agrarian social structures, as a large body of scholarship has shown, vary greatly within and across countries of the Global South.[6] This is nowhere more true than in India, whose roughly 600,000 villages vary tremendously in their economic foundations, degrees and patterns of inequality, and political histories.[7] In some regions, fertile triple-cropped land provides the basis for rural prosperity; in others, indebted farmers scratch a living from rain-fed fields and migrate to cities for much of the year. In a few small corners of the subcontinent one can find relatively egalitarian rural villages, but because of insufficient land reforms following Independence one mostly finds massive inequalities, correlated with caste and bisected by gender, that vary immensely in their particularities. And, finally, while some regions of rural India have a long history of political mobilization, others have never broken out of top-down patronage politics. Such variation profoundly affects the consequences of dispossession for farmers and their political responses to it.

A sociological approach to dispossession, then, can neither assume its contribution to progress nor romanticize the dispossessed. It must empirically examine how different forms of dispossession intersect with distinct agrarian milieux. By steering between the Scylla of high-modernist faith and the Charybdis of agrarian romanticism, this book attempts to chart such a course. Through an ethnographic and historical study of land dispossession in contemporary India, it advances a sociological theory of the relationship between land dispossession and capitalism.

Land dispossession, this book argues, is a social relation of coercive redistribution. Although mostly neglected by sociologists, this relationship exists in most social formations. It arises when those who control means of coercion—states, in many but not all cases—transfer portions of the earth's surface from one group of people to another. Such redistribution does not subside with the onward march of capitalism; on the contrary, capitalism creates systematic and unprecedented pressure to dispossess. But such dispossession remains mediated by states and takes different forms across both time and the uneven geographies of capitalist development. I suggest, therefore, that we can understand dispossession to be organized into socially and historically specific regimes. *The key to a comparative sociology of dispossession lies in understanding how distinct regimes of dispossession interact with diverse agrarian milieux that vary greatly in their economic foundations, social structures, and political histories.* This interaction generates very different political responses, ranging from willing compliance to militant and effective resistance. Thus, dispossession is not inevitable, but when it does "succeed," it yields qualitatively distinct trajectories of economic change and inequality that are not usefully reduced to the generic and normatively laden term "development." Against the homilies of "sentimental ruralists" and "brisk metropolitan progressives" (Williams 1985: 299), this book proposes a critical and comparative sociological lens.

Drawing on nineteen months of fieldwork, including participant observation, interviews, a village survey, and archival research, this book explains the emergence of a new regime of dispossession in post-liberalization India and examines its consequences for a village in the state of Rajasthan. It begins by showing that beneath the "land wars" of the 2000s lay a profound shift in the economic purposes driving land dispossession in India. After dispossessing land mostly for public-sector industry and infrastructure in the forty years after Independence, India's state governments began in the 1990s to dispossess land for private real estate and non-industrial growth. This restructuring of India's state governments into *land broker states* culminated during the real estate boom of the 2000s with SEZs. In 2005, a village I call Rajpura was one of nine villages to have its land dispossessed for the Mahindra World City, one of the first private SEZs to be built in North India. Most of the book is dedicated to examining the consequences of this private SEZ for dispossessed farmers in this rain-scarce, highly unequal, and politically quiet corner of Western India. Rajpura was a decidedly unidyllic village and precisely where one would expect such a project to be most welcomed. Observing the trajectories of Rajpura's diverse residents over a span of almost seven years, this book illuminates the process of socio-economic change and pattern of inequality that ensued. It reveals neither the timeless march of development nor the uniform predation of a peasant community. It shows instead a highly unequal trajectory of social change driven by real estate speculation rather than industrialization; the marginalization of rural labor more than its exploitation; and the withdrawal of the state's developmental ambitions into privileged elite enclaves only tenuously linked to their surroundings. The story of Rajpura's transformation, I suggest, is one of *dispossession without development*. It is a story, unfolding with local variation across rural India, of a non-idyllic village dispossessed by a state that has abandoned the broad social ambitions of the developmentalist era. And it is a story that compels us to see dispossession for what it is, without the obfuscations of development and other faiths.

Dispossession as Coercive Redistribution

As a term, "dispossession" is often used loosely and metaphorically, applied to a wide variety of phenomena and not distinguished from cognate terms. So, while this book does not seek to impose a singular definition on linguistic practice, it must begin by clarifying the particular kind of social relation it seeks to understand. The *Oxford English Dictionary* comes fairly close to my working definition: "the act of depriving someone of land, property, or other possessions." Appropriately, this definition implies an agent; it is not merely that people find themselves in a state of propertylessness, but that this state arises from someone depriving them. It is possible, of course, to be deprived by the impersonal workings of the market or by "acts of nature." Market-induced dispossession has been the focus of over a century of scholarship on the development of capitalism in peasant societies, which has long been seen to concentrate land and differentiate rural classes.[8] But this phenomenon is distinct from the type of directly coercive, state-orchestrated dispossession with which this book is concerned. Nor will this book discuss land loss through forces that are proximately natural, if ultimately human-induced.[9]

This book restricts the term "land dispossession" to situations in which those who control means of coercion—for the most part, states—transfer portions of the earth from one set of people to another. This conception of dispossession rests on its involuntary nature, whether or not the dispossessed are compensated.[10] Land dispossession is, in short, a social relation of coercive redistribution.

The question then arises of how land dispossession relates to other widely used terms: land grabs, displacement, enclosure, and acquisition. While more normatively charged, "land grab" will be used here as a lay synonym for "land dispossession." It also suggests a coercive process and its centrality to public discourse makes it difficult to avoid. The term also maps onto popular usage; farmers in Rajasthan used rough Hindi equivalents for "grab" to describe their own dispossession. Confusion arises when social scientists use "land deals" and "land grabs" interchangeably, which can conflate private purchases with state dispossession.[11]

While opponents of land dispossession prefer the emotively charged "grab," their exponents prefer euphemisms. The most popular has been "displacement." When large populations were dispossessed of their land and homes for dams and other capital investments of the 20th century, this was most commonly known as "development-induced displacement," distinguishing it from displacement by armed conflict. As social movements began to force the issue onto the agenda of international institutions like the World Bank in the 1980s, "displacement" became the term of choice in a burgeoning policy literature (cf. Cernea 1999). Applied social scientists began referring to displaced persons as "project affected persons" (PAPs) and devised policies for their "resettlement and rehabilitation" (R&R). Although "displacement" was usually applied to the same phenomenon this book is concerned with, the term lacks the active and relational sense of dispossession. Whereas dispossession makes it clear that coercion-wielding entities transfer land from one group of people to another, displacement appears to "just happen."[12] Most obscuring, however, is the coupling of displacement and development into a compound phrase. For "development-induced displacement" assumes precisely what needs to be examined: the extent to which the results of displacement are indeed "development." It obscures variation in dispossession's socio-economic effects and asserts by fiat what is contested on the ground.

A number of scholars have spoken of contemporary forms of land dispossession as "new enclosures."[13] The reference is to the English enclosures, the multi-century process by which the English gentry—ultimately with the aid of Parliament—deprived the peasantry of its common lands. I will turn shortly to how the enclosures have shaped theories of dispossession, but the specific historical reference lends the term an ambiguity. On the one hand, enclosure refers to the physical fencing of land. This was done with hedges and wooden fences in early modern England and is today more often accomplished with barbed wire and concrete.[14] But in the context of the English commons, to enclose was also to privatize, and this is where the confusion arises: many different property forms can be dispossessed, whether private, common, or complex hybrids.[15] Enclosure, then, can be seen as a subcategory of dispossession when it involves common property, or it can refer to the process of physically taking possession of any form of property.

Finally, there are various legal terms for the dispossession of private land: acquisition, compulsory purchase, condemnation, and eminent domain. Many countries have long had some provision for forcibly acquiring private land for "public purposes" (Reynolds 2010).[16] In India, eminent domain was introduced by the British in the 19th century, and the colonial-era LAA served as the legal basis for dispossessing private land until 2013.[17] "Land acquisition" is the term used by the Indian state and often in public debate. I will thus use it when discussing India's eminent domain laws, the administrative procedures for executing them, and the public debates that surround them. It should be kept in mind that while dispossession of public land proceeds on a different legal basis, it often accompanies the dispossession of private land. The degree to which dispossession proceeds legally is a historical variable: while violations surround this process in India, land dispossession is itself largely legal and carried out through routinized bureaucratic procedures.[18]

Having thus cleared a path through the terminological thicket, it is possible to see clearly the social relation this book is concerned with: the redistribution of land by owners of the means of coercion. I focus on dispossession by states, the predominant owners of the means of coercion in the contemporary world, leaving aside dispossession enacted by decentralized actors—mafias, militias, armed gangs, or landlords.[19] Although decentralized dispossession is a widespread phenomenon, state involvement brings a particular character to dispossession and must be analyzed separately. Not only is state-orchestrated dispossession likely to have a more discernable pattern—"regimeness," as I will call it—but it also directs resistance toward the arena of formal politics.

Further, the focus of this book is on *rural* land dispossession. While the urban-rural divide is blurry (Brenner 2013, 2014), and I will show that rural land dispossession in contemporary India is increasingly driven by real estate speculation emanating from cities, the dispossession of rural land is different in important respects from urban slum demolitions. Dispossessing farmland brings into play the complex class relations that organize agricultural production and, in many parts of the world, encounters a social unit—the village—with its particular forms of social and political life.[20] This book emphasizes the way in which agrarian social relations shape processes of dispossession and leaves rural-urban comparisons to future research.

Dispossession and Capitalism: Three Perspectives

The relationship between dispossession and capitalism has been relatively neglected. While the role of land dispossession under colonialism is widely acknowledged,[21] the dispossession of tens of millions of people for state-led "development" in the 20th century escaped the attention of almost every school of development sociology. This may reflect social science's relative neglect of space and geography (Harvey 1989; Lefebvre 1991; Coronil 1997; Foster 1999; Goldman and Shurman 2000), but it may also reflect the lack of widespread and effective opposition to dispossession during development theory's formative years. In countries emerging from colonial rule with popular nationalist parties, appeals by modernizing elites to "sacrifice for the nation" were particularly strong. Most Marxist scholars and parties were, for their own ideological reasons, similarly uncritical of "advancing the forces of production."

It was only when non-party social movements began resisting large dams with some visibility in the 1980s that scholars began documenting the plight of the displaced[22] and advancing critiques of "top-down" development (cf. Baviskar 1995; Scott 1998). Although still on the margins of development theory, a number of scholars produced exemplary studies of land dispossession for state-led (and often World Bank–funded) modernization schemes, contributing to the growing intellectual current of political ecology.[23] Yet just as these critiques of state-led development were coalescing, the majority of the world transformed the way it organized capital accumulation. Programs of "neoliberal" economic restructuring were implemented with great variation in degree, timing, and character across the developing world (Fourcade and Babb 2002; Evans and Sewell 2013), but all were premised on the assumption that state control over the economy should be diminished in favor of the market (Harvey 2005).

While sociologists were quick to point out that markets depend on state institutions and are always "embedded" in a multitude of social relations (Granovetter 1985; Block 2001; Krippner and Alvarez 2007), escalating conflicts over "land grabs" in the mid-2000s suggested a starker contradiction: deepening marketization was accompanied by increasing use of state power to dispossess private (and common) property.[24] Proliferating land grabs, and resistance to them, quickly generated a "land grab literature rush" (Oya 2013), which has yielded an efflorescence of empirical studies.[25] It has also renewed the search and need for a theoretical understanding of the relationship between dispossession and capitalism.

There are, I suggest, three main theories of this relationship. The first holds that dispossession is a necessary and inevitable cost of economic development. Matter-of-fact and embedded in common sense, this *modernization theory of dispossession* rests on the assumption that all growth constitutes "development" and on the normative assertion that aggregate "development" justifies the dispossession of less productive rural people. The second comes from classical Marxism and provides a twist on the same argument: the dispossession of rural people is an inevitable and progressive stage in the transition to capitalism. In this view, however, dispossession will ultimately be redeemed when working-class struggle enables the re-collectivization of property under socialism. I call this the *proletarian redemption theory of dispossession*. Both of these theories correspond to the dispossession-as-progress pole of the binary addressed previously. The third, which I call the *predatory theory of dispossession*, breaks with the assumption of progress. It posits that dispossession is a form of ongoing plunder of subaltern populations specific to the latest phase of neoliberal capitalism. While none of these theories will suffice, my own theoretical reconstruction proceeds from the third.

The Modernization Theory of Dispossession

According to the dominant view, dispossession is an unavoidable cost of economic development. No country has gotten rich without reducing the number of rural producers; and poor countries are simply going through today what rich countries went through long ago. If dispossession is the inevitable price of progress, those who oppose it are backward-looking romantics. This familiar argument suffers from two major shortcomings as a social scientific theory. First, it imbricates its empirical arguments with normative legitimations and a determinist conception of history. Second, it fails to capture empirical variation in the character of dispossession over time and space.

Because the modernization theory of dispossession is so deeply embedded in common sense, it is necessary to trace its contingent historical emergence. The theory originates in early modern England, where the landed gentry justified the enclosure of the commons, and the expulsion of the peasantry from it, by the "improvement" it would make possible (Neeson 1993). Improvement thus originally "referred to operations for monetary profit . . . and especially to operations on or connected to land, often the enclosing of common or waste land" (Williams 1976: 133). Improvement was central to John Locke's (1980) theory of property, which provided philosophical ammunition for the enclosure movement. Early political economists like John Steurt were even more explicit.[26] Adam Smith notably omitted the very visible hand of state dispossession—including the contemporaneous Highland Clearances of his native Scotland—from his theory of capitalism, but agreed that "the diminution of the number of cottagers, and other small occupiers of land" was "the immediate forerunner of improvement and better cultivation."[27] These were political interventions into a public debate whose outcome was uncertain. Even in the absence of adult franchise and with a parliament of landlords, it took centuries of bitter struggle for enclosure to prevail (Neeson 1993). But the fact that the English enclosures preceded the industrial revolution helped to legitimize subsequent episodes of dispossession.

Beyond the English countryside, the argument that "unproductive" agrarian land and people had to give way to improvement was justifying colonial conquest, plunder, and genocide. Dogmatic concepts of improvement were articulated alongside racist conceptions of Europe's "civilizing" mission to justify patently illiberal forms of colonial dispossession (cf. Rodney 1981; Banner 2005; Moore 2005; Gidwani 2008; Whitehead 2010).[28]

In the mid-20th century, improvement became "development" and was endowed with the aspirations of postcolonial nationalism. A tacit modernization theory of dispossession prevailed across the ideological spectrum, finding traction with "Third World" heads of state, development planners, social scientists, and revolutionaries. As James Scott (1998) has demonstrated, technocratic elites of all stripes imposed large-scale social engineering projects on rural populations, which promised improvements to the human condition but "typically required a vast public authority empowered to condemn private property [and] relocate people against their will" (Scott 1998: 95).[29] The large capital projects of "Third World" modernization—dams, steel towns, industrial estates, power plants, ports, and highways—required massive dispossession, but were justified by the promise of national development.

Social scientists largely failed to take note of this dispossession, but some offered theories that tacitly endorsed it. In the 1950s and 1960s, so-called modernization theorists argued that peasants were the fount of cultural and economic backwardness and the chief obstacle to modernization; it was incumbent upon the technocratic elite of the Third World to push it through over any objections from the countryside (Rostow 1959: 7).[30] Dependency theorists subsequently critiqued modernization theorists for ignoring external constraints to growth in "satellite" countries; but they also had little to say about the large-scale land dispossession involved in its promotion by "Third World" states.[31] While returning attention to the internal conditions for economic development, comparative political economists (Evans and Stephens 1988) also ignored land dispossession as a component of this development. But if the primary job of "developmental states" was to forge constructive relationships with capital in a joint project of economic transformation (e.g., Johnson 1982; Amsden 1989; Evans 1995; Chibber 2003; Kohli 2004), these projects were concretely instantiated in capital projects that dispossessed millions of people. If one does not find an explicit defense of dispossession in this scholarship, this is largely because the rural land dispossession these projects entailed was ignored. Even as the overriding concern for growth at all costs gave way to "social development," land dispossession was not addressed as an important mechanism of redistribution or cause of "entitlement failure" (Sen 1984; Sen 2000).[32]

As national development projects gave way to neoliberalism, the modernization theory of dispossession ironically resurfaced in more explicit form. While in theory, neoliberalism seeks to limit state intervention into the economy and restrict arbitrary infringements on private property (Hayek 1944),[33] its adoption in practice has often involved increasing violation of small private (and common) property in pursuit of economic growth.[34] After two decades of economic liberalization in India, otherwise market-friendly economists can thus be found insisting on the need for governments to dispossess land for private companies: "development cannot take place without changing the use of some land";[35] "the prosperity of the peasantry in the world always depends on the number of peasants going down";[36] and anyway "the overwhelming majority of farmers' children want to leave agriculture."[37] Thus, Amartya Sen concludes, "prohibiting the use of agricultural land for industries is self-defeating."[38]

The modernization theory of dispossession presents itself as irrefutable: who could argue that economic growth does not involve changing land uses and drawing people out of agriculture? But such arguments conflate changing land *use* with changing land *owners* and, thus, farmers *leaving* agriculture with farmers being *forced out* of it. We are then faced with the question of why otherwise liberal economists believe that government coercion is necessary to make land find its "highest and best use." The answers are pragmatic and filed under "market failure": small and fragmented landholdings, the explanation goes, make it costly or cumbersome to purchase land for large capital projects, and even a small number of holdouts can prevent contiguity (Banerjee et al. 2007: 1487; Chakravorty 2013: 118; Panagariya n.d.). Because in a market economy private companies are the main agents of economic growth, they too must be assisted in overcoming this obstacle.[39]

What specific purposes justify the use of state force for overcoming this obstacle? This is a political—not an economic or technical—question. And because modernization theorists do not distinguish between the different uses for which farmers should be forced to give their land, the implication is that *any* purpose representing a "higher value" than agriculture warrants dispossession. It is an argument for the unlimited upward redistribution of property.[40]

This normative bias leads to a critical analytical failing: because it treats all growth as the same, the modernization theory of dispossession cannot see how particular phases and forms of capitalist growth transform the nature and consequences of dispossession, or understand why land dispossession may become more or less politically explosive. The fallback claim that dispossession is inevitable is belied not only by the widespread success of farmers in preventing it, but by the need for an explicit modernization theory of dispossession.

Rather than *assume* that dispossession is a necessary and predetermined price of "development," we must recognize that it facilitates different forms of accumulation and associated class interests in different times and places. And if the economic purposes driving dispossession change, then the contribution of dispossession to "development" cannot be a constant; it is variable and subject to contestation. This perspective presents a challenge not only to advocates for capitalist modernization but also to its harshest critics.

The Proletarian Redemption Theory of Dispossession

Karl Marx argued that dispossession played a brutal role in the transition from a pre-capitalist to a capitalist society. But while he ridiculed the modernization theorists of his day for neglecting this violent history, he often seemed to share their assumption that the peasantry's "annihilation" was both unavoidable and desirable.[41] This was not because "improvement" was an end in itself, but because the dispossession of the peasantry through so-called "primitive accumulation" would ultimately be redeemed by the dispossession of capitalists.[42] Marx's argument assumed that dispossession: (1) was confined to the origins of capitalism; (2) created the material conditions for socialism; and (3) transformed peasants into a revolutionary working class. But these assumptions are respectively wrong, undiscriminating, and conjectural. This not only makes the concept of "primitive accumulation" inappropriate for contemporary land grabs; but it has historically turned many Marxists into de facto modernization theorists.

At the end of *Capital,* Marx critiques Adam Smith and other political economists for their ahistorical, even theological, account of the origins of capitalism. Smith had recognized theoretically that an advanced division of labor presumed a "previous" accumulation of "stock"; how otherwise would the owner of his fabled pin factory buy land, build the facility, purchase raw materials, and extend wages to workers *before* his pins could be sold on the market?[43] But Smith never answered how this previous accumulation came about; and did not ask why there were propertyless workers on hand to employ.[44] Given his view that the division of labor evolved naturally from human beings' "propensity to truck, barter and exchange" (Smith 1999: 117), the implication was that the enterprising accumulated stock while the slothful formed the working class. Marx called this a "nursery tale" and likened it to the theology of original sin. In contrast, he insisted that capital came into the world "dripping from head to toe, from every pore, with blood and dirt" (1977: 926). He then offered his own historical sketch of "so-called original accumulation" (*die sogenannte ursprüngliche Akkumulation*), which was consequentially mistranslated back into the English edition of *Capital* as "primitive accumulation" (Perelman 2000).

Marx's account of "primitive accumulation" addresses many processes but centers on the English enclosures and colonial plunder.[45] The relative importance of these to the birth of capitalism has been the subject of a long and polarized debate (cf. Hilton 1978; Brenner 1976, 1977; Wood 2002; Wallerstein 2011), but Marx saw them as complementary.[46] Dispossession of the English peasantry created capitalist social relations in agriculture by turning the land into capital and the peasants into wage laborers (Marx 1977: 875); and colonial plunder provided further start-up funds (the "stock") for industrial capitalism, which would absorb some of those dispossessed peasants. Importantly, however, Marx confined these processes of dispossession to the *initial* development of capitalism. Primitive accumulation was "the historical basis, instead of the historical result, of specifically capitalist production" (Marx 1977: 775).[47] Once capitalist social relations became firmly established, the "silent compulsion of the market" took over.[48]

Herein lies the problem: Marx analyzed primitive accumulation by its consequences—creating capitalism's pre-conditions—rather than its causes. Marx's analysis of the enclosures, for instance, devoted little attention to the economic forces motivating the gentry to enclose the commons. While Marx recognized that rising wool prices generated by the booming textile industry of Flanders "provided the direct impulse for these evictions" (Marx 1977: 879), he did not draw the logical conclusion from this: that *dispossession was a consequence and not just a cause of capitalist development.* But if capitalism itself created systematic pressures to dispossess land, the implication is that it would continue indefinitely, take many forms, vary across phases of capitalism, and encounter rural populations *already* unevenly absorbed into capitalist social relations. Given, moreover, Marx's view that capitalism's increasing capital-intensity would generate a growing "relative surplus population" that it could not employ,[49] the implication is that demand for land would become progressively uncoupled from demand for labor. But if Marx recognized this possibility, he never developed it.

And he adhered, in *Capital* at least, to the assumption that the dispossession of the English peasantry was a progressive step on the road to socialism. By neglecting the centuries-long struggle between the landed gentry and the peasantry that enclosure entailed (Thompson 1966, 1975; Neeson 1993), he also implied that it was inevitable. Focusing on consequence rather than cause, and with little attention to political struggle, Marx left a history of how capitalism developed in England but not a theory of how dispossession would continue under capitalism.

Marx ultimately backed away from the proposition that "primitive accumulation" was a necessary and inevitable stage for all societies (Shanin 1983)[50]; and one can find elsewhere in his writings a less teleological[51] and more "multi-linear" conception of historical change (Anderson 2010)—one that my own argument builds upon. However, Marxist debates over the origins of, and transitions to, capitalism in the "Third World" largely compounded the term's conceptual ambiguities and deterministic biases.[52] "Primitive accumulation," in this literature, became stretched to incorporate a variety of historical processes—such as class differentiation of the peasantry and the transfer of surpluses from agriculture to industry.[53] However defined, many Marxists continued to see primitive accumulation as a necessary stage that contributed to economic development in poor countries.[54] Even as revolutionary prospects receded, many cheered these processes along, seemingly still confident that capitalism was leading inexorably toward socialism.[55] By the new millennium, revisionist scholars began to argue that primitive accumulation was "ongoing" under capitalism rather than a stage (cf. Perelman 2000; De Angelis 2001, 2007; Hart 2002; Sanyal 2007; Moore 2015), but this did not resolve the term's conceptual ambiguity.[56]

In recent years, many scholars have applied the term "primitive accumulation" to contemporary land grabs (cf. Chatterjee 2008; Sassen 2010; Adnan 2013, 2015; Magdoff 2013),[57] but this is both confusing and misleading. It gives the impression that contemporary forms of land dispossession are aspects of the timeless transition from a pre-capitalist to a capitalist society.[58] To the contrary, most involve dispossessing land—*often already held within capitalist social relations*—for a variety of economic purposes that are orthogonal to the slow and geographically uneven development of capitalist agriculture. They reflect not an early stage of capitalism but advanced capitalist demands on land, including for financialized real estate speculation.[59] They take a myriad of sector-specific forms—whether dams, highways, mines, steel plants, Special Economic Zones, or upscale housing—that vary over time and place and have diverse socio-economic consequences. Driven by capitalist demands for land with little regard for what happens to the (often superfluous) labor power of the dispossessed, they have highly ambiguous consequences for class struggle.[60] This book will show that farmers dispossessed for a contemporary SEZ are unevenly proletarianized, underemployed, and complexly differentiated in an informal economy;

there is little ground for assuming that their dispossession has contributed to their radicalization or prepared the ground for socialism. Given the untenability of its assumptions, the proletarian redemption theory loses its distinctiveness from the modernization theory.

Breaking out of this conceptual impasse requires posing the question differently: not "What is the role of land dispossession in transitions to capitalism?" but "What is the role of land dispossession *within* capitalism?" This entails shifting attention from the transition between modes of production to changing regimes of dispossession within the capitalist mode of production.

Dispossession as Predation

Rather than dispossession being a necessary cost of development or stage in the transition to capitalism, a third approach sees it as the product of a particularly predatory neoliberal phase of capitalism. Exemplary of this approach is David Harvey's (2003, 2005) influential theory of "accumulation by dispossession" (ABD), though one can find parallels in other recent theorizations of "land grabs," "new enclosures," and "expulsions" (De Angelis 2007; Araghi 2009a, 2009b; McMichael 2012a, 2013; Sassen 2014). Usefully, Harvey dispatches with the assumption that dispossession is inevitable or historically progressive. Problematically, he builds his theory of dispossession with specific reference to his analysis of neoliberalism. In doing so, he overlooks the importance of land dispossession during prior phases of capitalism and fails to capture geographic variation within the neoliberal phase. Extending his concept to too many distinct processes, Harvey is vague about the mechanisms of land dispossession. And while Harvey does not romanticize peasants,[61] as some other theorists do, a high level of abstraction prevents him from capturing the diverse and unequal consequences of dispossession for rural people and the conditions under which they organize to prevent it.

Important foundations for the predatory approach can be found in the works of Rosa Luxemburg and Karl Polanyi. Luxemburg was the first to argue that dispossession was systematically connected to capitalist expansion by way of its demand for land, not labor.[62] She proposed that capitalism needed to continually use force against non-capitalist societies to access their means of production; and that it would collapse once it devoured them (Luxemburg 2003: 351). From a different perspective, Karl Polanyi (2001) argued that land commodification was central to laissez faire capitalism and also generative of political struggle. Since land is a "fictitious commodity"—it is not produced for sale on the market but is "an element of nature inextricably intertwined with man's institutions" (Polanyi 2001: 75, 187)—its commodification generates social dislocations that prompt "counter-movements" for social protection.[63]

Harvey (2003, 2005) has built on the insights of Luxemburg and Polanyi to advance his theory of accumulation by dispossession. Although he does not provide a definition, Harvey offers a variety of examples of ABD—from land dispossession to financial devaluations, intellectual property rights, and the privatization of public goods[64]—all of which, according his argument, provide an outlet for "over-accumulated capital" in the core economies of the West.[65] By releasing cheap assets for profitable use, land dispossession is one of several strategies to overcome capitalism's growing crisis of profitability. Importantly, Harvey's reconstruction recognizes dispossession to be an intrinsic aspect of fully developed—and indeed advanced—capitalism. This is the concept's main advancement upon primitive accumulation.[66]

But Harvey's analysis has two main shortcomings. First, his over-extension of the concept to include so many distinct forms of theft and fraud,[67] combined with a high level of abstraction, prevents him from grasping the sociological specificity of land dispossession. Land dispossession, I have argued, is a form of coercive redistribution mediated by states. As such, it is very directly determined by political struggle (Brenner 1977; De Angelis 2007).[68] By reading every instance of dispossession as a result of the global impulses of capital, Harvey fails to answer why and how impulses of capital translate into *dispossession* rather than merely commodification. Both Luxemburg and Polanyi suggested that dispossession might arise when there are obstacles to its commodification; but on behalf of whom and for what purposes are states willing to use force for overcoming these obstacles? A cursory examination of the historical record suggests great variation, which leads to the second problem.

Harvey's theory of land dispossession is based on his theory of neoliberalism. But land dispossession is, as he acknowledges, a much older phenomenon that varies greatly over history and geography. Understanding this variability would allow us to better understand what is unique about land dispossession in the neoliberal period compared to colonialism or state capitalism. It may be true, as Harvey suggests, that dispossession is increasing under neoliberalism; but given that in many instances (as I will show in India) it is driven largely by domestic capitalists in alliance with the state, it is not clear that "overaccumulated capital"—which Harvey sees as particularly afflicting advanced rather than emerging economies[69]—is the cause. Dispossession cannot, in general, be deduced from the sagging profits of Western companies or reduced to a "new imperialism."

These critiques are relevant to several other recent theorizations of "global land grabs." Whether seen as part of a global logic of "expulsion" (Sassen 2014) or a particular phase of the global food economy (Araghi 2009a, 2009b; McMichael 2012a, 2013),[70] the tendency has been to begin with hypothesized features of global capitalism instead, as I have suggested, with an understanding of dispossession. Land dispossession is a social relation of coercive redistribution. Far from being a product of "weak states" bowled over by global capital (Sassen 2014), it involves a deliberate use of state force to overcome obstacles to accumulation for purposes that vary enormously over time and space. And it affects not "commoners" (De Angelis 2007), "peasants" (Araghi 2009a; Shiva, Jani, and Fontana 2011; McMichael 2012a), or "small farmers" (Sassen 2014a) but heterogeneous agrarian classes that often have different interests vis-à-vis large capital projects. A sociological understanding of dispossession requires that we descend from the heights of abstraction to understand how regimes of dispossession collide with specific agrarian milieux.

Regimes of Dispossession and Agrarian Milieux

If dispossession is a social relation of coercive redistribution, the concept of regimes of dispossession helps us to capture how this relation varies over the different phases and uneven geographies of capitalist development. Analogous to a regime of production, which refers to the political apparatus for "securing and obscuring surplus value" in the labor process (Burawoy 1985), a regime of dispossession refers to the political apparatus for coercively redistributing land. While dispossession is typically justified by claims to the public interest in "development," regimes of dispossession can be differentiated by the specific economic purposes and associated class interests they serve. Thompson's description of the enclosures as "a plain enough case of class robbery" (Thompson 1966: 218) remains apt; the concept of regimes of dispossession highlights variation in the robbers and what they do with the loot.

Dispossession of private property is, in many contexts, legally constrained by eminent domain statutes to "public purposes." But states have great flexibility to define the "public purpose," and often amend (or simply flout) laws to suit their purpose in changing circumstances. Further, the judiciary is itself influenced by shifting opinions about what constitutes the public interest. Many states have, for long periods in their history, equated "public purpose" with projects of the state, limiting the forcible expropriation of land to infrastructure or defense. Equating the profit-making activities of private companies with the public interest characterizes particularly liberal historical regimes (such as India's present one), whose specific emergence must be explained. In either case, claims to the "public interest" in unequal societies are necessarily ideological. They proceed by synecdoche, attributing the interests of a part of society to the whole (Gramsci 1977). This is no less true of government infrastructure as of a private factory: a dam, highway, or airport inevitably benefits certain sections of the "public" while imposing disproportionate costs on others. While dominant classes tend to benefit disproportionately from dispossession under any particular regime, those specific classes or class fractions vary; as does the extent to which other classes share in the benefits.

While land dispossession can be orchestrated by decentralized wielders of coercion,[71] I conceive of regimes of dispossession as being organized at the level of states. [72] The specific level of the state is likely to vary. In India, authority to dispossess land rests with both the central and state governments, but it is primarily the responsibility of the latter. My analysis focuses on the state of Rajasthan within India, though I argue that basic elements of the two historical regimes I analyze can be identified across India's states.[73] Although it is possible to periodize aspects of capitalism at a global scale (Arrighi 1994),[74] there is too much variation in the precise causes and class interests driving dispossession in various national contexts to merit globally periodized regimes (cf. Araghi 2009a). Different countries—and regions within countries—have integrated to different degrees, at different times, and in different ways into global capitalism. This uneven development of capitalism results in varied *sectoral compositions of dispossession*. And because dispossession requires the use of coercion that is largely—if not entirely—monopolized by states, the nation-state and its subnational units are, in a postcolonial age, the most significant scales for organizing land dispossession, even where the recipients are multinational companies. In my view, this makes the "the" in "the global land grab" (Zoomers 2010; Margulis and Taylor 2013; Hall 2013a), "the new enclosures" (De Angelis 2007), or "the global enclosures" (Araghi 2009a) misleading.

Regimes of dispossession is a flexible concept intended to help us see patterns amid the seeming chaos of dispossession. It is ultimately useful for two main reasons. First, it replaces the assumption that dispossession is historically inevitable with a framework for comparative research into the politics of dispossession. Second, it replaces the assumptions that dispossession is either uniformly developmental or predatory with a framework for comparative research into its socio-economic effects. A sociology of dispossession can be advanced, I suggest, by examining how distinct regimes of dispossession interact with specific agrarian milieux.

From Inevitability to the Conditions of (Non-)Compliance

Dispossessing people of their land is ultimately a question of political authority, or of the ability of states to make people comply with their orders (Weber 1978: 212–215; Bendix 1947; Etzioni 1961). If *consent* is the appropriate term for long-term submission to exploitation (Gramsci 1977; Burawoy 1979), *compliance* captures the necessary and sufficient condition for the temporally discrete process of dispossession—that people are made to leave their land and no more. Dispossession does not require—and often does not produce—enduring consent to the existing social order. Conversely, non-compliance with dispossession does not necessarily imply dissent to that order. Farmers might, for example, have no qualms with an SEZ as such; they might just not want to give up their land for it (Nielsen 2010). As a short-term relationship requiring only temporary compliance, dispossession operates orthogonally to ongoing class hegemonies (Gramsci 1977).[75] Whereas exploitation requires enduring consent at the point of production, dispossession only requires one-time compliance at the point of enclosure.

Regimes of dispossession vary in the combination of means at their disposal for producing compliance. Because dispossession is inherently transparent—no farmer can have their land snatched without noticing—mystification is not one of them (De Angelis 2007). States must ensure dispossession through *explicit* forms of inducement: coercion, legitimization, and/or material compensation. All regimes of dispossession rely on the actual or threatened use of coercion. But regimes of dispossession vary in the extent to which they can supplement coercion with other inducements.

States almost always find it necessary to legitimize dispossession.[76] If the English gentry and parliament justified the enclosures by the "improvement" it made possible, contemporary regimes of dispossession rely on the derivative language of "development." A major determinant of the success and stability of a regime of dispossession is the extent to which its appeals to the public interest are convincing to the dispossessed and to a broader public. The capability of states to legitimatize dispossession hinges on the specific purposes and interests the dispossession serves. It is typically easier to legitimize dispossession when the perceived benefits are broad rather than narrow, when they accrue to nationals rather than foreigners and, as I will suggest, when they involve public rather than private entities. States also often find it easier to legitimize dispossession among dominant racial and ethnic groups when it targets dominated groups.[77]

In addition to coercion and legitimation, the third basis of compliance is material compensation. Given the often dramatic effects of land loss on people's livelihoods, combined with the difficulty of compensating for non-monetary values, compliance by material compensation is far trickier than it would appear. While there were scant incentives for English peasants to relinquish the commons, most contemporary societies require that those dispossessed of their private property be given some form of compensation. Liberal democracies typically base this compensation on an assessment of a property's "fair market value," though determining this in the absence of a voluntary transaction poses a problem. In recent decades, developing countries have sometimes augmented this compensation with explicit policies for "resettlement and rehabilitation." This often includes promises of employment, replacement land, or improved infrastructure and services (electricity, water, roads, schools, clinics, etc.). Promises can be politically important in eliciting compliance; if and when they are broken, it is typically too late for the dispossessed to get their land back. Both the types of promises made and the ability of states to deliver on them depend crucially on the kind of accumulation facilitated by dispossession. A large dam might make irrigated land an option; a manufacturing project, jobs; a real estate colony, land values. Different regimes of dispossession make possible different kinds and degrees of material incentives for eliciting compliance. Compliance to dispossession is thus achieved through historically specific combinations of coercion, compensation, and legitimacy.

But the same regime of dispossession is likely to generate different responses in different agrarian milieux. Attempts to dispossess land for the same kind of project can provoke militant resistance in one village and quiet compliance in another. They can also prompt different kinds of resistance: in one village demanding the total halting of a project, in another demanding higher compensation. These goals can, moreover, be expressed through diverse political ideologies. While many specific features of agrarian milieux may affect the politics of dispossession, this study will illuminate three: the value and degree of dependence upon agricultural livelihoods; patterns of social inequality; and political histories. As regimes of dispossession refract through agrarian milieux that vary along these dimensions, they are likely to generate a great variety of political responses.

Yet some regimes of dispossession are more formidable than others. The strength of a regime of dispossession is the probability that a given attempt to dispossess will be met with compliance.[78] When the probability of compliance sinks beneath a certain level, access to land can become a choke point for accumulation. At such junctures, which we see in India today, the "land question" is likely to enter into the center of national politics. There are roughly three possible resolutions to such a contradiction. The state can forge ahead with the regime through brute coercion; it can attempt to rescue the regime by transforming the means of compliance; or it can abandon the regime. Strong political resistance can make brute coercion increasingly difficult, elicit efforts at material compromise, or even render a regime unviable.

Far from being inevitable, then, land dispossession is the outcome of political struggles occurring under distinct social and historical conditions. The assumption of inevitability is based on an over-generalization from particularly formidable regimes of dispossession. Political (non-)compliance to dispossession is shaped by the interaction of regimes of dispossession and the sociological features of particular agrarian milieux.

From Development to Capitalist Trajectories

When dispossession is "successful," its result is not necessarily "development." While states have historically justified dispossession as serving the public interest in "development," state legitimations are a poor starting point for sociological analysis. While the term is impossible to escape, one should use it carefully in order to "avoid thinking the state with state thinking" (Bourdieu 2014: 106). Development is an essentially political concept that is defined and evaluated differently across social position. Its referent, moreover, has changed profoundly over time. During the mid-20th century, development referred to a set of conscious interventions by states and international institutions into the economies of "Third World" countries (Hart 2001, 2009; McMichael 2012b).[79] Variously described as statist, *dirigiste*, high-modernist, or developmentalist, the resulting forms of capitalism—of which there were many permutations—gave the state a large role in catalyzing economic transformation; prioritized key sectors such as manufacturing and agriculture; and involved moderate commitments to equitable growth and poverty alleviation. While these models had uneven success, the point is that development—especially in postcolonial contexts—referred to ambitions of social transformation that were broader than the promotion of private-sector growth at all costs. As political regimes across the world embraced, with great variation in speed and content, neoliberalism from the 1980s onward, they continued to appeal to development while abandoning its original referent. Prioritizing the growth of private capital, they increasingly relinquished state-developmentalist ambitions to control the market for social ends while devolving responsibility for those social ends onto civil society (Harvey 2005; Hart 2001, 2009).[80] In contrast to its professed ideology, "actually existing neoliberalism" (Brenner and Theodore 2002) has continued to involve large-scale state dispossession; this dispossession is still justified by appeals to development; but this now refers to distinct political economic projects. Attributing dispossession to the generic needs of development obscures such variation, which the concept of regimes of dispossession helps to highlight. If dispossession is driven by different purposes in distinct contexts, then its consequences are a variable, not a constant.

One must observe—not assume—those consequences. Once farmland has been turned into a dam, SEZ, factory, mine, or real estate project, one can observe the character of the accumulation it facilitates directly and indirectly, and the distribution of its costs and rewards. Instead of subsuming such variation into the generic category of development, we can compare the specific trajectories of capitalism dispossession generates. These trajectories of change can be rapid and dramatic. They involve not only specific changes in productive forces (manufacturing, mining, services, real estate, etc.) but also corresponding changes in inequality. Understanding these changes requires long-term fieldwork sensitive to both the subjective experience and the objective outcomes of dispossession. While large capital projects might elicit initial developmental "aspirations" among rural populations (cf. Cross 2014), the critical sociological question is whether these aspirations are realized and how this varies across social position.

Such analysis faces the twin traps outlined at the beginning. First, it must overcome the modernist sneer toward small agrarian production in order to take seriously what dispossession means to farmers (Humphries 1990). Where economists see straightforward transfer of land from lower to higher value land uses, the dispossessed see the transfer of their land (and everything attached to it) to someone else, and weigh this against their compensation, jobs, or other promises of "development."

The second trap is to see farmers or peasants as a homogenous class with the same interests. There are few if any agrarian communities in the contemporary world that resemble the idyll of harmonious peasants or "commoners."[81] Agrarian social structures in most parts of the world are, instead, marked by significant levels of social inequality. While collective property still exists in many regions of the world today, it often co-exists with private property and/or various forms of individual or family tenure. Failed land reforms in large parts of the Global South have left intact large inequalities in the distribution of land and agrarian assets,[82] which are also often associated with inequalities of race, caste, or ethnicity. These inequalities shape the abilities of dispossessed households to cope with—or even profit from—dispossession. Moreover, a growing literature has demonstrated that women very often bear disproportionate costs of land dispossession, though in ways that vary across projects, regionally specific patriarchies, and across other dimensions of inequality like class, caste, and race.[83] As different forms of dispossession refract through diverse ensembles of agrarian social relations, they produce qualitatively different patterns of economic change and inequality.

In the place of inevitable and developmental dispossession, then, this book proposes a comparative research program into the encounter between regimes of dispossession and particular agrarian milieux. Its contribution is a case study of the encounter between India's neoliberal regime of dispossession and a village in Rajasthan.

Milieu and Method

This book uses the extended case method (Burawoy 1998, 2009), which attempts to reconstruct theory through the extended observation of large social forces in small places. In this case, the theory is (most proximately) the predatory theory of dispossession; the social forces are those of dispossession in post-liberalization India; and the place is Rajpura, a village of over four hundred families in Rajasthan that, in 2005, had its land dispossessed for one of North India's first and largest Special Economic Zones.

Rajpura presented itself as a good case for several reasons. The first was that its farmers were already dispossessed when I arrived: while "land wars" were stopping SEZs across India, the Mahindra World City was operational and occupying most of Rajpura's agricultural land when I started my fieldwork in 2009. This allowed me to empirically study its effects at a time when the debate around SEZs was largely conjectural.[84] The second reason is analytical: Rajpura is a limit case for the modernization theory of dispossession. As a monsoon-dependent village with substantially diversified farmers, it was precisely the kind of village that should have benefited the most from such non-agricultural growth. The village was, moreover, dispossessed for an SEZ that actually attracted companies—unlike many that were abandoned after the financial crisis and turned into real estate projects pure and simple (CAG 2014). Reflecting the more general sectoral composition of India's SEZs, these companies were disproportionately from India's "knowledge economy": information technology (IT) and IT-enabled services (ITES). Finally, instead of the far more common below-market compensation, Rajpura's farmers were given one of the best compensation policies on offer in India. Rajpura was not a prosperous Green Revolution village; and the Mahindra World City was probably one of the best SEZs to be dispossessed for in India. This allows me to assess the modernization theory—by far the most dominant of the three—under conditions that are most generous toward it. This strength is also the case's main weakness: it provides conditions least generous toward the predatory theory of dispossession. Indeed, it has the danger of dramatically *understating* the damaging effects of dispossession toward farmers elsewhere in India. To the extent that above-average compensation in Rajpura also reduced the proportion of those strictly proletarianized by dispossession, it is also slightly less favorable to the theory of *proletarian redemption*. The compensating strength is that because many states have since been forced to adopt more "generous" compensation measures, Rajpura may be a prototype of the future. Chapter 9 places Rajpura within the comparative context of other such instances across India.

A single case yields insights unavailable to studies with a broader scope but lower resolution. Part of the insufficiencies of existing theories of dispossession, detailed earlier in the chapter, stems from the high level of abstraction at which they operate; they are theories of dispossession without micro-foundations (Burawoy 1989). The opposite danger is to remain stuck in local particularity while missing broader social forces: a shortcoming of many otherwise fine case studies of dispossession. Trying to connect the micro to macro, the extended case method proceeds under the premise that there "can be no microprocesses without macroforces, nor macroforces without microprocesses" (Burawoy 2009: 9). While the forces bearing down on Rajpura have far larger remit, it is in villages like Rajpura that the role of land dispossession in Indian capitalism and democracy is being played out, and fought out. Through the ethnographic observation of its microprocesses in a Rajasthani village, this book aims to better illuminate the macroforces of dispossession in contemporary India.

This extension from micro to macro is made possible by another extension: of observations over time (Burawoy 1998, 2009). I made several trips to Rajpura beginning in October of 2009, and moved into the village itself in January 2010. Over the next thirteen months—and shorter revisits spanning seven years—I observed a remarkably rapid process of social change that manifested itself in the diverse life trajectories of its residents. After making a tenuous and opportunistic contact with a Jaipur-based real estate broker with family ties to the village, described in the preface, I first obtained lodging in the house of a Brahmin village headman (*sarpanch*) in the Brahmin-dominated village of Shivpura. After a month of observing how the arrival of the SEZ was being opportunistically leveraged by upper-caste landholders, I escaped to the more sociologically representative—and thus far poorer—house of a Dalit family in the larger, mixed-caste village of Rajpura. A relatively large village that lost most of its land for the SEZ, Rajpura became the main focus of my ethnographic research, which also necessarily extended in less depth into adjacent villages.

With the *mohalla* of the Balai subcaste as my base, I branched out into the village's caste-based lanes, remaining fields, its main market, and its multiple *chai* stalls to document how very diverse villagers—ex-feudal landlords, capitalist farmers, marginal farmers, landless workers, livestock herders, potters, tea-sellers, land brokers, labor contractors, priests, shop owners, and so on—experienced the arrival of the Mahindra World City. My foreignness allowed me to move freely over Rajpura's caste divisions but not its gender divisions. The rigid gender norms of Rajasthani society initially restricted my conversations to men. These barriers lessened as I built relationships and gained trust—particularly in the Balai *mohalla* in which I lived—but did not recede, leaving fieldwork that was skewed toward the male public sphere. And because Rajpura was a large village of over four hundred families, it was impossible to know it in its entirety. Nevertheless, through immersion in the daily life of the village and countless conversations in homes, tea stalls, fields, and village lanes, diverse individual trajectories began to form into coherent social processes. To more precisely define the contours of these processes, I concluded my first round of fieldwork with a random-sample survey of ninety-four households in Rajpura and the three nearby villages of Shivpura, Jatpura, and Neempura. Adding these villages gave me a more complete sample of the local caste structure: while Rajpura had a large proportion of lower castes—called Scheduled Castes (SCs) and Otherwise Backward Classes (OBCs) in India—Shivpura was heavily Brahmin, and Jatpura heavily Jat. Adding Neempura, part of Rajpura's *panchayat* but not dispossessed for the SEZ, allowed me to sample more farmers who did not have their land acquired. Sampling 12% of the households in each village, which were selected randomly from local voting lists, the survey consisted of twenty-nine questions that captured household socio-economic status before and after the SEZ.[85] Descriptive statistics from the survey provide a quantitative architecture for my ethnographic findings. After concluding this fieldwork in February 2011, I returned for follow-up visits in the summers of 2012, 2014, and 2016. These were rich opportunities to observe significant transformations that would have been less visible in a shorter time-span.

My research was not, however, restricted to Rajpura and its immediate surroundings. While ethnographic studies often reify the external forces operating at the local level (Burawoy 2009: 250), I followed those forces from Rajpura to sites well beyond—including the corporate offices of the Mahindra World City, the small storefronts of real estate brokers on the nearby highway, global business consultancies in Gurgaon, and dozens of government offices in Sanganer (the sub-district headquarters), Jaipur, and New Delhi. I spent a week poring over forty years of documents in the dusty basement of the Rajasthan Industrial Development and Investment Corporation (RIICO). Right to Information (RTI) requests, filed by social activists in Jaipur, yielded a treasure trove of documents that painted a far more concrete understanding of the relationship between the Rajasthan government and the Mahindra World City than could be obtained through interviews. For comparative perspective, I interviewed government officials involved in land acquisition in six other states, visited a half dozen SEZs across India, and interviewed both their developers and dispossessed farmers where possible. I draw on these national and comparative observations in Chapters 2 and 9. All told, I conducted 116 formal interviews, not counting more numerous informal ethnographic conversations. These broader interviews and brief ethnographic visits periodically took me away from Rajpura for a few days or weeks at a time. While this involved some sacrifice in the continuity of ethnographic observations, the strategy had three compensating strengths. First, by opening up the black box of "state" and "capital" it allowed me to see dispossession as a politically contingent social relationship enacted by real people in boardrooms and government offices rather than as an ineluctable historical process. Second, returning to Rajpura after even short absences allowed me to see all the more sharply processes of social change that can be less perceptible in the continuous monotony of everyday life.[86] Third, it extended my observations over more time than would have been possible had I concentrated the village fieldwork in one stretch, a crucial consideration given the long gestation period of a large capital project. Extending observations over time allowed me to turn events, conversations, and practices into processes, while extending my observations over space helped me to connect these processes to larger social forces.

If my account of how India's neoliberal regime of dispossession has played out in Rajpura has inevitably particular components, the extended case method is based on the premise that "every particularity contains a generality" (Burawoy 1985: 18). Rajpura, I suggest, is a crucible for observing how dispossession under an exclusionary phase of capitalism is intersecting with the stark inequalities of rural India. And connecting the microprocesses of village life to the macroforces of 21st-century Indian capitalism allows for the final extension of the extended case method, from case to theory. For what I observed in Rajpura provided little basis for modernist triumphalism, revolutionary faith, or peasant romanticism.

Dispossession After Development: Argument and Outline

The main empirical argument of this book is that the causes and consequences of land dispossession in India have changed dramatically with the country's transition from state-led development to neoliberalism. Dispossession has, by the still-salient standards of the Nehruvian period, become less developmental. This helps to explain why India's present regime of dispossession is so politically tenuous. While the Indian state's response to this tenuousness has been to give farmers a stake in real estate speculation, this is a poor basis for development and will have uneven success politically. "Land wars" are a symptom of dispossession without development and will not disappear without a major redirection of India's political economy. To the extent that they can foster this redirection, farmer protests against land dispossession are agents of—rather than obstacles to—development.

Chapter 2 explains why the shift from state developmentalism to neoliberalism in India led to the genesis of a new regime of dispossession. Drawing on interviews with government officials, corporate executives, and a variety of archival and secondary sources, it shows how the Rajasthan state government quietly morphed into a land broker state beginning shortly after India commenced economic liberalization in the early 1990s. Until this point, the state government had largely acquired land for public-sector industry, infrastructure, and publicly developed housing. But as economic liberalization created new demands for rural land from the early 1990s onward, the pressure of inter-state competition and the lure of licit and illicit rents incentivized the Rajasthan government—like most of its counterparts across India—to begin acquiring land for any private purpose representing "growth," including real estate development, regardless of its broader developmental consequences. This new regime of dispossession culminated during the rapid economic boom of the mid-2000s when the central government's Special Economic Zone policy encouraged state governments to acquire unprecedentedly large swaths of land for tax-free and deregulated zones built and managed by the private sector. While SEZs were facing "land wars" across India, the Rajasthan government sought to avoid opposition by giving farmers a stake in the anticipated real estate bonanza: a consequential shift in mechanisms of compliance.

Chapter 3 reconstructs the pre-SEZ agrarian milieu of Rajpura. On the eve of its dispossession, Rajpura's economy was based on rain-fed cultivation and livestock-rearing, but water scarcity had pushed many farmers to partially diversify from agriculture. Sharp class, caste, and gender inequalities reflected the failures of the postcolonial Indian state to effectively redistribute land, invest in education and social welfare, and tackle entrenched forms of social domination that characterized rural Rajasthan under pre-independence princely rule. Unlike some parts of India, the village had little experience with collective protest and was politically dominated by alternating upper-caste men. These three factors, as the following chapters show, contributed to the ability of Rajasthan's land broker state to produce compliance to dispossession; and would affect the ability of Rajpura's farmers to benefit from the economic changes unleashed by the Mahindra World City.

Chapter 4 examines the dispossession of Rajpura's farmers for the Mahindra World City. It shows, first, how the aforementioned features of Rajpura's agrarian milieu facilitated the ability of the Rajasthan government to generate individualized compliance to dispossession through its market-based compensation policy. The chapter then examines the initial consequences of this dispossession for both the village and the Mahindra World City. Dispossession enabled Mahindra to arbitrage on the discrepancy between the cost of dispossessed land and its ultimate value as residential and commercial real estate—what I call the rate of accumulation by dispossession—and to establish a tax-free enclave for India's already booming "knowledge economy." Conversely, it generated a cascading *disaccumulation* of agrarian assets within Rajpura. Dispossession undermined direct access to means of subsistence, destroyed a remunerative livestock economy, worsened already acute water shortages, and imposed disproportionate costs on women. It was against these substantial livelihood losses that Rajpura's villagers weighed any gains from the economic changes generated by the Mahindra World City. The next three chapters examine those changes.

While it destroyed productive agrarian assets, the SEZ's major contribution to the local economy was a speculative land boom driven by domestic and global investors. Chapter 5—the most important of the book—examines how this real estate speculation dramatically transformed economic life and social inequality in Rajpura. While dispossessed farmers were given a stake in this speculation, their ability to profit from it was radically unequal. This chapter shows how prior endowments of economic, cultural, and social capital—rooted in the historic failures of land reform and a patriarchal system of landownership—shaped the ability of dispossessed farmers to profit from speculative land markets and reinvest capital gains in an informal economy dominated by rents and circulation. Rather than generating a fairly uniform proletarianization of the dispossessed, as often happened under projects of the Nehruvian state, the result was *differentiation by speculation*. A small fraction of the village, drawn disproportionately from the landed upper castes, became successful neo-rentiers; a majority of the lower-caste semiproletariat became further proletarianized; but a significant and mixed-caste intermediate stratum emerged as what I call petty asset managers, trying to prevent their proletarianization through small investments in land, petty commerce, and moneylending. Excluded altogether from this real estate economy were landless lower-caste households and, by virtue of their lack of independent land rights within households, women in general. So, while real estate speculation made some farmers extremely rich, arbitrary caste- and gender-based inequalities in the distribution of land made it a poor basis for inclusive economic transformation.

While real estate speculation was a differentiating force among Rajpura's dispossessed farmers, Chapter 6 shows that knowledge-intensive growth was so exclusionary for almost all agrarian classes that it made single-cropped agriculture and livestock-rearing look attractive. Rajpura's farmers almost unanimously lacked the requisite cultural capital for inclusion in the SEZ's IT/ITES industry. A small minority received low-paying and insecure work as gardeners, security guards, janitors, and drivers through a stratum of exploitative contractors. For almost no families did these jobs make up for lost agricultural assets. Government welfare and corporate social responsibility programs were ineffective substitutes for land, leaving many to wish they had it back. This non–labor intensive and exclusionary growth, I suggest, helps us understand why even small agrarian assets assume such importance for rural households in contemporary India. In a trajectory of capitalist growth that requires farmers' land more than their labor, and offers inadequately attractive exit routes from agriculture coupled with an inadequate welfare state, holding onto agrarian assets even while diversifying from agriculture—the semiproletarian condition—remains a highly preferred and prudent livelihood strategy.

In addition to marginalizing rural labor, the Mahindra World City was an enclave with few other benefits to surrounding villages. Chapter 7 shows how SEZs represent an abandonment of the developmental ambition of broad-based economic transformation and the retreat into private enclaves of elite accumulation. It shows, first, that public infrastructural investment by the Rajasthan government—in roads, electricity, and water—was entirely geared toward the needs of this emerging private corporate city with little concern for the welfare of surrounding rural populations. Private investment in the zone's export-oriented "knowledge economy," moreover, generated few productive linkages with the surrounding rural—but urbanizing—economy. While the first process relegated Rajpura's dispossessed farmers to a disinvested urbanizing village on the margins of the world city, the second confined them to a tertiary informal economy dominated by rents, petty trade, and usury. The findings of this and the previous two chapters, which are summarized in a brief reprise, demonstrate the exclusionary trajectory of capitalist growth facilitated by India's land broker states, which left a majority of dispossessed households in Rajpura—and a vast majority of lower-caste households—poorer and less food secure than before.

Chapter 8 examines the politics that followed dispossession in Rajpura, which was shaped by the conflicting forces outlined in the previous chapters. Although the Rajasthan government avoided an initial "land war" in Rajpura, the effects of dispossession combined with marginalization from good jobs and facilities inside the SEZ generated widespread anger. Such anger was filtered through an "agrarian populist" idiom, such as that implied by some predatory theories of dispossession, in which farmers as a whole are seen as the victims of outside urban forces. But this sense of shared victimization was undercut by the sharp inequalities land speculation had magnified *within* Rajpura. Differentiation by speculation divided interests and bulldozed the types of social relations that would be necessary for such collective action. In place of a populist upsurge or a radicalized proletariat in the making, there was a symbolic "war of words" (Scott 1985) and individualized forms of adaptation. While Rajpurans continued to aspire for inclusion into "development," their vision of development is structurally unattainable under the current trajectory of Indian capitalism. And this mismatch between subjective aspirations and objective possibilities (Bourdieu 1984) will not only shape politics in Rajpura going forward, but provides crucial insight into the politics of dispossession in contemporary India.

Chapter 9 concludes by arguing that the case of Rajpura provides several insights into the causes and thus future trajectory of India's endemic "land wars"; and the implications of these land wars for development. First and foremost, it suggests that the exclusionary trajectory of capitalism in contemporary India is the structural underpinning of farmer protests. Rent-heavy, non–labor absorbing, and highly enclaved growth makes holding onto land and livestock—even in rain-scarce and monsoon-dependent regions—a highly desirable and prudent livelihood strategy. And if land prices are the *only* material incentive for relinquishing land, those land prices must be high to elicit compliance. Second, therefore, while the political stability of India's neoliberal regime of dispossession now rests on its ability to substitute land prices for inclusive growth, those prices are not in most places high enough to reliably secure compliance—even after a major and ostensibly "pro-farmer" overhaul of India's Land Acquisition

Act. Third, moreover, it will be far harder to orchestrate such a compromise in agrarian milieux that do not resemble Rajpura: where agricultural profitability and dependence are higher; where inequalities are more muted; and where histories of peasant activism are more militant. Given these obstacles to a material compromise and the long-gone ability of the Indian state to make farmers "sacrifice for the nation," there remains the option of brute coercion. But the increasing political saliency of dispossession in India's electoral democracy is making it difficult to take farmers' land by gunpoint. India's neoliberal regime of dispossession is, and will likely remain, politically tenuous. Beyond obstructing it for concrete material reasons, anti-dispossession movements are politically diverse, reflect the agrarian milieu from which they emerge, and do not share a common program. Yet the case of Rajpura helps us to see that these protests are not obstructions of progress, but powerful checks on an exclusionary economic trajectory.

2

Genesis of the Land Broker State

> All nations seized by the capitalist mode of production are periodically seized by fits of giddiness in which they try to accomplish the money-making without the mediation of the production process.
>
> —Karl Marx (1981: 137)

> They take [land] from us and give to others. They kick us out and sell to other people. What meaning is there in this?
>
> —Mohanlal Saini, Rajpura

When I met Mohanlal Saini, barbed wire separated him from his former land, his house was demolished, and the public land where his cattle grazed sat under a Deutsche Bank office. Mohanlal was one of thousands of farmers from nine villages to have their land dispossessed for the Mahindra World City (MWC). Located 25 km from the state capital Jaipur, the MWC was the first and largest private Special Economic Zone (SEZ) to be built in Rajasthan. Developed by the real estate subsidiary of India's blue chip Mahindra Group, it was also advertised as the largest Information Technology (IT) SEZ in India. In addition to campuses for IT and Business Process Outsourcing (BPO) firms and four other zones for export-oriented industries, the MWC would feature a "Lifestyle Zone" with elite residential colonies, private schools, hospitals, parks, and shopping malls. As landlord of this private city, Mahindra would resell plots of land to private companies and build high-end residential and commercial real estate. To facilitate the project, the Rajasthan government dispossessed 2,000 acres of private land and 1,000 acres of public grazing land for the company. Mohanlal's bewilderment, expressed in the preceding epigraph, that the government would take his land in order to "sell to other people," pinpoints the puzzle of this chapter: when and why did the Rajasthan government become a land broker for private capitalists?

What struck Mohanlal as strange has been naturalized by scholars who see India's land grabs of the past few decades as reflecting the homogenous needs of "development" (Chakravorty 2013) or the timeless unfolding of "primitive accumulation" (Sanyal 2007; Chatterjee 2008). Such approaches fail, I have argued, to capture changing political economies of land dispossession across phases of capitalism. Meanwhile, those who see land grabs as a form of predation specific to neoliberalism cannot account for the way that dispossession has transformed from the developmentalist to the neoliberal era. This chapter explains why India's shift from state-directed capitalism to neoliberalism in the early 1990s led to the genesis of a new regime of dispossession.

From roughly 1947 to 1991, the Rajasthan government—like its counterparts across India—overwhelmingly dispossessed land for public-sector industrial and infrastructural projects. This *developmentalist regime of dispossession* was restricted by the aims of central planning and served the purpose of material expansion on a national scale. Its archetypical forms were public-sector dams, industrial estates, and mines. Land dispossession in Rajasthan was largely reflective of the national trend, though limited by the state's scarce water resources and relatively slow pace of industrialization.

In the early 1990s, India's central government embarked on a process of economic liberalization that prioritized rapid economic growth through private investment. This radically accelerated the private demand for land across much of India, particularly for real estate and non-manufacturing industries. This demand, however, confronted the supply barrier of a large small-holding peasantry and "imperfect" rural land markets. A combination of fierce interstate competition for investment and the lure of licit and illicit rents incentivized India's state governments—who have primary discretion over land—to help private capital overcome this barrier. They became, in short, *land broker states.* For land broker states, any form of private profit contributing to growth became a justification for dispossessing farmers. Indeed, under this new regime, arbitraging on under-valued land—maximizing what I call the *rate of accumulation by dispossession*—became a "public purpose" devoid of any broader considerations of "development." Whereas the developmentalist regime dispossessed to produce commodities upon land, this neoliberal regime dispossesses merely to commodify land—often without, as Marx put it, "the mediation of the production process" (1981: 137). In Rajasthan, I show how this neoliberal regime of dispossession began to emerge in the 1990s as parastatal agencies formed during the developmentalist period transformed into instruments for dispossessing rural land for private real estate capital. The Rajasthan State Industrial Development and Investment Corporation (RIICO) evolved from builder of public-sector industrial estates to land agent for private and decreasingly industrial capital. The Jaipur Development Authority (JDA), meanwhile, morphed from urban planning agency into a machine for transferring agricultural land to private builders. By the 2000s, the activities of both had substantially converged and the two agencies teamed up to facilitate one of the first private SEZs in North India.

The Developmentalist Regime of Dispossession

When India achieved independence in 1947, "Rajputana" was a constellation of twenty-two princely kingdoms. The majority of these kingdoms were founded by Rajput "warrior" castes and alternately subordinated to the Mughal, Maratha, and British Empires. Considered not to be worth the cost of direct colonization, the British opted to keep these relatively arid and resource-poor states under a form of indirect rule known as "paramountcy."[1] Under this "ambiguous conception of sovereignty," Rajputana's princely states paid tribute and ceded foreign policy to the British, but retained substantial internal autonomy until India's Independence in 1947, when they were consolidated into the modern state of Rajasthan (Rudolph and Rudolph 1984: 3; Stern 1988). Rajput rule left beautiful sandstone forts and a romantic mystique that annually draws millions of Indian and foreign tourists to the state, including to the "heritage hotels" of Rajput heirs. It also left an economically underdeveloped state with feudal agrarian social relations, almost no industry, little infrastructure, and nominal primary education.

In the 1950s, Rajasthan was integrated into India's postcolonial development project. India's version of this economic model is often misleadingly termed "Nehruvian socialism," after India's first prime minister. Although Jawaharlal Nehru elicited the Indian parliament's commitment to a "socialistic pattern of society," little socialization or redistribution of property was attempted or achieved. Dominant agrarian classes in the Congress thwarted redistributive land reforms in the 1950s (Frankel 2005), Nehru himself quickly repressed labor radicalism (Chibber 2003), and nationalization of private industry was limited to coal, banking, and insurance (which Indira Gandhi brought under state control in the 1970s). India's post-1947 economic model can more accurately be described as developmentalist state capitalism: private industry was tightly regulated through a complex licensing system, the "commanding heights" of the economy were reserved for the public sector, and the imperative of rapid economic growth was leavened with modest efforts to alleviate poverty (Frankel 2005; Kohli 2012).

The challenge facing this development project was to plug the colonial "drain" of wealth and build an "autarkic, self-sufficient national economy" (Goswami 2004: 280). While building this economy marked an important break with the extractivism of colonial capitalism, it shared the need for dispossessing rural land for economic growth. The mechanisms for doing so were bequeathed by the colonial state.

The Colonial Legacy

As the British established territorial sovereignty in the subcontinent, colonial authorities re-engineered India's diverse property systems. This principally involved instituting private property in arable land and asserting state control over forest, grazing, and "waste" land (Guha 1989, 1996; Gadgil and Guha 1993; Sivaramakrishnan 1999; Gidwani 2008; Kashwan 2017). While it extracted natural resources from "state" land and taxed agriculture on private land, transporting these surpluses involved building roads, canals, ports, and ultimately railways. Building this circulatory infrastructure, which was often financed by shareholders in London, required means for requisitioning the private property the colonial state was simultaneously sanctifying. Beginning with the Bengal Regulation Act of 1824, the British introduced the principle of eminent domain to India, establishing the means to forcibly acquire private land for a "public purpose." This culminated, after a series of amendments, in the Land Acquisition Act (LAA) of 1894—which, though amended several times, remained the chief legal instrument for expropriating private land in India until 2014. Its key features were a broad definition of the "public purposes" for which land could be compulsorily acquired, including for private companies,[2] and the requirement that landowners be compensated at the land's "fair market value." Assessing that value proved difficult and prompted multiple revisions. But the LAA established the crucial principle that compensation would be based on the land's previous use—often as agricultural land—and not take into consideration the land's intended use. It contained no provisions for resettling the dispossessed, provided little scope for entertaining objections, and gave almost unlimited discretion to colonial District Collectors (Ramanathan 2008; Krishnan 2014; Ramesh and Khan 2015).

Rajasthan's princely states were largely insulated from these transformations of land tenure and from the British Land Acquisition Act. Forests and grazing land remained under customary tenure, while arable land was held under various forms of feudal tenure, detailed in the next chapter. Although the British urged the Rajas to survey and settle arable land in the early 20th century, this only proceeded on a significant scale after Independence (Government of India 1950: 34; Stern 1988). While the Rajas took land as they saw fit—for roads, salt-works, and relatively minor irrigation projects—the most notable land acquisition occurred for the railways. Jaipur State, for example, acquired land for the imperial railway arteries and its own state-owned railway, apparently with little or no compensation paid to dispossessed cultivators (Stern 1988: 191).[3] But as the princely states merged with independent India, the consolidated Rajasthan state inherited the colonial state's more bureaucratized powers of eminent domain over private land, as well as control over large amounts of "public land" that were de facto inhabited and utilized by millions of agro-pastoralists.

National Development by Dispossession

While preserving the legal mechanisms of dispossession bequeathed by the colonial state, the Indian state would use them to advance postcolonial capitalism. Whereas land dispossession under the Raj served extraction by metropolitan capital, in the post-independence period it served the project of material expansion on a national scale (Goswami 2004). Although eminent domain was briefly and controversially used to expropriate large landlords and undertake modest land reforms (Merillat 1970; Sud 2012)—the limits of which are explored in the next chapter—this use was quickly dwarfed by efforts to dispossess rural land for public-sector industry and irrigation infrastructure, the key spatial forms of Nehruvian planning.

While taking its cues from New Delhi, Rajasthan's implementation of the Nehruvian development project was middling and constrained by its history and geography. Its state machinery was new and marked by the princely legacy of condescension toward commerce.[4] Rajasthan's arid to semi-arid climate and dearth of sizeable rivers furnished relatively few dam sites, and lack of water resources restrained the impact of the Green Revolution. The state was landlocked and had no ports. Without deposits of coal and iron ore, it also had no steel or heavy metals industry. Until an industrial growth spurt in the 1980s, the state's economy remained concentrated in agriculture and "traditional sectors" (e.g., handicrafts, gems, and jewelry) and growth consistently trailed the Indian average (World Bank 2006: 4). Still, Rajasthan pursued the state-led development project framed by New Delhi. As elsewhere, this involved dispossessing a very large number of rural people.

Large dams were the single largest source of dispossession in postcolonial Rajasthan and India (Mathur 1997: 5; Fernandes 2008). Dams were the paradigmatic form of state-led development and potent symbols of national progress. But damming river valleys was not possible without flooding the homes, fields, and forests of millions of people. In the 1950s, Rajasthan moved swiftly to develop its relatively few potential dam sites, which were almost entirely in the south and southeastern part of the state. While there is no official count of the number of people dispossessed by large dams in the state, existing data suggests that over 25,000 families from hundreds of villages lost their land for just six of Rajasthan's biggest dams.[5] Since most were located in forested hilly tracts of south Rajasthan, the dispossessed were disproportionately Bhil *adivasis* (indigenous groups categorized by the Indian government as "Scheduled Tribes"). Northwest Rajasthan, meanwhile, was the recipient of one of the largest irrigation projects in postcolonial India: the Indira Gandhi Canal (IGNP), a World Bank–funded mega-project that involved building 8,000 kilometers of canals to "green" the Tar Desert with water from Punjab and Himachal Pradesh. This monumental project transformed thousands of square miles of inhospitable desert—much of it common grazing land supporting semi-nomadic pastoralists—into thousands of private plots irrigated by canal and supplied with Green Revolution inputs (Goldman 1994). While there are no estimates of the original inhabitants dispossessed for the canal, Michael Goldman (1994) has vividly documented the privatization of common grazing land and destruction of village institutions this involved. To feed the IGNP, moreover, 30,000 families were dispossessed from ninety-four villages for the Pong Dam in Himachal Pradesh (Mathur 1995b: 2).

After large dams, the major source of dispossession in postcolonial Rajasthan was public-sector industry. India's Second Five Year Plan (1956–1961) famously called for rapid industrialization with an emphasis on heavy industries in the public sector (Chakravarty 1987; Zachariah 2005). Although Rajasthan had none of the flagship "steel towns" that displaced hundreds of villages in other states (Burman 1968; Roy 2007; Parry and Struempell 2008; Struempell 2014), it began to slowly industrialize and develop its mineral resources in the 1960s. Like other states, it formed parastatal agencies to catalyze these efforts. In 1969, it formed the Rajasthan State Industrial and Mineral Development Corporation, which in 1980 was spliced into the Rajasthan State Mineral Development Corporation (RSMDC) and the Rajasthan State Industrial Development and Investment Corporation (RIICO). RSMDC facilitated the exploitation of Rajasthan's mineral deposits, along with large public sector firms like Hindustan Zinc. RIICO's principle task was to acquire land using the LAA, develop industrial estates and lease plots to public- and private-sector industries, to which it also provided cheap credit.[6] Between its 1969 formation and 1999, RIICO acquired a relatively modest 25,000 acres of land—from an unknown number of people—for 175 industrial estates spread across Rajasthan.[7] Its activities began to pick up in the 1980s when industrial growth in Delhi's National Capital Region spilled over into eastern Rajasthan.

While Rajasthan was one of the least urbanized states in India, it formed urban improvement trusts for its largest cities in the 1950s and gave them power to compulsorily acquire land for planned urban development. In 1970, the state government formed the Rajasthan Housing Board, which was given similar powers to develop affordable housing. In 1982, this power was extended to the Jaipur Development Authority (JDA), and subsequently to similar authorities for Rajasthan's next largest cities. Modeled on the Delhi Development Authority (DDA), which was founded in the 1950s, the JDA's purpose was to promote planned urban development in the state capital. In addition to the power of eminent domain, it was given ownership over all public land in Jaipur's urbanizable limits, which mostly consisted of the grazing commons of peri-urban villages. While founded on the cusp of liberalization, the JDA would become a major instrument of dispossessing farmers for private real estate interests in the neoliberal period.

As elsewhere in India,[8] those dispossessed by development projects in Rajasthan were pitifully compensated, seldom resettled much less "rehabilitated" to their previous standard of living,[9] and almost always further impoverished. Compensation was, to begin with, scandalously low. While the LAA required that landowners be compensated at "market value" plus a "solatium" of 15%, land valuation was in practice highly arbitrary. Land records were poorly maintained, irrigated land was often categorized as unirrigated or barren, payments could be delayed for years, and those without formal title—a common occurrence in many *adivasi* areas—received no compensation at all. Houses, trees, and wells were undervalued; grazing commons and forest land were not valued at all. Many were shoved off with meager cash compensation and left to their fate. Resettlement, when it occurred, was often a cruel joke. While those displaced for irrigation projects were often promised replacement land, it was seldom irrigated and often barren. Resettlement sites were often poorly constructed, far from existing villages, and devoid of basic necessities like water, schools, and health clinics.[10] Faced with this dismal situation, some attempted to move back to higher land in their original villages, where they were treated as encroachers and subject to harassment by government officials.[11] Perhaps no one fared worse than the Pong Dam oustees: driven from their homes and land in the relatively lush foothills of the Himalayas, they were allotted barren IGNP plots in "unlivable" sites in the Rajasthan desert without amenities or support.[12] While these plots would take years to make cultivable, the rules governing their allotment required that their owners take immediate possession and have them under plow within a year. Making matters worse, local "land mafias" encroached upon them through "murder, looting, and arson" (Mathur 1997: 10), seemingly in connivance with government officials. When they could not or would not shift to these sites, their allotments were simply canceled (Mathur 1995b). The minority who stayed, meanwhile, suffered from the many failures of the project itself: shoddy construction, lack of village amenities, insufficient state support, the concentration of land in the hands of rich and absentee owners, and unforeseen water-logging and salinization that rendered a large section of the command area infertile (Goldman 1994). This Kafkaesque nightmare, perhaps an inevitable byproduct of "high-modernist" social and environmental engineering at this scale (Scott 1998), is only an extreme version of what many of the displaced suffered; and many of those displaced by other dams in Rajasthan were offered land in the IGNP canal area! While we know less about them, those dispossessed for mining and conservation projects appeared to have fared little better (Sharma 1995; Mathur 1997). The one existing study of those dispossessed for a RIICO industrial estate suggests that they were undercompensated and that while the estate attracted almost 400 companies and generated 40,000 jobs, dispossessed families received few of them while their villages became dumping grounds for toxic pollution (Srivastava 1995).

It should have been possible for the state to do a better job at including the dispossessed in the subsequent agricultural and industrial growth. That it did not is surely due to the fact that the dispossessed were either relatively small in number compared to the beneficiaries and/or from politically marginalized populations. This is supported by the fact that politically influential groups among the dispossessed sometimes managed to gain preferential treatment.[13]

Rajasthan's moderate economic growth in the developmentalist period was thus subsidized by the dispossession and impoverishment of a large but unknown number of rural people. Scholars have estimated the all-India figure to be somewhere between 25 and 60 million and have documented a similarly abysmal record of resettlement and rehabilitation (cf. Fernandes and Thukral 1989; Thukral 1992; Fernandes and Paranjpye 1997; Cernea 1999; Fernandes 2008). Whether dispossession contributed to "development" in this period is a matter of perspective, in other words, whether one stood in the command area of the dam or with one's house under a reservoir; with a public-sector job or pulling a rickshaw in the nearest slum. The historical claim of this chapter is simply that this was a distinct regime of dispossession, shaped by a developmentalist project that was different in several respects from its neoliberal successor.

First, the major projects driving dispossession in this period were planned and managed by the public sector. This is not because it was illegal to dispossess land for private companies. The liberal LAA, formulated in large part to facilitate British railway companies (Krishnan 2014), allowed the government to acquire land for private companies. Indeed, this right was solidified through a 1963 amendment overturning a Supreme Court decision that struck down the Uttar Pradesh government's acquisition of 10 acres for a private textile factory. In his majority decision, Justice J. Wanchoo had argued that a private industry did not constitute a public purpose and worried that such a practice would make the government "a general agent for companies to acquire lands . . . for private profit."[14] But while the controversial amendment to overturn his decision clarified the legality of government land acquisition for private companies, the prevailing development model ensured that it remained limited in practice.

By reserving the "commanding heights" of the economy to the public sector, India's industrial policy ensured that it was mostly public-sector corporations that required large tracts of land for greenfield projects. Lighter industries open to private investment typically required less land, and after the 1960s were mostly allotted leased land inside public-sector industrial estates (and subject to regulations discussed shortly). While the Indian state inherited a private mining sector, post-independence exploration and extraction was dominated by the public sector. Most importantly, until the 1990s, "Infrastructure was naturally seen as the exclusive responsibility of the public sector" (Ahluwalia 1998: 257). Roads, ports, highways, airports, and power plants thus created no scope for transferring land to private companies. Industrial estates were government-developed and managed by their public-sector landlords. Large dams were built by powerful government agencies or river-basin parastatals modeled on the Tennessee Valley Authority (Klingensmith 2007; Goldman 1994).[15] Although often funded and advised by the World Bank, such authorities were criticized for expanding state power over rural areas and centralizing control over their natural resources (Goldman 1994; Baviskar 1995). While some land dispossession for private companies occurred during the Nehruvian period, this was dwarfed by the large "nation-building" projects of the public sector. And while dispossession for state projects facilitated private accumulation in a capitalist economy, this largely occurred through the mediation of public-sector infrastructure rather than the direct transfer of land to private corporations. The government, as a former chief secretary of Rajasthan recalled, "was not as much willing to acquire land for private people."[16] All of this reflected the statist ethos of Nehruvian planning. Justice Wanchoo's fears *would* be realized; but not for another three decades.

Second, the state largely dispossessed land for projects that were narrowly productive in orientation and often imposed rules to restrict speculation. The goal of Indian planning was not to increase economic activity in general but to prioritize the rapid expansion of heavy industry and agriculture, which were considered central to national "self-reliance." Public-sector industry—whether in estates, "steel towns," or stand-alone locations—would provide the building blocks of an industrial society; public-sector mining was made to serve its needs; and dams provided a portion of the electricity, while catalyzing agricultural capitalism in the countryside. Industrial estates, in sharp contrast to post-liberalization SEZs, were narrowly industrial and their land rents flowed to the public sector. In the industrial townships built to house public-sector workers, "Urban planning decisions about how much land to acquire and how many houses to build were shaped by a single calculation: how many workers does it take to produce one million tons of steel ingots" (Roy 2007: 140). Even housing development was a state-dominated affair and included provisions for affordability; indeed, the purpose of creating urban improvement trusts and development authorities with the power of eminent domain was to *control* private speculation on urban and peri-urban land (Merillat 1970: 224; Jain 2009: 65–69; Ghertner 2015: 26), quite the opposite from today. Banking land was intended to prevent speculators from driving up the cost of planned development; and the expansion of public-sector housing—for example by the Rajasthan Housing Board—was meant to control prices by expanding supply. Government control over urbanizable land was also intended to ensure that land appreciation driven by public infrastructure investment could be recouped by the public sector (Jain 2009: 65–69).[17] Anti-speculation measures were also commonly adopted in the command area of dams, inside industrial estates, and in the vicinity of India's planned state capitals (Kalia 1999: 35, 127). Reflecting a developmentalist "land to the tiller ethos," land allotments in the IGNP command area were given on a priority basis to the regional poor and landless, who were prohibited from selling their land for the first ten years (Goldman 1994: 170). RIICO similarly had rules mandating that industrial plots be put to productive use; and when sold, a fixed percentage of the profits would revert to RIICO. Government agencies, jealous of their prerogatives and emboldened by the status granted to the public sector under Nehruvian planning, did not consider it their responsibility to dispossess farmers for the capital gains of private companies.

Of course, state controls on paper did not always translate into practice. Government officials proved alert to the opportunities for rent-seeking these projects offered, and many of these rules were bent or evaded. Private companies did get land inside industrial estates and, seemingly with the collusion of officials, evaded restrictions on speculation.[18] Likewise, restrictions on speculation in the IGNP command area were circumvented by powerful elites purchasing "power of attorney" from poor allottees in connivance with project officials, generating an "ebullient black market . . . for desert real estate," which became more bullish when the restrictions were scrapped altogether in 1987 (Goldman 1994: 172). Urban development authorities did a poor job of building affordable housing and were accused of abetting land speculation from their inception (Srivastava 2015: 59–60). State-managed capitalism was still capitalism, and it is important to recognize the continuities between present and past regimes of dispossession: we will see that these practices paved the way for the unrestricted land profiteering of the neoliberal period. But land profiteering was, until the 1990s, restricted by state controls and much more closely tethered to production. The idea that land should be dispossessed for any private purpose representing a higher value land use was not yet ascendant.[19]

Third, state control over these projects came with various kinds of developmental commitments that were broader than economic growth per se. One of the most important was "balanced regional development," the idea that economic development should be spread evenly over the country in order to reach "backward" areas. In the context of Europe, Neil Brenner (2004) has termed this mid-century geographical imaginary "spatial Keynesianism": in the context of postcolonial India, we might call it "spatial Nehruvianism." An abiding concern of nationalist economic thinkers since the 1930s (Zachariah 2005: 218), this principle was a response to the highly uneven geography of colonial capitalism (Goswami 2004: 130)[20] and prominently reflected in India's Five Year Plans (Ahluwalia 1998: 262). Concretely, this commitment to geographical equity shaped the allocation of the industrial licenses required to start or expand businesses. It was also evident in the siting of industrial areas. Contrasting his agency's industrial areas with private SEZs, a RIICO official explained, "Business will only acquire land in fast-moving regions. But being a government agency, we also have to look at slow-moving regions."[21] Trying to bring investment to "backward areas" often involved providing liberal equity, cheap credit, and land rebates on investments in "tribal areas" and "no industry districts" (RIICO 1988a).[22] The commitment is also observable in the extensive geography of irrigation projects, which spread their tentacles of canals far into the countryside in order to green "barren" land. While state-led development never achieved balanced regional development—an impossibility within a capitalist economy no matter how tightly controlled—its efforts to check the inequality of the market contrast markedly, as Chapter 7 will show, with the post-liberalization surrender to geographic inequality and the retreat into private enclaves of elite accumulation.

A related commitment was to labor-intensive growth. While the "Mahalanobis model" of prioritizing heavy industry was criticized at the time for its capital intensity, Indian planning did make significant efforts to generate large-scale employment. As Parry (2003: 222) notes, planning priorities of the time emphasized employment rather than profit in the public sector, which would allow at least a small fraction of the dispossessed to be absorbed into the privileged public-sector labor force. Industrial estates gave preferential land allotment to labor-intensive industries (RIICO 1993). These efforts, made possible by India's relatively autarkic trade policies combined with the prevailing state of technology, were only moderately successful and did not come close to absorbing India's working population. Yet they again stand in sharp contrast to their relinquishment by the post-liberalization state and the consequent surrender to "jobless growth." And the fact that many of the jobs they created were in the public sector made it possible, where the political desire existed, to extend them to dispossessed populations.[23]

Finally, the developmentalist regime of dispossession was very successful at producing compliance for more than three decades. There is very little recorded evidence of strong opposition to Rajasthan's early dams or other infrastructure projects (Mathur 1995b; Mathur 1997). As one revenue official recalled of RIICO's industrial estates, "At that time, we took a lot of land from farmers and there was hardly any protest."[24] The almost complete lack of evidence about the opinions of the dispossessed in Rajasthan and elsewhere in India—especially during the early post-independence decades—limit our ability to explain why. Given the pitiful compensation on offer, the main material incentives were promises of inclusion in the resulting growth, whether irrigated land or industrial jobs. While such promises were often broken, they were plausible given the growth model and may have been politically effective. Still, the dispossessed were being asked, as Nehru told the oustees of one dam, to "sacrifice for the nation." Such normative persuasion could draw on the full force of postcolonial nationalism (Goswami 2004; Zachariah 2005). What Ramachandra Guha has called the "overwhelming consensus in favour of a heavy industry-oriented, state-supported model of development" (Guha 2007) lent widespread public legitimacy to projects like large dams (Khagram 2004: 35; Guha 2007: 224–225) and steel towns (Roy 2007: 140).[25] This legitimacy is inextricable from the fact that dams promised electricity and irrigation to hundreds of thousands of farmers in their command areas while public-sector industry promised secure formal-sector jobs. Whether this legitimacy really extended to those dispossessed for these projects remains unclear.[26] The more judicious conclusion, I believe, is that postcolonial nationalism made it extremely difficult to fight these projects—no matter what the dispossessed thought.[27] If and when farmers did not want to give up their land for these projects, the overwhelming public support for them greatly constrained the terms on which farmers could articulate opposition and severely limited their ability to attract outside support.[28] Most villagers probably saw that they had no choice. And if they had thoughts of resisting, they were quickly met with police force.[29] In several instances, dam authorities simply closed the spill gates to flood recalcitrant villagers out of their homes. Addressing those to be submerged by the IGNP-feeding Pong Dam in the 1960s, Finance Minister (and future Prime Minister) Morarji Desai warned, "[W]e will request you to move from your houses after the dam comes up. If you move, it will be good; otherwise, we shall release the waters and drown you all."[30]

This "sacrifice for the nation . . . or else" approach was highly effective. It was not until the 1970s that activists armed with discourses of indigenous rights and environmental protection started to raise concerns about displacement and "destructive development." The struggles against the Tehri and Narmada dams pioneered the way for anti-dispossession "people's movements" in India (Kothari 1984; Omvedt 1993; Routledge 1993). While less documented, opposition to large dams also emerged in Rajasthan in the 1980s, most notably against the Bisalpur Dam, which received inspiration and support from the Narmada anti-dam struggle (Mathur 1997: 26). Those to be displaced by several other dam projects in the state also received NGO support (I. C. Srivastava 1995; Hemadri 1995). None of these efforts succeeded in stopping dispossession, however, and at most they achieved modest improvements to compensation and resettlement. The development model would itself give way before social movements could significantly impede dispossession executed on its behalf.

To summarize, between Independence and economic liberalization the Rajasthan government largely dispossessed land for public-sector industry and infrastructure projects. These projects reflected the principles of Nehruvian state planning: they prioritized production while seeking to control speculation and were guided by developmentalist commitments to balanced regional development and labor absorption. The state produced compliance to dispossession for these purposes largely through powerful appeals to national development backed by police force. While this regime facilitated significant economic expansion compared to the colonial/princely era, we know that its gains disproportionately but not exclusively accrued to India's "dominant proprietary classes": the national bourgeoisie, large farmers, and state officials themselves (Bardhan 1984; see also Nilsen 2010). While it was relatively uncommon to directly dispossess land for private companies, land dispossession still served private capital indirectly by providing inputs, creating infrastructure, and building heavy public-sector industries that created downstream opportunities for private investment (Chibber 2003: 208). The large capital projects of this era were, moreover, often poorly executed, ran into huge cost-overruns,[31] and encountered enormous ecological and logistical problems that may be inherent to what Scott (1998) calls "high-modernist" social engineering. Most importantly, they were steeply subsidized by the brutal and fairly uniform impoverishment of millions of dispossessed people. The staggering human toll of dispossession during this period, almost entirely absent from the mainstream development literature, should be kept squarely in mind. This was no golden age of dispossession that actually did serve the "public interest." It was just a different regime of dispossession in the service of a distinct phase of capitalism.

The Neoliberal Regime of Dispossession

If the Nehruvian state dispossessed land for the public more than the private sector, and for productive purposes while trying to limit private speculation, the neoliberal regime of dispossession is defined by the removal of such limits, and the willingness of states to dispossess land for any private purpose that contributes to economic growth, no matter how speculative or non-labor absorbing. The following sections explain why the adoption of neoliberal economic policies at the national level precipitated this new regime of dispossession in Rajasthan.

Land in Demand

The liberalization of India's economy began with tentative steps toward domestic deregulation in the 1980s (Kohli 2002). A balance-of-payments crisis in 1991 created the opportunity for India's pro-reform political elite to initiate a more thoroughgoing—if phased and stealthy (Jenkins 1999)—program of reforms. These reforms began to dismantle the model of state-regulated capitalism that had prevailed since Independence. The complex system of industrial licensing was abolished, public-sector investment was curtailed, and the private sector was given a free hand to enter new sectors and expand capacity. Trade was significantly liberalized and foreign investment courted. The financial sector was gradually liberalized: private investors were allowed into the previously nationalized banking sector, liquidity requirements and interest rate controls were relaxed, priority-sector lending was reduced, and non-resident Indians (NRIs) and foreign institutional investors were allowed into Indian capital markets for the first time (Joshi and Little 1996; Jenkins 1999; Chandrasekhar and Ghosh 2002).

These reforms transformed the Indian economy in ways that dramatically changed the demand for rural land. Most importantly, liberalization rapidly reversed the predominance of the public sector in the Indian economy. The share of private investment in total paid-up capital steadily increased from less than 30% at the end of the 1980s to roughly 70% by the end of the 1990s (Kohli 2012: 45). Consequently, as the Indian economy grew over that decade, and dramatically so in the mid-2000s, it was private corporations rather than public-sector undertakings (PSUs) that would increasingly require land for industry, infrastructure, real estate, and extraction.

The sectoral composition of India's economic growth also began to shift and, with it, the sources of demand for land. India's manufacturing sector was not dramatically stimulated by neoliberal reforms and has remained sluggish in relative terms (Bardhan 2010; Kohli 2012). As Figure 2.1 shows, the share of manufacturing in India's GDP began losing ground to business services and so-called "FIRE" industries—finance, insurance, and real estate—beginning in the 1990s, and was surpassed by the mid-2000s. While manufacturing accounted for 59% of all new capital projects in 1995, it accounted for only 17% in 2015.[32]

More than labor-intensive manufacturing, India's post-liberalization growth has been propelled by Information Technology (IT) and Business Process Outsourcing (BPO, a component of what is also called IT-enabled services or ITES) (Bardhan 2010; Gupta and Kumar 2012). The ascendance of India's IT/BPO sector is by now a well-known story. Supported strongly by the Indian government since the 1980s, the industry made early inroads into software development and, by the 1990s, had turned India into a popular offshoring destination for "back-office" services (Upadhya 2016: Ch. 1). Major multinational

Figure 2.1 The growth of FIRE and service industries relative to manufacturing in India.
Source: Ministry of Statistics and Programme Implementation, Government of India.

corporations (MNCs), beginning with American Express, British Airways, and General Electric, started to offshore various parts of their business operations to India to arbitrage on labor costs, which were typically 70% cheaper than in Western countries. In addition to MNC subsidiaries, a range of independent (Indian and foreign) service providers, including software technology firms, moved into the market. The BPO sector grew rapidly in the 1990s and even faster in the 2000s, as outsourcing became standard business practice for Western corporations (Arora et al. 2001; Kapur 2002; Dossani and Kenney 2007; Bardhan 2010). Between 1998 and 2012, revenues from the IT/BPO sector expanded from 1.2% to 7.5% of India's GDP, and its share of total exports ballooned from 4% to 25% (NASSCOM 2012).

Although the IT/BPO sector still only accounted for a relatively small share of India's GDP (Kohli 2012: 119), its phenomenal growth contributed to a boom in demand for commercial real estate (Goldman 2011; Searle 2016: 31). With older Indian cities unable to provide the "world-class" office space and infrastructure required by multinational corporations (Searle 2016: 31), much of this demand became channeled into greenfield campuses and high-tech parks on their rural peripheries, swelling the footprint of cities like Bangalore and Hyderabad, and populating new satellite cities like Gurgaon (Goldman 2011; Searle 2016). By the mid-2000s, the IT/BPO industry was leading the rush into SEZs.

This phenomenal growth of the "knowledge economy" dovetailed with a second generation of reforms that liberalized India's infrastructure and real estate sectors. Until the early 1990s, the creation of infrastructure was assumed to be a public-sector responsibility financed by government spending. India's Eighth Five Year Plan, formulated in 1992, anticipated that "the public sector will continue to play a dominant role" in infrastructure creation, but for the first time opened the door for private participation:

> if private initiative comes forward to participate in creating such infrastructure like power plants, roads, bridges, medium and minor irrigation projects, social housing, industrial estates, on reasonable terms and with full protection of people's interests, such initiative must be positively encouraged (Government of India 1992: para 1.4.26).

As the decade wore on, Indian planners became convinced that sustaining India's growth rate required dramatic infrastructural expansion, and that it was impossible or undesirable for the public sector to provide the needed investment. The result was privatization of the infrastructure sector (Ahluwalia 1998; IDFC 2008), beginning with a series of policies to attract private investment into power (1992), roads (1997), and ports (1997). By the Eleventh Five Year Plan (2007–2012), the Planning Commission projected that India would need $320 billion in infrastructure investments to avoid bottlenecks, and that 75% of this investment would come from private sources (Rastogi 2008: 1). In practice, investment in infrastructure almost quadrupled over the 2000s with 37% of that investment coming from the private sector (Gulati 2011: 380).[33] Public-private partnerships (PPP) became the preferred institutional form for investment in power, telecom, roads, railways, and all manner of physical and "social" infrastructure. Crucially, compensating private investors with excess land and/or development rights became an increasingly common form of cost recovery in these arrangements—whether for roads, airports, or affordable housing (Ahluwalia 1998; IDFC 2008, 2009). The introduction of privately developed SEZs after 2000, to be discussed shortly, simply represented an application of this principle to industrial infrastructure. The ability to make real estate profits through infrastructure investment increased its attractiveness to private investors, who could now buy shares of infrastructure assets through special investment funds.[34] The line between infrastructure, typically considered a "public work," and real estate became blurred.

The privatization of infrastructure was thus synergistic with the liberalization and dramatic growth of Indian real estate. Until the 1990s, urban development was a state-dominated affair. Public housing boards and urban development authorities retained significant control over residential construction; the Urban Land (Ceiling and Regulation) Act allowed the government to expropriate vacant private landholdings exceeding a certain limit[35]; regulations sought to check land speculation and assure housing for the poor; and formal credit from the nationalized banking sector was unavailable to private builders (Searle 2016: 29). However, after liberalization in the early 1990s, the Indian government passed a series of policies that encouraged private investment in housing.[36] As Searle writes, "Since the liberalization of the economy, the model of state-dominated urban development has crumbled nationally as states and municipalities, urged by the central government, have opened urban development to private corporations" (Searle 2016: 29).

Crucial to this liberalization of housing development has been the loosening of restrictions on bank lending to private developers. By 2002, private developers were allowed to obtain financing for construction from foreign investors, and this policy was further liberalized after 2005 (Searle 2016: 30). Credit expansion, combined with the booming demand for commercial office space by India's IT industry and pent-up demand for housing by a burgeoning middle class (itself augmented by the IT industry), precipitated a real estate boom by the mid-2000s. Between 2001 and 2011, housing finance expanded by a factor of eight, and real estate values increased by at least a factor of five (2.5 times the rate of inflation) (Chakravorty 2013); the latter a very conservative estimate given that sale prices are systematically under-reported to avoid taxes, making real estate a huge sink for black money (Kumar 2002). Flat prices in India's largest cities rivaled or surpassed those in Western metropolises,[37] while smaller cities and large towns also experienced dramatic booms. The constrained supply of land in urban areas meant that much of this demand spilled into peri-urban and rural areas where global, national, and regional builders—including large conglomerates that quickly diversified into real estate—began to buy up farmland to construct housing colonies, and middle-class and non-resident Indians bought up plots for residences and as speculative investments. Much of this "demand," as subsequent chapters will show, was purely speculative (see also Searle 2016). The result has been rural land values that rival those in the United States (Chakravorty 2013).

The liberalization of India's industrial, infrastructural, and real estate sectors culminated with India's SEZs during the 2000s. As juridical entities, SEZs were simply industrial estates governed by more liberal economic policies. In this respect, they had an antecedent in Export Processing Zones (EPZs), which evolved as a way to enable foreign companies to exploit cheap labor in "Third

World" countries by creating islands of political stability, good infrastructure, and business-friendly economic policies.[38] India developed its first EPZ in Kandla, Gujarat, in 1967, followed by six more over the subsequent decades. But India's EPZs were small, government-developed industrial estates[39] and represented a marginal experiment at export-oriented growth within the context of import-substituting industrialization (Chibber 2003: 198).[40] When the Indian government passed an SEZ Policy (2000) and the SEZ Act (2005), it sought to correct for these "deficiencies" with a more liberal set of financial incentives—income tax holidays, tariff waivers, and duty-free imports—and a streamlined regulatory environment.

But the real novelty of India's SEZs was that private companies were encouraged to develop, maintain, and effectively govern them on a for-profit basis. In contrast to China's government-built SEZs, India's SEZs represented a radically privatized way of building industrial infrastructure in which corporate developers would replace government agencies. This policy was justified by the argument that the Indian government could not itself build the infrastructure on the scale envisioned and reflected the overall push toward developing infrastructure on a public-private partnership (PPP) basis (IDFC 2008). But as a Commerce Ministry official pointed out, India's SEZ model "is not strictly PPP because the government is not putting a single penny in. It's purely privatized."[41]

Privatizing SEZ development was pushed forward by real estate companies who saw in SEZs an opportunity for windfall returns at a particularly favorable moment in India's neoliberal growth trajectory. While the manufacturing sector lobbied for the liberal concessions that were made available to exporting companies within SEZs, real estate companies and large corporate houses lobbied for the opportunity to privately develop them.[42] Crucially, the SEZ Act only required that 35% of the land acquired for SEZs be used for the manufacturing of goods or the rendering of services, giving developers freedom with the rest—after protests against them quickly emerged, the "processing area" was increased to 50% (Jenkins 2014: 46–47). Since the highest-value land use is housing, most developers saw SEZs as an opportunity to build satellite cities on cheap land at the urban periphery during the unprecedented real estate boom of the mid-2000s. SEZs thus became outlets for speculative real estate capital at the peak of India's land boom, which explains the scale and speed with which they spread across the country—464 were approved in the first sixteen months and the total quickly approached 600.

In sum, the process of economic liberalization that began in the 1990s created "a voracious appetite for space to meet the demands of industrialization, infrastructure building, urban expansion and resource extraction" (Ghatak and Ghose 2011: 65).[43] This demand grew steadily over the 1990s, receded somewhat between 1997 and the early 2000s in the aftermath of the East Asian financial crisis, and ascended to new heights in the mid-2000s as India's growth rate reached 9% and a liberalized real estate market entered a dramatic boom. This boom spread well beyond India's large metropolises, engulfing relatively sleepy "Tier-2"[44] cities like Jaipur and driving road-front urbanization far into rural India. And in contrast to the land requirements of India's state-led growth model, this new demand for land was overwhelmingly private and decreasingly industrial, much less agricultural.

The question remains: why would increasing demand for land translate into increased *dispossession* rather than just a booming land *market*?

The Supply Obstacle

This new demand for land increased the significance of an old obstacle: rural land markets dominated by a small-holding peasantry. It is often observed that land is a unique commodity because it is finite, non-producible, and has location-specific qualities that make it imperfectly substitutable (Hall 2013b). For development projects that are "site-bound" (Hirschman 1967), this means that specific pieces of land are required either for their bio-physical or locational properties. Even "footloose" projects that have some latitude in location require contiguity. From the demand point of view, this means that capital cannot simply go wherever there are willing sellers.

There are, conversely, several reasons why market demand does not always call forth willing sellers. Landowners value particular parcels of land for both economic and social reasons. It is in this sociological sense that I interpret Polanyi's (2001) observation that land is a "fictitious" commodity. Because it is not brought into the world with the purpose of being sold, attempts to reduce it to a commodity run into historically sedimented forms of valuation that are not reducible to exchange value (Polanyi 2001: 187). Farmers value land in multiple ways—as home, patrimony, security, and as a source of autonomy, status, identity, and community—that are not easily or necessarily translatable into price. While such valuations of land are often glibly dismissed as "emotional attachments," they can also be economically prudent. Even where farmers would in principle like to exit agriculture, they are often reluctant to surrender land where non-farm economic opportunities appear unpromising—which, as Chapters 6 and 7 suggest, they are in India today. The upshot is that the existence of alienable private property across most of rural India is no guarantee of a purely capitalist land market.[45] While a capitalist looking to purchase hundreds of acres in rural India will surely find some sellers, they will also surely find holdouts.

This difficulty of consolidating large tracts of land is compounded by land fragmentation. Landholdings in India are among the smallest in the world and are only shrinking with the relentless march of generational subdivision. Of the

101 million operational holdings in rural India in 2003, 70% were less than one hectare (NSS 2006). In Rajpura alone, the land acquired for the Mahindra World City was previously divided into 2,950 parcels (*khasras*) owned by 391 different families.[46] And the average landholding in Rajasthan is three times larger than the national average, making the problem far more acute elsewhere.[47] Land fragmentation, moreover, multiplies the likelihood of legal disputes in the context of shoddy land records and a creaking judicial system. While a comparatively large portion of India's rural land is surveyed and settled as private property, land records are often ambiguous. Joint ownership complicates titles and, for various historical reasons—including low levels of literacy and government corruption and inaccessibility—older generations of farmers did not always register subdivisions or sales. Increasing land values multiply the resulting disputes, which are estimated to affect 28% of peri-urban land parcels (World Bank 2007: 2). These disputes can take years or even decades to resolve in India's backlogged courts, during which time construction or sale can be frozen by court injunction, delaying projects indefinitely.[48]

So while economic liberalization increased private demand for rural land, India's rural land markets do not provide "an open field" for the circulation of capital (Harvey 2006b: 271). Although these features of India's land markets existed under the developmentalist regime, they began to pose a larger problem after liberalization as private demand accelerated.

This provided the rationale for increased state involvement in land acquisition for private companies. Any capitalist looking to establish a large greenfield project in rural India would insist that the government acquire land for them. As a Mahindra World City executive explained:

> [Purchasing land] is always difficult. . . . You have to negotiate with too many people and you always find a maverick. Say you want to buy 100 acres, if you find someone who is smart and educated, he says, "I'm not going to sell my land." So government has to take it. . . . You have to do it through government. They are the necessary evil.[49]

This view was repeated by every private developer, consultant, and industry representative I interviewed over the course of my research. It reflected the consistent demand of Indian industry, summarized by the Confederation of Indian Industries, that "Government cannot absolve its responsibility in land acquisition" (CII 2011). Government officials I interviewed in Rajasthan and six other Indian states almost unanimously repeated it.[50]

Nevertheless, this does not explain the state's willingness to mobilize coercion to make these projects possible. To understand why state governments began, post-liberalization, to help private capital overcome the barrier of rural land markets on an unprecedented scale and for an expanded range of purposes, it is necessary to appreciate the way economic liberalization restructured the relationship between capital and subnational states.

Competing to Dispossess

By loosening the central government's control over the economy, liberalization greatly intensified the competition for investment among India's state governments (Jenkins 1999; Rudolph and Rudolph 2001). The abolition of industrial licensing—the process by which the central government approved and determined the location of new industrial undertakings—gave private investors the freedom to decide where to invest. Now having to compete for mobile capital rather than lobby for central government licenses and investments (Sinha 2005), state governments came under pressure to offer increasingly liberal policies and concessions to investors. In the early 1990s, state governments passed new industrial policies outlining these incentives, opened investment promotion bureaus, and began actively courting private and foreign investment (Rudolph and Rudolph 2001; Sud 2012). Signing Memorandums of Understanding (MoUs) with private and foreign companies signaled the ability of political leaders to bring "development" to their states.

Rajasthan slowly followed suit. An early step came in 1987, when the state government formed a Bureau of Industrial Promotion (BIP) to help attract investors, with a particular emphasis on non-resident Indians (NRIs) (RIICO 1988b).[51] More substantial reform came in 1994, when the Rajasthan government passed a new industrial policy which sought to simplify government clearances, attract private investment into infrastructure, and provide more generous financial incentives to attract footloose capital (Government of Rajasthan 1994; Bhargava 1995). The chief minister began traveling to New York and London to attract NRI investment (RIICO 1994a). Increasingly liberal industrial policies followed in 1998 and 2004, promising speedier approvals, more incentives for private investment in infrastructure, and concessions to targeted industries. In 2003, the government passed an SEZ policy that offered exemptions from all state taxes to companies inside SEZs; promised to provide water, electricity, and highway connectivity at government expense; committed to delegating the power of Labour Commissioner to the regional SEZ Development Commissioner (who would ostensibly be more pro-industry); and promised "single window clearance" for all approvals. Passed in the twilight of the Ashok Gehlot Congress government, this policy would be implemented with great vigor by his successor. In 2004, Vasundhara Raje of the conservative Bharatiya Janata Party (BJP) was elected as chief minister and oversaw a more muscular phase of liberalization. Raje, who descended from the Scindia royal family of Gwalior, aggressively courted private investors, pushed large PPP infrastructure projects, and passed a series of policies to facilitate the real estate sector, which was starting to boom in Rajasthan. She personally negotiated the arrival of the Mahindra World City and forcefully promoted Rajasthan in the inter-state competition for mobile capital.

Brokering land, as Nikita Sud (2009, 2012) has similarly observed in Gujarat, has become central to this competition.[52] Given the barriers to amassing large chunks of land on the market, companies began to insist that state governments provide it, and such commitments became a regular feature of MoUs across India. According to both government officials and industry representatives, the ability of state governments to furnish this land is of critical importance in the inter-state competition for investment. As a former chief secretary of Rajasthan told me, land is "the number one factor" in attracting industry.[53] A major chamber of commerce official confirmed: "It is the most important factor in deciding where to invest."[54] The ability of states to dispossess farmers for private capital is now a key criterion of their economic competitiveness.

This criterion only increased in importance in the late 2000s as acquiring land became more difficult in the face of farmer opposition. Most famously, the opposition to land acquisition for Tata Motors' Nano car factory in Singur, West Bengal, led to the project being shifted to Sanand, Gujarat, where then Chief Minister Narendra Modi made the required 1,000 acres available within a few weeks at a concessionary price (Sud 2012: 92–93). The high-profile relocation of the Nano factory reinforced perceptions of West Bengal as hostile to business, while shoring up Gujarat's business-friendly image. The lesson was not lost on other states. As a former head of RIICO put it, "state governments vie with each other to be as friendly to the private sector as possible. . . . Why did Tata go to Gujarat? Because there is a hue and cry in West Bengal and Gujarat served it to them on a platter. If you are not able to do it, you are not seen as pro-industry."[55] Eager to appear pro-industry, Rajasthan's SEZ policy promised from the beginning to acquire land for private developers using the emergency clause of the LAA, which allowed it to acquire land at two weeks' notice with no hearing of objections (Government of Rajasthan 2003).

Inter-state competition not only created pressure for state governments to expropriate land for private investors; it also created pressure for them to do so cheaply. As a land acquisition officer for RIICO bluntly put it: "If we give market price, then industrialists won't come."[56] Providing investors with cheap land meant maintaining low compensation to farmers, which was still made possible by the Land Acquisition Act. Government-fixed compensation rates continued to be much less than the actual market rate for multiple reasons: a rigid land classification system (which meant assessing land only at its agricultural value), the systematic undervaluation of land sales to avoid Stamp Duty, and the LAA's prohibition on considering the land's prospective use when determining compensation. Such undervaluation made it possible to offer land to private companies at below-market prices. Public grazing land could be thrown into the bargain even more cheaply since it could be acquired by administrative fiat with no compensation to existing users. Combined, these mechanisms of state dispossession create large gaps between the cost of government-acquired land and its actual or potential market value. Whereas in the developmentalist period these mechanisms of undervaluation were used to keep down the cost of public-sector infrastructure and industry, post-liberalization they have become enormous mechanisms for private arbitrage on land.

I call this ratio between the artificially low cost of government-acquired land and its ultimate market appreciation the "rate of accumulation by dispossession." Figure 2.2 provides a conceptual illustration. The lower value (P1) is the compensation the state pays to farmers. The middle value (P2) is the price at which the state resells the land to a private investor. The upper value (P3) is the ultimate market appreciation of the land after it is acquired and handed over to a private capitalist. The latter can only be provisionally calculated at any given point in time. The crucial point is that under India's neoliberal regime of dispossession, capturing the rate of accumulation by dispossession—the discrepancy between P1 and P3—has itself become a major purpose of dispossession. Interstate competition militates toward an expansion of this rate as states seek to provide capitalists with the cheapest land possible.

But there is variation in how much of the rate of accumulation by dispossession is made available to private investors (the private increment), and how much is retained by the land broker state itself (the public increment). Using the

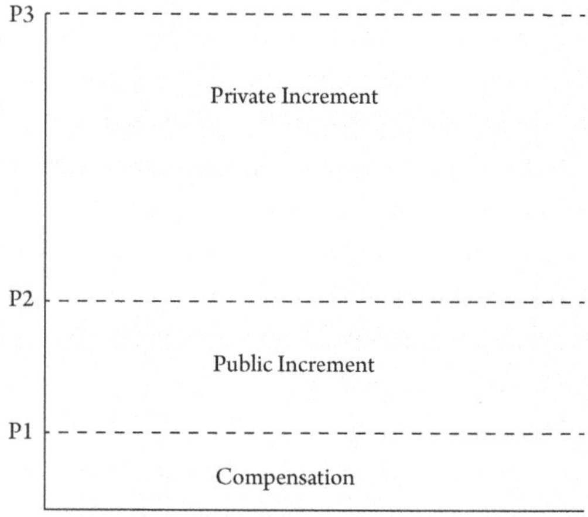

Private Rate of ABD = P3/P2 × 100
Public Rate of ABD = P2/P1 × 100
Total Rate of ABD = P3/P1 × 100

Figure 2.2 The rate of accumulation by dispossession.

state machinery to enable private arbitrage on land opened opportunities not just for private capital but also for the state and its office-holders.

Rents: Licit and Illicit

The transformation of state governments into land broker states was further incentivized by the vast opportunities for licit and illicit income this generated. One aspect of this—the *public rate of accumulation by dispossession*—is legal and reflects the difference between the compensation the state pays to farmers (P1) and the price at which it sells the same land to capitalists (P2).

Government agencies or parastatals—principally industrial development corporations and urban development authorities—take a cut for their acquisition services and any infrastructure they add before reselling it. In public-private partnerships, the state's contribution of land can also form the basis for its equity in a project ("land for equity"). The increment kept by the public agency varies significantly. Promotional agencies like industrial development corporations keep this increment relatively low in order to attract investors, while urban development authorities appear to keep a larger increment for themselves.[57] But even in these cases, cheaply acquired farmland leaves significant room to earn a profit even while handing it to private investors at less than market value. The income from this land brokering constitutes a significant and growing source of government revenue, as I will show shortly in the case of Rajasthan's parastatal agencies.

But it is not only government coffers that are stuffed by an expansion of the state's role in dispossessing land. The incentive of getting into the land brokerage business did not only arise from the motivations of politicians and bureaucrats to "bring development" to their states nor from the need for government revenue. It also arose from the lucrative opportunities for illicit rents that a deepening state role in land dispossession made possible—especially during an unprecedented real estate boom when, as the *Economist* (2014a) put it, "Property became a multi-billion-dollar business governed by officials paid a pittance."[58] The magnitude of unofficial rents that can be extracted through the acquisition and allocation of land in post-liberalization India has made the much-maligned "license-permit-quota Raj" look quaint.

Politicians and bureaucrats involved in the negotiations and planning that precede the public announcement of projects possess a very valuable commodity: knowledge about where land prices will suddenly escalate exponentially by the mere fact of a project being announced in their vicinity. The first and most obvious way to cash in on this knowledge is to buy land in the area for oneself, suitably disguised by registering it in the name of extended kin, cronies, or *benami* (front; literally "without name") companies.[59] The second is to distribute this information to private investors, lower level officials, friends, and family in return for kickbacks and favors.[60]

Another lucrative source of rents is to redraw project boundaries to benefit particular landowners. Slightly shifting the layout of a highway or SEZ in one direction or another has dramatic ramifications for land values. A hundred yards this way and one's land is acquired at a below-market rate; a hundred yards the other way and one can reap the windfall from highway- or SEZ-front property. Allegations of manipulating project boundaries are legion.[61] Finally, land dispossession for large capital projects generates land speculation on surrounding farmland, and the buyers of this farmland must go through government agencies to have it converted from agricultural to commercial or residential status, and to obtain various building permits. This may be the single largest source of illicit revenue for urban development authority officials and the politicians who appoint them.[62] Many people believe it provides the bulk of campaign finances for Indian elections. And this is only the higher level corruption: village, subdistrict, and district land record officials (*patwaris*) routinely demand bribes from those wishing to register land transactions or resolve problematic titles. Elected *panchayat* heads (*sarpanch*), as Chapter 5 shows, also have ways to get a cut. While direct evidence about specific instances of such "corruption" is difficult to obtain, I will provide indirect evidence of its existence in the case of the Mahindra World City. Its magnitude is unquantifiable but clearly immense.[63]

Rather than seeing these illicit appropriations as the "corruption" of errant officials,[64] we should view them as part of a chain of rentiership made possible by the state's new land brokering role in post-liberalization India. While economic liberalization was supposed to reduce the scope for such "unproductive rent-seeking" (Kreuger 1974; Bhagwati 1982), the concomitant expansion of state land dispossession it has generated has greatly expanded the scope for public and private, legal and illegal accumulation through dispossession (see also Chandra 2015). The broad range of actors with a stake in this game—a true "public-private partnership"—helps to ensure its reproduction.

Land broker states thus emerged out of a conjuncture of several forces: the problem posed by an escalating demand for land confronting the supply barrier of rural land markets; the pressure exerted by inter-state competition for state governments to overcome this barrier by dispossessing farmers; and the licit and illicit revenue that such a role made available to state institutions, their office-holders, and politicians. Under this new regime, dispossession has both increased in scale and dramatically changed in character. While significant subnational variation persists in the scale and the economic sectors driving dispossession, the pressure to dispossess land cheaply for private capital is general and intense. This is evidenced by the scale of the land broker state in Rajasthan, a relatively underdeveloped and landlocked state with no major metropolis, but that has nevertheless aggressively courted private capital with dispossessed land in the post-liberalization era.

While state policies have set the framework for this new regime, it is the parastatal agencies formed during the developmentalist period that have become its main instruments. I now turn to how RIICO and the JDA transformed into administrative machines for dispossessing rural land for private capital.

The "Industrial" Development Corporation

Immediately after economic liberalization began in the early 1990s, the Rajasthan Industrial Development and Investment Corporation began to substantially expand the scale and scope of its activities. After acquiring 10,056 acres of land in the 1980s, RIICO's land acquisition doubled to 22,931 acres in the 1990s.[65] Struggling to keep up with "skyrocketing' demand" (RIICO 1990), it set ambitious yearly land acquisition targets and instituted a land banking system to plan for future requirements. Not only did RIICO begin to acquire more land, but its land acquisition began to expand far beyond the public-sector industrial areas that were, until then, its bread and butter.

Rajasthan's new investment policy of 1994 included the radical decision "to allow [the] private sector to establish and maintain industrial areas" (RIICO 1994a). This policy, which would have entailed the state acquiring land for private builders to develop and resell as industrial plots—as would eventually happen in SEZs—was never effectively carried out and RIICO continued to be the sole developer and landlord of industrial areas. But declaring that "the thrust is now on privatization in Rajasthan" (RIICO1994b), RIICO began to bring in private builders to construct housing townships and other facilities in and around their industrial areas on "a turn-key basis" (RIICO 1995a). Its industrial areas thus stopped being exclusively industrial. In 1994, RIICO approved a five-star luxury hotel in its Jaisalmer industrial area (RIICO 1994c) and began to place more emphasis on tourism and industries closer to real estate than manufacturing. In 1995, it advertised that it was looking for investors in "hotels, motels, golf courses, gyms, sports complexes, health centres, zoos/botanical gardens, skating rinks, educational institutions . . . housing colonies, New Townships" (RIICO 1995b). In the same year, it acquired land for two amusement parks for "water related games, artificial sea waves, fast food, conference hall, golf course and resort" (RIICO 1995c). It announced that "apart from industrial infrastructure, a new drive has been launched to develop social infrastructure" like housing townships around industrial areas with the help of private-sector builders (RIICO 1996). The line between industrial production and real estate was becoming blurred under the euphemism of "social infrastructure," making any form of private profit a justification for dispossession.

Industrial areas also became more outward-looking as the emphasis shifted to attracting outside and foreign investment and promoting exports. Beginning modestly in the late 1980s and increasing substantially in the early 1990s, RIICO started signing Memoranda of Understanding (MoUs) with foreign companies. And after the new investment policy of 1994, RIICO announced eight proposed "export promotion industrial parks" (EPIPs), a central government scheme in which export-oriented companies would receive special concessions like liberalized enforcement of labor laws,[66] anticipating features of SEZs (RIICO 1994a). In 1998, RIICO also started to provide land and buildings for export-oriented software technology parks (RIICO 1998). Industrial areas thus became increasingly oriented toward external investments and markets.

Along with these changes, the Nehruvian social commitments embedded in the way RIICO produced industrial space started to attenuate. A 1994 RIICO newsletter summarily announced, "rebates in industrial areas rationalized" (RIICO 1994d): subsidized land prices to small entrepreneurs would be replaced by subsidies for favored industries (Information Technology and Biotechnology) and a graded system that provided the cheapest land to the biggest investors—for example, offering land rebates of 60% to "very prestigious investments" of over Rs 100 million and to any Fortune 500 company.[67] Under the guise of "simplifying procedures" for entrepreneurs, many of the regulations restricting speculation on industrial plots were scrapped.[68] Land was now being dispossessed and transferred to capital absent the veneer of Nehruvian developmentalism.

As liberalization progressed, the old-fashioned industrial estate thus began to mutate in ways that significantly shed its association with the developmentalist regime of dispossession. Aspects of industrial area development were privatized as state governments became facilitators rather than direct undertakers of investment. The strong emphasis on productive, labor-intensive manufacturing became diluted as land was increasingly expropriated for any economic purpose, like real estate or tourism, that constituted a higher value land use than agriculture. Industrial areas became less about promoting homegrown entrepreneurship and more about attracting external investment and, to some extent, promoting exports. Finally, the social commitments that had previously shaped the development and allocation of industrial land started to wane, and were replaced by the overriding purpose of attracting large corporate investments.

All of this translated into significant revenues for RIICO, which began returning handsome dividends to the state government. One year into liberalization in 1992, RIICO—which derived most of its revenue from acquiring and developing land for industry—announced its "highest ever profit" (RIICO 1992) and reported new record profits almost every year for the rest of the decade. Its net before-tax profit in 2010–2011 was over $40 million (RIICO 2011: 3). As one RIICO official put it, "we are money-making primarily because we have land. And Rajasthan has seen a great boom in land prices over [the] last 7–8 years."[69] With 39% of the planned Delhi–Mumbai Industrial Corridor set to pass through Rajasthan, RIICO was anticipating further expansion. If not notoriously corrupt, RIICO is no stranger to charges of impropriety[70]; even its officials acknowledge that advance information about projects creates substantial opportunities for illicit rents. As a former high-level official conceded, "We might say something in a meeting and it doesn't get announced until six weeks later. It sneaks out."[71]

As the 2000s economic boom washed through Rajasthan, RIICO thus became an instrument for dispossessing unprecedented areas of rural land for a broad range of economic purposes. Its activities thus began to merge with that of urban development authorities.

The Urban "Development" Authority

Founded on the cusp of liberalization, the Jaipur Development Authority's commitment to "socialist" urban planning was brief and perfunctory. During the 1980s, the JDA embarked on several large extensions of Jaipur city that involved substantial land acquisition. Although done under the auspices of planned urban expansion and the creation of affordable housing, they were poorly planned, generated little affordable housing, and ended up transferring significant amounts of land to private builders.[72] Several were held up in litigation by farmers angered by poor compensation. Almost from its inception, the JDA was publicly criticized for its corruption and ineptitude.[73] Over the course of the 1990s, the scale of its activities and the scope of its operations expanded. By the time of the real estate boom of the mid-2000s, it was broadly recognized as an instrument for converting rural land into private real estate. It embarked on plans to acquire land for a Film City, a Sports City, a Hotel Land Bank "to meet the requirements of the tourism industry," and a 143-kilometer ring road that would be built on a PPP model that incentivized private investors with adjacent real estate (JDA 2011).

With land as its primary source of revenue,[74] the post-liberalization land boom in Jaipur incentivized the JDA to continually expand its urbanizable limits. When the JDA was created in 1982, these limits incorporated 335 villages. In 1997, the JDA added 153 villages to its jurisdiction, and added another 247 at the height of the real estate boom in 2005, bringing thousands of hectares of village grazing land into its land bank for selling to private investors.[75] As one government official put it, "They just snatched that common land and sold it."[76] Figure 2.3 shows the revenues the JDA derived from this procedure. In 2001–2002, the JDA was already earning a handsome revenue of over $20 million

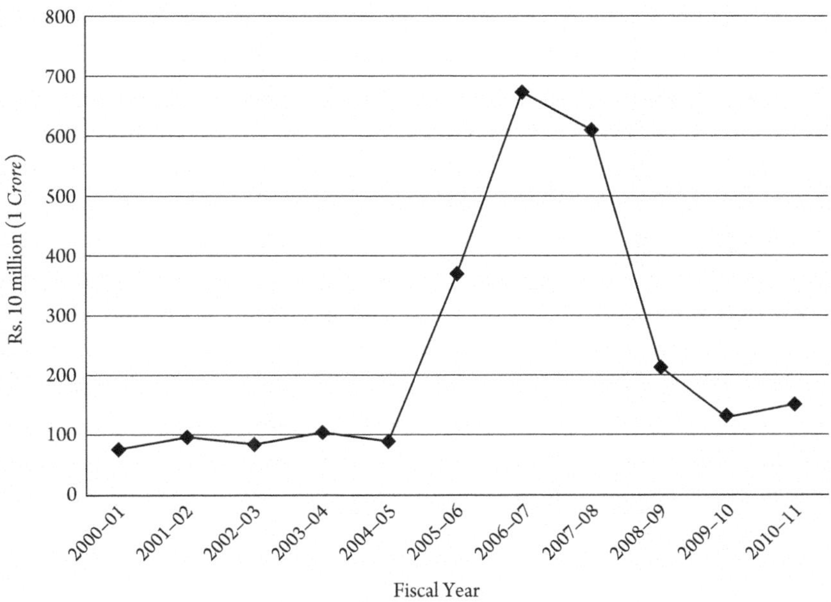

Figure 2.3 Public rate of ABD: Annual revenue from JDA plot sales. Source: JDA Records.

(Rs. 100 *crore*) per year by selling plots from its land bank. The combination of more land and higher prices produced a nine-fold increase in revenue to over $134 million (Rs. 671 *crore*) in 2006–2007. As one of its own officials remarked, "With extension of [its] land bank, JDA was making gold."[77] Income from land sales in most years covered over 100% of the JDA's operating budget and accounted for more than three times the municipal property tax (Sridhar, Gu, and Yao 2013: 141). According to critics within the government, it could have made a lot more: instead of auctioning land to the highest bidder, the JDA in many cases allotted land to influential individuals and institutions at subsidized rates.[78] Such foregone revenue notwithstanding, the dispossession of public grazing land from villagers subsidized the JDA's infrastructural spending in Jaipur as well as the profits of private builders. This created both a massive organizational incentive and a strong set of private interests behind dispossessing as much land as possible and brokering it to whoever desired it, for whatever purpose: whether housing townships, malls, or private farmhouses for the wealthy.

It also created massive opportunities for illicit rent-seeking through the avenues described previously: advance information about projects that enable land arbitrage; and bribes for land conversation, zoning exemptions, township approvals, and building approvals. Regarding the first, one official of the Jaipur Development Authority forthrightly explained, "The information starts with the commissioner and seven to eight people, then eventually gets to everyone."[79] Land conversion through the "90B" clause in the state revenue code was a notorious cash cow. As a former revenue official put it, referring to the vernacular unit of agricultural land, it allowed the government to "make money per *bigha*."[80] One Jaipur real estate investor frankly described delivering a briefcase of cash to the JDA for converting agricultural land to commercial.

Drifting from its original purpose of planned development and affordable housing, the JDA thus became a tool for grabbing land for the real estate industry. In 2005, the JDA teamed up with RIICO and commenced to acquire land from Rajpura and eight other villages for one of the largest projects in its history. The Mahindra World City would be the culmination, for both agencies, of a decade-long shift from a developmentalist to a neoliberal regime of dispossession. But while SEZs elsewhere were bogged down by land wars, both agencies had been experimenting with a compensation policy that would help the MWC avoid such a fate.

Compensation by Speculation

If the developmentalist regime dispossessed land with promises of development and little in the way of compensation, this began to change post-liberalization in response to growing farmer opposition. Although Rajasthan did not experience the explosive farmer protests of other states, as early as the 1990s its agencies were having greater difficulty acquiring land, largely due to legal challenges by farmers. And the problem only became more acute by the 2000s. As one RIICO official put it, "Land acquisition is actually not a very comfortable position nowadays. There is so much litigation, so many things . . . opposition is there everywhere."[81] A land acquisition officer conceded, "Today, land acquisition has become very difficult." Although RIICO's industrial estates were not immune to challenge, he explained that it was more difficult with private projects like SEZs "because it's private companies, they think you're taking land from us poor people and giving it to the rich." Farmers, he explained, often could not see the benefit they would derive from these projects. And if you offered them below-market compensation for any project, he explained, they would petition the courts.[82]

Such difficulties prompted the Rajasthan government to settle on a different approach to compensation, especially for urban-industrial projects. The Rajasthan Housing Board had, as early as 1989, experimented with giving dispossessed farmers small plots of land in the proposed development—at first equivalent to only a small fraction of their original land (Kumat 1995: 39). This policy was credited with greatly expediting acquisition for a housing development in Jodhpur (Kumat 1995) and was subsequently adopted by other agencies. By the early 1990s, the JDA was offering villagers developed plots that were 25% the size of their original land—though in a more peripheral and hardly "developed" location, the premise was that a smaller amount of developed land would be worth more than the original farmland. By the end of the decade, RIICO was also offering farmers in the periphery of its more urban industrial estates the option of receiving plots of developed land. Although one of the policy's formulators professed that it came from a genuine concern for farmers, he was also blunt that its intention was to "soften opposition."[83] A RIICO official described it as "buying peace."[84]

The next chapter will examine how this policy works in practice. The key observation for now is that, faced with increasing non-compliance, Rajasthan's land broker state slowly stopped appealing to farmers' nationalism and, instead, began enlisting them as financial subjects. This approach to eliciting compliance would become more widespread in the aftermath of growing farmer protests in the late 2000s, but Rajasthan was ahead of the curve when the SEZ boom arrived in the mid-2000s. And this would partly explain why, as the next chapter shows, the Mahindra World City was up and running while SEZs elsewhere were stuck in land acquisition purgatory.

Conclusion

This chapter has traced the emergence of a new regime of dispossession in post-liberalization Rajasthan. It has explained the transition from a developmentalist to a neoliberal regime of dispossession as the product of: a dramatic post-liberalization increase in the private demand for land; the supply barrier posed by small rural property and "insufficiently" capitalist land markets; the pressure of accelerating inter-state competition on states to overcome this problem with dispossession; and the licit and illicit rents such a role makes possible for state institutions and their office-holders. The result has been the restructuring of the state government, through its parastatal agencies, into a land broker for private capital. This neoliberal regime of dispossession is defined not just by an increasing scale of dispossession but by a qualitative expansion of the economic activities for which the state will forcibly dispossess land from farmers. No longer just dispossessing land for public-sector projects of productive material expansion, the state has turned to dispossessing farmers for private real estate capital. As a shorthand, we can characterize this as a shift from a regime of dispossessing "land for production" to one of "land for the market." No longer is land dispossessed just for the production of commodities, but increasingly for the commodification of land itself. This makes the "rate of accumulation by dispossession," the discrepancy between the price paid to farmers and its ultimate market value, a main motivation for—and sufficient justification of—dispossessing farmers.

India's SEZs were the apotheosis of this new regime of dispossession. India's SEZ Policy of 2000 encouraged state governments to acquire unprecedentedly large swaths of land for private companies with the minimal requirement that 35% of their land area be used for export-oriented "processing." Even before the policy could be turned into a law, the Rajasthan government jumped at the opportunity. And this, in short, is what brought the Mahindra World City to Mohanlal's doorstep in 2005.

3

Rajpura

The future of India lies in its villages.

—M. K. Gandhi

What is the village but a sink of localism, a den of ignorance, narrow-mindedness and communalism?

—Dr. B. R. Ambedkar

In 2005, Rajasthan's land broker state arrived in Rajpura; until then a village of about four hundred households predominantly engaged in rain-fed agriculture and animal husbandry. Its reception and the process of change that followed can only be understood in light of the pre-existing agrarian milieu it encountered. This chapter, consequently, sketches in historical perspective the agrarian milieu of Rajpura. It emphasizes three salient features of that milieu. First, on the eve of its dispossession, Rajpura was a monsoon-dependent village where the majority of people still depended on cultivation and a relatively profitable livestock economy, but where declining rains had forced most farmers to diversify. Second, Rajpura was no harmonious village republic, but a highly unequal agrarian milieu divided along lines of class, caste, and gender. These sharp inequalities reflected the failures of the postcolonial Indian state to effectively redistribute land and tackle entrenched forms of social domination that were the main legacies of princely rule. Third, this agrarian structure was the basis of a pattern of "big man" politics that gave Rajpurans limited experience with peasant insurgency before the SEZ arrived. These three factors, as the following chapters show, facilitated the ability of Rajasthan's land broker state to produce compliance to dispossession; and would affect the ability of Rajpura's farmers to benefit from the economic changes unleashed by the Mahindra World City.

Rajpura Under the Rajputs

Until 1947, Rajpura was the seat of a minor *jagir* (estate) in the princely state of Jaipur. One of the most powerful of the twenty-two kingdoms that comprised "Rajputana," Jaipur was founded in the 12th century through a series of military conquests by "warrior-caste" (*kshatriya*) Rajputs over pre-existing Meena chiefdoms. A Rajput named Dhola Rai from the Kucchawa lineage of Rajputs—which claimed descent from the second son of Rama, hero of the Ramayana epic—left Gwalior[1] and established a kingdom in Dausa. Dhola Rai's grandson subsequently established a new capital 50 km to the west at Amber (also known as Dhoondar), building a fort on the hills overlooking present-day Jaipur. Although imprecise in his dates and details, British chronicler James Tod (1997[1829]: 281) was probably right in describing the founding of Amber as "a case of simple usurpation" that involved "filling the reservoirs in which the Meenas bathed with their dead bodies."[2]

Amber became a tributary of the Mughal Empire in the mid-16th century and remained a relatively small kingdom until the 18th, when Mughal power began to collapse. Seizing the opportunity, Maharaja Savai Jai Singh oversaw Amber's expansion into one of the most powerful states in Rajputana. Jai Singh's crowning achievement was the construction of Jaipur as the first planned city in North India. But the British Empire soon replaced the Mughal, and in 1803 Jaipur State acceded to a "protection" treaty with the East India Company, followed by a more enduring one in 1818, thus becoming a tributary of the British and subject to its system of indirect rule known as paramountcy (Stern 1988), which deprived the princes of their foreign policy and left them with a supervised domestic autonomy (Rudolph and Rudolph 1984: 3). Although subject to intermittent interference by British agents, Jaipur State remained administratively distinct and relatively autonomous from British-ruled India (Stern 1988; Rudolph and Rudolph 1984: 4). While the *durbar* (court) made modest overtures in the direction of modern statehood in the first half of the 20th century (Stern 1988),[3] Jaipur remained a hereditary monarchy until India's Independence in 1947. Political authority rested with the royal family in Jaipur but was exercised on a day-to-day basis through the lesser Rajput nobility in the countryside.

This political structure rested upon, and was built to ensure, the extraction of grain and labor from peasants. Although long a center for gems and banking, Jaipur had little manufacturing base until the Second World War, and the state's economy remained overwhelmingly agricultural. A semi-arid region with little surface water and almost all of its rainfall concentrated in three summer months, small-scale irrigation was made possible by hand-dug open wells powered by draft animals.[4] Cultivation of millet and sorghum was synergistic with livestock rearing, which was central to peasant livelihoods. Yields depended on the erratic annual monsoon, and several consecutive droughts could bring catastrophic famines, as they did in 1899–1900 when thousands left their villages to beg for food in Jaipur, many of them dying in the streets (Kacchawaha 1992).[5]

Scholars have been hard-pressed not to call this social system feudal, although some have objected to the application of this European term to Indian conditions.[6] While keeping in mind important differences—principally the clan structure underlying Rajput rule—we can describe the social relations of production in Rajpura and much of Rajasthan at this time as feudal, if we take that to mean simply that the dominant classes expropriated economic surplus by virtue of their political power in a system of parcellized sovereignty (Anderson 1974:19). Under the *jagirdari* system—the form of land tenure that prevailed in Rajpura and approximately 60% of Rajputana (Government of Rajasthan 1959: 7)[7]—Rajput clansmen received hereditary revenue rights over landed estates from the prince (Chakravarti 1975: 31). The *jagirdars*—also known by the more generic term *thakur* (Habib 2002: 79)—were the rulers and landlords of the villages comprising their *jagir,* which they were free to exploit so long as they paid the requisite tribute to the prince who in turn paid tribute to the British.[8] On the basis of their local monopolies of violence, *jagirdars* extracted rent, a great variety of taxes and cesses (*laag baag*), and corvée labor (*begaar*) from their subjects. Rent could be as high as one half of the crop taken from the field or threshing floor, and villagers had to pay taxes to the *thakur* for just about everything: houses and cattle, grass and reeds, pasturage, wood, dung, and even marriages and deaths (Government of India 1950; Rosin 1978: 470).[9] The *jagirdars* themselves took more interest in conspicuous consumption and displays of religiosity than agricultural improvement (Rosin 1978: 471). In addition to filling British coffers, this system of absolute surplus extraction maintained the *jagirdars* and Jaipur nobility in leisurely affluence, visible today in the magnificent forts that dot Rajasthan's landscape and the decorative arts that fill its museums. It correspondingly maintained the peasantry in grinding poverty.[10]

Rajpura's last *thakur,* Jagat Singh, claimed descent from a brother of the Maharaja of Jaipur, from whom they received their *jagir* of fourteen villages.[11] Many in Rajpura—like the villagers in nearby Ajmer studied by Gold and Gujar (2002)—remembered the *thakur's* rule as brutally exploitative, even if the failures of the postcolonial state occasionally elicited nostalgia. When I asked older villagers what these times were like, they usually mentioned taxes, corvée labor, and poverty. While the large cultivating castes typically focused on the share of grain the *thakur* took, Dalits emphasized their extreme poverty and the various caste indignities they suffered—like having to drink well water from an arms-length spout. Legitimated by an ideology of divinely ordained rule, this exploitation was backed up by the *thakur's* stockpile of weapons.

While the *thakur* occupied the pinnacle of the agrarian class structure, the peasantry was itself highly differentiated. In the hereditary caste-based division of labor, Jats specialized in cultivation and controlled the most land. Brahmins had large tenancies and some independent land grants, while those that fulfilled priestly duties had rights to cultivate temple land. A smaller number of Kumavats and Ahirs were also significant cultivators in addition to being masons and herders, respectively. Two lineages of Jain merchants sold provisions and provided credit. Malis were "gardeners" and medium-sized cultivators, while Gujjars specialized in livestock rearing. Other "service castes" cultivated smaller parcels of land or none at all while practicing caste-based occupations in return for grain—the so-called *jajmani* system. The various caste-wise occupations are detailed in Table 3.1 and grouped according to their categorization by the post-independence Indian state.

Rajpura in Postcolonial India

The Limits of Agrarian Reform

After Independence, the twenty-two princely states of Rajputana—considered by the new government as "centres of feudal autocracy" and bulwarks of British power—were abolished and consolidated into the modern state of Rajasthan.[12] A series of land reform laws in the 1950s and 1960s abolished the *thakur's* role as tax intermediary, redistributed "land to the tiller," and imposed land ceilings. These reforms brought Rajpura's cultivators into a direct relationship with the state as land owners (*khatedars*) and ended the *thakur's* various exactions. But they fell far short—as they did across Rajasthan (Singh 1964; Chakravarti 1975; Rosin 1987) and most of India (Herring 1983; Frankel 2005)—of establishing an egalitarian distribution of property. Like *jagirdars* across Rajasthan (Singh 1964; Chakravarti 1975; Rosin 1987), Jagat Singh and his family used a variety of techniques to evade land ceilings, most notably putting land in the names of extended family and trusted retainers, thereby preventing a large portion of their *jagir* from being resumed by the state and redistributed. By the admission of the *thakur's* grandson, Mahinder Singh, the family still controlled at least 375 hectares (1,500 bighas) in 2005.[13] While Rajasthan's land reforms were supposed to abolish absentee landlords, Jagat Singh and his family continued to reside in their magnificent compound (*haveli*) in Jaipur, where they also owned several surrounding city blocks, and continued to extract rent from sharecropping tenants for the half century between Independence and the arrival of the SEZ.

Aside from failing to undermine the economic power of Rajpura's feudal lord, post-independence land reforms favored the large cultivating castes. In Rajpura,

Table 3.1 **Castes and "Traditional" Occupations in Rajpura**

General Castes
Bania (merchant)
Brahmin (priest; most cultivated)
Rajput (warrior-landlord)
Otherwise Backward Classes (OBC)
Ahir (cultivator and herder)
Darji (tailor)
Gujjar (herder)
Jat (cultivator)
Khati (carpenter)
Kumhar (potter)
Kumavat (farmer and mason)
Lakhera (bangle maker)
Mali (gardener)
Muslims (blanket makers)
Nai (barber)
Raona Rajput ("illegitimate" Rajput)
Soni (goldsmith)
Scheduled Tribes (ST)
Dhanka (basket and rope maker)
Meena (village guard)
Scheduled Castes (SC)
Balai (weaver)
Bavariya (hunter)
Beirwa (leather worker)
Daroga (domestic servant)
Dhobi (washerman)
Khatik (butcher)
Naik (soldiers and midwives)
Regar (shoe maker)
Sangat (sweeper)

as in much of Rajasthan, Jats were the largest beneficiaries (Chakravarti 1975; Rosin 1987). As the largest cultivating caste in the "traditional" division of labor and one that was both politically aware and organized at the state level (Sisson 1969, 1972; Stern 1988), Jats were the most successful at converting their large tenancies into private property during land settlement procedures that were often manipulated by the coercion and bribery of Rajputs (Singh 1964;

Chakravarti 1975). Kumavats and Brahmins benefited similarly, and these castes established themselves as substantial farmers in the post-independence decades. Among the General Castes, the merchant (*bania*) castes alone did not come out of the land reforms as a landed class, though some subsequently acquired small holdings through purchases and usury. Malis (gardeners) typically had less land than Jats and Brahmins, but more than the other service castes that would come to be grouped under the official category of Otherwise Backward Classes (OBCs). By virtue of both cultivating less land under princely rule and their lack of power to defend their tenancies at the time of settlement, the lower castes—designated as Scheduled Castes (SC) and Scheduled Tribes (ST) by the government—emerged from land reforms with the least land. Among the lower castes, the Meenas (considered a Scheduled Tribe) were alone in having a few families with significant holdings. So, while post-independence land reform in Rajpura undermined feudal landlordism, it left intact large caste-based inequalities in the distribution of land.

This highly unequal caste-based distribution of land changed only marginally—mainly through subdivision and sales to meet contingent expenditures (Bailey 1957)—between Independence and the SEZs' arrival in 2005. The third column of Table 3.2 illustrates the distribution of land among various caste categories in 2005, as reported in my 2011 survey of ninety-four households in four villages. The large outlier not included in the survey was the single family of the former Rajput *thakur*, whose 375 hectare holding was almost one-hundred times larger than the all-household average. Beneath the *thakur's* large absentee holding, Jat families in the four villages surveyed held on average 7.3 hectares of land, General Castes (mostly Brahmins, and a few Jain merchants) 4.6 hectares, OBCs 3.3 (with 10% landless), and the SC/STs 2.2 (with 15% landless). So, while the lower castes emerged from post-independence land reforms with more land than in many other parts of India (which reflected in part the larger landholdings of rain-scarce Rajasthan), they were largely betrayed by the egalitarian promises of land reform. While SC/STs constituted 35% of the population, they owned just 15% of the land.[14,15]

Differentiation, Diversification, and Development Failure

Petty commodity production on this unequal land base led to a corresponding concentration of agricultural assets but did not result in large-scale capitalist agriculture. Given the local insecurity of the monsoons and the lack of irrigation, adoption of Green Revolution technology was late and limited, and capitalist relations of production muted. Before the SEZ's arrival, 91% of families self-cultivated, while only 18% hired labor for at least some part of the year (see Figure 3.1). Because single-cropped agriculture did not allow for

Table 3.2 **Pre-SEZ Socio-economic Attributes of Households by Caste**

Caste	*Households in sample No. (%)*	*Average landholding (ha)*	*Landless (%)*	*Owned shop or business (%)*	*Formal employment (%)*	*Formal employment or business outside village (%)*	*Informal wage labor (%)*	*Education ≥ 10th class (%)*
General	24 (26%)	4.6	0	54	50	58	8	83
Jat	16 (17%)	7.3	0	44	31	44	13	69
OBC	21 (22%)	3.0	10	43	14	19	48	43
SC/ST	33 (35%)	2.2	15	15	9	6	85	24
All	94 (100%)	4.0	7	37	24	29	45	50

Note: The table captures the percentage of households, not individuals, with these characteristics. Landholdings are the undivided family holdings, not the stake of individual siblings. If at least one household member has a business, formal employment, did informal wage labor, or had education past the tenth standard, this is recorded as an attribute of the household (though, as I make clear, these are typically attributes of men within the household). An earlier version of this table appeared in Levien (2011). Reprinted with permission from John Wiley and Sons.

the maintenance of permanent farm laborers, this agricultural wage labor was seasonal and concentrated during the harvest. For those with land in excess to family labor, the dominant form of surplus expropriation was rent-in-kind sharecropping with rents fixed at one-third or two-thirds of the *kharif* (summer/monsoon) crop depending on whether the tenant or landlord advanced the costs of production (for the winter *rabi* crop it was one-fourth or three-fourths). Aside from the *thakur's* large absentee holdings, 8% of farmers leased out land, mostly Brahmins and Banias (merchants) pre-occupied with businesses and urban employment. Over 30% of Jats leased in land to consolidate economies of scale in production; with capital to invest, they were usually able to retain two-thirds of the harvest for themselves. A similar percentage of SC/ST households leased in land out of necessity; with less capital, they more often retained only one-third of the harvest.

While rains had decreased and groundwater levels were rapidly receding, the upper castes were also more likely to have irrigated land. This reflected both their capture of better land during land reforms and their greater ability to invest in wells—at first hand-dug open wells, and subsequently the tubewells that spread rapidly across Jaipur district in the 1990s (Birkenholtz 2008). Thus, while 46% of Brahmin families and 44% of Jat families reported receiving two crops on at least part of their land before the SEZ arrived, only 32% of OBCs and 27% of

Figure 3.1 Family harvesting millet crop on land outside SEZ. Photo by author.

SC/STs did so. As for the next most important agrarian asset, 69% of Jat families owned a tractor compared to only 9% of SC/ST families, who were forced to rent tractors from the dominant castes.

Most significant for rural livelihoods in Rajpura was the commercial livestock economy that depended on this dryland cultivation. A large grazing commons of over 1,000 acres—categorized as *panchayat* controlled *gocher* ("pasture") and *savai chak* ("unculturable waste")—and the customary practice of making the stubble of the millet harvest a "seasonal commons" (Jodha 1985: 252) allowed most families in Rajpura to maintain livestock, including buffalo, cows, goats, sheep, and a few camels (see Figure 3.2). As in most of Rajasthan, livestock rearing was a crucial source of nutrition and income, as well as a liquid form of savings and insurance against drought (cf. Jodha 1985; Robbins 1998; Brara 2006). Rajpura's proximity to Jaipur made it well-positioned, especially after an all-weather road was built in the 1980s, for commercial milk production as the so-called "white revolution" turned Jaipur District into the top producer of buffalo milk in the state (Government of Rajasthan 2009: 201). One buffalo cost approximately $1,000 to purchase and could generate $40 to $60 in net income per month, almost equivalent to the monthly wage of an unskilled worker. With a smaller upfront investment and lower fodder requirements, goats could fetch a more modest income after meeting household requirements, and a family raising a dozen might expect

Figure 3.2 Village grazing land. Photo by author.

a similar income. But while livestock rearing was crucial to the reproduction and income of most families, skewed land distribution left an unequal basis for accumulation.

Larger landholders not only had greater means to purchase livestock, but also could produce the fodder necessary to maintain animals throughout the year. This gave the large landed castes a particular advantage in maintaining more expensive and lucrative buffalo (see also Brara 2006: 163). Before the SEZ's arrival, Brahmins owned on average fifteen buffalo and Jats owned seven and a half, while SC/ST families had less than two. The latter depended more heavily on the low-cost goat—the "poor man's cow"—for household consumption and income. So, although livestock rearing was important for most families, Brahmins and Jats become significant commercial milk producers while lower castes sold much smaller surpluses over their domestic requirement. Jats and Brahmins also, significantly, moved into distribution, transporting other villagers' milk by motorbike to dairies in Jaipur.

Increasing rain scarcity and generational subdivision pushed Rajpura's residents to diversify from agriculture in the decades after Independence, but unequal landholdings provided a starkly unequal basis for doing so. As seen elsewhere in India, the dominant castes used the surpluses from their more extensive agricultural operations to invest in education, start small businesses, and obtain non-farm employment (Harriss 1991; Harriss-White and Janakarajan 1997; Jeffrey and Lerche 2000; Jeffrey 2001), giving them an economic foothold in the city. As Table 3.2 shows, the large landholding Jat caste invested substantially in small businesses (with 44% of families having a shop or business before the SEZ arrived), many of which were extensions of their agricultural enterprises. Many became milk middlemen, while others set up tractor parts or repair stores near the highway. Jats also invested in education and were moderately successful in obtaining formal-sector employment (defined as salaried—rather than casual—employment in either the public or private sector), with 31% of families having one such position in the household. All told, this diversification provided 44% of Jat households with a non-casual economic foothold outside of the village.

Brahmins pursued a similar strategy of off-farm diversification but with even more success and with greater emphasis on education. A few Brahmins in Shivpura appeared to have been among the first in the village to obtain industrial jobs in Jaipur during the 1960s. Many subsequently became milk middlemen, and some went a step further by setting up dairies, sweet shops, or *chai* stalls in Jaipur. Others ran provision stores, started private schools, bought tourist taxis, or opened travel agencies. All told, 54% of General Caste (overwhelmingly Brahmin) families had set up a shop or business by 2005. Fifty percent also had a formal-sector job, which reflected the fact that 80% of General Caste families had a member educated past the tenth standard (compared to 69% of Jat families). Almost 60% of General Caste families thus received substantial income from non-agricultural activities outside of the village. Not all Brahmins were diversified or particularly well off, but for many the village was becoming a unit of residence more than a source of livelihood.

While lower-caste villagers also diversified out of agriculture, they did so out of necessity as unskilled wage laborers. While 43% of OBC households had a small business, which was on par with the Jats, these were mostly village shops that reflected their hereditary caste occupation (barbers, potters, bangle makers, ironmongers, carpenters, etc.): they were typically less lucrative and much less likely to be in the city. With only 43% of families having a member educated past the tenth standard, OBCs had a much lower incidence of formal-sector employment at 14%. Almost half of OBC families were dependent to some extent on informal wage labor. SC and ST households were predictably the least successful in their diversification: with little formal-sector employment (9% of families) and few businesses (15% of families), only 6% of SC/ST families had an urban economic foothold outside of the village besides casual wage labor, which 85% of families were dependent upon. The vast majority of the lower castes were thus semiproletarians: while not landless, their small holdings forced them to supplement agricultural income with wage labor for at least part of the year.[16] Although a very small minority managed to obtain public-sector employment by virtue of government reservations, for the vast majority this was casual and temporary manual labor in construction, handicrafts, or other industries in Jaipur, the RIICO industrial estate in nearby Bagaru, or the block printing mills of Sanganer (in roughly that order). Low-paid, strenuous, and without the autonomy afforded by farming, such work was resorted to only out of necessity. When the rains were good, people worked less.

In Rajpura, Nehruvian developmentalism thus modified but did not transform the highly unequal agrarian order of princely rule. The failure of the postcolonial state to undermine the caste-based pattern of land ownership left a highly unequal distribution of economic assets, which provided the basis for further inequalities in what, following Bourdieu (1984), we can call cultural and social capital. Concentrated landholdings and other forms of economic capital created the basis for unequal educational attainment. Perhaps less obviously, unequal off-farm diversification generated a highly unequal distribution of social networks that could confer real or potential material benefits (Bourdieu 1984; Bourdieu 1986: 248).[17] The high proportion of Brahmins and Jats with non-menial jobs and businesses outside of the village, illustrated in Table 3.2, provided them with higher quality urban networks that, we will see, could be lucratively monetized in the post-SEZ land boom.

At the time of the SEZ's arrival in 2005, then, Rajpura was a diversifying village but one whose foundation was still dryland agriculture. At a distance of 25 km from Jaipur, Rajpura was far enough to have experienced only modest urbanization of land use (although it was technically included in the urbanizable limits of Jaipur after 1997) but close enough that farmers could diversify into the urban economy without migration. This diversification was made necessary by the lack of water. Although Jaipur district was the fourth-most irrigated in Rajasthan (Government of Rajasthan 2009: 187), only 27% of the farmland in Rajpura was irrigated prior to the arrival of the SEZ (Census of India 2001). Like two-thirds of India's farmland (World Bank 2014), Rajpura's agricultural fields were largely monsoon-dependent. Decreasing rains and lack of irrigation made agriculture less viable as a standalone occupation, although it was fairly remunerative when the rains were good. The minority with irrigated land could benefit from the nearby Jaipur market for winter vegetable cultivation. Agricultural production was neither as precarious as in arid Western Rajasthan nor as prosperous as in much of the fertile Gangetic Plain to the East. It provided most families with crucial means of subsistence and income that varied by holding and access to irrigation. Importantly, however, the commercial milk and livestock rearing that was synergistic with this dryland cultivation *was* relatively profitable, allowing the dominant castes to accumulate and the lower castes to meet household needs and earn a modest income.

Like much of rural India, Rajpura suffered from the Nehruvian state's failure to invest in rural infrastructure, health, and education (cf. Sen 2000; Dreze and Sen 2013; Kohli 2013). While the village received electricity and an all-weather (though not paved) road during the 1980s, electricity supply was erratic, the vast majority of houses were earthen (*kaccha*), and the nearest emergency room was still in Jaipur. Primary education was, upon Independence, almost non-existent[18]; and by the end of the developmentalist period it was still very poor. Most villagers believed that little was taught in the government schools, and those who could afford it sent their children to marginally better private schools. According to the 2001 Census, only 45% of villagers and 29% of women in Rajpura were literate—compared to a national rural literacy rate of 59% and a female rural literacy rate of 46% (Census of India 2001). Although some upper castes were investing in education and making use of the—mostly low-quality—private colleges that were proliferating around Jaipur, half of all families did not have a single member educated past the tenth standard. No one spoke more than a few phrases of English, the key to upward mobility in India's "new economy." This would leave Rajpura poorly prepared to benefit from an Information Technology SEZ, as Chapter 6 will illustrate.

But the ability of villagers to profit from real estate speculation once the Mahindra World City arrived in 2005 would be determined by the village's internal class structure. And this structure can be schematically summarized as follows: at the top, a large and absentee Rajput landlord that controlled almost one hundred times the average-sized landholding; medium and rich farmers (mostly Jat and Brahmin) undertaking commercial but largely unirrigated cultivation with family and seasonal wage labor that was synergistic with milk production and complemented by small businesses and urban jobs; a layer of smaller farmers (poor Jats and Brahmins and better-off OBCs) that could largely reproduce their families through farming and livestock without necessarily accumulating; a numerically large semiproletariat drawn from OBCs and SC/STs, which supplemented small agricultural holdings and livestock rearing with wage labor, traditional occupations, and a few small businesses; and finally, a small landless class, exclusively OBC and SC/ST, dependent entirely on wage labor and/or traditional occupations. Although significant intra-caste inequalities existed, caste was a good predicator of class, as Table 3.2 indicates. While there were some relatively poor Jats and Brahmins, there were no rich Dalits.

In addition to being the best predictor of class, caste continued to operate as a means of social and symbolic domination. Although some castes gave up their hereditary occupations in the post-independence decades, the village remained organized into caste-segregated neighborhoods, caste endogamy prevailed, and inter-caste dining was limited. Upper castes would not drink from the same vessel as lower castes, who were usually given plastic cups at *chai* stalls. Although caste indignities against the "upper" Dalit subcastes—especially the Balais, some of whom had adopted Sanskritization as an avenue of upward mobility (Srinivas 1966)—had attenuated but not disappeared, untouchability still operated with particular force against the village sweepers (derogatorily known as *bhangis*), who could not go into temples, sat alone during weddings, and whose compensation of leftover *rotis* was dropped into their hands from above to prevent "pollution." It was also evident in the common prejudices of other villagers toward Beirwas, Bawariyas, and Regars. This routinized discrimination and segregation did not, we will see, disappear in a tide of modernization once the SEZ arrived.

The Regional Patriarchy

Rajasthan is also notorious for its inequalities *within* households. Class and caste inequalities intersected with starkly patriarchal gender relations. Rajasthan ranks below the national average in most indicators of gender disparity (World Bank 2006: 11), and Rajpura ranks lower than the state average on most counts. In 2001, there were 897 women to every 1,000 men in Rajpura, which was even lower than the state-wide average of 906, itself below the national average of 927 (Census of India 2001; World Bank 2006: 11). We have seen that in 2001, only

29% of women in Rajpura were literate compared to 59% of men (and 46% of rural women in India). Gender segregation prevailed in everyday life, with women rarely seen alone in village-wide public spaces such as the market or *chai* stalls, and usually veiled (with a *ghunghat*) when in the presence of non-related men. Rajasthan has historically been at the center of controversies over *sati* (self-immolation on a husband's funeral pyre) and while it has been over seventy years since the last *sati* in Rajpura, there is a popular village temple, built in the 1980s, that commemorates the event, which lives on in village lore as an example of devotion and sacrifice.[19] While these facts attest to the prevalent patriarchal relations in the region, several components of male domination proved most pertinent to the process of land dispossession.

In patrilocal Rajasthani villages, women move from their natal to marital household and typically lack independent land rights in both. Although the Hindu Succession Act of 1956 gave Hindu women limited inheritance rights to their husband's property (as widows), and a 2005 amendment extended equal inheritance rights to daughters, in practice there remains a strong cultural bias against female inheritance of agricultural land.[20] A combination of factors—including economic dependence, social confinement, fears of jeopardizing ties with natal families, and straightforward coercion—militate against women demanding these rights (Agarwal 1994: 261). While exclusion from land rights is ostensibly compensated by dowries, these (typically moveable) assets are often controlled by in-laws and husbands and do not necessarily provide women with independent economic assets (Agarwal 1988, 1994). Even as widows, women's inherited land rights are vulnerable and likely to be de facto controlled by male relatives (Agarwal 1994: 254–259). This patriarchal system of land tenure is particularly strong in Rajasthan (Agarwal 1994). Its effect is to give men control over the disposition of land and the proceeds from it. In Rajpura, this became highly consequential after the SEZ's arrival.

Although largely excluded from land ownership, women had some limited control over earnings from livestock (see also Brara 2006: 184–187). However, they carried a heavy burden of productive and reproductive work. Women did the most exhausting work in the gendered division of labor in agriculture. While men plowed and sprayed pesticides, women did much of the labor-intensive planting, weeding, and harvesting. Women performed the vast majority of all household work—gathering fuel and fodder; preparing food; and caring for children. Outside of the household economy, the gender division of labor varied markedly by caste. Upper-caste men confined women to the home and family agricultural fields as a point of honor, as did those aspiring households who could afford to forego women's wages. Lower-caste men could not afford this distinction, poverty forcing both women and men of these households into casual wage labor. When they did work, women were concentrated in the lowest paid and most precarious forms of construction and agricultural labor: according to the 2001 Census, women comprised 34% of the village's workers but 58% of its marginal laborers and 65% of its marginal agricultural laborers (Census of India 2001). Consequently, the socio-economic attributes of households summarized in Table 3.2 obscure deep inequalities within. The economic, cultural, and social capital of Rajpura's households were, to a large extent, attributes of their men.

Gender inequalities thus intersected with class and caste inequalities to produce a comprehensively unequal agrarian order. Such vast inequalities were the starting point for the sweeping changes that followed the arrival of the Mahindra World City. They were also the underpinnings of a pattern of politics that importantly shaped subsequent responses to those changes.

Big Man Politics

Princely rule and the failures of the postcolonial state left Rajpura not only with a highly stratified agrarian social order, but also with limited experience of collective politics. Rajasthan's princely states feature infrequently in the historiography of India's agrarian uprisings (Verghese 2015).[21] The major documented rebellions within Jaipur State occurred in the northern and historically distinct region of Shekhawati,[22] and I have found no evidence—in written archives or collective memory—of such a mobilization in Rajpura. Like most of rural Rajasthan, Rajpura also remained relatively insulated from the broader political and intellectual ferment of Indian nationalism (Rudolph and Rudolph 1984). The Congress made limited and late attempts to penetrate the princely states, and its base was limited to the urban upper castes and the Jats of some districts (Sisson 1972; Stern 1988). Civil society was almost non-existent, the media highly circumscribed, and literacy rates extremely low (Rudolph and Rudolph 1984). A few notable individuals from Rajpura were reputedly involved in anti-*jagirdar* political activity around the time of independence. But the bulk of Rajpurans, although undoubtedly experienced in time-honored peasant techniques of "everyday resistance" (Scott 1985), entered independence without the strong "repertoire" of collective action (Tilly 1993) found in some parts of India (Baviskar 1995; Guha 1999; Sundar 2007).

Independence turned Rajpura's residents from subjects to de jure citizens, but did not end the *thakur's* political writ in the village. Although his official position as *thakur* was eliminated by 1952 and subsequently replaced with an elected local government (*panchayati raj*), Jagat Singh managed to secure the position of village *sarpanch* (headman) for another two-and-a-half decades and even became *pradhan* (head of the sub-district). It was only in 1975 that a Brahmin Ayurvedic doctor educated in Jaipur, Banvarilal Sharma, effectively challenged his leadership. Sharma's first significant accomplishment was to persuade the Rajasthan state to confiscate the arms with which the *thakur's* men terrorized opponents. During his second term in the 1980s, Sharma lobbied to get a water pipeline constructed to bring drinking water to Rajpura from a nearby village and also persuaded the state administration to extend the electricity grid from Shivpura, which was closer to the highway, to Rajpura and adjacent villages. But Sharma's election did not eliminate the *thakur's* power in the village, and the two rivals alternated office almost without interruption until 2005. The exception was a single term by a Regar woman who was elected on a ticket reserved by law for a Scheduled Caste woman,[23] and who was widely considered to be a compromise pick of Sharma and Singh. Notably absent from the list of Rajpura *sarpanches* are Jats, whose political assertion has been pronounced elsewhere across Rajasthan and North India (cf. Jaffrelot 2003; Jaffrelot and Robins 2009). Although Jats achieved significant economic success in post-independence Rajpura, they were not able to capture local political power by virtue of their dispersal across several panchayats and their location in outlying hamlets (*dhanis*) that were somewhat isolated from OBC- and SC-dominated Rajpura. As to why the village's SC and OBC majority repeatedly returned two upper-caste men to power for most of a half century, the unanimous explanation I received from lower-caste respondents was that no one from their caste had the money to win elections or the education and connections to "bring development." The Dalit political assertion seen elsewhere in North India—most notably in Uttar Pradesh and Bihar—has been notably muted in Rajasthan (Jaffrelot 2003: 69–76, 352–354) and was not very evident in Rajpura. Rajpura also experienced none of the populist agrarian assertion that occurred elsewhere in North India beginning in the 1980s (Byres 1988; Omvedt 1993; Brass 1995; Varshney 1995; Gupta 1998; Witsoe 2013). Women were almost entirely excluded from local politics except when government-mandated reservations resulted in a figurehead women *sarpanch*, and the public sphere was implacably patriarchal. Local politics was based on the ability of "big men" (*bare admi*) to "bring development."

In 2005, Laduram Meena became the latest "big man" when he was elected as *sarpanch* in a year when the seat was reserved for Scheduled Tribes. Although classified as a Scheduled Tribe, the Meenas—traditionally village watchmen—have been successful in post-independence Rajasthan by virtue of their political mobilization and success in obtaining government jobs through reservations. Laduram was a moderate sized landholder, but had become a land broker about five years before, setting up a partnership with Shiv Choudhary, a young Jat from a wealthy landholding family. Laduram's election as village *sarpanch* just as the SEZ was arriving in Rajpura proved fortuitous, as we will see, for his real estate business—but not for many of the villagers he ostensibly represented.

While village politics was largely based on local patronage, party affiliation in state and national politics was divided between the Congress and BJP. Scheduled Castes largely voted for the Congress, while General Castes and some OBCs eventually turned toward the BJP. Only a handful of village elites were actively involved in state politics: all of the *sarpanches* were (initially) members of Congress, while one of the Bania shopkeepers was a BJP party worker. Among youth, I encountered far more skepticism toward politicians of both parties than active engagement in party politics. While the village's land was acquired by the BJP government of Vasundhara Raje, when I arrived in 2009 she had just been defeated by the Congress' Ashok Gehlot. For reasons I explore in Chapter 8, support for the BJP at the state level was growing during my fieldwork despite mounting grievances in the village vis-à-vis the SEZ, which Raje initiated. But while most families did not actively participate in state or national politics between elections, village *chai* stalls were sites of vigorous public debates on the merits of parties, politicians, and events of the day.

Scholars have observed that popular memories of collective resistance strongly influence contemporary agrarian politics (Baviskar 1995; Sundar 2007). Many of the most tenacious struggles against land dispossession in contemporary India have arisen in places with prior histories of peasant mobilization (Levien 2013; Jenkins et al. 2014). Rajpura's history was, in this respect, muted. When the Rajasthan government arrived in 2005 to acquire Rajpura's land for the Mahindra World City, its job was made easier by a deeply unequal agrarian order without a strong history of political mobilization.

Conclusion

This chapter has outlined in historical perspective the agrarian milieu that would be dispossessed for, and refashioned by, the Mahindra World City. At the time of its dispossession, Rajpura was a largely agricultural village with a relatively profitable livestock economy. But it was also one in which decreasing rains and the relentless march of subdivision had forced many to diversify. Farmers were looking for better opportunities, but those opportunities were not nearly plentiful enough for most to leave farming—and the most attractive off-farm opportunities were out of reach for the majority, in part because of very low levels of education.

It is impossible to romanticize the social relations of pre-SEZ Rajpura, which still bore the heavy imprint of princely rule. The failures of the post-independence Indian state to redistribute land left intact vast caste-based inequalities in the distribution of the principal means of agricultural production.

These inequalities in agricultural assets provided an unequal basis for off-farm diversification in the post-independence decades. And this diversification provided dominant landowning groups—principally Brahmins and Jats in addition to the family of the former Rajput *thakur*—with large advantages in cultural capital (education) and social capital (extra-village social networks). Articulated with these caste-class inequalities was a deeply patriarchal system of landownership and pattern of social relations. These stark social inequalities were, in turn, conducive to a kind of top-down patronage politics that left Rajpura's farmers without a strong history of collective action.

Placing the chapters that follow in this historical perspective will help us to understand why the arrival of India's much heralded "new economy" in a rain-scarce village of Rajasthan was neither unanimously welcomed as development nor collectively rejected as plunder. Supporting neither Gandhi's rural romanticism nor Ambedkar's dismissal, the story that emerges from this collision between a neoliberal regime of dispossession and a 21st-century Rajasthani village is a far more uneven and contradictory one: of gains and losses; continuity and change; winners and losers; hope and disappointment; and a compounding in the present of development failures past.

4

Dispossession

In 2004, plans were under way to turn Rajpura into a World City. Although Rajpura's farmers were unaware of it, the Rajasthan government was in negotiations with the then $7 billion Mahindra and Mahindra Company to make their village ground zero for one of the largest Special Economic Zones in North India.[1] While Rajpura's farmers would have known Mahindra as the country's largest manufacturer of tractors, the diversified conglomerate had—like many of India's industrial houses—moved into real estate in the late 1990s with its subsidiary Mahindra Gesco Developers Ltd. (later changed to Mahindra Lifespaces).[2] Mahindra had already built the first private SEZ in India, the 1,300-acre Mahindra World City Chennai.[3] Vasundhara Raje, Rajasthan's aggressively pro-business Chief Minister of the Bharatiya Janata Party (BJP), was keen to establish something similar in Rajasthan.

On July 4, 2005, the Rajasthan Government signed a Memorandum of Understanding with Mahindra to establish the Mahindra World City (MWC) Jaipur. Under the terms of the agreement, Mahindra would be solely responsible for developing and running the SEZ and obtaining most of the financing, while RIICO would provide land and retain a minority stake in the project (subsequently established as 26%). Anticipating the project to bring $3 billion of investment to the state, the Rajasthan government committed to building new roads for the SEZ, supplying it with adequate power and water (estimated at half a million gallons per day), exempting it from Stamp Duty on land transactions, and helping it to obtain regulatory approvals.[4] Most importantly, it committed to acquiring for Mahindra 1,050 acres of government (grazing) land and 2,000 acres of private land near the Jaipur-Ajmer section of National Highway 8.[5] The Jaipur Development Authority would hand over the grazing land, which was technically in its jurisdiction, and acquire the private land from farmers.

This chapter examines the subsequent dispossession of Rajpura. It begins by showing how compliance to dispossession was produced and then examines the initial consequences of this dispossession, both for the village and for the MWC. It demonstrates, first, that Rajasthan's land broker state avoided a "land war" in

Rajpura by absorbing farmers into land speculation. It did so through the policy, discussed at the end of Chapter 2, of allocating dispossessed farmers small plots of developed land near the SEZ. This highly consequential compensation policy interacted with the features of Rajpura's agrarian milieu specified in the previous chapter to avoid farmer protests, allowing the MWC to become one of the first operational SEZs in North India. Taking us inside this world city, I then show how the dispossession of Rajpura's farmers enabled a combination of real estate arbitrage by the SEZ developer and the establishment of a tax haven for IT/BPO companies. While subsequent chapters examine the consequences of this pattern of growth for dispossessed farmers via land markets, labor markets, and infrastructure provision, this chapter shows how the immediate flipside of this accumulation inside the SEZ was a dramatic *disaccumulation* of productive assets in Rajpura. Although IT campuses and high-end real estate constituted a "higher value" land use than dryland agriculture, the loss of farm incomes, livestock, housing, water, and other means of subsistence was highly consequential for local livelihoods and was disproportionately felt by women. It was against these substantial losses that Rajpura's villagers weighed any gains from the MWC.

Compliance

In 2004, Rajpura experienced a mysterious surge in land prices. It began with a few brokers looking to buy land. The public announcement of the MWC was still almost a year away, and few in Rajpura knew why anyone was interested in their rain-fed farmland. The trickle of brokers soon turned into a torrent. A shopkeeper recalled:

> Outsiders started coming to buy the land, all of a sudden! They were looking for farmers, asking "whose land is this?" Night after night the market was a carnival (*mela*). Some were giving food and liquor. People didn't know about the SEZ. They found out after. It came in the newspaper, later. Later notices [of land acquisition] came . . . *after* the brokers.

Village land records indicate that sixty-nine farmers in Rajpura sold their land in 2004, compared to 10 in 2003. These were mostly indebted lower-caste farmers who were enticed by an unprecedented increase in land prices—from $4,000 per bigha to $5,000 and then $6,000. These sums would seem paltry within months, but no one knew what was coming and brokers deliberately spread misinformation. Rumors circulated that a government project was planned, some said an airport. Brokers told farmers that it was better to sell than get nothing from the government. Dispatched by those with inside knowledge of the planned SEZ, these brokers would make windfall gains by buying up cheap land from unsuspecting farmers.

Eventually, a signboard for the project was posted in the village. As one young farmer recalled, "We saw a board that said SEZ. But we didn't know what an SEZ was. Then it started coming in the papers." After announcements in the local Hindi dailies, farmers came to understand that an SEZ—pronounced "sej" locally—was to be established in Rajpura, though most had no clue what a "sej" was, much less what it would mean for them. Finally, notices arrived in legalistic Hindi telling farmers that their land would be forcibly acquired by the JDA and that, as compensation, they could either receive a fixed cash payment or plots of developed commercial-residential land adjacent to the SEZ. Initially, farmers were promised plots that would be 15% the size of their original farmland; this would later be raised to 25% after lobbying by the local MLA (Member of Legislative Assembly). These plots would be allocated in large areas developed by the JDA adjacent to the MWC, zoned for urban use, and developed with the necessary infrastructure. The intent, as one high-level government official frankly described it, was to "soften opposition" and "buy consent."

The policy did not buy "consent," but it did soften opposition. It did so most importantly by transforming dispossession from a collective relation to the state into an individualized relation with the market. While the threat of state dispossession loomed, farmers were faced with individual choices about whether and when to sell their rights to compensation plots. Many farmers—especially among the poor and less educated lower castes—did not have the means to wait and had no idea what an SEZ was, much less what it would do to local land values. Outside investors, brokers, and some savvy farmers did: they quickly calculated that these plots would be more valuable than the original farmland once multinational companies came to the village and, as brokers, persuaded less savvy farmers to sell. Once the government started land acquisition proceedings, registration of land sales in the footprint of the SEZ was frozen[6], but brokers circumvented this by executing "power of attorney" contracts through which they could buy farmers' rights to their future compensation plots. Soon there was a burgeoning market for these not-yet-built compensation plots and by the time I arrived in 2009, approximately three-fourths of them had already been sold to outside investors.[7] The sellers, as the next chapter shows, were disproportionately poor and lower caste.

By selling their compensation plots out of various combinations of necessity, fear, misinformation, desire, and calculation that differed by household, many farmers tacitly complied with their dispossession. More savvy farmers shrewdly calculated that they would profit from the project by letting their plots appreciate or by becoming brokers and were thus enlisted as active supporters. The next chapter will observe in detail the divergent strategies and highly unequal outcomes that resulted. The point for now is that aside from a few individual holdouts—discussed further in Chapter 8—no organized opposition emerged to the initial land acquisition. The JDA was able to transfer 3,000 acres of land to the Mahindra World City as "land wars" raged across rural India. Figure 4.1 illustrates the basic layout of the SEZ and the compensation plots in relation to the four villages in my survey.

With the violent clash over the proposed SEZ in Nandigram still fresh, India's national media took notice (Sarkar 2008). Asked for the key to the MWC's success, a Mahindra executive explained to NDTV that land acquisition was "done on a negotiated basis with the farmers" and that the state government "sat down and talked with the farmers," resulting in a "fair deal for the landowners" (*NDTV* 2008). No one in Rajpura—aside from then *sarpanch* Laduram Meena, who admitted to being at a meeting with government officials and Mahindra executives—recalled any negotiation or even a consultation; whether it was a fair deal was fiercely disputed, as we shall see. The decision to locate an SEZ in Rajpura was taken by the Rajasthan government in negotiation with Mahindra: villagers' consent was neither sought nor granted.[8] Rather, the government's market-based compensation scheme worked by absorbing farmers

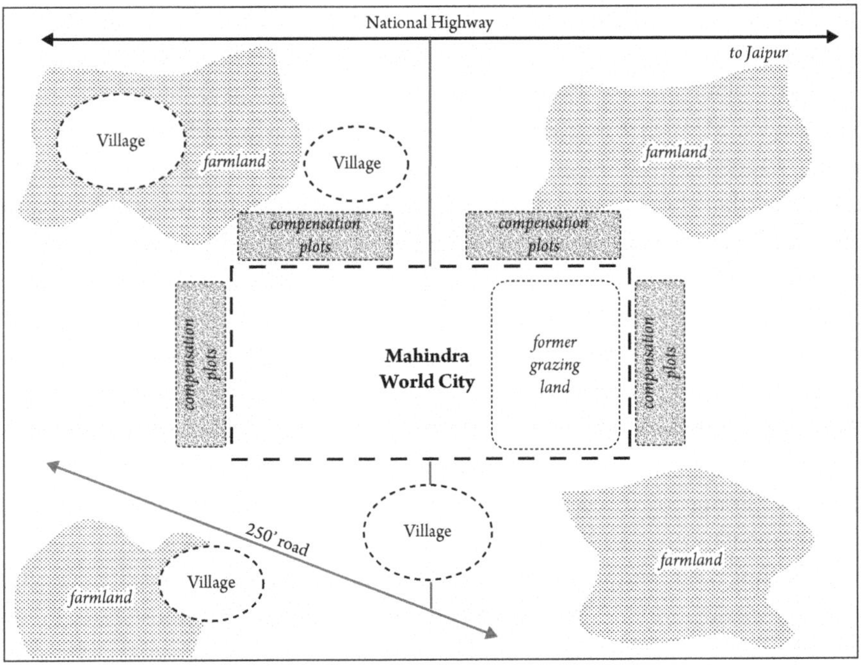

Figure 4.1 Stylized map of Mahindra World City and villages surveyed. Design courtesy of Jia-Ching Chen.

into the process of real estate speculation, which individualized farmers' relation to the SEZ and fractured their interests along the lines of pre-existing inequalities. This fracturing would only deepen with time.

Accumulation

Rajpura's farm and grazing land thus became a "world city." No old-fashioned industrial estate, MWC's marketing materials described it as an "integrated industrial city" where one could "work, live, learn and play." Its centerpiece would be a 700-acre zone for Information Technology and Enabled Services (IT/ITES), anchored by a campus for Bangalore-based Infosys and described as the biggest in India. It would also have smaller zones for light engineering, gems and jewelry, handicrafts, and apparel. Contiguous with but technically distinct from the SEZ, Mahindra would develop a 500-acre Domestic Tariff Area (DTA) to provide the same infrastructure for non-exporting companies. Once the zone attained a critical mass of industries and employees, Mahindra planned to use 1,000 acres to build a "Lifestyle Zone." The Lifestyle Zone would make the SEZ a complete satellite city with upscale residential colonies, shopping malls, schools, hospitals, and recreational space—all the amenities for the white-collar employees working in the zone. In place of the drab instrumental aesthetic of a RIICO industrial estate, the MWC was designed by architectural and landscaping consultancies from Singapore for the "world class" aesthetic (Ghertner 2015). Thanks to a grant from the Clinton Climate Initiative for Sustainable Development, it boasted green technology such as LED and solar lights, and "recycled water."

Such were the plans as laid out in slick marketing brochures. The profit model was fairly straightforward.

SEZ Development: The Rate of Accumulation by Dispossession

As one Mahindra official frankly described their business model, "You can say our product is developed land parcels."[9] With 3,000 acres of land in possession, Mahindra employed construction companies to level it, build roads, and install water, electricity, and data connectivity. It then began reselling this land by the square meter on a long-term lease basis to companies looking to establish office buildings or factories in the zone. Roughly half of its "land parcels" would be developed into luxury residential space and associated commercial development in the Lifestyle Zone. As noted, the SEZ Act only required that developers use 50% of the land for productive purposes. It was this freedom with the other 50% that provided the key incentive for Mahindra and other private SEZ investors.

A MWC manager made it clear that while they might make moderate profits on reselling industrial land, the Lifestyle Zone "will be our bread and butter."[10]

As SEZ developer, Mahindra's strategy was thus to maximize the discrepancy between the artificially low price of dispossessed agricultural land and its ultimate value as industrial, commercial, and residential real estate. I have called this ratio between the cost of state-acquired land and its ultimate appreciation the rate of accumulation by dispossession. Through interviews and government documents obtained through India's Right to Information Act, I was able to provisionally estimate this rate for the MWC.[11] Mahindra paid the government of Rajasthan an average of Rs 1,020,567 per acre of land.[12] To be generous to Mahindra, we can add its per acre land development cost to this initial land price: a Mahindra manager told me that this was approximately Rs 3,000,000 per acre.[13] In 2010, Mahindra was selling long-term leases for developed industrial land to companies for Rs 2,500 per sq. meter, or Rs 10,117,150 per acre.[14] While the residential zone was not yet developed, we can take the price of plots in nearby residential colonies as a proxy. By 2016, plots in the nearby Jaipur Greens residential colony were starting at Rs 14,500 per square yard—or over Rs 70,180,000 per acre. By virtue of being given dispossessed land from the Rajasthan government, then, Mahindra was netting over Rs 6 million ($120,000) per acre on industrial land. Barring a collapse of the real estate market, it would net at least Rs 66 million ($1.32 million) per acre in the residential area. The rate of accumulation by dispossession was roughly 250% on the industrial land and would likely be more than 1,745% in the "Lifestyle Zone." Since they assume no further price rise, these are conservative estimates.

While "adding value" through infrastructure creation, an SEZ developer thus derives windfall profits from the mere fact that the state is willing to give it cheap land dispossessed from farmers. There is nothing illegal about this procedure; this incentive for private SEZ development was envisioned by the SEZ Act itself and was taken for granted by government officials and corporate executives as the business model for many forms of Public Private Partnership (PPP) infrastructure. India's Land Acquisition Act allowed the government broad discretion to acquire land for private companies for purposes it deemed in the public interest. Dispossession for India's SEZs was, as the previous chapter demonstrated, the fruition of a decade-and-a-half shift in how India's Land Acquisition Act was used in practice. The routinization of such land brokering explains the complete freedom with which Mahindra officials shared this information.

The MWC was not, as some scholars have interpreted SEZs, a "neo-colonial" land grab, nor did it contribute to the "foreignization of space" (Zoomers 2010) or a "disassembling" of national territory (Sassen 2013). Mahindra was not only one of India's oldest industrial houses but was financing the SEZ through internal accruals and loans from the State Bank of India.[15] The available data suggest that relatively little foreign investment has come into India's SEZs generally.[16] India's SEZs are not the product of a weak state being bowled over by foreign capital (Sassen 2014) but of a relatively strong state put in the service of a mature domestic capitalist class: one that moved with alacrity to capture windfall rents during the real estate boom of the 2000s.

The Rajasthan government also had its own independent interests in the MWC. Aside from the licit revenue that would accrue to RIICO through its minority stake and to the JDA for reselling the land to Mahindra and developing adjacent land, the MWC also provided ample opportunity for illicit rent-seeking. The most direct evidence of this, detailed in the next chapter, is the tremendous boom in land sales that occurred in adjacent villages in 2004—one year before the SEZ was announced. A suspiciously large number of the purchasing companies do not come up on any Internet search. Government documents, moreover, reveal that the project's exact boundaries were shifted multiple times. A hotel owner whose land was acquired for the MWC filed a case accusing the government of shifting the project's boundary to benefit a large private developer. An independent commission formed to investigate alleged irregularities in land deals under Raje's administration pointedly directed questions at the JDA to this effect—until the commission was unceremoniously folded down by a court order.[17] Such accusations will probably remain unproven, but there is little doubt that the MWC was a massive stimulus to the public-private partnership in rent-seeking that defines the land broker state.

But the MWC was more than a real estate colony. The SEZ Act required that developers attract exporting companies that would generate net foreign exchange. The MWC's residential real estate business presumed, moreover, a sufficiently proximate white-collar work force to buy its high-end flats. At 25 km from Jaipur, this demand could not, in the near term, come solely from the city's peri-urban expansion. Mahindra needed exporting companies as capitalist tenants. India's knowledge economy, as a Mahindra annual report noted,[18] provided the natural synergy.

Tax Haven for the Knowledge Economy

If the stated intent of India's SEZs was to stimulate manufacturing, they have instead been disproportionately inhabited by the already dynamic IT/ITES sector (Palit and Bhattacharjee 2008). The MWC reflected this larger trend. Although a multi-purpose SEZ, the 700-acre IT/ITES zone was its centerpiece and the only zone that was operational for most of my fieldwork. Seven years after land acquisition, the other zones were developing extremely slowly: only one textile plant and one small engineering firm had opened by 2012. By 2014, JCB had set up a plant to build earth-moving equipment in the Domestic Tariff Area. The State Bank of India and ICICI, India's largest public- and private-sector banks respectively, had also bought land in the DTA, but neither had started construction, in part because, as Chapter 8 will discuss, one family was refusing to surrender its land. For most of my fieldwork, only Infosys and Deutsche Bank were operational, with the vast majority of the land dispossessed for the Mahindra World City sitting vacant.

Chief Minister Raje and the Mahindra executives had been keen on attracting Infosys, the $7.9-billion Indian IT and BPO giant, as the anchor investor. The darling of India's knowledge economy, it was Infosys's motto—"win in a flat world"—that provided the inspiration for Thomas Friedman's (2006) paean to globalization. As of 2011, Infosys had bought 190 acres in the MWC—"flattening" a good chunk of Rajpura's grazing land. Its business services division—Infosys BPO—was employing approximately 600 English-speaking youth with bachelor's degrees to do back-office finance, accounting, human resource, and insurance work for corporations in the United States, European Union, and Australia. In addition to expanding its BPO operations, the parent company, Infosys Technologies, was planning to set up a major software campus on the site.[19] In the Silicon Valley/Bangalore model, the campus would be a self-contained enclave with its own food courts and recreational space.

Even before Infosys was up and running, Deutsche Bank's in-house BPO division moved into a campus built for them by Mahindra to undertake the back-office accounting work for its global investment banking business. As of 2010, it was employing approximately 500 people to do the necessary manual accounting for Deutsche Bank's transactions in global equity, debt, foreign exchange, and commodities markets.[20] While other large IT companies had bought land in the MWC, the 2008 financial crisis prompted them to delay construction, and put a damper on the expansion plans of Infosys and Deutsche Bank.

The SEZ's attraction for these already-thriving "knowledge economy" firms was straightforward. While the IT sector already enjoyed a range of tax breaks, export subsidies, and labor deregulation under the Software Technology Parks of India (STPI) policy, these were set to expire. India's SEZ Act provided a variety of incentives that were moderately stronger than those enjoyed under the prevailing STPI policy: income tax holidays, duty-free imports, exemption from sales, service, and the minimum alternative tax, and "single-window clearance" for all central approvals. While India's labor laws were still technically applicable inside SEZs, they would be arbitrated by a single and typically industry-friendly bureaucrat called the "development commissioner." But because the IT/ITES industry was already exempted from unionization, it was the tax and tariff incentives that were more significant. Government officials admitted that they had no way to check whether companies were merely shifting existing units into SEZs to capture these tax breaks.[21]

While Jaipur was not a major hub for IT/BPO companies, its main attraction was a large supply of the low-cost educated labor upon which the offshoring enterprise rests. The main operating cost of BPO companies in particular is the wages of moderately skilled middle class labor that is able and willing to undertake data entry, accounting, and other "back office" work on night shifts corresponding to the markets of their foreign clients. While over 90% of such employment was captured by seven leading cities—Bangalore, Mumbai, the National Capital Region of Delhi, Hyderabad, Pune, Chennai, and Kolkata—increasing costs of living in these metros were driving up wages and eroding profit margins. Second-tier cities with a sufficient pool of labor skilled in computers and rudimentary accounting—and proficiency in English for jobs that require direct interaction with clients—were becoming increasingly attractive (NASSCOM and A.T. Kearney 2008). According to NASSCOM (2010), 58% of the total IT-BPO workforce came from "non–Tier 1 cities," suggesting the possibility that they could be captured more cheaply at their source. Companies could capitalize on the desire of BPO workers to live in their hometowns and pay them 75% of the wages offered in India's large metros.[22] Labor recruited from elsewhere, as one Infosys manager told me, need only be paid according to local costs of living.[23] Jaipur had gone through an education boom over the previous decade, and was thus awash in young graduates willing to work nights for a starting salary of approximately $200/month.

With both Infosys and Deutsche Bank looking to expand operations, Mahindra was able to offer them sufficient land with high-quality "plug-n-play" infrastructure—roads, water, power, electricity, connectivity, etc.—with plenty of room to expand. The MWC was close to a major expressway linking Mumbai and Delhi, a planned ring road, and the newly renovated Jaipur International Airport. Land prices were lower than in many Tier 1 cities, and the Rajasthan government's Stamp Duty exemption amounted to a 7% discount. Given these incentives, the Mahindra World City quickly sold out the first phase (383 acres) of its IT zone.[24]

So while Mahindra was the SEZ's landlord, IT companies were its main tenants. While the former accumulated through land arbitrage, the latter accumulated through labor arbitrage. The two were synergistic, as the surplus value generated within the IT firms provided demand for the converted farmland as their "spatial basis of operations" (Marx 1982: 916) while also driving demand for residential real estate. Both the SEZ developer and the knowledge-economy lessees received tremendous tax breaks.

The difference between India's new private SEZs and the old public-sector industrial estates can now be fully appreciated. Whereas the Rajasthan government previously developed industrial infrastructure itself, it was now a mere land broker and facilitator, providing cheap land and subsidies to private capitalists. Whereas public entities like RIICO had an incentive to acquire the minimum amount of land required for industrial production (to minimize their sunk capital), private SEZ developers like Mahindra had the incentive to make their zones as large as possible to maximize their profit on cheaply acquired land. Whereas RIICO industrial estates embodied the productivism of Nehruvian planning, the Mahindra World City would be a private satellite city for middle-class consumption. In the place of spatial Nehruvianism, with its intent of spreading investment evenly across the national territory, the private SEZ represented a retreat into elite private enclaves—what Graham (2000) calls "premium networked spaces" (see also Brenner 2004: 246)—as a strategy for promoting infrastructural investment. And instead of prioritizing labor-intensive industrialization, the Mahindra World City, like a majority of India's SEZs, was to be disproportionately inhabited by the "knowledge economy." The Mahindra World City, in short, represented a complete departure from state-driven developmentalism.

This pattern of growth would be highly consequential for Rajpura's dispossessed farmers. Its major consequence, as Chapter 5 demonstrates, was a dramatic real estate boom that would engulf Rajpura but refract through its agrarian social structure to very unequal effect. Beyond that, as Chapters 6 and 7 show, it largely marginalized their labor and excluded them from its "world class" infrastructure and amenities. Its most immediate consequence, however, was to destroy the pre-existing agricultural economy.

Disaccumulation

When I arrived in 2009, most of Rajpura's land was already inside the Mahindra World City and its agricultural economy decimated. But according to the government and corporate officials I interviewed, there was nothing to decimate. On my first trip inside the SEZ, a group of managers and engineers explained to me that the land in Rajpura was "barren," and joked that when they first arrived there was "nothing but goats, camels, and prickly bushes" that got caught in one's pants.[25] A promotional video on the MWC's website made a similar point: it showed pictures of cracked earth overlaid with flashing text that read "hostile environment conditions," "barren land," "lack of potable groundwater," and "highly alkaline soils."[26] A government official concurred: "the land that was acquired was unirrigated. It was barren land, so it's not a loss."[27] Contrasted with the "development" the SEZ claimed to be bringing, such representations of the landscape justified the dispossession of nine villages in the minds of government officials and Mahindra executives.

"Improvement" and "development" have, as Chapter 1 illustrated, been the principal legitimizations for land dispossession since at least the English enclosures. And these legitimations rest on portraying "traditional" land uses as unproductive and its users as "backward."[28] In India, economists have argued that because agricultural growth is stagnant, it is imperative to transfer land—by force, when necessary—from agriculture to higher value uses (Banerjee et al.

2007; Bardhan 2011; Chakravorty 2013). And while some have expressed concern about acquiring "fertile" irrigated land, few express qualms about converting the type of unirrigated land found in Rajpura. Compared to millet cultivation and livestock rearing, a "world city" filled with multinational companies was surely the land's "highest and best use." But utilitarian analysis evades the question: higher value for whom? While the following two chapters will examine the implications of the MWC's real estate and knowledge intensive growth for dispossessed farmers, the starting point is a measured assessment of what was lost. And Rajpura's residents made it very clear that something was lost.

Although semi-arid and susceptible to water scarcity, agriculture in Rajpura provided most families with crucial means of subsistence. The single crop that most families received from their land provided them with significant portions of their grain requirements for the year (varying, of course, by landholdings and the quality of the monsoons), and left many with a marketable surplus. Pearl millet (*bajra*), grown in Rajasthan for several thousand years and well-adapted to drought-prone environments, was the staple crop and consumed the most acreage. Made into *rotis* and a butter-milk porridge (*raabdi*) in the winter, *bajra* most importantly provided fodder for livestock in the dry months. Lesser acreage was devoted to other grains like sorghum (*juvar*) and corn, lentils and others pulses, oil seeds such as mustard, sesame, and peanuts (a large cash crop in Jaipur district),[29] and various non-water intensive vegetables that could be sold to the nearby Jaipur market. With a decent monsoon, these crops could yield substantial income.[30] For the minority with enough water for a second crop—a not insignificant 32% of families in my survey—winter wheat and vegetable cultivation could be quite remunerative.[31]

Cultivation of millet was synergistic with the rearing of livestock, which was both more stable and more profitable. The village's large tract of grazing land could support livestock for much of the winter, while the post-harvest stubble and stored fodder could be used through the summer. Milk and milk products—*ghee* (clarified butter), *dahi* (yogurt), and *chaach* (buttermilk)—were central to local diets, providing protein and balancing the oily and hot vegetable dishes that were consumed with thick *roti* twice a day. Given Rajpura's proximity to the Jaipur market and increasing prices during the 2000s (more on which shortly), milk production contributed more to economic accumulation than the direct sale of agricultural produce. One buffalo, as we saw, could yield Rs 2,000 to 3,000 ($40–$60) per month, while a dozen goats could earn roughly the same amount as a casual laborer. In addition to being the main source of agricultural income for Rajpura's cultivators, livestock rearing was the chief occupation of pastoral specialists—most prominently the Gujjars—who depended almost entirely on the village commons for supporting their herds of goat and sheep.

While providing fodder was its most valuable use, the village commons also furnished fuel, edible shrubs, and medicinal plants. *Neem* trees provided goat fodder, soap, and medicine, and were used for brushing teeth. *Babul* trees provided firewood and fodder and were a crucial ingredient of the local country liquor. *Kachriya* was dried and eaten as a vegetable, while *sangra* and *kair* were made into pickles (these might have been the prickly bushes that got caught in the pants of Mahindra officials). In her study of the effects of the English enclosures, Humphries (1990: 32) observes that, "Taxonomies of the products that could be hunted and gathered for consumption, or sale, or as the raw materials for some handicraft production, usually receive a condescending sneer." But these minor forest uses complemented cultivation and livestock rearing to form an agrarian economy that furnished most of Rajpura's villagers with a significant portion of their subsistence needs. While highly valued by all, this subsistence cushion was particularly important for the lower-caste semiproletariat, whose only other source of income was erratic and poorly paid manual labor.

When their land was dispossessed for the Mahindra World City, cultivators lost their farm incomes and direct access to grain, lentils (*daal*), and vegetables. Expropriation of the village grazing land, combined with the loss of stubble and fodder from farmland, undermined the livestock economy. Profitable milk production depended on both—purchasing fodder (at Rs 200 per 40-kg *maund*) dramatically reduced profit margins. Many families, now confined to house plots, no longer had the space to keep animals for stall feeding. Goat rearing, with its already low margins, was hardly economical with purchased tree fodder. The result was a massive liquidation of animals.

Table 4.1 demonstrates the effect of land dispossession on household livestock holdings for the three villages (Rajpura, Shivpura, and Jatpura) in my sample that lost land to the SEZ. The first thing to notice is that land dispossession led to the loss of two-thirds of the total livestock population in these villages.[32] Given this large and roughly simultaneous divestment, many farmers received fire sale prices.

Table 4.1 **Average Livestock Holdings by Caste before and after SEZ**

Caste (No. of Households)	*Buffalo*		*Cows*		*Goat*		*Sheep*		*Total Animals*	
	Before	*After*	*Before*	*After*	*Before*	*After*	*Before*	*After*	*Before*	*After*
General (24)	14.96	4.96	4.38	2.25	0.08	0	0	0	19.41	7.21
Jat (9)	6.56	5.56	1.78	1.00	8.11	3.11	0	0	16.44	9.67
OBC (21)	5.81	1.57	2.76	0.52	11.14	1.38	7.29	2.00	27.00	5.62
SC/ST (29)	1.69	0.86	0.83	0.28	5.86	1.93	1.38	0	9.76	3.07
All (83)	7.10	2.73	2.45	1.00	5.77	1.37	2.33	0.52	17.64	5.63

But aggregate figures do not capture the differential consequences of this disaccumulation across class and caste. For Jats and Brahmins (the only livestock-owning General Caste in the sample), dispossession dramatically reduced the volume and profitability of their commercial milk production. Brahmin buffalo holdings were reduced from an average of fifteen per family to five, while Jat buffalo herds dropped more moderately from 6.5 to 5.5. That Brahmin and Jat herds were reduced to roughly the same level suggests that dispossession did not affect the wealthy agricultural castes linearly, but established a new and lower ceiling. The ability of Jats and Brahmins to hang onto even this many buffalo was a testament to their larger landholdings (which left them with more land outside of the SEZ), higher incomes (to purchase fodder), and larger houses (which gave them more space for stall feeding). Nevertheless, the dominant castes still suffered large absolute losses in livestock income, and even those who were otherwise supportive of the SEZ complained vociferously about the loss of grazing land.

With smaller holdings and less off-farm income, OBC households—and especially the livestock-specialist Gujjars—were devastated by the enclosure of the village grazing commons. OBCs saw their buffalo holdings drop from 5.81 to 1.57 per family and were forced to liquidate almost 90% of their goats and 75% of their sheep. Those that tried to maintain their animals, like the landless Ranadevi and Gopal Lal Gujjar, had to purchase fodder from farmers who still had land. The going rate was Rs 200 per tree, which translated into roughly Rs 50 per day for their eighteen goats, slashing their daily income from an already meager Rs 120 ($2.40) to a precarious Rs 70 ($1.40) per day. The new dearth of local fodder forced them and other herding families to search for it farther afield, increasing their itinerancy with attendant consequences for their children's education. Another Gujjar family lost not only the fodder but the small plot of land on which they kept their eight camels. The village potters (*Kumhars*) found it more difficult to access cow dung, as well as wood and clay.

If the lower castes lost the least absolutely, they lost the most relatively. Owning a cow, buffalo, or small herd of goats moderated the penury of the lower-caste semiproletariat, providing their families with milk and, in some cases, a small supplemental income. Dispossession thus deprived these households of the slender margin separating them from total wage dependence and extreme poverty.

Dispossession thus not only eliminated farm incomes, but deprived Rajpura's farmers of direct access to means of subsistence. Everything, the ubiquitous complaint went, now had to be bought or bargained for (*mol karna*). Vegetable vendors started to appear in the Rajpura market, and many families now bought their milk in small plastic packets from the multiplying provision stores. It was the further bad luck of Rajpura's residents to become dependent on the market for their subsistence during the dramatic food price inflation of the late 2000s.

Over the latter half of the decade, food prices were increasing annually by 10%, with higher increases in protein foods (milk, lentils, eggs, meat) and vegetables (Gulati and Saini 2013)—items not covered by the Public Distribution System. Given these dramatic increases, most families were unable to purchase food (particularly non-grains) equivalent to what they used to receive from their land and livestock. As one farmer expressed an extremely common sentiment, "Before we got fodder, grain. We've lost everything. Cows, buffalo, goats, everything is gone. We're sitting here unemployed. You get some money, spend it, then what? Before in our village food was plentiful. *Ghee*, milk, buttermilk. Now there isn't even milk for *chai*." While this hardship would probably be temporary—though lasting years—for those who were waiting to sell their compensation plots, it would be more enduring for those experiencing downward mobility.

The aggregate effects of dispossession on food security will be discussed in Chapter 7 after examining the mediating effects of real estate speculation, employment, and other economic changes generated by the SEZ. But the effect of dispossession on food consumption was daily apparent to me in the undernourishment of the three children of Mahesh and Lada, with whom I ate for most of my fieldwork. Without their fields and livestock, they depended on *roti* made with Public Distribution System grain and market-bought vegetable dishes (*sabzis*), with little *daal* (which had reached a very high Rs 80 per kg) and almost none of the dairy products that usually complete the Rajasthani diet. Economic diversification and, as we will see in the next chapter, greater success at utilizing their compensation plots in Rajpura's booming property market cushioned the blow for many of the wealthy upper castes. My one month of meals in the house of the Brahmin sweet shop owner, farmer, and former *sarpanch* Bansilal Sharma—consisting of *ghee*-slathered *rotis*, plenty of *daal*, tall glasses of *chaach*, and buttermilk dishes like *kadhi* and *rabdi*—made a stark contrast with the scarce protein in Lada and Mahesh's house.

Fuel also became scarce. Almost all families fired their earthen stoves (*chulas*) with wood collected from the grazing land, or with cow dung from their livestock. Dispossession created a shortage of both, increasing the daily household burdens for women who had to search longer and harder for fuel—the exception being those families that received enough in compensation to opt out of the problem by switching to gas stoves.

While most of the land acquired for the SEZ was agricultural and skirted the dense village settlements, those families living on their farmland and in the more scattered hamlets (*dhanis*) also lost their homes. Low compensation prices for houses on acquired farmland created widespread disaffection. Suresh Sharma, who I watched gradually shift his house to a compensation plot before the old one was bulldozed, complained that he was being compensated $2,000 for his big stucco compound that accommodated a large joint family. Notwithstanding the fact that farmers generally wanted to use compensation money to upgrade their houses, it was also true that houses were being compensated below their replacement cost. Farmers who had to use one of their compensation plots for housing also had to forego its real estate value. With land prices spiraling, buying new plots in the village was prohibitive and the displaced were effectively priced out of the local market.

More brutal was the eviction of lower-caste families living on the village grazing land without title. Multiple SC and OBC families lived on the *panchayat* land that the Rajasthan government transferred to Mahindra. This included several Mali and Gujjar households, whose *mohallas* sat between the SEZ proper and the Domestic Tariff Area that was slated to be filled with a JCB factory and prominent Indian banks. It also included the entire hamlet of the Bavariyas, who had been living on the village grazing land for at least seven generations without title. Designated a "criminal tribe" by the British, Bavariyas still carried the stigma of a "denotified and nomadic tribe" (Radhakrishna 2001)—which, in addition to their lack of legal standing, helped to delegitimize their residency claims. Previously hunters in the *jajmani* system, they now made their living through casual wage labor, and raised chickens, rabbits, and goats on the side. They were extremely poor, discriminated against in the allocation of government development spending—a majority did not even have ration cards and their hamlet had neither electricity nor a handpump—and socially dominated by the Jats that controlled their *panchayat* (adjacent to Rajpura's).

Because they lived so far out into the old village grazing land, I only met the Bavariyas in the summer of 2012 when the approximately seventy-person hamlet was facing imminent eviction. The *panchayat* land underneath them had been transferred to the SEZ, whose boundary wall was being constructed through the hamlet, the trees around them had been cut, and their cremation ground enclosed. They had had to sell the majority of their sixty-odd goats because of lack of fodder; most of their chickens mysteriously became ill and died. Their only source of information about the SEZ was daily threats from its security guards. Their main hope was that the government would give them an alternative house plot to live on, and provide them with electricity and water. As an extremely gaunt old man articulated their modest demand, "It would be best to stay here. If not, somewhere they should give space to live."

When I returned in June, 2014, a JCB factory stood on part of their former hamlet—in a dark irony, manufacturing the very machine used to demolish their homes. It was with some difficulty that I tracked down a few of the scattered families. They were temporarily taking shelter in the condemned and abandoned two-room hut of a Jat farmer who had moved elsewhere with his compensation money. In March, a construction crew had arrived with police protection and bulldozed their houses. The police destroyed many of their belongings, set their homes on fire, and *lathi* charged the men, mercilessly beating a young man who now had a metal rod in his knee. The Bavariyas received no compensation from the government, which considered them encroachers. A few families were living in tents on the small plot of a relative near Bagaru; those camping at the Jat's house had nowhere to go, and their temporary shelter would soon be demolished.

Land dispossession also worsened Rajpura's already acute shortage of potable water. Those government handpumps in Rajpura that were not dry were saline. Farmers used to get "sweet water" from a pipeline—the one established by Banvarilal Sharma—which came from a better endowed village on the other side of the SEZ. Although there was some disagreement on whether it was already going dry, the SEZ severed that connection. Farmers meanwhile lost their wells along with their farmland. The village water-catchment tank (*taalaab*), built generations ago on *panchayat* land to recharge groundwater and provide drinking water for livestock, was now under the SEZ. Greatly compounding the problem was that the Mahindra World City was itself facing water shortages for part of the year, prompting Mahindra and its construction contractors, as will be discussed in Chapter 7, to purchase water from local villagers—including former *sarpanch* Laduram Meena—who took to selling scarce groundwater, pumped out of private tubewells drilled with land money, to Mahindra at $3 per 500-liter tanker.

The upshot was that Rajpura's groundwater was disappearing fast, and most families now had to purchase water from tankers, commercializing yet another necessity. In addition to being an economic hardship, this was shaping up to be a public health catastrophe. Much of the tanker water that Rajpura's residents were buying—as well as that provided free by the *panchayat* during the summer months—was coming from a village close to the town of Sanganer. This village only had a water surplus because its aquifers were recharged by industrial effluent from the town's several hundred block printing mills. Toxic dyes released from the mills without mitigation into ravines were seeping into the groundwater of neighboring villages. Although no one had tested the water in the village or the tankers, Jaipur-based scientists found that Sanganer's waste water contained higher than permissible levels of heavy metals and various toxic chemicals (Joshi and Kumar 2011). Village residents believed that the water was "dirty" and complained of multiple health ailments. The MWC did not create Rajpura's water problems but certainly exacerbated them—and neither it nor the Rajasthan government would do anything to solve them.

Finally, Rajpura's residents lost other incalculable social goods. Sacred groves (*oran*), the cremation grounds of several Hindu castes, a Muslim burial ground (*kabristaan*), and several temples and shrines fell inside the SEZ.

Dispossession, in sum, deprived Rajpura's cultivators of direct access to means of production, subsistence, and intangible forms of social wealth. The combined loss of arable land and the village grazing commons forced a disaccumulation of livestock, created fuel and water shortages, endangered health, and infringed on other social goods. Of all of these values, only privately titled land was compensated. Utilization of this compensation in a booming real estate market and its reinvestment will be examined in the next chapter. What should be appreciated at this stage is that the reduction of the entire structure of agrarian production and reproduction in Rajpura to the exchange value of private land was a simplifying fiction (Polanyi 2001). Left out of this calculus was the entire set of spatial practices that rested upon the combination of private and public land, and which collapsed like a house of cards upon dispossession, triggering a chain of unintended consequences and costs.

This catalogue of dispossession's tangible and intangible costs is not meant to suggest that what was destroyed was an idyllic and self-sustaining agrarian community. Chapter 3 showed how Rajpura's deep class inequalities closely corresponded with caste, which also continued to operate as a form of social domination. Both dimensions of inequality intersected with a starkly patriarchal social order in which women rarely had independent land rights, were not deemed worthy of an education, and were largely relegated from the public sphere. But we must reject the simplistic terms of opposition, which have been rehashed for centuries (Williams 1985), between agrarian romanticism and ruthless modernism. Rajpura was, on the eve of its dispossession, neither a community of sustainable "small peasants" (Shiva, Jani, and Fontana 2011) nor a "hollowed village" (Gupta 2009). It was a struggling but not doomed village where 400-plus families lived and made an important part of their living with the very unequal resources bequeathed by the past. Dispossession affected the village as a whole but did so unequally.

While the landed upper castes in Rajpura lost the most in absolute terms, they also had more to fall back upon—and were the best positioned to profit from the SEZ-induced real estate boom. With their small plots of land and handful of livestock as their only buffer against landless penury, the lower-caste semiproletariat lost relatively the most and, as we will see, gained the least from inclusion into the real estate boom. The landless were, however, differentiated by their dependence on the village commons.

Rajpura's sweepers were mostly indifferent toward the SEZ. At the very lowest rung of the village social hierarchy, their small cluster of houses sat at the far eastern edge of the village. The Sangat women cleaned the open gutters of the village in exchange for *rotis* that even other Dalits dropped into their hands to avoid "pollution." Until recently they were not allowed to drink *chai* at village stalls, and even now were served in plastic cups. The men were casual laborers, though the father of one family had a government job in an Ayurvedic hospital. Only one of the four Sangat families in Rajpura had any land, and most had no cattle.

They had no land to lose nor to leverage in the post-SEZ land boom. Since they did not own cattle, they were not affected by the enclosure of the grazing land. As one Sangat women put it, "It did not make any difference."

Even more indifferent to the SEZ were the village musicians. The lower-caste Ranas lived in small, run-down brick houses on the west side of the village. Entirely landless, they spent eight months of the year playing at village weddings throughout the region, making $2 to $4 per performance. In the offseason, they did casual labor, made wooden cots, and kept a goat and a few chickens. Although one of their children had ambitions to study, he dropped out to help his family make cots. Aside from having to sell one sheep due to lack of fodder, the SEZ had not affected their lives: they remained extremely poor.

Land dispossession was a tremendous blow, however, to landless herding families, to those like the Bavariyas who lived without title on *panchayat* land, and to anyone that had even the smallest amount of land and livestock. Everyone in the village was affected by the intensifying water shortage. But one cannot be dispossessed of what one does not have: in Rajpura, and probably in most locales, the totally assetless were indifferent to dispossession. Integrated into a regional labor market, they did not depend on agriculture for a living and some harbored modest hopes that the SEZ would bring better employment. Chapter 6 examines whether it did. But with nothing to lose, the fully proletarianized saw any gains as a bonus.

To anticipate the findings of the following chapters, it was neither the wealthiest farmers nor the poorest landless laborers but rather the poor *semi*proletariat that lost the most from dispossession. The assetless proletariat were—aside from those living on or off the village commons—largely indifferent to dispossession while a significant number of farmers (disproportionately upper-caste and landed) utilized their compensation plots to good effect and emerged as neo-rentiers or, more commonly, what I will call petty asset managers. So, while Rajpura's cultivators were universally stripped of their means of subsistence and production, some were included in the dramatic SEZ-induced real estate boom that swept through their village. The differentiated outcome from this speculation, examined in the next chapter, greatly complicates the usual equation of dispossession with proletarianization.

Dispossession also refracted through patriarchal social relations in ways that were no less tragic for being predictable. Women suffered disproportionately from land dispossession, albeit with important variation by class and caste. Every woman whose opinion I was able to gauge regretted the loss of their agricultural land, their livestock, and its produce. Although losing agricultural land in one sense relieved women of their disproportionate share of agricultural work, women in Rajpura were far more concerned with the loss of grain and dairy products, and many repeatedly complained that they were now "unemployed" (*berozgar*).[33] Studies of the gendered effects of land dispossession often find that in addition to undermining women's economic activities and autonomous sources of income (WCD 2000: 114; Dewan 2008: 130; Pandey and Rout 2004: 21; Mehta 2009: 19–20), land loss increases the burden of women's reproductive labor (Humphries 1990; Thukral 1996). This was the case in Rajpura, as loss of the common land and arable fields increased the work entailed in obtaining fuel and fodder. But class mitigated this burden, as better-off households were able to buy their way out of the problem with gas stoves and purchased fodder. Chapter 5 further examines how women were marginalized by the real estate economy while Chapter 6 assesses the consequences of the SEZ for the gender division of paid labor.

So, while dispossession inflicted harms that were felt in common by a plurality of Rajpura's residents, intersecting inequalities of class, caste, and gender apportioned those harms through the grooves of existing social relations.

Conclusion

I argued in Chapter 1 that dispossession is, first and foremost, a form of redistribution; that the socio-economic consequences of this redistribution are a variable rather than a constant; and that it should not therefore be assumed that its outcome is "development." While the Rajasthan state had long dispossessed farmers for public-sector industry and infrastructure, Rajpura's farmers were dispossessed for a "world city" that enabled private capitalists to reap windfall profits through real estate speculation and build a tax haven for relatively non-labor-intensive industries. This dispossession certainly contributed to growth—but a peculiar pattern of growth that, as subsequent chapters will argue, was particularly unpromising as a form of broad-based economic transformation. And for Rajpura's villagers, it came at a large cost. Dispossession initiated a cascading process of disaccumulation for most villagers, which translated into lost income, food, water, and shelter. Chapters 6 and 7 will demonstrate how these losses far outweighed the meager employment and infrastructural facilities generated by the Mahindra World City for local villagers.

This chapter began by showing how individualized absorption into speculative land markets created the initial compliance to dispossession in Rajpura. We now turn to how Rajpura's vast inequalities ultimately shaped the distribution of rewards from real estate speculation, the Mahindra World City's main contribution to the local economy.

5

Differentiation by Speculation

What we call land is an element of nature inextricably interwoven with man's institutions. To isolate it and form a market for it was perhaps the weirdest of all the undertakings of our ancestors.

—Karl Polanyi (2001: 187)

We didn't know what property was.

—Farmer, Rajpura

If the Mahindra World City initially arrived in Rajpura as a mysterious surge in land prices, the transformation of farmland into real estate quickly became the dominant fact of village life. The prospect of multinational companies—including the giants of India's IT/ITES sector—establishing their offices on land hitherto used for rain-fed agriculture unleashed a speculative land boom that radiated out from the SEZ and far into surrounding villages. Because the SEZ operated as an enclave of high-end services and real estate that generated few productive linkages and minimal local employment (as Chapters 6 and 7 will demonstrate), it was this real estate boom that most profoundly reshaped life in Rajpura. As investment capital from Jaipur, Delhi, and Dubai descended upon Rajpura's farmland, its former cultivators were swept into a radically new economic milieu driven by land prices and subject to the convulsions of global financial markets.

The peculiarity of real estate speculation as a driver of rural transformation is not well studied. Agrarian political economy has, over the last century, largely devoted itself to studying, "whether, and how, capital is seizing ahold of agriculture" (Kautsky 1988 [1899]: 12). It was the emergence of capitalist agriculture in peasant societies that was expected to drive economic development (Preobrazhensky 1965; Brenner 1976; Byres 1991), differentiate rural classes (Lenin 1964), and spur peasant politics—whether revolutionary (Moore 1966; Wolf 1999[1969]; Paige 1975) or "everyday" (Scott 1985). Whether and how each was occurring preoccupied scholars of the "agrarian question" for most of the twentieth century.[1]

While this question still has relevance,[2] the process of agrarian change unleashed by the Mahindra World City in Rajpura was quite different. Rajpura and eight other villages were dispossessed for a privatized satellite city. Mahindra's business model was to arbitrage on the difference between the cost of forcibly acquired rural land and its ultimate value as urban real estate. The zone's location on farmland 25 km outside of Jaipur enticed real estate investors to villages that had previously seen little non-agricultural demand. The resulting real estate boom was dramatic, and entirely orthogonal to the muted commercialization of agriculture in this semi-arid region. Capital came to seize the land, not agriculture.

This chapter shows how real estate speculation refracted through Rajpura's pre-existing class, caste, and gender relations to reshape the lives of its residents. The sheer sums of money that flowed through Rajpura in the years following the SEZ's arrival were vast, and even dispossessed farmers were given a stake in the bonanza by the Rajasthan government's compensation policy. This chapter demonstrates, however, the mechanisms by which inequalities bequeathed by the past undermined the prospects for inclusion in the present. It shows how the radically unequal distribution of economic, cultural, and social capital—rooted in the failures of land reform—shaped the ability of Rajpura's residents to profit from land commodification, and to reinvest capital gains into what remained an informal economy of petty trade, usury, and land speculation. I call the resulting pattern of inequality *differentiation by speculation*. While the poor and lower-caste semiproletariat have largely been pushed down into the informal subproletariat, and previously comfortable agrarian classes have become unimaginably wealthy neo-rentiers, a large and differentiated group of petty speculators, brokers, and business owners now forms a complex intermediate stratum of what I call petty asset managers. Caste-associated economic inequalities have—in the aggregate—been reconstituted around non-agricultural wealth, while gender inequalities expressed in land rights, the division of labor, and intra-household well-being have arguably intensified. So, while the prospect of easy capital gains excited the "aspirations" or "dreams" of many villagers (Cross 2014), the ability of Rajpura's residents to realize their aspirations has been radically unequal.

Dispossessed for a form of economic growth requiring their land but not their labor, Rajpurans' life chances have come to be shaped by their own uneven capacities to commodify land, and to otherwise survive in a non-industrial informal economy. Polanyi's observation that the commodification of land is a historically "weird" undertaking highlights the peculiarity of this pattern of change, which looks qualitatively different from the agricultural and industrial capitalism that drove dispossession in the period of state-led development.

A Land Boom in Rajpura

Brokers with inside knowledge started streaming into Rajpura to buy land roughly a year before the SEZ was announced. Once the government announced the SEZ in 2005, the stream turned into a torrent. Investors descended from Jaipur, Delhi, Mumbai, and unidentifiable points beyond. Dozens of national and regional real estate developers bought farmland for luxury housing colonies in the SEZ's vicinity. Dubai-based Emaar—builder of the Burj Khalifa—purchased hundreds of *bighas* in a joint venture with Delhi-based MGF. All roads leading to Rajpura became littered with billboards for luxury residential developments: Jaipur Greens, Omaxe City, Aastha SEZ View, Unique Dreams, and more. Wealthy individuals and politicians bought land through dozens of *benami* (shell; literally "without name") companies.[3] Smaller investors, including middle class families from Jaipur and non-resident Indians (NRIs), bought up plots and flats inside the not-yet-existent residential complexes. Small brokerage offices proliferated, and the brick and concrete walls of Rajpura were plastered with fliers advertising property dealers.

As Figure 5.1 shows, land sales in Rajpura quickly and dramatically exceeded historic levels. From a pre-SEZ high of ten transactions per year in 2003, land sales exploded to sixty-nine in 2004 and reached a peak of

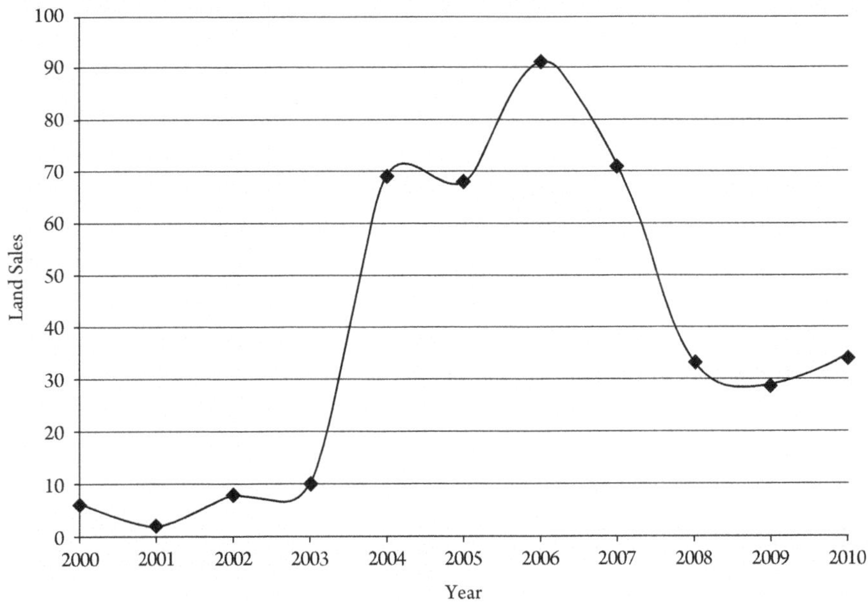

Figure 5.1 Land sales in Rajpura, 2000–2010. Source: Rajpura land records. An earlier version of this table appeared in Levien (2011). Reprinted with permission from John Wiley and Sons.

ninety-one in 2006. This nine-fold increase drove a surge in land prices from roughly $16,000 per hectare before the SEZ to over $280,000 per hectare for farmland near the SEZ in 2008.[4] The Jaipur Greens residential colony was soon selling as-yet-undeveloped plots for as high as $123 per square meter (over $1.2 million per hectare), while two-bedroom flats in the Unique Dreams apartment towers were selling for $56,000. Most buyers were not end-users but investors looking to flip properties. All were banking on the probability that the SEZ would fuel residential demand, effectively extending Jaipur to this rural hinterland.

A market quickly emerged for the not-yet-constructed compensation plots allotted to dispossessed farmers. Under the Rajasthan government's compensation policy, to recall, dispossessed farmers were allotted compensation plots zoned for residential and commercial use that were one-fourth the acreage of their previous farms. The premise was that including farmers in the land speculation would avoid the kind of "land war" bogging down SEZs elsewhere in the country. The Jaipur Development Authority was to equip the plots with roads, water, and power. Long before the plots had a physical existence—as late as 2012 they were nothing more than patches of vacant scrubland divided by white boundary markers (see Figure 5.2)—they had a brisk market for their exchange value. Brokers facilitated the sale of these plots to outside investors using "power

Figure 5.2 The compensation plots. Photo by author.

of attorney" contracts in which farmers sold the rights to their forthcoming government compensation. During my initial fieldwork (late 2009 to early 2011), the plots were selling for about $60 to $70 per square meter (or $600,000–$700,000 per hectare) and brokers estimated that two-thirds to three-fourths of them had already been sold. By 2014, the plots had shot up to an astonishing $300 to $400 per square meter.

As early as 2004, a stratum of local land brokers (*dalals*) emerged with great alacrity to facilitate the sale of farmland and compensation plots. These brokers were local farmers who used their social networks in Jaipur to form partnerships with city brokers who represented investors. The local broker was, in the words of one Jaipur-based investor, "the most important link among the chain." The farmer-cum-broker provided the local knowledge of who had land to sell, and what property was disputed. Just as importantly, they used their local standing to build trust between the farmer and buyer. This trust-building often required recruiting sub-brokers from within the seller's caste, and usually involved repeated house visits and affirmations of good faith over *chai* and *beedis* (cheap country cigarettes). While a single transaction could involve as many as five *dalals*, it most commonly involved two—a representative of the buyer and of the seller. If the *dalal* was the sole representative of the party, he received 2% commission for this service, which could translate into thousands of dollars per sale. *Dalals* with their own capital—or pooling their money in partnership—could engage in the more lucrative practice of providing advances for a sale agreement and finding an outside buyer to conclude the purchase at a higher price. Many young and middle-aged farmers jumped at the opportunity. As Aseem, a private school principal in Shivpura put it, "You get Rs 3,000 [per month] working, and people see that as a *dalal* you get Rs 10,000 all at once." It was a common joke in the village that "every family has a *dalal*." My survey revealed that 14% of households contained a broker, though it is likely that there was underreporting—for reasons that will become clear. At the height of the boom, these brokers mobbed the village land records office and the *tehsil* (sub-district) headquarters from morning to night trying to register land sales, for which the *patwari* (land records official) also took a cut. As is common throughout India, these land transactions were recorded at their government-assessed value to minimize the Stamp Duty. The tremendous sums of cash generated by this real estate boom were thus almost entirely "black" (unaccounted for tax purposes) and could not be deposited in the bank.

This speculative land boom, like many across the world, went temporarily bust in 2008. The US financial crisis rippled through India and made its way to Rajpura. The Mahindra World City, which became operational that year, came to a grinding halt as companies who bought land postponed their investments. Around the SEZ, residential demand dried up, prices slightly dipped, and, as

Figure 5.1 illustrates, land transactions declined dramatically from the previous year. Rajpura's former farmland was, for most of my fieldwork, a suspended landscape of half-built residential colonies grazed upon by goats. While prices did not decline too precipitously and demand started to pick up by 2012, the four-year lull was a significant interruption of the speculative boom, and an unwelcome eventuality to all those in Rajpura who still had a stake in it. Some brokers found themselves exposed with purchase agreements for land they could not find buyers for at the agreed price. Many others dropped out of the market, retreating to their new homes to live off their commission. Those waiting for a good time to liquidate their compensation plots or farmland decided to wait until the "market returned." Life was in a state of suspension when I arrived in 2009, with many voicing doubts that the SEZ would expand beyond a few companies. Elsewhere across the country, over 400 approved SEZs had yet to become operational and dozens were seeking "denotification" (CAG 2014). For Rajpura's ex-farmers, the capriciousness of monsoons and crop markets had been replaced by a new form of volatility.

But the crash was preceded by three to four boom years that fundamentally reshaped the respective fortunes of Rajpura's residents. And by 2014 boom times had returned, spurred by SEZ expansion. It would be difficult to overstate the impact of this land boom on the village, and the centrality that land speculation assumed in its economic and social life. As land price inflation dwarfed other forms of income, where one stood in relation to the real estate market became the chief determinant of one's socio-economic trajectory. Land prices and the details of land transactions became ubiquitous features of *chai* stall conversations, which were peppered with talk of "*bighas*" and "*lakhs*."[5] Land sales became the main point of tension, envy, and gossip within and between families. Such personal dramas unfolded in tandem with the transformation of the landscape as farmland was "cut" up for plots and demarcated with low brick walls; residential colonies and private colleges rose above mounds of cut millet; store-fronts for property brokerages proliferated; the Rajpura market swelled with new shops and multi-storey buildings; and a handful of magnificent concrete and marble bungalows began to appear in *mohallas* that a few years prior had only earthen homes. Traffic through the Rajpura market grew, and the BMWs and Audis of middle class investors from Jaipur started appearing on the village's rutted roads. The land boom, in short, unleashed a sudden and rapid socio-spatial transformation of Rajpura.

Differentiation by Speculation

The point of departure for this transformation was the pre-existing and highly unequal class, caste, and gender relations that shaped life chances in Rajpura before the SEZ arrived. Chapter 3 demonstrated how land reforms in the 1950s and 1960s failed to fully transform the agrarian social structures of princely rule, and left highly unequal starting points for economic diversification in subsequent decades. At the time of the SEZ's arrival, distributions of economic capital (landholdings, livestock, tractors, wells, and off-farm jobs and businesses), cultural capital (formal education and business acumen), and social capital (social networks formed through non-menial work or businesses outside of the village) were highly skewed and corresponded tightly with caste. A deeply patriarchal order, moreover, ensured male control over land and most other assets within households. When the Rajasthan government acquired their land for the SEZ in 2005, Rajpura's residents thus had vastly unequal resources with which to profit from the government's compensation policy and the larger process of land speculation.

Among the hundreds of stories of "winners" and "losers" I came across, some were surprising. Several Brahmin families were entirely left behind by the real estate economy because the government classified the land they cultivated as "temple land." Conversely, I was astonished to realize that Rajpura's washerman (*dhobi*) had become a prosperous broker and that by 2014 a few Dalits were sitting on several *crores* (Rs 10 million; approximately $200,000) worth of land. Such stories could be isolated to tell a heartening tale of upward mobility, if not exactly entrepreneurship (Kapur et al. 2014). Indeed, real estate speculation introduced more fluidity into the resulting pattern of social inequality than is typically seen within agricultural capitalism; in some cases, market savvy and connections (cultural and social capital) could make up for lack of economic capital, and astronomical price increases meant that an owner of even a few *bighas* could profit handsomely if they were able to wait out the market. Sheer luck also played a role. But we should be clear from the outset about the aggregate pattern.

As Table 5.1 demonstrates, the capacity of Rajpura's families to profit from real estate speculation corresponded fairly tightly with their initial social positions. Based on my survey of ninety-four households in Rajpura and three adjoining villages, the table demonstrates the caste-wise outcome of farmers' ability to profit from land markets (it excludes the outlier of Rajpura's *thakur*). It shows that at the time of my survey in 2011, the majority of lower-caste (SC and ST) families had already sold their plots while the majority of upper castes were shrewdly hanging on to them. While 82% of SC/STs and 58% of OBCs had already sold, only 25% of Jats and 19% of General (upper) Castes had done so.[6] The majority of the latter who did *not* sell would ultimately be the major winners. But even when they did sell, the upper castes received more money per hectare than their lower-caste counterparts: General Castes received a median sale price for their plots that was $12,000 more per hectare than SC/STs, and

Table 5.1 **Ability of Different Castes to Profit from Land Markets**

Caste	*Households who had Land Acquired (n=49)*		*All Households in Sample (N=94)*
	Sold plot as of Jan. 2011 (%)	*Median Price $1,000 per ha.*	*Land Broker (%)*
General	19	64	21
Jat	25	60	25
OBCs	58	56	10
SC/ST	82	52	6
Avg. (Weighted)	51	56	14

Note: The columns "Sold Plot" and "Median Price" are calculated as a percentage of those households who had land acquired for the SEZ and were thus allocated plots (n = 49). The total number of Jats in this subsample is small (n = 4) and, therefore, these figures should be treated as less precise than for the other castes (though their relative magnitude corresponds with the ethnographic data presented in this chapter). An earlier version of this table appeared in Levien (2011). Reprinted with permission from John Wiley and Sons.

every step down in the caste groupings depicted in Table 5.1 is associated with a $4,000 decrease in per hectare land price.[7] Finally, the data show that the upper castes were over-represented among the land brokers earning commission off the plot and land sales of others: 21% of General Caste families and 25% of Jat families contained a broker compared to only 10% of OBC families and 6% of SC/ST families. Not only were the upper castes better able to profit from the sale of their own land, but they were also better able to capture rents from the sale of other villagers' land.

The class positions at the end of these unequal trajectories were complex and difficult to categorize. In what follows, I try to put some conceptual order on the post-SEZ trajectories of Rajpura's residents by organizing them into four categories: neo-rentiers, petty asset managers, the proletarianized, and the excluded.

For reasons more fully explained in Chapter 7, the most common avenues of reinvestment for farmers was in more land (for the purpose of becoming absentee landlords and/or speculators), small shops, transportation, and moneylending. Differentiation thus proceeded almost entirely by success in recycling capital gains into an informal economy in which rent and circulation predominated over production. The distinction between neo-rentiers and petty asset managers was thus largely quantitative: the former comprised a significant minority of local landholders who vastly expanded their capital through real estate speculation and brokerage and reinvested their earnings into more land, trade, and usury, while the latter churned smaller amounts of capital between similar avenues of investment.[8] While the neo-rentiers were on a definitively upward trajectory, many of the petty asset managers were tenuously reproducing themselves just above or below the status quo ante, struggling to avoid proletarianization. Such has been the fate of the majority of the land-poor lower castes, for whom the earnings from land commodification have not been sufficient to counter their loss of land and livestock. These proletarianized families have experienced a straightforward downward trajectory from marginal farmers or semiproletariat to landless wage laborers. Finally, there is the excluded: the landless proletariat who had no (private) land to lose, but also therefore nothing to leverage in the post-SEZ land boom. The excluded were themselves divided by their dependence on the village commons: those who grazed or had houses on village land were among the most devastated by dispossession; while those with no livestock and a house in the village proper were indifferent toward it.

These categories blurred on their edges and families moved through them as their fortunes rose or fell. What follows is a snapshot of this ongoing movement, covering the roughly six-and-a-half-years separating my first and last rounds of fieldwork. These household trajectories obscure, however, the almost universal marginalization of women from the real estate economy.

The Neo-Rentiers

It is perhaps unsurprising that the most successful rentier of the present is that of the past. Mahinder Singh, as we saw in Chapter 3, is the grandson of Rajpura's last *thakur* (landlord-ruler). While Jagat Singh lost his role as the hereditary *jagirdar* of Rajpura after Independence, he managed to evade land ceiling reforms and retain effective control over at least 375 hectares (1,500 *bighas*), compared to the average village holding of 4 hectares.[9] *Thakursahab*—as villagers still called him—continued to extract rent-in-kind from his tenant cultivators for over a half century after Independence, and continued his domination of village politics for decades. The wealth extracted from generations of Rajpura's cultivators put Mahinder through elite schools in Jaipur and Baroda. After graduating college, he became an investment banker with Citibank in Mumbai. When I moved to Rajpura, Mahinder had just returned to his ancestral *thikana* to take up the role of acting village *sarpanch*—his mother was elected on a ticket reserved for women, and then ostensibly took ill. His career move from *haute finance* to de facto village headman was anomalous, but made good business sense. Mahinder was shrewdly transforming his family's former *jagir* into a real estate fortune.

Because he lived at his family's *haveli* in Jaipur and made only irregular trips to the village, it took me a few months to track Mahinder down. After getting his cell phone number from a member of his retinue, he told me to meet him "at my fort," which he preferred to the official *panchayat* office. Inside its turreted ramparts was a several-story (now largely vacant) palace, a grass lawn, and several out-buildings—all maintained by an old family retainer. Over this and subsequent meetings, the only during my village fieldwork conducted in English, Mahinder matter-of-factly explained his many business interests—sometimes, to my discomfort, keeping a long line of supplicants waiting.

While a significant portion of the land owned or controlled by his family was acquired for the SEZ,[10] he had received so many compensation plots, he explained, "it's crazy." He had not sold any of them, confident that they would appreciate, perhaps spectacularly, once the SEZ took off. In the meantime, he was still collecting rent-in-kind from his sharecroppers on his remaining land; indeed, he was even collecting rent on land *inside* the SEZ that was technically no longer his (a phenomenon I discuss in Chapter 8). Mahinder even bought additional land on the village's outskirts, which he turned into his own real estate colony. Royal Residencies, which I passed regularly on my evening walks, was a forlorn patch of empty plots demarcated with posts and no signs of life except grazing cattle. Mahinder informed me, nevertheless, that it was completely sold out. He started a construction company, which had a contract to build a portion of the SEZ's boundary wall. Given the scale of his operations, I assumed that brokering was too small-change for him, but he corrected this misimpression, explaining "Why not?" His elite urban contacts coupled with his standing in the village ensured him a steady stream of commission from Rajpura's land sales. As icing on the cake, he occasionally rented out his fort to film and TV crews.

If he could still capitalize on the romantic aura surrounding the Rajput nobility, Mahinder had made a spectacularly successful conversion from feudal aristocracy to capitalist real estate mogul. Combining his substantial inheritance of landed property, the cultural capital from his elite education and business training, and his social networks that span Rajasthani aristocracy and Mumbai high finance, Mahinder was deftly shifting his family's fortunes from pre-capitalist to capitalist ground rent. His role as village *sarpanch* was synergistic with his brokerage business—as it was for his predecessor Laduram Meena.

Being from the non-dominant Meena "tribe," Laduram's ascent was somewhat less conventional. Although designated a Scheduled Tribe, a section of Meenas have enjoyed upward mobility in Rajasthan because of their strong political mobilization for reservations in public-sector jobs and higher education. Laduram got involved early with the Congress Party and when the SEZ arrived in 2005 he was fortuitously positioned as village *sarpanch*, having been elected on a ticket reserved for ST candidates. Laduram had more land than most Meenas—38 *bighas* according to Rajpura's records. Most significantly, in 2000 he had started a small real estate partnership with Shiv Choudhary, a young, wealthy Jat whose family owned 100 *bighas*. At the time there was no demand for land in the village, and the two brokered land around Jaipur.

Many villagers alleged that, as *sarpanch,* Laduram took a hefty bribe for not opposing the transfer of village grazing land to the SEZ—one of his own nephews estimated it to be as much as Rs. 10 *crore* ($2 million). Laduram maintained that the government did not need *panchayat* approval for the acquisition. Government documents obtained through the Right to Information Act by Banvarilal Sharma—the muckraking political opponent of both Laduram and Mahinder—indicate that Laduram made illegal allocations of now highly valuable *panchayat* land to various individuals, and then bought some of it back. But whether or not Laduram accepted bribes or otherwise abused his office, he certainly took early and great advantage of the SEZ-induced land boom.

When I first interviewed Laduram, he was four months out of office and had just returned from a pilgrimage to the Kumbh Mela in Haridwar. Workers were building an addition to his large, well-furnished house. While portraying himself as a defender of the village's interests vis-à-vis the SEZ, he was frank with me about his business dealings. He explained that at the height of the boom between 2005 and 2008, he was facilitating 50 deals per month. He had extensive networks in Jaipur due to his pre-existing real estate business and Congress party affiliation. His real estate partnership—which operated from an office with tinted glass windows in the village market—brought in smaller *dalal*s to share in the commission when they needed someone more closely acquainted with the seller. Laduram used these property deals, many villagers claimed, as a form of political patronage, distributing commission opportunities or information to gain the political support of key people in different castes. Indeed, Laduram's extensive contacts and access to information—of current prices, potential buyers, the plans of the SEZ—led many villagers "to sit near him" in village parlance. But rather than using his networks and knowledge to defend the village's interest as a whole vis-à-vis the SEZ, Laduram made a massive amount of wealth alienating the land of fellow villagers, many of whom—as we will see—later felt cheated.

Laduram dissimulated about the extent of his newly gained wealth, but I was able to confirm that he had recycled his real estate earnings into the purchase of at least 50 *bighas* of new farmland, many commercial and residential plots around the SEZ and Jaipur, a petrol pump license, a large building in the Rajpura market he rented out as shops and migrant labor accommodation, a "farmhouse," and several more shops in a nearby town. Laduram also bought two corner plots of land abutting the "250-Foot Road," one of which he had already turned into a marriage garden—a lucrative business in the village after the land boom. He and his nephew had a "water supply" business selling groundwater to Mahindra and other villagers. When I returned to the village in 2014, construction had just been completed on his four-story student hostel, which towered anomalously above the village market—a shrewd response to the opening of two private colleges on farmland just outside Rajpura. He, his sons, and his nephews disposed of surplus cash through old-fashioned village moneylending at the prevailing 24–36% per annum. He was easily a dollar millionaire. In addition to his pilgrimage to Haridwar, he sponsored regular *pujas* at his privately built Shiva temple, donated to the village's Hanuman festival, and sponsored occasional feasts—the time-honored laundering of morally ambiguous wealth. But while Laduram had parlayed his prior economic capital, business acumen, and above all his social networks to dramatically expand his economic capital, his political capital did not fare so well in the process. Laduram's dual role as village *sarpanch* and chief land broker, as Chapter 8 details, earned him many detractors who felt that he cheated the poor and "sold the village."

If Laduram and Mahinder were the "big men" in the local real estate market, other large-landholding families attained previously unimaginable wealth by selling compensation plots and land, and then setting themselves up as substantial rentiers, merchants and moneylenders. As the prime beneficiaries of post-independence land reforms, Jats and Brahmins were also the major beneficiaries of the post-SEZ land boom. Not only did they have the most land to speculate on, but their prior diversification gave them the means and savvy to wait out the market; and the networks to become brokers.

Jagdish Choudhary of Jatpura was a spectacular example of a dispossessed farmer turning compensation plots into a fortune. Like many Jat families, his family had already diversified: Jagdish was pursuing a college degree while his brother worked in the diamond business in Jaipur. When their 24 *bighas* of land was acquired for the SEZ, they waited a few years until their compensation plots had appreciated, and then sold them for a magnificent $580,000. With this money, they built a large concrete and marble house in the village, and purchased 170 *bighas* of land in a village 10 km away, which they leased out to tenants. While they planned to collect one-third of a crop in the near term, they really purchased the land because it was 10 km from the national highway, where its real estate value was sure to go up. Jagdish's family had thus ascended from mid-sized farmers to large absentee landlords and speculators.

Other Jats in Neempura and the outlying *dhanis* of Rajpura had the good fortune of having large holdings just a few kilometers outside of the SEZ's footprint. Brothers Chimanlal and Haldiram Choudhary, who I met while surveying Neempura, were sitting atop a gold mine in the form of 80 *bighas* of farmland. When I first approached their homestead at midday, the two were leaning against one of a dozen neat *bolis* of fodder, surrounded by twenty or so buffalo. Pastoral appearances concealed a real estate fortune. In 2008, they explained, they sold 12 *bighas* of land for $192,000. They used that money to expand the house of their joint family and to buy 15 *bighas* of land in a village 10 km away, which Chimanlal's son used to start a brick kiln employing 300 laborers—one of the only classically "productive" investments of land money I encountered. While the fathers were illiterate, one son had a BA and another was a tractor mechanic in a commercial agglomeration along the highway. While their savvy decision to sell a small portion of their farm paid off massively, it was their net worth that was shocking. With land prices in Neempura at around $40,000 per *bigha* in 2011 (it had doubled again by 2014), they were sitting on land that was worth approximately $2.7 million. Chimanlal explained their change in fortune: "Before we had bitter water and the price of our land was Rs 50,000. Now it's twenty to thirty *lakh* and we can buy sweet water." Sitting in their white *kurtas* and orange turbans, faces withered from decades of cultivation in the Rajasthan sun, their glee was transparent. Many of their fellow Jat villagers were similarly selling off land in small parcels at good prices while letting the majority of their holdings appreciate.

Because Brahmins had the highest levels of education and were the most successful in obtaining formal-sector jobs outside of the village, when the SEZ arrived, most knew what to do. Those who lost land for the SEZ were mostly waiting for their compensation plots to appreciate and/or planning to start businesses on them when constructed; their main complaint was that the JDA was slow in building the infrastructure. Those with land outside of the SEZ were following a strategy similar to the Jats: waiting or selling small portions of their land at high prices.

My one-month sojourn in Brahmin-majority Shivpura introduced me to many such successful speculators. My initial landlord, Bansilal Sharma, was one of them. Former Shivpura *sarpanch* and proprietor of a sweet shop in Jaipur, Bansilal had 2 of his 20 *bighas* acquired, had deftly moved into the brokerage business, and planned to use his compensation plots to start a business while letting his remaining farmland appreciate. In Shivpura, such shrewd navigation of land markets was not anomalous: most farmers were still holding out even five years after the SEZ's arrival. As the Shivpura *chaiwala* Kailash Sharma explained, "Buyers come, but people here are not selling. They're demanding Rs 2 *crore*!" At Kailash's *chai* stall, one young Brahmin who worked for an insurance company told me that agents for the Omaxe City residential colony would come to his house "daily" to inquire about their family's 12 *bighas*. Forming a graph with his hands, Ramesh Sharma confidently explained that, "Until the graph reaches 90%, we won't sell." If they sold before that, they would have to buy land in a "backward area," by which he meant an area where the land had merely agricultural value. For him, an educated white-collar worker from a farming family, the agrarian landscape was divided into "backward" and "forward" areas based on their potential exchange value. His ability to formally visualize a temporal graph of prices—even if these are ultimately uncertain (and I am still not clear what the slope of his line represented)—bespoke a familiarity with market mechanisms not shared by many fellow villagers. He was reluctant to sell his farmland only because he was shrewdly calculating how to maximize its exchange value.

While most in Shivpura were delaying gratification, a few fantastic mansions indicated those who had already cashed out. One magnificent structure drew me to Gangaram Sharma, fifty-two, of Shipvura, who I tracked down at his highway-side motorcycle parts shop. Gangaram had sold 8 of his 14 *bighas* of land to the Omaxe City developers for approximately $500,000. Aside from building the mansion—two stories, four colonnades, a car park, and large reflective glass windows (see Figure 5.3)—he bought 94 *bighas* in a village 33 km away, which he was leasing to tenants, at least until it appreciated. He estimated that his remaining land was worth Rs 2.5 *crore* ($500,000).

Not all Brahmins and Jats were successful speculators. Those with small holdings and no off-farm income had to sell more rapidly; and those who had their houses acquired for the SEZ were forced to use their compensation plots for replacement housing. Many were extremely disgruntled about the SEZ because of the lack of employment, the slow pace at which the JDA was developing their plots, and because they thought they should be able to sell their land freely in the market. Conversely, not all successful speculators came from dominant castes. The land boom produced some startling "rags to riches" stories, even if they were proportionately and absolutely few in number.

Figure 5.3 Neo-rentier mansion. Photo by author.

Kanaram Regar and his two sons ran a vegetable stand in the Rajpura market, and it took me a while to figure out that these Dalit *sabziwalas* had a higher net worth than most middle class families in the United States. Crucially, they started out with 13 *bighas* of land, significantly more than the average Regar holding of 3 *bighas*. But when their land was acquired for the SEZ, they waited long enough to get a handsome—if still retrospectively low—price of $20,000 per *bigha*. They used that money to buy land in three or four locations, and had already sold one parcel for a small profit—having bought the land at $9,000 per *bigha*, they sold it for $12,500. They bought the vegetable stand, one of the small handful in the market that now catered to dispossessed farmers who could no longer meet their subsistence needs, and to the "outsiders"—especially drivers and migrant laborers—who now passed through the market. Even more shrewdly, they used some of the cash from the land sale to buy a van for transporting produce from the wholesale vegetable market 15 km away, which allowed them to become distributors for other village vendors. Their integrated vegetable business made them about $800 per month. Kanaram's older son was also a labor contractor and, after building a new house, the family was renting out their old one to Bihari migrant laborers. Kanaram's was thus one of the few Regar families to have thrived in the new post-SEZ dispensation; as Kanaram observed of his fellow caste members, "they have no land and are unemployed." But the upward mobility of even a few Dalits like Kanaram attests to a modicum of fluidity that did not exist within the old agrarian economy.

Such fluidity was also evident in the equally successful—if less salubrious—case of Mohan Nayak. Some men with newfound cash in their pockets quickly developed a taste for meat and drink, and their desire to bring me on their forays led me to Mohan's roadside *dhaba* (small eatery). While Nayaks traced their heritage to Rajputs—in whose armies they served—their socio-economic status at Independence was low, and they were categorized as SCs. Mohan had the good luck of having some land near the "250 Foot Road," part of which he sold to start the *dhaba*. Men would bring him raw meat from the butcher, and drink country or "English" liquor while his young cooks prepared it. His *dhaba* also, I belatedly learned, served as a "sex hotel" of sorts. When I returned to the village in 2014, Mohan had built a large "A.C. hotel" (meaning air-conditioned) for this purpose, with rooms reputedly costing $100 per night. Mohan had thus leveraged land values into a lucrative livelihood as hotelier for the sex trade, catering to the less reputable consumer demands of other successful speculators.

Overlapping with the successful speculators were the brokers, who become rich not through—or not just through—selling their own land but through facilitating the sale of others'. Land brokers connect distant buyers with local sellers and, in the context of poor land records and backlogged courts, build trust between them.[11]

Although many brokers were large landholders, brokerage required neither land nor capital for working on commission. While it required a modicum of business acumen, it did not require formal education—a fact only slightly exaggerated by the common joke that many brokers "can't write their own name, but know how to calculate commission." What brokers did require was social networks that could connect them to buyers or brokers in the city—a fact that *dalals* themselves often repeated, and that was incidentally reinforced by their numerous attempts to enlist me into land deals. When I demurred, explaining that I had little savings or business acumen, they assured me that neither was necessary, I just needed to "bring in an excellent outside party." Brokerage was a business based on social capital, understood not as a collective stock of norms and trust (Putnam 1993, 1995) but as individual access to networks of unequal value (Bourdieu 1986, 1990). By virtue of their off-farm diversification, upper castes had more extensive and higher value networks. And beneath the meta-*dalals* like Mahinder and Laduram were a significant stratum of medium-sized Jat and Brahmin *dalals* who earned substantial commission brokering farmland and compensation plots.

When the SEZ arrived, milk middlemen already had the urban contacts—as well as the motorbikes—necessary for making a quick and lucrative transition into land brokerage. Lalsingh Choudhary was a good example. A fifty-year-old Jat farmer from Neempura, Lalsingh owned 60 *bighas* of land between him and two brothers. Although uneducated, he used contacts from his milk distribution operations in Jaipur to become a large broker during the real estate boom, cutting fifty deals, sometimes on commission, and sometimes more lucratively advancing the money himself before arranging for an outside buyer. He reinvested his earnings into 25 additional *bighas* of land in a village 20 km away that he leased to sharecroppers, urban plots, and a cold drinks business in Jaipur, as well as a tubewell, tractor, and water tanker with which he sold groundwater to Mahindra. He bought a car, became a moneylender, and was sitting on a small real estate fortune to boot.

Putting urban connections to opportunistic use as the real estate boom arrived was the common pattern for almost every *dalal* I spoke with. Gangaram Choudhary, a young Jat from a family with 50 *bighas* of land, had been working as a driver in Jaipur before using those contacts to broker about twenty to twenty-five deals, from which he claims to have earned $12,000 (surely an under-estimate). Fellow Jat Mahinder Choudhary leveraged his contacts as a milk-middleman to do four to five deals, netting approximately $10,000, which he reinvested in a cold drink and juice shop in Rajpura's market that fetched him $500 per month. One Brahmin *dalal* reported making his contacts through the customers of his sweet shop in Jaipur, in which he is a partner with Bansilal Sharma. Another *dalal* made his contacts through previous work in a Jaipur jewelry shop, another through a retail cement business he owned in Jaipur, another through his *chai* stall in Mansarovar (an extension of Jaipur built in the 1980s), and one young Brahmin through his MA in political science. Of the few who did not make their contacts in Jaipur, several did so as owners of village *chai* stalls—the obvious points of entry for an outside *dalal* looking to buy land.

I encountered only one *dalal* who made his contacts through manual labor, highlighting the importance of the quality and not simply the existence of social networks. Santosh Balai, a lower-caste *dalal* who ran a small pirate DVD shop in the village, explained that he was doing wage labor in Jaipur and told his boss that he could help him buy land near the SEZ. While his example demonstrates some fluidity in who could create a connection and tap into real estate rents, he had only managed to do two or three deals. For the most part, the networks that mattered were built through non-manual work and business experience outside of the village. While there were some lower-caste brokers, they were few in number, typically operated on a much smaller scale, and were often brought into a deal when needed to build a connection with a seller from their own caste. I did not encounter a single broker among the "lower" *jatis* of Dalits: the Beirwas, Regars, or Sangats.

Brokers thus converted their social capital—itself the byproduct of prior off-farm diversification—into much greater economic capital. Their extra-village social networks enabled them to tap into the chain of rentiership generated by the SEZ, appropriating substantial commission from the alienation of village land and investing that money into further land purchases, usury, and trade. Once the SEZ's growth slowed, many of them applied their experience brokering land around Jaipur's planned ring road. Their alacrity in turning their social relations into capital made brokers highly controversial figures, as Chapter 8 demonstrates.

By way of land speculation and brokerage a fraction of villagers in and around Rajpura thus established themselves as neo-rentiers. While most were comparatively well off in the pre-SEZ agricultural order and had successfully diversified into non-farm occupations, they were now wealthy beyond imagination. The bulk of their income came from capitalist or pre-capitalist ground-rent, interest from loans, profits from small mercantile establishments, or commissions from land sales. Choosing to retain their village residence, they lived in flashy multi-storey houses, drove cars, educated their children in Jaipur, and spent money liberally on marriages and displays of Hindu piety. In village parlance, they were "sitting in the A.C."

The Proletarianized

In stark contrast to the neo-rentiers were those who were completely proletarianized and further impoverished by dispossession. This included the vast majority of the Dalit semiproletariat, especially the Regars and Beirwas. Regars were the largest single caste in Rajpura, while a smaller number of Beirwas lived in two *dhanis* outside of Rajpura and Neempura. The median experience of families in these castes was fairly straightforward proletarianization, by which I mean that they were deprived of all means of production and subsistence, not that they necessarily found regular employment (Denning 2010). While they were poor and semiproletarianized before the SEZ, their small pieces of land had provided their families with crucial means of subsistence to supplement meager and irregular wages from manual labor. With their small holdings dispossessed for the SEZ, they lost non-market access to grain, vegetables, fodder, milk products, as well as small agricultural incomes. At the same time, they were the least well-equipped to profit from selling their compensation plots. With micro-holdings divided between multiple brothers, the pressure of large debts, little market savvy, and *dalals* as their main source of information about the SEZ, they typically sold their land quickly and cheaply, and were the least able to convert their money into an alternative livelihood. They were the last to learn the potential value of their compensation plots and land, which typically happened after they had been liquidated. Their downward trajectories were depressingly similar, lacking the diversity of the upward ones.

Chitramal Regar's case epitomizes this straightforward impoverishment of the already poor. A forty-year-old bullock cart driver from Rajpura, Chitramal and his family had 3 *bighas* of land divided between six brothers, all of which were acquired for the SEZ. In need of money, the family sold their compensation plots early to a village broker for $42,000. Divided between six brothers, the money was not enough to buy new land after paying off their substantial debts. Chitramal regrets selling the plots but explained that he is illiterate and didn't know what an SEZ was, much less what it would do to land prices. He was bitter at the broker who "sold us cheaply." Before, he at least got food from the land, but now he relies solely on his meager income transporting goods between villages in his bullock cart, a dying business with the influx of trucks and tractor-trolleys. He is sliding deeper into debt and wishes he had the land back.

Dinesh Regar's story is similar and more clearly illustrates the malevolent agency of upper-caste brokers. Dinesh and his two brothers together had 6 *bighas* of land, and all of it was acquired for the SEZ. They sold their compensation plots quickly, but Dinesh says they were tricked by a broker into selling all 6 *bighas* for a very cheap $18,000 when they thought they were only selling 3. He explained that he is illiterate and "the broker deceived us" and "snatched" their land. In addition to losing their land, they had to sell their five buffalo for want of fodder and now had to do "a lot more" wage labor. Unable to get work in the SEZ, he worked through a contractor in Jaipur. When I asked what he had done with his share of the land money, he said, "What is three *lakhs* ($6,000)? We had to spend it on marriages. . . . It's been a complete loss for us."

Mangal Ram Regar is a forty-year-old who shared 6 *bighas* with six brothers. Five of the *bighas* were acquired and they sold the compensation rights early for a mere $8,000 per *bigha*. This went quickly on expenses and marriages. There wasn't enough left to build a house, much less to buy other land. He and all his brothers were now totally dependent on casual labor in Jaipur, getting work for about fifteen to twenty days of the month and earning $2 to $3 per day. While they had one *bigha* left, they owed the whole crop to the Jain shopkeeper. Because they didn't have enough money to buy food, small debts had accumulated. Although Mangal Ram had five goats before, the loss of fodder forced him to sell the weakened animals cheaply to the Khatik (butcher). With just one cow left, they had only enough milk for *chai*. While Mangal Ram was illiterate, his two sons, ages 10 and 11, were studying, but he was unsure how long he could keep them in school.

In the Beirwa *dhanis* where land was not forcibly acquired, there were many families who were nevertheless pushed by debt and induced by brokers into selling their land *very* cheaply. The three Beirwa land sellers in my survey received a paltry average price of $5,200 per *bigha*. The most tragic example I encountered was Gopalal Beirwa, an illiterate sixty-year-old man who, faced with mounting debts and expenses, was induced into selling all of his 3.5 *bighas* of land to a broker for a shockingly small $3,500 per *bigha* (about one-tenth of the prevailing price at the time). He was unaware of the new post-SEZ land prices and needed money to pay off debts. Gopalal was able to build a modest concrete house and drill a well for drinking water. But he now had no land, three fewer goats, and less food. He was angry at the broker who, he belatedly recognized, had deceived him.

Such cases of further proletarianization and impoverishment, different only in the details, constitute the *majority* of families in the land-poor lower castes. Despite some notable success stories, Table 5.1 demonstrated that SC/ST families were the least able to capitalize on their plots and enter into the brokerage economy. Not only did they start out with the least land upon which to speculate, but large debts and lack of off-farm diversification gave them little ability to wait out the property market, while illiteracy and lack of market savvy further facilitated their exploitation by brokers. Most had no idea what an SEZ was, much less what it would do to property markets; indeed, as the epigram suggests, while land sales had been a part of village life for a half century, "property" as a distinct domain of business was unfamiliar to most until the SEZ's arrival. Treating one's land as a purely financial asset is a learning process, not an attribute of human nature, and success goes to those who learn the fastest. Most Dalits had learned too late, leaving them with insufficient capital to invest in replacement assets. While they used compensation money to pay off large debts, those debts were piling up again—further enriching the expanding class of neo-rentier moneylenders. No longer possessing any assets to lessen the necessity of wage labor, they were now part of the precarious class of "wage hunters and gatherers" (Breman 1994) moving from one temporary construction site to another. Because most did not find work in the SEZ, as the next chapter shows, they took the bus early to Jaipur and nearby towns and came back in the evenings. I was often only able to find them in the evenings when they were dusty and exhausted from a day of hauling stones or mixing concrete, or on days when they were not lucky enough to find work at all. Of all of Rajpura's residents, it was this Dalit semiproletariat that arguably lost the most from the arrival of the Mahindra World City. Dispossessed of the small agrarian assets that moderated their penury, they were now squarely part of a precarious and underemployed landless class.

Petty Asset Managers

Between the relatively few who become magnificently wealthy neo-rentiers and those who dropped into the landless proletariat, there was a less-easy-to-categorize middle ground. By way of many specific routes through land commodification and reinvestment of capital gains, these farmers replaced their dispossessed farmland with alternative assets that had at least temporarily prevented their proletarianization. Some simply bought replacement farmland—often less fertile—in far-off villages, where they became absentee landlords, collecting fairly marginal rent-in-kind from local sharecroppers. Others invested in land or small urban plots for short-term capital gains, expanded their houses to rent out rooms, or started small informal businesses of highly variable profitability. Some dabbled in small-time brokerage and a few fortuitously held onto appreciating plots or land. What separates them from the proletarianized is that—through slightly greater economic means, business savvy, or sheer luck—they emerged from the process of dispossession with replacement assets. Many of them shuffled these relatively small assets across different investment classes with remarkable frequency. Although most were unable to entirely abandon wage labor, they aspired to live entirely from rent, interest, or mercantile profit. For those who had fulfilled this aspiration, "work" consisted entirely of cutting deals and moving assets, the chief tools of the trade being a mobile phone and motorbike. This category included some relatively poor or uneducated Jats and Brahmins, many OBCs, and some better-off Dalits.

When the SEZ arrived, Ram Kishore Prajapat was a semiproletarianized farmer who still practiced his caste occupation of making clay pots. As luck would have it, his 4 *bighas* of land abutted the new "250 Foot Road" that the government was building to connect the SEZ to the Jaipur International Airport, but the land was not forcibly acquired. Ram Kishore sold the land to a buyer for

$50,000 dollars—in retrospect, a fairly low price—who subsequently sold it to Laduram Meena for his marriage garden. When I first spoke with Ram Kishore he was a tenant for Laduram on his former land, putting up half the costs in return for half the harvest. But he was also the absentee landlord of 22 *bighas* of land that he had bought in a more rural area 60 km away. A tenant in his own village and an absentee landlord in another, he still did irregular construction labor and made pots for a few months of the year—although this became less profitable after enclosure of the village grazing land made his raw materials scarce. He had also bought a small portable kiosk (typically used to sell tobacco), though at the time of my fieldwork it was sitting empty. While he lost income from the enclosure of the commons, he turned four *bighas* of land into twenty-two, even if it was in a distant village. Uncertainties remained: will the rent from the new land keep him afloat, or its real estate value appreciate? Will something come of his small kiosk? Or will the uneducated potter be gradually forced into manual wage labor? Although it is still too soon to tell, Ram Kishore's case illustrates the ability of a small-holding OBC—who, it should be emphasized, escaped the process of dispossession—to engage land markets for a modest if uncertain ascent.

The Balai *mohalla* I lived in was a particularly rich site for observing petty asset managers, the variation among them, and the thin line separating them from the assetless proletariat. Small-holding and semiproletarianized farmers at the time of the SEZ's arrival, the Balais nevertheless had slightly more land than other Dalit subcastes. In the context of extremely high land values, this gave them more room to maneuver. But there was great inequality in how families in the *mohalla*—and even brothers within families—parlayed their holdings into new livelihoods.

Sanjay Bunkar was one of the more successful and enterprising of the *mohalla's* young men. Sanjay's father was an illiterate farmer and carpenter, one of six brothers that shared 23 *bighas* of land, 5 of which were acquired by the government for the 250 Foot Road. They waited until 2007 and sold their compensation plots for a comparatively good $24,000 per *bigha*. Sanjay's father used most of his share to pay off loans, marry off Sanjay's sister, and build a modest brick and concrete house. Sanjay, who was in his late twenties and had studied through the twelfth standard (a relatively anomalous achievement among Balais), used about $1,700 of it to start a tire puncture shop on the corner of their land, which had a prime location at the intersection of the old village road and the new 250 Foot Rd. His business was relatively profitable, netting him about $200 per month. Sanjay went through numerous other jobs while I was there—photographer, driver for a private engineering college and for Deutsche Bank—but his main aspiration was to build a hotel on his family's remaining land, which by 2014 was worth a small fortune. Sanjay explained that they didn't sell the land early because "we knew the road was coming," information which

I suspected came from his uncle, the deputy *sarpanch* under Laduram Meena. While Sanjay was a tireless worker, his upward trajectory was greatly aided by his education, the information provided by his uncle's political connections, and the sheer luck of having remaining land just outside of the SEZ. Although continuously hustling and moving across jobs for most of my fieldwork, he seemed likely—barring a collapse of the real estate market—to become a successful rentier and realize his ambition to "sit in the A.C."

Prabhu Balai's post-SEZ experience was more straightforward and representative. A member of the village's other Balai *mohalla* and in his late sixties, Prabhu had his 12 *bighas* of land acquired for the SEZ. He sold his compensation plots quickly and used the money to buy 10 *bighas* of land in another village 10 km away, which he himself was cultivating. Like the old land, the new land had no irrigation, but it was less fertile and very inconvenient to cultivate. Prabhu had come out of the land acquisition process with two fewer *bighas* of less fertile and more remote land. Besides farming that land during the monsoon season, both he and his only son were unemployed; he considered the SEZ a complete loss. Rather than being incorporated into the urbanizing new economy, Prabhu was being forced to move further into the rural hinterland where soils were poorer and off-farm opportunities more scarce.

If Sanjay was possibly on his way to neo-rentier status and Prabhu treading water, Mahesh and Lada Bunkar were engaged in a constant struggle to avoid proletarianization. Having lived with Mahesh, Lada, and their three young children for most of my fieldwork, I gained a more intimate understanding of their changing circumstances than any other family in Rajpura. Their daily struggles, shifting survival strategies, and multiple changes of fortune illustrate the thin line between self-employed petty asset manager and impoverished proletarian.

Before the SEZ's arrival, Mahesh and his two brothers owned 25 *bighas* of land between them. Cultivating this land was insufficient to sustain the family, and Mahesh had tried his hand at door-to-door vegetable selling and construction contracting while he and Lada also did seasonal agricultural labor. While the family lost all 25 *bighas* to the Mahindra World City, they were only compensated for seven because of an ambiguous title on the rest. With substantial debts and "no idea what a 'sej' was," they sold their compensation plots quickly for a relatively cheap $14,000 per *bigha*. The brothers used their respective shares to replace their earthen homes with concrete houses and to jointly buy 10 *bighas* of much less productive farmland 20 km into the interior. It proved difficult to supervise the tenant from afar, and they received only meager rent-in-kind. When I first arrived at their house in early 2010, Mahesh was unemployed and, after a kidney stone operation, reluctant to undertake manual labor. The family's concrete house was already showing significant signs of wear, though it had a small fridge, a TV, a gas stovetop, and Mahesh's motorbike parked in the courtyard.

The money had run out and the family was falling ever more deeply into debt. While officially classified as "Above Poverty Line" (APL) because of their assets, their diet told another story. Their two daily meals consisted of watery *sabzis* made with market-bought vegetables, and *rotis* made with wheat from the Public Distribution System—which they received at a less subsidized rate due to their APL classification. They had lost all the dairy products they used to receive from their livestock, and consumed very little *daal*. Their three young children, and particularly their daughter Sapna, were clearly under-nourished.

While only partially literate and not particularly business savvy, Mahesh thought he had found a solution to his family's problems when Lada's cousin from another village invited him to help broker a land deal in Rajpura. While most of Lada's family were very poor, Rajesh had established himself as a small-time broker and wanted to use some of his earnings to flip a plot in Rajpura. For several weeks, Rajesh pulled up to the house in his jeep to work out the details. Rajesh would advance the "earnest money" to the seller, and then try to unload the plot to an outside investor at a higher price. Mahesh would act as his local *dalal*, making a connection with a seller in Rajpura, earning 1% commission on the deal. Mahesh was excited about the idea of making the equivalent of several months of wages without much work. He found a lower-caste widow, also a Balai, who wanted to sell her compensation plots. She and her son were, in turn, represented by Santosh Balai, the pirate DVD shop proprietor encountered earlier. After many meetings and affirmations of good will expressed over cups of *chai* and shared *beedis*, a purchase agreement was struck between the brokers—the widow herself sat on the floor outside with the women of Mahesh's family—to buy the plot for $26,000, a relatively cheap price because there was a family dispute over its ownership. Within a few months, Rajesh had found an outside buyer willing to take it for $46,000, netting $14,000 after registration costs, the usual cut for the *patwari*, and a $3,000 bribe to JDA officials for clarifying the title. But the deal ultimately turned sour: Rajesh refused to pay Mahesh 1% of the full purchase price, arguing that the transaction costs that he advanced should be subtracted from the total. Mahesh earned less than he anticipated and fell out with Lada's cousin. After the exaggerated professions of good faith and kinship that had cemented the deal, Mahesh ruefully observed, "The relationship has been ruined." His family added some milk products back into their diet for a month or two, but the income was insufficient to make a dent in their rising debt.

While land brokerage did not work out, Mahesh had invested some of his remaining compensation money in a residential plot on the outskirts of a small town. But within a few years, cash flow problems, intensified by large medical debts for Lada and his mother, forced him to sell the plot at a small loss. His next idea was to become a landlord, and he borrowed $8,000 from a moneylender to add an extra story to his house. Two private colleges had sprouted up and when I returned in 2012, four students were renting the upstairs rooms. But the $130 Mahesh was collecting in rent did not even cover the monthly interest he owed to the moneylender. My own premium rent was only a momentary help. His hopes turned to a storefront that he bought from his brother, who lived a few houses away, for $3,000. The storefront, which jutted out from the side of his brother's house and faced the village road, sat empty.

With Mahesh's experiments in rentiership largely failing, the family's only income was Lada's periodic wages from the National Rural Employment Guarantee Scheme, which, due to Mahinder's indifference as *sarpanch*, was only being fitfully implemented in the *panchayat*. The family was sliding deeper into debt and Mahesh was struggling to keep moneylenders at bay. Mahesh's last resort was to look for work in the SEZ, where he thought a contactor would be able to get him work as a security guard. However, it wound up being a janitorial job, which in addition to paying only $60 a month, would have represented a step backward in social standing. He was unemployed when I left the village in 2012.

When I returned in 2014, Mahesh had reinvented himself as a vegetable vendor. He had taken a loan of $11,500 to purchase a small lorry to transport vegetables from the government market near Sanganer to the village. Off at the crack of dawn, Mahesh would return in the late morning with baskets of the lowest grade vegetables. The family worked together to separate out the unsellable vegetables and by the afternoon Mahesh would make a round of the village before parking in the Rajpura market. Competition was stiff. In addition to three vegetable carts, another truck identical to Mahesh's parked nearby. To add insult to injury, his brother Kheemu Ram—with whom he'd had a falling out over the storefront—was working for his competitor. On good days, Mahesh was upbeat, claiming he had made Rs 1,000 ($20)—though it was often unclear whether such estimates factored in all his costs, such as petrol and the interest on his loans, which came to about $6 per day. Some days he would make only $2, and on others be stuck with $20 to $30 in unsold vegetables. When I sat down with him to do a back-of-the-envelope calculation, we concluded he was making just under $5 a day; higher than unskilled wage labor, but inadequate to make progress on his debt. Lada was no longer working on NREGA, which Mahinder had stopped implementing in the *panchayat*, and she too had recently undergone surgery for kidney stones, which had cost them almost $300. Mahesh was anxious, and had taken to drinking after years of sobriety. His hopes now rested on the unproductive farmland he had bought about 25 km away—the government had just announced an industrial estate nearby, which had increased the land value. He also estimated that the storefront he had bought from his brother was now worth Rs 10 *lakh* ($20,000). This was, in fact, the source of their quarrel—the brother was now demanding more money for the storefront he had sold to Mahesh at Rs 1.5 *lakh*.

If things appeared slightly more hopeful for Mahesh and Lada during my last visit, they seemed anything but stable. Highly in debt, and just keeping their heads above water through increasingly risky investments, Mahesh and Lada were toeing the fragile line between a stable foothold in the informal economy and a precarious descent into proletarianization. While tempted by the possibility of living from rents instead of wage labor, Mahesh lacked the prior endowments of capital, entrepreneurial savvy, and social networks that would allow him to make the multiple conversions of land into cash and cash into other means of livelihood. While his and Lada's house looked much nicer than the average earthen home—which had led the government to classify them as APL—they were cash poor and food insecure. As prophylactics against proletarianization, Mahesh's forays into rentiership had so far proven to be of small and uncertain value. For much of the five years that I followed their lives, Lada had in essence already been proletarianized, providing the waged—as well as reproductive—labor that kept the family afloat. While the economic changes sweeping the village might throw a lucky break their way, it seems equally possible that time will pull their family fully into the precariously employed proletariat.

The Excluded

The preceding sections showed how Rajpura's private *landholders* were absorbed into speculative land markets to extremely uneven effect; but what happened to those with no land at all? We saw that before the SEZ's arrival, 7% of families in Rajpura, Shivpura, Neempura, and Jatpura were landless, and these were exclusively among the SC/ST and OBC castes. Most worked in construction and other forms of low-wage manual work outside of the village, while some also performed "traditional" caste-based occupations and seasonal agricultural labor. While none benefited from the rising land market, their relation to the SEZ varied by dependence on non-private land.

Rajpura's sweepers and musicians, as the previous chapter showed, had no land to lose or to leverage in the land boom. They lost nothing through dispossession and gained nothing through real estate speculation. The Bavariyas, by contrast, lost a great deal when they were evicted from their homes on the village common land without compensation. While dispossession for many farmers in Rajpura was rendered less violent by their incorporation into the land boom, the eviction of the Bavariyas deprived them of the slender non-titled assets—their homes and grazing land—that moderated their destitution. No longer even possessing homes in Rajpura, they were entirely excluded from the ensuing economic changes and likely turned into paupers. Chapter 3 also illustrated how the enclosure of Rajpura's commons was a large blow to many other landless families. Sedentary and transhumant herding families lost access to the grazing commons and received no compensation. Several SC and OBC families—including most of the Mali *mohalla*—also lived on *panchayat* land that fell within the SEZ boundary, and would soon be evicted without compensation.

A tale of two *chai* stalls demonstrates another mechanism of exclusion as well as the extra-legal means by which it could occasionally be reversed. The first *chaiwala*, Ranjan Gujjar, was being squeezed out of his customary location not by government dispossession but by the pressures of land commodification. Ranjan's small *chai* stall had sat for years on an unused narrow strip of land between the village road and the potter Ram Kishore's land. Landless, Ranjan supported his family on about $3 per day from the straw-and-stone *chai* stand, from which he also fixed motorcycle tire punctures and sold small quantities of petrol. But Ranjan's situation became tenuous once Ram Kishore sold the land beneath him to another buyer who then sold it to Laduram Meena. When I returned to the village in the summer of 2012, there was a concrete wall where the *chai* stall used to stand: Laduram had kicked him off to build his marriage garden. The stall was now on another marginal strip between the marriage garden and the 250 Foot Road. "He can also throw me off from here," Ranjan explained. "The land is his up to the road." The process of land commodification was thus encroaching on previously unvalued spaces that by custom allowed the landless poor to make a living.

The second *chaiwala*, Balu Singh Gujjar, lived on *panchayat* land and operated a stall in the center of the Rajpura market. Rajpura was actually the natal village of his wife, who had run off with the brother of one of his customers just before I arrived. Although moderately worried about losing his home in Rajpura—a very small one-room structure with a bed and a propane burner situated on *panchayat* land—for most of my fieldwork Balu Singh's main complaint pertained to the land under his *chai* stall. Like Ranjan, Balu Singh lacked title, but in 2009 he was one of the beneficiaries of Laduram's (probably illegal) allocation of *panchayat* land in the lead-up to the 2009 election. While the plot was only 9 × 10 meters, its central location made it worth—in Balu Singh's estimation—about $30,000 to $40,000. The problem was that because the *panchayat* secretary refused to sign them, these allocations had questionable legal standing. When I first arrived, Balu Singh was dismayed that Mahinder, as new *sarpanch*, would not recognize their legality. But about nine months later, through machinations I never got to the bottom of, Balu Singh reported that he had received the title to the plot. He was now angry that he was being refused a construction permit because of a proposed traffic circle. But his ability to establish (legally questionable) ownership of his plot set the stage for a possible ascent into petty rentiership.

Legal ambiguity was a mechanism of exclusion for many families, some of them not poor. We saw that Mahesh and his brothers did not receive compensation for the majority of their full holding because of an unclear title. A significant minority of farmers had unclear titles for various reasons including illiteracy, corruption, and distance from government administration. When the government acquired their land, they were denied compensation until their cases could be settled, which can take decades unless one is prepared to pay hefty bribes. A lawyer told Mahesh that his case could be resolved with a bribe of Rs 1 *crore* ($200,000), an amount far out of his range. But it was not just the poor and lower castes that were stuck in legal limbo. Some of the priestly Brahmin families found that their land was classified as temple land or was being claimed by temple trusts. In Rajpura, Hariram Sharma and family were the *pujaris* of a small village temple that doubled as their home and provision shop. When their 8 *bighas* of land were acquired for the SEZ, they were told that it belonged to the Rajasthan government's Devasthan (religious land) Department. They claim that the confusion arose because their grandfather's name was Badrinarayan, another name for Vishnu, to whom the temple's main shrine is dedicated. Although they were moderately well off in the pre-SEZ scenario, they were excluded from the process of land commodification and continued to live in the small stone temple surrounded by the concrete houses of OBC neighbors. In Shivpura, the young Brahmin *chai* stall proprietor Kailash Sharma had received no compensation for his acquired farmland because a temple trust had emerged to claim it after the SEZ arrived. The property boom prompted all kinds of people, including extended family who had long ago migrated to the city, to claim newly valuable property, tying up land and compensation plots in legal disputes.

But if the land boom excluded those households without effective private property rights, it also excluded those with a tenuous claim on the property of their own household.

Real Estate and Patriarchy

Patriarchal property ownership coupled with female exclusion from the public sphere made real estate speculation a men's game. While land loss had disproportionate consequences for women, their lack of independent land rights excluded them from the real estate economy (cf. Agarwal 1994). This exclusion was reinforced—here as elsewhere in India—by land acquisition laws and policies that assign compensation to male "heads of household" (Thukral 1996; Mehta and Srinivasan 2000; Mehta 2009). Women's informal influence over the disposition of land and compensation plots varied by household; but ultimately the decision of whether or not to sell rested with men. It was men who negotiated land deals, served as brokers, and collected the cash. As we saw in Mahesh's land deal, even when land or plots were in the name of a widow, male relatives negotiated the sale and probably controlled the proceeds.

The sale of land and plots then put unprecedented sums of cash in the hands of men who were often, at the same time, rendered unemployed. One consequence, which appears with frequency in studies of land dispossession (cf. Mehta and Srinivasan 2000; Colson 1999), was that some men misspent these earnings in a variety of ways. While alcoholism and domestic abuse were prevalent before the SEZ, it was a common complaint among women in Rajpura that men were drinking more, and that this drinking was leading to greater domestic violence. Lada, an outspoken informant on such matters, explained: "Before they drank, but not that much. Money has come, and now they drink morning and night." Kamla Devi Nayak, surrounded by several daughters, similarly explained: "Before they were doing work . . . it was better. . . . [Now] if they make Rs 100, it's only with a fight that they give Rs 50." There are few secrets in a village, and domestic violence was not one of them. Mahesh's brother, according to Lada, took his land money and "wasted it all drinking"; he mercilessly beat his wife, who often came to Lada's house for food and companionship. Boduram, their next-door neighbor, sold his land extremely cheaply and sat at home drinking while his wife did construction labor, the proceeds from which he expropriated for more alcohol.

We should not conclude from this that men generally frittered away land earnings on alcohol; most did not and for those who did, it was often a response to, rather than a cause of, their dwindling fortunes. But men's control over real estate earnings did tilt the balance of household power even further in their favor. And when the money ran out, many men were reluctant to accept the necessity of returning to hard manual labor. Once the dust settled and Lada and Mahesh had no more income, Mahesh was not interested in the low-paying jobs available to him. He spent his days riding his motorcycle, talking at *chai* stalls, and contemplating his series of less-than-successful investments as Lada did construction labor to make ends meet. While women in upwardly mobile households were often confined to *purdah*, those in the struggling families were subjected to heightened intra-household exploitation. This seemed particularly acute among those households which received just enough cash to raise men's expectations, but not enough to permanently avoid a descent into the landless proletariat—a descent which happened first for women and then for men.

The infusion of cash from land sales also had the perverse effect of drastically ratcheting up wedding expenses, including dowry levels. One family in the Balai *mohalla* spent $7,000 on their daughter's wedding while I was there; a relatively poor Brahmin family spent $20,000. These lavish weddings—involving more elaborate food and sweets, more guests and more expensive "gifts"—enriched the village goldsmith and the successful land speculators who invested in marriage gardens and tent and party supply businesses (discussed more in Chapter 7) but put a squeeze on the "losers" from the SEZ, who had little savings and income, but who felt compelled to take massive loans from moneylenders to maintain status. Lada fretted about having to spend that much some day on her daughter Sapna's wedding, observing "Our wedding for two sisters cost Rs 10,000. Now its Rs 10 *lakh*. People got money, so they spend that much. Now the poor also have to do it." As one lower-caste man explained, "Before people would pay Rs 20,000 to 30,000 for an excellent wedding. Now it's at least 10 *lakhs*. They'll want a four-wheeler, cooler, gold, and silver. The boy will want a motorcycle. Before, dowry was five kitchen utensils (*bartan*) and some clothes. . . . For the poor man, marrying [one's children] has become difficult. If there are three or four girls, he'll die." As the last comment indicates, escalating dowry levels increase the financial cost of girls, a worrying development in a region that already had one "missing" woman for every ten men (Census of India 2001).

It is possible that as urbanization in these villages progresses, some forms of patriarchal social relations might attenuate. The main evidence I found to support this was from the census, which reported an increase in female literacy in Rajpura from 29% in 2001 to 46% in 2011, which was slightly higher than the 11% increase observed in rural Rajasthan as a whole. I otherwise found little ethnographic evidence that the SEZ's arrival was eroding Rajasthan's rigid gender relations. In important respects, the land-centered form of accumulation widened already stark gender inequalities.

Conclusion

As a torrent of domestic and global capital descended upon Rajpura's single-cropped farmland, its former cultivators were swept into a dramatic land boom. Rather than being entirely excluded by below-market government compensation, as has been the typical lot of dispossessed farmers in India, Rajpura's landowners were included in the bonanza by the government's compensation scheme. The purpose of this scheme was to avoid the type of "land war" afflicting SEZs and other large capital projects across India. In this sense, it was a "success." If dispossession can often create an instrumental solidarity between otherwise unequal agrarian classes (cf. Baviskar 1995; Levien 2013), the Rajasthan government's market-based compensation policy avoided organized opposition in part by absorbing farmers into the process of land speculation. Chapter 8 will discuss how this affected politics in Rajpura subsequent to dispossession, while Chapter 9 will discuss the implications of this success for India's "land wars" more generally. But this chapter has begun to examine its socio-economic consequences. And these consequences, it must be emphasized, were better in Rajpura than in many contemporary instances of forcible land dispossession. The inclusion of landed farmers into an astronomically hot real estate market—in a region, moreover, where landholdings were three times larger than the national average[12]—generated far more "winners" in Rajpura than is the norm. This made the Mahindra World City probably the best SEZ for which to be dispossessed in all of India during the 2000s. But this chapter also demonstrates that real estate speculation is a poor basis for inclusive economic transformation.

Real estate speculation proceeds upon distributions of land that reflect arbitrary but longstanding historical inequalities. While the nature and extent of those inequalities vary across the diverse agrarian social structures of India, they are almost everywhere pronounced due to the failures of the Indian state to undertake effective redistributive land reform in the decades after Independence (cf. Frankel 2005). Caste-based inequalities in land ownership provided the basis across most of India in the post-Independence decades for cumulative inequalities in agricultural capital and off-farm diversification, and in the acquisition of cultural and social capital,[13] all factors that we have seen to be crucial in the ability to profit from land markets. Cutting across these class-caste inequalities are entrenched patriarchal social relations in which women lack independent land rights and are often excluded from the public sphere of commercial activity (Agarwal 1994). While we can expect land commodification to produce distinct patterns of differentiation across specific patterns of social inequality, there are almost no places in India where it encounters a remotely equitable distribution of property. As India's rising land markets reach more corners of rural India—on the outskirts of cities and towns, near coastal development, and adjacent to large infrastructure projects—differentiation by speculation is becoming an important mechanism by which India's market-led order is compounding the inequalities left by state-led development.

In Rajpura, real estate speculation intersected with a deeply unequal agrarian milieu—marked by the enduring legacy of princely rule—to expand those inequalities in complex and novel ways. Rajpura's feudal lord of yesterday is its real estate mogul today, while the dominant agricultural castes—principally Jats and Brahmins—have disproportionately become successful speculators and brokers. The novelty is that a non-trivial number of low and intermediate caste marginal farmers wound up not as pauperized laborers but as petty asset managers, while a few even became wealthy neo-rentiers. Small plots of dramatically appreciating land—usually in combination with greater-than-average market savvy, a fortuitous connection, or sheer luck—became a lottery ticket for some. But the majority of Rajpura's poorer and lower-caste villagers, faced with economic compulsion and operating with less information[14] and market savvy, liquidated their assets relatively quickly and cheaply, leaving them proletarianized and impoverished. This was the experience of the vast majority of the already poor Dalit semiproletariat. It is not possible, however, to generalize about how Dalits fared from this process (cf. Cross 2014).[15] While landed Dalits fared much worse than upper castes, they were also internally differentiated by land values—as illustrated by the divergent outcomes among Balais, and between the Balais and Regars. And while landless Dalits were universally excluded from upward mobility via real estate, they were differentiated by their losses. Those with no agricultural assets, like the village sweepers, did not lose anything (and were thus moderately hopeful about the SEZ), while landless grazers and the Bavariyas (who were living on the village land without title) were evicted without compensation and were thus further impoverished. Intersecting, meanwhile, with this relatively complex pattern of inequality between households was the almost universal exclusion of women from the real estate economy, a boost to gender inequality in already intensely patriarchal Rajasthan. Real estate speculation thus expanded the deep inequalities left by state-led development and excluded significant sections of the population.[16] Large inequalities in land ownership—and the broader social inequalities with which it is associated—make land speculation, even in a rising market, a poor basis for inclusive growth.

And it is, as Rajpura's farmers discovered in 2008, speculation. The global financial crisis brought land transactions in Rajpura to a grinding halt for several years. Land prices started to inch up again by 2012 and increased again dramatically by 2014. It may be, as Chakravorty (2013: 163) argues, that India has entered permanently into a new "land price regime," which Rajpura's large and petty rentier stratum can ride to a life of leisure "in the A.C." It may also be the case that Rajpura is sitting atop a large asset price bubble of the kind that has persistently characterized capitalism over the past four hundred years (Kindleberger and Aliber 2011).[17] What is certain is that Rajpura's future is now tied to the convulsions of global financial markets. Land prices have replaced the weather as the main source of volatility.

Whether prices go up, down, or both, there remains the question of what, besides land values, will sustain Rajpura's erstwhile farmers and their descendants into the future; for land rents proved to be the main basis upon which villagers could be included in the financialized and "knowledge-intensive" capitalism that consumed their land. Bracketing real estate, Rajpura's farmers were almost completely marginalized from the economic growth taking place inside the Mahindra World City.

6

Peasants in a Knowledge Economy

In information technology we may have finally found the engine that can drive India's takeoff and transform our country.

—Gurcharan Das (2002: xvii)

The misery of being exploited by capitalists is nothing compared to the misery of not being exploited at all.

—Joan Robinson (1962: 45)

Six days a week at around 5:00 pm, dozens of white SUVs stir up dust as they come flying down the village road, past women and children leading their livestock home for the night and men having their late afternoon *chai*. After a large blue sign for the Mahindra World City Special Economic Zone, they turn left into a security checkpoint where guards check drivers' IDs and inspect the cars' underbellies with mirrors. Once through the gates, the cars deposit their cargo—educated middle-class youth from Jaipur—into their respective office buildings. As night settles over Rajpura, these "knowledge professionals" sit down at their work stations to manipulate symbols for multinational clients in the Western hemisphere.

If real estate speculation washed over Rajpura to highly unequal effect, this chapter asks: how did Rajpura's dispossessed farmers fit into the export-oriented "knowledge economy" that provided the SEZ's ostensible purpose? As Chapter 2 illustrated, the Mahindra World City's IT/ITES focus reflected the broader pattern of India's SEZs and, more generally, its post-liberalization growth, which has been driven by high-skill services more than by manufacturing. While many have, like Gurcharan Das cited at the opening of this chapter, celebrated India's "knowledge economy" or "services revolution" (cf. World Bank 2004; Friedman 2006; Joshi 2009), others worry about the implications of skill-intensive rather than labor-intensive growth for a country with a large, undereducated, and underemployed rural population (cf. Bardhan 2010; Dreze and Sen 2013; Mitra 2013). So far there has been little ethnographic research into the implications of India's dynamic knowledge economy for rural India, where over 60% of the population still resides.[1] Research on labor in India's IT/ITES industry has focused on the "knowledge professionals" that perform the core programming, processing, and service work for their multinational clients (Upadhya 2007; Upadhya and Vasavi 2008; Radhakrishnan 2011; Upadhya 2016), but almost nothing has been written about the indirect jobs in support functions—security guards, janitors, gardeners, drivers, and so on—that are more likely to be filled by poor, moderately educated rural Indians. Even though India's SEZs have been disproportionately inhabited by the "knowledge economy," there has been little discussion of the consequences of this *sectoral composition of dispossession*. This chapter thus seeks to ethnographically illustrate the consequences of knowledge-intensive growth for Rajpura's dispossessed farmers.[2]

If we bracket the unequal gains from real estate speculation examined in the last chapter, this chapter argues that "knowledge-intensive" growth was so exclusionary for almost all agrarian classes in Rajpura that it made single-cropped agriculture and livestock rearing look attractive. Whether illiterate or college educated, Rajpura's dispossessed farmers unanimously lacked the requisite cultural capital for inclusion in the SEZ's IT/ITES industry. Dispossessed of their means of production, their labor was largely superfluous to the "knowledge economy" taking root on their former land. A small minority received low-paying and insecure work as gardeners, security guards, janitors, and drivers through a stratum of contractors that mediate between the zone's core economic activity and rural workers. Rural women, when they sought and received work, were slotted into the most casual and low-paying of these positions. For no landed families did these jobs make up for lost agricultural assets. Nor were government welfare programs an effective substitute. This chapter thus helps us to understand why India's exclusionary growth reinforces the value of even small agrarian assets. In a trajectory of capitalist growth that offers inadequately attractive exit routes from agriculture, the *semi*proletarian condition is far preferable to the proletarian.

So, while real estate speculation differentiated Rajpura's dispossessed farmers, knowledge-intensive growth generally marginalized them. While the first fed off the inequalities within the village, the second underscored the inequalities between the zone's urban (corporate and individual) beneficiaries and the village as a whole. While Rajpura's highly differentiated petty commodity producers were not literally "peasants" at the time of the SEZ's arrival, the chapter's metaphorical title is intended to capture their peripheral and subordinate position in the SEZ's division of labor.

Dispossessed and Surplus to Capital's Requirement

Rajpura's residents were, as seen in Chapter 3, already partially dependent on off-farm employment before the MWC arrived. Pushed by declining water levels and subdivision, a majority of households simultaneously pursued non-agricultural footholds while relying on agrarian assets for household reproduction and, varying by farm size, accumulation. Given their unequal starting points, households diversified with very uneven effect: landed upper castes more successfully invested in education, small businesses, and formal-sector jobs while the less educated lower-caste semiproletariat depended on casual wage labor. Both segments of this diversifying peasantry faced a hostile and unpromising labor market. While the poor semiproletariat was chronically underemployed in low-paying manual labor, the village's college graduates were also unable to find jobs commensurate with their expectations. No one considered casual wage labor an attractive option, and even that was in short supply. When the SEZ was announced, many hoped that it would bring better and more regular employment to the village, while land loss increased the need for it among the proletarianized. But no matter how they fared in the post-SEZ land market, virtually everyone in Rajpura was disappointed with the post-SEZ labor market.

By far the single largest—almost universal—complaint of Rajpura's residents toward the SEZ was that they had been rendered "unemployed" (*berozgar*) and that all the work was going to "outsiders" (*baaharwale*). My survey—conducted six years after land acquisition and three years after the SEZ's first unit became operational—found that only 18% of families who were dispossessed for the SEZ (and 14% of families overall) had at least *one* member employed for *any duration* in the SEZ. As many of these families—and in particular women—pointed out, this was only one job (typically for a male son) when the whole family was rendered "unemployed" by the loss of land and livestock. While exclusion from the SEZ's core jobs arises from the disjuncture between knowledge-intensive growth and the poor educational levels of rural India, exclusion from low-wage manual labor—most notably construction—stems from the advantage to employers of a "footloose" migratory labor system (Breman 1996).

Devalued Degrees

Core jobs in the IT/ITES sector require educational credentials that are scarce in rural Rajasthan. Entry-level "knowledge professionals" in BPO firms require, at minimum, a bachelor's degree. A Deutsche Bank manager explained to me that the firm hired mostly young people with a bachelor of commerce, an MBA, or a certified accountancy degree, although good English speaking ability was not required. At Infosys, a manager explained, "They need to have a normal graduate degree from any discipline . . . and should have some working knowledge of computers and a little accounting knowledge." Because they mainly work for international clients, he added, "As a matter of policy, we do not recruit people who do not speak English." This meant that their workforce came from the "middle class" and not the "lower middle class [which] doesn't speak English." Although much BPO work does not require more than basic computer skills to perform, scholars have pointed out that IT/ITES firms prefer to hire over-qualified candidates to increase their attractiveness to foreign multinationals, a marketing strategy made possible by the relative scarcity of salaried white-collar work in India (Upadhya and Vasavi 2008). In addition to formal credentials, IT/ITES firms also "look for people who will fit into the globalized work atmosphere," which involves an assessment of "cultural capital and social skills" (Upadhya 2011: 172)—markers, in other words, of class distinction (Bourdieu 1984) that, in India, are closely bound up with caste (Deshpande 2011). These factors help to explain why India's IT/ITES workforce is largely urban, middle class, and upper caste (Upadhyay 2007, 2016; Radhakrishnan 2011). Even for relatively privileged urban youth, obtaining IT/ITES jobs is challenging (Nisbett 2013).

The consequence is that even the most educated of Rajpura's residents were excluded from the zone's "knowledge economy." We saw that only 56% of Rajpura's population over six years of age was literate and only 50% of households contained at least one person who had passed the tenth standard.[3] There was a significant and growing contingent of young men who had obtained undergraduate degrees, but the majority of these were from new private colleges of mediocre quality and reputation, which had proliferated around Jaipur in the mid-2000s after the central government liberalized private investment in higher education.[4] Some earned certificates from vocational training programs, computer training courses, prep courses, and other forms of private but non-accredited education that do not carry much weight with MNC employers. Almost no one in the village spoke more than a few phrases of English, including the teachers in the "English medium" schools. The result was that I did not find a single village resident employed as a "knowledge professional" in Infosys or Deutsche Bank. In fact, the canteen operator inside Deutsche Bank preferred to hire from Jaipur because, in his view, village youth did not have the "manners" to serve the zone's middle-class employees. Considered to be uncouth rustics, Rajpura's youth lacked not only the formal credentials but the corporeal bearing considered necessary for service work in a "world city."[5]

While Rajpura's poor and uneducated residents knew that these jobs were not for them, those with college degrees felt particularly pained at being denied them. Craig Jeffrey (2010) has poignantly documented the malaise of educated but unemployed youth in India, "passing time" as they wait—often in vain—for their credentials to translate into secure salaried work (see also Jeffrey, Jeffery, and Jeffery 2008). "Time pass" was indeed endemic in Rajpura and a common way in which unemployed youth—educated and uneducated—described their melancholic limbo. The village's *chai* stalls were daily filled with young men, as were the village's many modestly profitable shops; whether selling phone cards, cutting hair, or hawking vegetables, many young "entrepreneurs" considered their small businesses a "time pass" until they could find better work. The arrival in their village of an SEZ with some of the largest multinationals operating in India certainly incited their aspirations (Cross 2014), which made their lack of realization all the more painful. It was commonly observed that good work in the SEZ was only going to "educated people," "hi-fi people," "diplomawale," "Jaipurwale," and "outsiders."

Although middle-aged farmers were clearly unemployable within the knowledge economy, many—particularly Brahmins and Jats—had invested heavily in their children's education. And even those who ultimately did well in real estate were extremely aggrieved at the lack of employment for their children. That youth with BA and MA degrees—including a few from government universities—could not get hired in the SEZ was a source of widespread dissatisfaction among children and parents alike. Although we will see that the SEZ created some low-paying jobs for security guards, drivers, gardeners, and construction workers—and even these were few in number—these were not the kinds of jobs that most uneducated youth were looking for, much less those with college degrees.

Villagers made an important distinction between *mazduri* (low-paid casual labor that was generally disdained) and the more sought-after *naukri* (salaried employment) or *dhandha* (occupation).[6] Not only was *mazduri* insecure and low-paying, but it lacked the status of *naukri*—which, among other considerations was important for making a good marriage. Kana Ram Choudhary, a relatively prosperous Jat farmer who had 13 of his 30 *bighas* acquired, made the point well when I interviewed him at his house. One of his sons had an MA, another a BA, and the other had passed tenth standard. Pulling one of them over, he said, "Look at him, he's educated. He has no occupation (*dhandha*). What's he going to do?" "Time pass is happening," the son confirmed. When I asked if he would do wage labor (*mazduri*) in the SEZ, Kana Ram replied, "Educated people won't do jobs cleaning the bathroom. How can someone educated in computers clean gutters?"

Disappointment at the absence of *naukri* was not limited to the upper castes or to BA graduates. When I asked Sanjay Bunkar, an entrepreneurial young Dalit with a "tenth pass," whether people were slowly getting *naukri* in the SEZ, his response was, "What *naukri*? People here are getting *mazduri*. . . . In the SEZ, they make us security guards." Sherpal Naik had similarly passed the tenth standard and, as his parents proudly emphasized, "knew how to work computers." Sherpal had taken a computer class, learned how to do data entry on Excel, and wanted to find work utilizing those skills. Instead he had just come back from a stint of pipe-fitting work in New Delhi, and was now working as a security guard at a factory in Bagaru for Rs 4,000 ($80) per month. His family's entire farm had gone into the SEZ. "They open up here. They don't give us any jobs. We have to go 15 to 25 kilometers away for work," he complained. Asim Hussein, who passed twelfth standard but did not finish college and ran his own vegetable business, remarked more caustically, "They only employ people as gardeners and janitors. They don't employ educated youth. They have screwed us." When I asked a Brahmin farmer with three educated and unemployed children whether they would take work as security guards, he responded, "Everyone wants to do something *according to their qualification*."

The problem, of course, was that the "qualifications" of Rajpura's youth had less value than they believed. The educational attainment that farming families thought entitled them to jobs in the SEZ—BAs, BCOMs, or even MAs from small private universities, much less computer training certificates from private institutes—did not carry the same value in the eyes of large multinational IT/ITES companies. Private-sector jobs were not subject to reservations for lower-caste candidates, and the patronage networks typically used by the agrarian elite to secure employment (cf. Jeffrey and Lerche 2000) had no traction in the corporate sector. So, while the expansion of private higher education had increased their expectations, Rajpura's youth had bought devalued credentials. This "structural mismatch between aspirations and real probabilities" (Bourdieu 1984: 144) was captured astutely by Aseem, principal of Shivpura's "English medium" school: "People are not getting work according to their thinking. These big companies come and they think all their problems will be solved. . . . A computer degree: Mahindra considers this very little. But to people here it seems really big."

It is not simply that Rajpura's youth lacked the requisite education for the service economy. In the context of anemic job creation, educational expansion inevitably fuels credential inflation; and it is the rural youth in places like Rajpura, occupying a relatively dominated position in the field of cultural capital, who find themselves holding the most devalued degrees (see Bourdieu 1984). It is this structural reality that leads some youth, such as Rajpura barber Mukesh Sen, to doubt the value of education altogether. In the unemployment of his peers, Mukesh saw a justification for his own lack of education: "Studying is useless in India. You study for fifteen years, *fifteen years* of expenses and then you don't even get a job. . . . [In the SEZ], the good jobs are going to Jaipurwale, people here carry stones . . . and even that they don't get." Although a majority of youth were still deeply committed to pursuing education, dreams of inclusion in the SEZ's new economy were already giving way to the melancholy of "broken trajectories" (Bourdieu 1984: 150; see also Willis 1977).

No Locals Allowed

As Mukesh's parting observation suggests, Rajpura's educated youth were not the only ones who saw their labor largely superfluous to the needs of the Mahindra World City. While Rajpura's minority of educated youth were excluded from high-end jobs as "knowledge professionals," the bulk of the village's uneducated labor force was excluded from even low-paying jobs by another mechanism: the longstanding and widely observed preference of employers for migrant workers (cf. Breman 1994, 1996, 2007). The largest number of unskilled jobs created by the SEZ were in constructing the SEZ's buildings, boundary walls, and roads. But the vast majority of workers—by most estimates three-quarters—were migrants shipped in from other states or districts. At the Mahindra World City, I encountered work gangs from Tamil Nadu, Bihar, Uttar Pradesh, Madhya Pradesh, Karnataka, West Bengal, and several districts of Rajasthan. Many of these migrants were landless or land poor, and lived for the duration of their contract—from a few weeks to a few years—in makeshift tent encampments near the SEZ boundary wall without sanitation, electricity, or a good water source. As observed elsewhere (Breman 1996; 2007), contractors explained that the main advantage of hiring migrants was their disconnection from the local community. They did not miss work for weddings, festivals, or family matters. And they could not draw on local support for disputes with employers. As Breman (2007: 184–185) puts it, employers' "clear preference for outside rather than local labour . . . is part of a strategy to keep down the cost of production, and is based on the simple conviction that outsiders are more obedient and easy to discipline than local employees." This strategy is made possible by the existence, at the national level, of an immense pool of underemployed workers. Its consequence is a huge pan-India floating labor force that serves to suppress wages and enforce mobility. For farmers who are dispossessed for large capital projects, this "migratory labor system" (Burawoy 1976) steers "local" work to "outsiders" and forces locals to seek work "outside."

When two small factories finally opened up in the Handicrafts and Light Engineering zones of the MWC—one making handicraft textiles and the other knitting needles—this migratory labor system ensured that most of these jobs also didn't go to dispossessed farmers. When I returned to the village in 2012 to discover that these factories had opened, I was curious whether they had altered the pattern of knowledge-intensive growth and absorbed Rajpura's residents into manufacturing jobs. But the factories were relatively small and also mostly hiring non-locals. While the textile factory owner had indicated potential interest in enlisting local women into piece-rate sewing, this did not materialize. The only person in Rajpura I met who was working in the textile company was Asit Sharma, the educated son of a village *pujari* who had gotten work as a cutter. But he was ultimately fired after missing work for his uncle's funeral. The only person I met working in the knitting tool factory was a young supervisor from U.P. who rented a room from Lada and Mahesh. He explained to me that his employer did not hire locals because, "Local people will fight. [The managers] think that if something happens, they will come back with 10 people. So, they'd rather hire people from outside. . . ." He would not have gotten hired in his own village: "Everyone has to go somewhere else." By 2016 a JCB factory had opened but, as Asim Hussein reported, it was the same story: "No locals allowed."

The point is not that workers from elsewhere in India—including extremely poor landless migrants—were less deserving of work than Rajpura's residents. But it must be understood that this "footloose" labor system ensures that those dispossessed for large capital projects and those employed by them are different people. Even if Mahindra cared to give preferential treatment to locals, its own labor demands were minimal and it could hardly force its tenant companies to comply. So while "outsiders" took the work in Rajpura, Rajpurans had to look outside. This spatial separation of dispossession and exploitation, obscured by aggregate measures of employment, greatly reduces the attractiveness of surrendering one's land for industry. As Chapter 9 discusses, this fact is politically consequential.

Dispossessed and Under-Exploited

Knowledge-intensive growth thus largely excluded Rajpura's workforce and made little dent in their chronic underemployment. Stripped of their land and dependent on the market for survival, a majority of Rajpura's ex-farmers found no more buyers for their labor power than before the SEZ arrived. It is not simply, as Joan Robinson quipped, that being exploited is better than not being exploited; if given the choice, Rajpura's farmers would avoid casual wage labor at all costs. But if one is to be dispossessed, the aphorism certainly holds true. Rajpura's farmers were dispossessed and *under*-exploited. And their predicament was a reflection in miniature of a much larger problem, which is that India's trajectory of capitalist growth requires rural land far more than rural labor. Accelerating dispossession for non-labor intensive growth contributes to the systematic expansion of what Marx (1977: 982) called a "surplus population," understood not as a specific class of people but as the aggregate existence of labor power in excess of capitalism's requirement.[7] This existence exerts downward pressure on the livelihoods of heterogeneous classes—whether diversifying rich farmers faced with an overly competitive market for white-collar work, or unskilled neophyte proletarians looking for non-existent manufacturing jobs. It pushes a large fraction of dispossessed people into informal methods of self-employment, as the next chapter observes. And it marginally adds to the ability of capital to maintain low wages and insecure conditions among the actually employed—as Marx emphasized. Such was the situation of the minority of Rajpura's dispossessed farmers who actually did find work inside the Mahindra World City.

"Eaten in the Middle": Precarious Labor in a World City

Excluded from "core" jobs in the knowledge economy, the limited work available to Rajpura's ex-farmers inside the SEZ was indirect, low-paying, temporary, and insecure. In addition to construction, this included work as security guards, gardeners, janitors, "office boys," or drivers. Such jobs were not extended directly from the large multinational companies in the zone, but were—as per the common and longstanding practice of decentralized labor recruitment in India (cf. Breman 1990; Chandavarkar 1994; Breman 1996; Breman 2007; De Neve 2014; Pattenden 2016)—outsourced to a network of contractors, locally referred to as *thekedars*.[8] While small *thekedars* are often themselves precariously situated one step up from their workers (Breman 2007: 216; De Neve 2014), their ubiquitous existence and use by employers assures a flexible and precarious workforce (Breman 2007; Pattenden 2016: 75–77). *Thekedars* were used in all the jobs available to Rajpura's ex-farmers, and were synonymous with temporary and low-paying work. As *dalals* mediated the land market, so *thekedars* mediated the labor market, separating the formal from the informal economy and taking their share of the wages flowing from the former to the latter.

In construction, the majority of *thekedars* were from other states or districts of Rajasthan, from which they recruited their workers. For building the SEZ infrastructure and buildings, Mahindra and its tenant companies hired construction companies—several from Bangalore—who in turn hired dozens of labor contractors to recruit workers. These fly-by-night contractors came from all corners of India, mobilizing groups of ten to thirty workers—typically from their home region, village, or even extended kin. At any given time, there could be fifty different contractors working on different parts of the SEZ, each operating on a separate contract of different duration. Some contracts went through a large *thekedar*, who sub-contracted out specific jobs to smaller *thekedars*. Like the chain of land brokerage, these contractor chains were based on relations of mutual acquaintance (*jaan pehechaan*). Although the majority of *thekedars* were from outside of Rajpura, a handful of locals were able to tap into these networks and mobilize local workers. One, Gopal Meena—who drove Laduram Meena's water delivery tractor and staffed his clothing shop—was able to arrange for outside workers. Gopal had met a Bihari *thekedar*, and sent him with an advance of Rs 20,000 to bring back an extra twenty workers from Bihar. That Gopal would take the trouble of recruiting workers from the opposite side of India rather than from Rajpura attests to the depth of preference for migrants. For six months, Gopal's gang helped to build the Deutsche Bank office.

Thekedars had to respond to fluctuating labor demands and, operating beneath the radar of labor laws, could hire and fire at will. As one *thekedar* explained to me, sometimes he needed ten, sometimes fifteen, sometimes twenty-five workers—so he had to send unnecessary workers back to their villages accordingly. *Thekedars'* own income was determined through a few different arrangements. In some cases, *thekedars* were paid so much per worker—Gopal was paid Rs 10 per worker per day on top of a base salary of Rs 100 per day (totaling Rs 300 per day). Others reported being paid Rs 300 per worker per day, keeping about half of that after paying wages. In other cases, the *thekedar* was paid according to the work done—so much per square foot of road, for example—and pocketed the difference. A small *thekedar* might also act as foreman (*mistri*), though these could also be separate people paid a slightly better wage of Rs 200 to Rs 250. For unskilled workers, wages varied slightly across work gangs, but for most of my fieldwork they were between Rs 110 and Rs 150 ($2.20–$3.00) for men, and Rs 15 to Rs 30 less than that for women.

Workers told me that the vast majority of workers in the SEZ were from outside of Rajasthan, with one putting the number at about 75%. I have already spoken of the miserable conditions of these migrant workers, who lived in barebones tent encampments near the SEZ boundary walls or, in the case of some single men, packed into rented rooms. These migrant workers were, for the most part, landless or land-poor, and when they came to the Rajpura market to buy provisions, their tattered clothing stood out from all but the poorest of Rajpura's inhabitants. On several occasions, I observed young children working with their parents, although sometimes they were left under the supervision of older or ill workers in the tent encampments. For these "wage hunters and gatherers" (Breman 1994), the SEZ was just one more temporary construction site, no better or worse than any across the subcontinent. For Rajpura's residents, their presence was another sign of the SEZ's benefits going to "outsiders."

This footloose migratory system left only a small amount of irregular work for people in Rajpura, taken mostly by those proletarianized by land loss, including some lower-caste women. These jobs were the last resort of downwardly mobile ex-farmers. Several women in the Balai *mohalla* worked for a contractor now and again, including Lada during the height of her and Mahesh's financial difficulties.

The work was difficult, low paying, and irregular, often lasting just a few weeks at time. Demand for construction workers is notoriously volatile, fluctuating both seasonally and cyclically. Work in the MWC stopped in the rainy season, contracted to a trickle after the global financial crisis paralyzed investment, and picked up again only after 2012. There were no safety precautions and *thekedars* easily escaped liability. After one Rajpura youth had his leg crushed under a stone slab, his contractor ran off to avoid paying hospital bills. Another laborer reported being denied Rs 10,000 in back wages after missing work due to a death in the family. With dozens of temporary and easily replaceable work gangs from different states, each speaking different languages and under contracts of different duration, it seemed impossible to organize a union or press claims on *thekedars*, who could dissolve and re-form overnight.[9]

Cheetur Joggi made this point clear enough when I met him and some of his co-workers from Shivpura as they were walking out of the MWC gates one evening. Cheetur was the most outspoken and wasted no time in telling me that work inside the SEZ was "not right." He was routinely underpaid by Rs 10 to Rs 30 and on one occasion tried to organize his fellow workers against a previous contractor who was not paying them for overtime. He and fifteen co-workers sat down on the job, but the Rajasthani contractor fired them all. "You try to form a union, they fire you and get others from outside." Eventually he got hired by another contractor from Delhi, who he approached outside the MWC gates. Carrying stones and dirt in the Rajasthani sun was unpleasant work, but being landless and uneducated he had no choice; good work in the SEZ was for "high profile" people. As if on cue, a Deutsche Bank SUV whizzed past us carrying a group of young "knowledge professionals" into the SEZ. Cheetur wryly observed, "We don't speak to the educated big people. We stay very far from the big people." With that, he and his co-workers started off on the several-kilometers walk home. On top of the all-too-familiar precarity of casual wage laborers in India, Cheetur's story illustrates the acutely perceived social distance between local workers and the "big people" who were the SEZ's privileged workforce.

More significant than temporary construction work—though not necessarily higher paying—was the ongoing support work necessary for the functioning of the SEZ: principally security guards, gardeners, housekeepers, and drivers. These jobs also operated through contractors and were thus temporary and insecure; but because they were regular while they lasted, a larger portion of the workforce was recruited locally. The different jobs were farmed out to different contractors, some regional and others national. The jobs were insecure and low-paying at around Rs 3,000 to Rs 4,500 ($60 to $90) per month.

Security guard work was by far the most prevalent. "Manned guarding" is the cornerstone of India's $7 billion and rapidly growing private security industry (Ernst & Young 2013). Islands of wealth in a sea of poverty require protection, and India's corporations and middle classes are loath to entrust this task to an undermanned—and reputedly corrupt and inefficient—police force.[10] The result is that installations of India's new economy, such as SEZs, outsource their security needs to thousands of private security firms, mostly in the unorganized sector, who supply armies of poorly paid security guards recruited from villages and slums. A highly competitive industry based almost entirely on labor cost, private security margins depend on keeping their guards poorly paid and vulnerable.[11] There is almost no scope for upward mobility; the farthest one can go is becoming a supervisor with a modest pay bump.[12]

A small platoon of village youth thus constituted the front line in protecting the Mahindra World City from external threats—including their fellow villagers. They were hired on short-term contracts (most for one year) by several private security firms hired by either the MWC or its tenant companies. When I first arrived, guards were paid Rs 4,500 for twelve hours of work; when I returned in 2012, shifts had just been reduced to eight hours and wages slashed to Rs 3,500. At just over $2 per day, this poverty wage was no better than casual construction labor, although more regular and less grueling. Job security was nonexistent, and villagers complained of several rounds of layoffs, in which locals were replaced with outsiders (possibly due to events I discuss in Chapter 8).[13]

None of the security guards I spoke to were enamored with their work. One, Bhagwan Gujjar, was a twenty-year-old son of a camel herder who lived in a *kaccha* house across the village road from the Balai *mohalla*. His brother had dropped out of school early and took care of the camels, though because of the SEZ they had lost the plot where they kept the camels and now had to purchase more fodder. Bhagwan had made it past the tenth standard and had hopes of landing a government job. He was pursuing a correspondence course in Jaipur while working nights guarding the SEZ's boundary wall. I would see him leave for his shift in the early evening, freshly bathed in a clean and pressed uniform, and return in the morning red-eyed and exhausted. He had just gotten married when wages were cut to Rs 3,500, and shortly thereafter I saw him negotiating a Rs 5,000 loan with Laduram's nephew. When I asked him if he liked the work, he responded "no one likes it." He and his fellow guards would like to do computer work, but they are uneducated and don't speak English. I once asked him if it ever felt strange that he was guarding his former land. "Yes, it does seem strange. Our land is in there. They took our grazing land, so people can't keep animals. High-level people work in there on computers. We can't work in there because we're uneducated." He added that he would like to "talk to the outsiders who come, like I am talking to you," but even that was not allowed.

While Bhagwan "aspired to exit agriculture," it was not so he could become a security guard. Coming from a camel-herding family with little economic or cultural capital, it required tremendous effort to pursue the correspondence course he was taking while working night shifts. He was under no illusions that his meager wages could support his entire family, for whom the camels remained an important source of livelihood. His low wages and mounting debt were not a promising start for a new family. I could not predict what his correspondence course might yield, but his window for escaping life in low-wage manual labor was shrinking. While Bhagwan longed for some kind of inclusion in the SEZ—even conversation with the "high-profile" people, from which he thought he might learn something useful—he acutely perceived, like Cheetur Joggi, the social exclusion that accompanied his economic marginalization.

Even lower paid than security guards were housekeepers, who made Rs 3,000 to Rs 3,500 and were predictably recruited from the lowest castes. In Rajpura, these jobs were mostly taken by young Dalit men, especially from the sweeper caste. We have seen that the four Sangat households were among the poorest in the village, and continued to suffer the most severely from caste discrimination. Aside from one family whose father had a government job supervising sanitary workers in an Ayurvedic hospital, they mostly depended on casual wage labor in addition to the *rotis* collected by the women for cleaning the village drains. Because three of the four families were completely landless, they lost nothing from the SEZ, and any benefits to come their way were a bonus. The only benefit so far was that the young men had gotten sanitation jobs inside the SEZ—not good jobs, but at least close to the village. One mother whose two sons received sanitation work in Deutsche Bank observed, "The SEZ is good for us, the children have received employment." One of her sons was less sanguine. It was low-paying, temporary, offered no paid sick leave, provided no prospects of upward mobility, and conveyed little status. "They [also] don't give respect. . . . What's to like? Time pass." Although the sweepers had not gained much, they lost nothing and had little reason to mourn the passing of the old village order. Dalits with even a little bit of land, however, could not be convinced that these jobs compensated for their current landlessness.

Drivers were the best off among the SEZ's informal workforce, though making a reasonable wage from driving depended on becoming a self-employed car owner without high interest payments. A majority of the drivers for Mahindra and the various SEZ units were from outside of the village, but it was possible to obtain a contract with the companies if one could afford to purchase the requisite SUV. Failing that, one might find work driving for a car owner, typically making a monthly wage of about Rs 4,000 ($80). It was possible to make more as a car owner—something that was open only to those in Rajpura with enough land money to purchase a $20,000 vehicle or to obtain the necessary financing. But it was not a high-margin business, especially if one had to purchase the car on credit, and many did not factor in their ability to meet maintenance costs. During the period covered by my fieldwork, there were two to three cars parked in the Balai *mohalla*: one was not owned by the driver, one was bought partly on credit and partly with land money, and the other was purchased entirely through credit (but was quickly sold). Prakash Bunkar's attempt to make a go at driving illustrates the tenuousness of these efforts and why real estate rather than employment was the main chance for upward mobility in Rajpura.

At the time of the SEZ's arrival, Prakash was a semiproletarianized farmer-laborer. His father and three uncles had 18 *bighas* of land between the four of them, and Prakash spent some of his youth in Madhya Pradesh, where his father had migrated to do construction labor. After moving back to Rajpura, Prakash's family cultivated their small piece of land while he worked for fifteen years in the block printing mills of Sanganer—back-breaking work that paid slightly more than construction labor. Prakash's father was compelled by debts to sell some of their land cheaply long before the SEZ arrived. The family's remaining 18 *bighas* were taken for the SEZ, and the brothers sold most—but crucially not all—of their compensation plots for a higher-than-median $18,000 per *bigha*. After paying off debts, the brothers collectively bought 20 *bighas* of land at a very distant 140 km away. They collected one-third of a monsoon crop from tenants, but the income was minimal and divided between four brothers who each had multiple children.

Prakash used his share of what remained to buy a very old jeep. After not getting much work as a freelance driver, he decided to sell the jeep and buy a new Chevrolet SUV that would allow him to chauffeur for Deutsche Bank. The car cost $18,000; he obtained formal financing for $10,000 by mortgaging his land and paid the rest in cash, part of which came from selling his jeep and the rest from a village moneylender (himself recycling land earnings). As my first spell of fieldwork was coming to an end, I watched Prakash inaugurate the car with a ceremonial *puja* (prayer ritual); he planned to hire a driver rather than drive the vehicle himself. When I returned one year later, he was driving nights from 8:00 pm until 7:00 am, making four trips back and forth to Jaipur, while his nephew drove the car during the day shift. When I asked him if he was making good money, his response was, "Money? What money? Exploitation is happening." Prakash was paid a fixed rate per kilometer that he thought was far too low and did not factor in fuel and maintenance costs. With high interest payments on his car, chauffeuring was less remunerative than he had hoped. When we sat down with a calculator to work out his monthly costs and income, we concluded that he was making a little less than $100 per month. This was slightly less than working in the block printing mills, although it was easier on his body. But without land to provide subsistence needs, expenses had gone up. Prakash concluded, "We don't save anything."

By 2014, Prakash's prospects had brightened, but not because of work. His earnings were still low and his car was in bad shape. But his ability to hold onto one compensation plot proved fortuitous; although tiny, it had appreciated almost *tenfold* in the preceding two years. It was perhaps Prakash's broader experience outside of Rajpura, gained as a laborer in Madhya Pradesh, that gave him the wherewithal not to liquidate all of his compensation plots. Whatever the reason, Prakash's small plot may prove to be a lottery ticket out of his difficulties. What his experience shows, however, is the meager and precarious employment available to dispossessed farmers inside the SEZ. Real estate profits, not wages, provided the chief opportunity for upward mobility in Rajpura, as unequal as that opportunity proved to be.

In sum, the jobs available to dispossessed farmers inside the SEZ were low-paying, indirect, and insecure; while they were a marginal bonus to the landless (reducing the transportation costs to similar low-paying jobs in Jaipur), in no one's eyes did they compensate for lost land. As several people put it, such work "had no meaning."[14] Wages from *mazduri* were woefully insufficient to transfer entire families out of agriculture; this would require the regular, salaried work for which people in Rajpura reserved the term *naukri.* The SEZ only offered *mazduri,* defined by the mediation of contractors who ensured their insecurity and "ate" part of their salaries as commission. Rajpura's residents desired to be included in the SEZ's formal workforce, but they were separated from that workforce by great social distance and a seemingly impermeable layer of contractors.

Rural Women in the Knowledge Economy

Because the shift from agriculture to wage labor is often seen as liberating for women, it would be fair to ask whether even the *mazduri* generated by the SEZ had more meaning for women. While a complex literature exists on the gendered consequences of labor-intensive manufacturing zones,[15] scholarship on gender in India's "new" or "knowledge" economy has focused on "knowledge professionals" (Mukherjee 2008; Fuller and Narasimhan 2008; Radkhakrishnan 2011). Given the significantly lower levels of education among women in Rajpura—the female literacy rate was 29% in 2001—it goes without saying that they were, like rural men, entirely excluded from "core jobs" in the zone's IT/ITES companies.[16] To the extent that women's labor in Rajpura was absorbed by the SEZ at all, it was into the subcontracted casual wage labor described previously. But the need to take such work varied significantly by class and caste.

For upper-caste women, loss of agricultural land meant almost complete confinement to the home (*purdah*), since working outside of the house was both economically unnecessary and considered to be beneath their caste status. This included probably all of the Brahmin and Bania families and many Jat families. During my one-month stay in Bansilal Sharma's house, the women of the large

Brahmin joint compound—including a daughter-in-law with a BA degree—spent their days busily milking and feeding the remaining buffalo, cleaning the house, washing clothes, and preparing food while the men worked until late at night in their Jaipur milk business. Although they bemoaned being "unemployed"—their hard work at home notwithstanding—there was no question of them working outside; it was, as several Brahmin men put it, "a matter of honor." When I asked Puneeta, one of Bansilal's daughters-in-law, if there was any benefit in not having to work so hard in the fields anymore, she replied, "Yes, there is both a loss and a benefit. We've gotten some rest, but it's a bigger loss. We used to get grain, fodder, everything from the fields."

While all women I spoke with bemoaned the loss of land and livestock, the post-dispossession gender division of labor was very different in poor, lower-caste households. The previous chapter illustrated that women were often the first in downwardly mobile families to be proletarianized: while men pursued a range of strategies to avoid descent into unskilled casual labor, women in those households were often the first to go looking for work. When they found work, it was invariably on the lowest rung of the informal labor force, earning lower wages than men. Women were excluded by gender norms from work as security guards or drivers, so the only work open to them inside the SEZ was in gardening or housekeeping; although some village women received such work, I did not meet any in Rajpura. All the women from Rajpura working in the SEZ who I met were doing construction work for private contractors, for which they were paid Rs 10 to Rs 30 less than men per day. In the Balai *mohalla,* Lada and at least a half-dozen women did irregular construction work for a contractor—a few weeks here, a month there—in or around the SEZ. But this private-sector construction work remained relatively scarce compared to lower paying work on India's National Rural Employment Guarantee Scheme, when the latter was being implemented (more on which shortly). So, while loss of agricultural land turned many upper-caste women into unemployed "housewives," it pushed many lower-caste women into the precariously employed proletariat. Several weeks after my conversation with Puneeta, I asked Kamla Devi Nayak, a lower-caste woman whose family had lost their land to the SEZ, whether she and her daughters had "gotten some rest," as Puneeta had suggested. Her reply was, "What rest? We carry stones under the hot sun."

If India's "knowledge economy" has created better—if not uncomplicated—career opportunities for educated middle-class women (Fuller and Narasimhan 2008; Radhakrishnan 2011), its consequences for rural women in Rajpura have been less inspiring. While land loss for the zone reinforced *purdah* among upper-caste women, it pushed lower-caste women into the casualized, low-paid workforce. Although such "increased labor force participation" is often seen as a gain for gender equality, it was not celebrated in Rajpura. Faced with increased reproductive work at home and precarious work in the market, I did not find a single woman who believed that these jobs compensated for lost land.

The Right to Work Comes and Goes

Five years after land dispossession, Rajpura's largest employer was not the Mahindra World City but the central government. The Mahatma Gandhi National Rural Employment Guarantee Act (MGNREGA), passed a few months after the SEZ Act in 2005, ostensibly guaranteed every rural household one hundred days of work per year at the minimum wage (at the time, Rs. 100 per day in Rajasthan). Funded by the central government, the program would be implemented by state governments through village *panchayats* who would devise local public works projects in collaboration with block and district officials, supervise workers, and maintain "muster rolls" that determine payments. The law required *panchayats* to provide the requisite one hundred days of work to anyone who requested it. By 2008, NREGA (as it is generally known) had been rolled out in all 615 districts of India. Providing over 216 billion workdays to 45 million rural households in 2009–2010, it was the largest public works project in the world. If Rajpura's farmers were dispossessed of land and underemployed in the private sector, to what extent did this massive job scheme offer a public-sector safety net?

When I arrived in Rajpura in 2009, participation in the job scheme was widespread. In 2010, 647 households in the *panchayat* had job cards, and 522 were recorded as having worked for some duration. My survey found that 51% of households and 76% of SC/ST households had worked in the scheme. Large work gangs, almost entirely of women, could be seen carrying dirt and stones, improving roads, and digging rain catchment *taalaabs* in projects that typically ran for a few weeks to a month at a time. Heavy female participation in the scheme appeared to arise partly from the work's proximity to home, and to its low wages compared to the private construction work more readily available to men. While only 13% of General Caste households utilized the scheme, participation was otherwise fairly broad and not limited to the very poor. Those proletarianized by land loss depended heavily on NREGA income as a supplement to casual wage labor for private *thekedars*, but so did the petty asset managers who, even if they possessed small means of production (a plot or far-off piece of land), still often lacked regular income. Even 56% of Jat families utilized the scheme, which was likely a reflection of being "land poor"; that is, being without a regular income as their plots and land appreciated. From what I could tell, every household in the Balai *mohalla* sent someone to work in NREGA.

Some scholars have suggested that NREGA and other social welfare programs—which seemed, for a brief period under the first UPA government, to be expanding—should be seen as explicit attempts to manage the "surplus populations" driven from the land but not needed by "corporate capital." Building on the work of Kalyan Sanyal (2007), Partha Chatterjee (2008) has prominently argued that "under present globally prevailing normative ideas," it is "considered unacceptable that those who are dispossessed of their means of labour because of the primitive accumulation of capital should have no means of subsistence." As a consequence, "governmental agencies have to find the resources to, as it were, reverse the consequences of primitive accumulation by providing alternative means of livelihood to those who have lost them" (Chatterjee 2008: 55). Although I have already argued that "primitive accumulation" is an inadequate term for the changing forms of land dispossession under capitalism, the account thus far would otherwise seem to support the second aspect of the Sanyal-Chatterjee hypothesis. After being dispossessed for the Mahindra World City, Rajpura's farmers found their labor largely superfluous to its knowledge economy, and dependent in large numbers on a government welfare scheme.

But this conception has two important shortcomings. The first is the obvious one that Rs 10,000 ($200) per year—assuming perfect implementation—in no way "reverses" the effects of land dispossession; Rajpura's farmers would have expected more in yearly income from one good buffalo. NREGA wages were welcome but insufficient to reproduce households or obviate their need for selling labor power on the market. The second shortcoming of the Sanyal-Chatterjee argument, however, is that NREGA never reflected "prevailing normative commitments" to ensure the survival of the dispossessed, but was a contingent political accomplishment (Baviskar and Sundar 2008) that, in Rajpura, was relatively short-lived.

From the beginning, many villagers claimed that the *panchayat* officials implementing the program were stuffing the rolls with ghost workers and pocketing a portion of their wages. As early as 2010, women complained that they were being underpaid—often only receiving Rs 90 per day or less. But this was still the golden age of NREGA: within a few years, political reaction to the program at the central and state level emboldened already hostile local officials to effectively kill the program. Rajasthan's *sarpanches* and *gram sevaks* launched a series of protests against mandatory government audits of the program during my fieldwork,[17] which succeeded in ensuring that no such audit took place in Rajpura—or most of Rajasthan. Meanwhile, the central government began to withhold payments and gradually under-fund the program (Ghosh 2015). By 2012, most women in Rajpura had stopped going because they weren't being paid. Lada and ten other women she worked with went to the bank for a payment to find that it had been cut without explanation. Livid, she explained, "They cut fourteen days of work. We carry dirt in the open sun, work so hard, then they don't give [wages]," adding later that "they are thieves." Women in the

Bavariya hamlet, desperately in need of work, also complained that the money "gets eaten in the middle;" it was no longer running in their (neighboring) *panchayat*. When I asked *sarpanch* Mahinder Singh in 2012 why the program was not running, he responded, "It's a flop show. It's a fraudulent scheme to kill the skilled labor of India. . . . As of now it is not running. I have stopped it. It will resume after the rainy season." When I returned two years later, villagers told me it had not been running for two years. While Mahinder was hostile to the program from the beginning, the shifting balance of power toward the "neoliberal faction" within the central government, coupled with the successful mobilization against oversight by local officials in Rajasthan, allowed him to kill the project with impunity.[18] The village would anyway soon be classified as a small town, and thus outside of NREGA's purview. As fast as the right to work had come to Rajpura, so it went.

The normative commitments of India's political leaders toward the dispossessed have been overstated. India's social welfare system remains inadequate for significantly ameliorating—much less reversing—the effects of dispossession.

NGOs to the Rescue?

Having taken villagers' land without providing them work, Mahindra offered corporate social responsibility (CSR). MWC officials seemed, in my interviews with them, genuinely enthusiastic about their philanthropic work in Rajpura.[19] Their first major intervention was to hire a national NGO, which I will call the Youth Foundation, to run vocational training classes for Rajpura's youth, with priority given to those whose land was acquired. Operating from a compound adjoining Rajpura's main temple, the Youth Foundation commenced to train batches of approximately one hundred students at a time in customer care, reception, and marketing for a tuition of Rs 500 ($10). The youth I spoke with paid the tuition in the hopes of gaining a job in the SEZ, but were sorely disappointed. As a Brahmin youth from Shivpura put it: "We didn't receive a benefit, it was a loss." They paid the fees and wasted time going back and forth, "and now we're sitting here unemployed." Foundation officials acknowledged this disappointment. Although they claimed to have placed 108 of 128 trainees in jobs (which I could not confirm), these were admittedly in low-paid private-sector work in Jaipur, and none were in the SEZ. A Youth Foundation official explained that it was almost impossible to place their students in SEZ jobs because their "mental levels were very low." Because they could not speak English they were "unsuited to call center work." Where the Youth Foundation did try to place them—with small private companies in Jaipur—did not provide the wages Rajpura's youth were looking for, required long daily commutes, and did not confer the status required to make good marriages. By December 2010, the Foundation had closed its doors in Rajpura.

Youth Foundation's efforts may have been sincere, if patronizing. But they had little chance of overcoming the structural gulf between Rajpura's young men and core jobs in India's knowledge economy. The premise of vocational training, an increasingly popular CSR initiative in the context of land acquisition in India, is that "qualifications make their own openings" (Willis 1977: 127) and that the gulf between "under-educated" or "under-skilled" job-seekers and more remunerative jobs can be overcome by investment in "human capital." But if investment in human capital might, over the long-term, attract further investment and higher-skilled employment (Sen 2000), it remains a positional good whose supply does not itself generate demand (Bourdieu 1984). Where economic growth does not generate a sufficient number of jobs for those being ejected from agriculture, the most it can accomplish is to shape who gets what jobs (Willis 1977). And while manufacturing may have been a more feasible leap for Rajpura's youth, there was little prospect that a several-month computer and soft-skills course could provide a springboard into the knowledge economy.

While it proved impossible to offer Rajpura's youth quality jobs in the SEZ, a second effort centered on helping them become entrepreneurs. Mahindra brought in two trainers from the Technology Business Incubator (TBI), an undertaking sponsored by the central government's National Science and Technology Entrepreneurship Development Board (NSTEDB), an institution whose mission is to "help promote knowledge driven and technology intensive enterprises" and "to convert 'job-seekers' into 'job-generators.'"[20] I had noticed the small building with TBI's logo near the SEZ, but had never seen its gate open. It was thus relatively late in my fieldwork when I met Santosh and Pradeep, the two trainers, during an interview at the MWC offices. In addition to overseeing the training program for male entrepreneurs under the guise of TBI, Santosh and Pradeep moonlighted for a Hindu-inflected social service organization I will call the All-India Self-Reliance and Awakening Movement (AISAM). Mahindra also engaged the two social workers, under the auspices of AISAM, to organize self-help groups among women in Rajpura—"to inculcate some kind of entrepreneurial spirit. Skill development. . . . Like making soap"—and to undertake what Santosh described as "moral education" and a Mahindra engineer referred to as "social engineering." When I asked the latter what this meant, he explained, "As industrial activity starts, lots of other activities—criminality, liquor—also come into the society" and thus arose the need to "eradicate social evils." About the type of education they provided, Santosh clarified: "You can say human values. Kindness, culture. About freedom fighters. We promote Indian culture." "Don't people know about Indian culture in this village," I asked? "Very little." As for the main problems in the village, he ticked off: "an illiterate public.

Education standard is low. Drinking wine. Cleanness, sanitation. . . . There is a lot of dirtiness."

By the time I met Santosh, TBI's original goal of creating tech-savvy entrepreneurs had already been abandoned and the program reoriented as a training program for security guards, electricians, mechanics, and plumbers. Half the trainees were guards, Santosh explained, because that was what the companies in the SEZ wanted. He invited me to a graduation ceremony for trainees the following day.

Inside the TBI gates, a temporary stage had been erected in front of rows of plastic chairs. Mahindra executives were late and, while we waited, the two trainers coached and prepped the young men. Santosh and Pradeep lectured their relatively aloof audience about self-help, thrift, and discipline. Their boss at TBI then arrived and delivered a valedictory:

> Your land has been sold for Mahindra World City, you've got lots of money, are using it also. But it will eventually finish. So before that happens . . . TBI thought of training youth as security guards. Realistically speaking, you can't become doctors or engineers at this age. So if we train you and give you skills . . . skills will be needed by these companies.

He asked a guard to stand up and say what he learned. The young guard remained sheepishly silent, and finally let out a laugh. He was told to sit down. A young guard next to me explained, "We learned yoga. Nothing related to work." They already had the security guard jobs before the training but now needed the "certificate" to maintain their employment. An electrician similarly insisted that he did not learn anything; he was already a practicing electrician but thought the certificate might help him with future employers.

Mahindra officials finally showed up in white SUVs and were escorted to chairs on stage. Office workers filed behind and placed several glossy Mahindra World City signs behind the dais. Santosh and Pradeep asked the security guards to stand up and recite what they learned, and then asked women from the new self-help groups how much money they had saved. A woman reported that each of the twelve members had saved Rs 50 ($1), which was greeted with applause. Santosh and Pradeep announced that Mahindra would be providing their group with a sewing machine. Their boss gushed about the Mahindra World City, how many companies were coming, and how many jobs people will get. He concluded: "The situation here was that there was absolutely no development." But development is coming, "and the people here will be included." A Mahindra engineer added, "The world's biggest companies are coming, you will not lose from this. You will be included, while keeping your traditions." The highest ranking executive, a South Indian, concluded in faltering Hindi: "We will do everything we can for these villages." Young women handed bouquets of plastic flowers to the Mahindra executives amid flashing cameras. The ceremony broke for *chai* and *samosas* and the VIPs filed back into the SUVs.

After the ceremony, I asked Santosh more about the self-help groups. He explained, it is "the group which helps themselves." The initiative had two components: training women to make soap, sew, and become beauticians; and helping them pool savings into a collective account from which they could take small business loans (micro-credit). The women had to pay Rs 600 ($12) for the training, and make an initial deposit of Rs 50 to start the credit fund. Once they had contributed Rs 300, they could borrow three times that amount, which had to be paid off within six months at 2% monthly interest. He invited me to the self-help group inauguration the following day.

As it turned out, the Balai *mohalla* was one of two singled out for a self-help group. The barber's house next to the home of Mahesh and Lada was abuzz with preparations. When I walked in, Santosh was giving the women instructions about the decorations and tutoring them on the names of the different executives, and in what order they should be given *tika* (vermilion paste applied to the forehead). The women had prepared a big "welcome" sign on the ground with the colored sand used to make *rangolis* during Diwali. A chart on the wall read "Self-Help Group" in Hindi and listed the women's contributions to the savings pool. The daughter of the house, Meera, appeared to be the most enthusiastic. Her father sat in a chair looking bemused, and said he had "no clue" what to make of it. Sanjay was telling someone to go fetch water and then suddenly barked, "Stand up. They're coming." The SUVs had pulled up the *mohalla's* narrow lane, and the same executives from the day before, with the addition of a textile industrialist, walked onto the veranda where *namastes* were exchanged and *tika* applied. Everyone filed into a modest concrete room where the men, who sat on plastic chairs, issued forth on the condition of women in Rajasthan while the women sat quietly on the floor. One of the Mahindra executives spoke of the value of women having work they could do from home. The visibly impatient industrialist, who had been talking on his cell phone, got to the point: what kind of machines had they learned to use? What kind of stitching could they do? The industrialist's handicrafts company would be exporting abroad, a Mahindra executive explained, so the work had to be high quality. The meeting concluded with the reiterated promise of a sewing machine.

Whether training the local women to become a sub-contracted workforce for the coming textile factory was the original motivation behind the self-help group or a tack-on remains unclear. As of 2016—almost six years later—the group had not received its promised sewing machine and none of its members had gotten any sewing work. What is clear is that there was a disconnect between the stated intent of the SHG's organizers and sponsors and the understanding of the women themselves, which became clear as soon as the SUVs pulled away. Pushpa, a middle-aged woman who lived across the lane from Mahesh and Lada and who was officially part of the self-help group, asked me what it was all about. "We didn't understand. We're illiterate. All those who were sitting in there are educated." When I explained what I understood, she said, "I'm not going to sew. If I can't sew, will I lose my money to the group?" She thought that the main benefit of the group would be taking loans, which she could use to pay her daughter's wedding expenses. I explained, using the information Santosh had provided me, that the interest rate was 2% monthly—the same as village moneylenders—and it had to be paid off within 6 months. She said you can't pay back a wedding loan in six months; her daughter's wedding had cost Rs 3.5 *lakh* ($7,000).

Later, I asked Lada and Pushpa what benefit they got from their training as beauticians. Does anyone go to a beautician in the village, I asked? "No," they said, but they used the course to apply "fairness cream" to each other. As for the other suggested routes to entrepreneurship, Lada shrewdly cut to the point:

> Tell me one thing: if all the women in the village are going to be selling clothes, then who will buy them? And then they told me that I should learn to make soap. But you can get soap in the store. Who will buy it from me? They say they will bring us work, but I don't believe them.

Lada withdrew from the course after eighteen days. The organizers later told her she could still get the "certificate" if she paid the remaining money but, she asked earnestly, "How can I get a certificate? I didn't learn to sew."

While the women used the self-help group for their own purposes, only in the minds of its organizers did their participation represent "development." It would not have occurred to them that the "group" (*samuha*) compensated for their loss of land and livestock, or that these were in the same category of reality.

The Importance of Being *Semi*proletarian

Neither the small amount of low-paid work in the SEZ, nor NREGA nor NGO interventions could replace the value of lost land in Rajpura. As in many parts of rural India, and especially those defined by dryland agriculture, the land itself could not support most households in Rajpura before the SEZ's arrival; but it was the foundational piece in diversified livelihoods in which no single piece could. Its dispossession was unevenly traumatic, as we have seen. The landed upper castes had more to fall back on, and moved with great alacrity into real estate and self-employment. Lower-caste smallholders lost their small cushions against full proletarianization and were forced to place their fates fully in a capricious labor market. While real estate was a differentiating factor, for no one in Rajpura did employment inside the SEZ come close to replacing the value of the land they had lost. Almost everyone in Rajpura stressed the importance of having land *while* diversifying from agriculture—in short, being semiproletarian.

The attractiveness of the semiproletarian condition vis-à-vis the proletarian is partly a straightforward economic calculation. As Mangalchand Choudhary, a Jat youth, pointed out to me, you can get Rs 2,000 to Rs 3,000 per month selling the milk from one buffalo; if you have two buffalo, that is more income than the monthly wage of an Infosys security guard. "Whoever has two buffalo, they won't do it! They'll take it easy," he explained. Gopal Bora Sharma made a similar calculation. Although relatively lucky to have a skilled job as an electrician, which paid a marginally better Rs 5,000 per month (still temporary and through a contractor), he was unhappy with the deal. His family had 1.5 of their three *bighas* acquired, and had to sell three buffalo. The monthly income from those three buffalo was Rs 7,000 to Rs 8,000, which means that "income has gone down." He concluded, "It's a big loss and the loss is bigger than the benefit." Such low-paying jobs did not make up for livestock, much less land. And this helps to explain why the shift from agropastoralist to Infosys security guard did not strike many as "progress."

But there is more to it than lost income. Casual wage labor (*mazduri*), it must be underscored, was universally repellent to Rajpura's farmers. All things being equal, farmers preferred to cultivate their own land over working for others. This was partly because *mazduri* had, in their estimation, a very low drudgery-to-reward ratio.[21] Even when it yielded higher cash income, *mazduri* required far more sustained physical labor than agriculture's periodic intensity. This was particularly true for men, who relegated women to the more grueling agricultural tasks like planting and weeding. But no one I spoke with in Rajpura, women included, preferred doing casual wage labor to working one's own land. This preference was inseparable from the autonomy and status provided by even small amounts of land. "Being one's own boss" and "nobody's slave" were phrases I heard repeatedly. While high-wage formal work could certainly change the equation, casual wage labor—low-paying, grueling, subject to the dictates of employers, and offering no prospects for upward mobility—was an unfortunate necessity to be minimized, not an opportunity to be utilized. Rajpura's semiproletarians sought wage labor when they needed it, and withdrew from the labor market when they could afford it. More land meant less work, as did more rain: as one youth put it, "If there is water, people like working less." A mango seller thus articulated his hierarchy of (dis)utility: "If I get work, I work. If I don't get work, I do this [sell mangos]. If we get crops, I rest." The next chapter turns to the strategy of self-employment as an alternative to wage labor. But the point to be established here is that no one preferred casual wage labor to working their own land, even small amounts of which were highly valued prophylactics against the radical dependence and drudgery of the fully proletarian condition. Such preferences did not reflect a "traditional" mentality impervious to the profit motive (Weber 1958: 60) but a fairly straightforward assessment that, if it was not absolutely necessary, the money afforded by casual labor was not worth the hassle.

Judged by the conjoined standards of income and autonomy, the jobs made available to dispossessed farmers were no compensation for lost land. If their land had not been acquired, these jobs would have been matter-of-factly viewed as supplementary income that could absorb the labor of a young family member, no better or worse than similarly bad-paying jobs in Jaipur, but with the advantage of being closer to home. Indeed, this is how farmers from surrounding villages whose lands weren't acquired felt about these jobs, as did those who had no land to lose. But for the dispossessed, these jobs were inadequate recompense. Not only did few families get them, but one member earning Rs 3,500 to Rs 4,000 could not sustain a nuclear family, much less a joint one. Such incomes were inadequate to replace the means of subsistence provided by land and livestock, especially during a period of rampant food price inflation. This was made clear to me by a group of middle-aged farmers on my second day in Rajpura. After listening to their complaints about the loss of their land and livestock and the lack of employment in the SEZ, I asked them whether they would rather have the land back or a job in the SEZ. "Both," they answered, refusing my dichotomization. In the absence of full employment for the household or a stable family wage, they needed land *and* work.

This assessment was not limited to older men. It is often argued that younger generations do not value farming and want to leave agriculture and the village behind (cf. Gupta 2009; Bardhan 2011). Defending government land acquisition for industry, Bardhan cites a survey purporting to show that "the overwhelming majority of farmers' children want to leave agriculture" (Bardhan 2011: 56). While it is true that many youth wanted to leave agriculture in Rajpura, it was not so that they could become casual laborers. Reality did not provide them with the abstract choice between agriculture and urban employment, but a far more constrained set of options.[22] None wanted to give up their land for the low-quality employment that was available to them in the SEZ. All understood that such employment could not support their entire families. And, contrary to common perception, many preferred agriculture to manual wage labor.

When I asked two Jat youth, Mangalchand and Ajay, what was better, farming or working as a security guard in the SEZ, they responded without hesitation, "Farming is better. It is work of the home (*ghar ka kaam*), one's own (*khud ka*). With that work [as security guard], you have to go and stay there nine hours, spend one hour going and one hour coming. You go home and sleep, that's it." This was no way to live, in their estimation. Such perceptions were not limited to Jats, who have a reputation as dedicated agriculturalists. Many young men in Rajpura similarly contrasted the work available to them with what they lost from the SEZ, and few thought it was a good trade. One Regar youth explained, "Say we get security guard work over there. You get Rs 3,500. A household cannot run on Rs 3,500. And they don't give that. And we don't get fodder." Sherpal Naik, a young OBC man who has not been able to find work in the SEZ, remarked on another occasion, "When we had land, we were happy. We got grain, kept animals, got milk, butter, and buttermilk. Ever since the land was sold, we have had trouble. Now we have to purchase even buttermilk." Allowing for the exaggerations of nostalgia, it was clear to me that most youth did value land ownership and the quality of food and security it provided their families. They also saw land as the basis for autonomous futures inside or outside farming. As one youth put it, "If we have land, we can do anything. Start a business, farm. Without land we can't do anything." Not only were available jobs in the SEZ—scarce as they were—insufficient to compensate for lost land and livestock and incapable of providing a promising route out of agriculture, but youth clearly saw the land's value as means of production. Dispossession represented a radical narrowing of future possibilities.

It is this micro-reality of the semiproletarian condition that renders meaningless generalities about farmers' desires to exit agriculture. Rajpura's youth wanted to leave agriculture for salaried jobs, not waged labor: for *naukri*, not *mazduri*. If *naukri* could alter the equation, no one thought *mazduri* was worth sacrificing land for. Faced with a non-labor-intensive trajectory of capitalist growth in which unskilled landless workers face a precarious life of "wage hunters and gatherers," it seemed far preferable—indeed, extremely prudent—to hold onto even small plots of unirrigated land and livestock. While Rajpura's residents did not, as we saw, organize to oppose land dispossession for the Mahindra World City, subsequent disappointment at the quantity and quality of work available to them in the SEZ led many to wish they had the land back. As one young Balai man put it: "The land has gone, we haven't received employment. . . . It was better before Mahindra came. We had land."

Conclusion

One would be hard pressed to identify a less promising form of economic growth for rural India than "knowledge-intensive" services. As a sector requiring education and skills that are in short supply in India's villages—a product of woeful investment in rural education over six decades (Dreze and Sen 2013)—and that is incapable of generating the sheer number of jobs required for pulling a growing rural population out of agriculture, India's much heralded IT/ITES economy is an exceedingly poor basis for broad-based "development." We have seen that it has almost entirely bypassed Rajpura, where even the most educated youth are still considered "unemployable" in its core jobs. Dispossessed for an enclave of India's "knowledge economy," Rajpura's farmers were superfluous to its labor requirements. Because of India's "footloose" migrant labor system, even the vast majority of construction jobs went to "outsiders." A small minority found temporary and subcontracted support positions as security guards, gardeners, drivers, and janitors. These jobs in no way compensated for lost land and livestock, a reality illustrated by the fact that a job as an Infosys security guard paid less than the monthly income from two buffalo (and had a much shorter lifespan). Social welfare programs—though welcome while they were running—did little to replace land as a basis of household reproduction and security against a hostile labor market. Dispossessed of their land and livestock for real estate and knowledge-intensive growth that required their land but not their labor; dependent on the market for consumption at a time of drastic food inflation; confronted with the beating back of a major social welfare program that could have moderately cushioned the blow; Rajpurans became the object of Corporate Social Responsibility. These CSR initiatives represented, at best, a complete misreading of the village's socio-economic hardships. Vocational training had no chance of bridging the gap between Rajpura's youth and the core jobs in the SEZ, and the promotion of self-help and entrepreneurship as a path to "self-sufficiency" was a cruel joke in the wake of being dispossessed of their productive assets. So, while real estate speculation ultimately differentiated the fates of Rajpura's residents, knowledge-intensive growth was almost uniformly exclusionary.

Marxists have historically seen dispossession as the process of creating a class of wage laborers. As Chapter 1 demonstrated, this functionalist logic takes the consequences of dispossession for its cause. Contemporary land grabs are driven by advanced capitalist demands for land. And in India, as in many parts of the Global South (Li 2010b), accelerating land dispossession is accompanied by decelerating labor absorption in the context of an already massive oversupply of labor. By the mid-19th century, Marx had already observed the tendency of capitalism to progressively displace labor with technology and thus generate an ever-expanding "population which is superfluous to capital's average requirements" (Marx 1977: 982). This "relative surplus population" could be augmented in "the more striking form of the extrusion of workers already employed, or the less evident, but not less real, form of a greater difficulty in absorbing the additional working population through its customary outlets" (1977: 983). While the former is most evident in the deindustrializing North, the latter is the crux of dispossession in the "late industrializing" South: while rural populations are being thrown from the land in increasing numbers, industrialization is far less labor-absorbing today than during Europe's industrial revolution (Rodrik 2016). This gap between labor power separated from the land and absorbed into wage labor existed under the developmentalist regime, but was somewhat ameliorated by the *relative* labor-intensity of industrial projects during that era combined with the capacity of the public sector—sometimes acted upon—to prioritize hiring the dispossessed (Parasuraman 1999; Parry and Struempell 2008). Under neoliberalism, this gap is only expanding by virtue of India's increasingly "jobless growth," which is especially non-labor-intensive by comparative and historical standards (Gupta and Kumar 2012; Verma 2012; Mitra 2013). Rajpura's dispossessed farmers joined the massive and growing body of people that India's trajectory of capitalist growth cannot absorb into regular wage labor. The consequent importance of the semiproletarian condition, Chapter 9 will argue, is a major structural factor underlying India's "land wars."

In Rajpura, large-scale employment of dispossessed farmers could have tipped the scales of local opinion in the SEZ's favor; instead, its absence was a source of widespread anger. As Shivpura *chaiwala* Kailash Sharma put it, "If people got work it would be great. But we're not getting any." He then added: "We can't even go inside."

7

On the Margins of a World City

Neither will the city save the country nor the country the city.
—Raymond Williams (1985: 301)

From the roof of Lada and Mahesh's house, where I slept along with their sons on summer nights, one could see over the *thakur's* fort to the illuminated offices and streetlamps of the Mahindra World City. As the village slept, Deutsche Bank's transactions in global commodity, currency, and stock markets were being settled from gleaming office buildings on Rajpura's former grazing land. During the day, village life continued on almost indifferently to the "new economy" that was taking shape a few hundred yards away (see Figure 7.1). A 10-foot boundary wall and a platoon of security guards stood between Rajpura and the Mahindra World City.[1]

Striking spatial divisions such as this make it tempting to conclude that contemporary India has two separate economies: a modern capitalist one for large corporations and the middle classes; and a non-capitalist or "need" economy for those excluded from the circuits of capital (Sanyal 2007; Chatterjee 2008). Such a conclusion, which builds upon the "dual economy" theories of the 1950s, mistakes the unevenness of capitalist development for its incompleteness (Chibber 2013).[2] Rajpura's farmers were already integrated into capitalism before the SEZ through markets for their produce (especially milk), and a majority sold their labor—at least periodically—for a wage. After losing their land and livestock, Rajpura's farmers were only more dependent on markets—including a globally integrated real estate market—for their survival. The Mahindra World City's boundary wall does not divide a capitalist from non-capitalist economy; rather, it marks the radical unevenness of capitalist development when left to its own devices.

The Mahindra World City is an enclave. By "enclave" I do not mean simply that it is governed by an "exceptional" regulatory regime (Ong 2006). It is the raison d'être of SEZs to provide a more liberal economic climate than what prevails in the rest of the country. But tax, trade, and regulatory concessions were of little

Figure 7.1 Grazing on the SEZ's periphery. Photo by author.

significance for villagers; and moderately liberalized labor laws were little noticed by rural workers who were never protected by them in the first place (Cross 2010)[3] and were, moreover, largely left unemployed by the SEZ. More salient were the ways in which the SEZ concentrated investment within its borders and generated few productive linkages to its immediate environment. This chapter combines Stephen Graham's (2000) and Neil Brenner's (2004) insights about the spatial concentration of infrastructural investment under neoliberalism and Albert Hirschman's (1958, 2013) concept of linkage effects to explain why the Mahindra World City did not initiate broad-based economic transformation in Rajpura.

First, it shows that the Mahindra World City is a private enclave of "world class" infrastructure that is largely disconnected from surrounding villages. Not only were the MWC's own investments in infrastructure and services confined within its boundary walls, but public infrastructural investment by the Rajasthan government—in roads, electricity, and water—was entirely geared toward the needs of this emerging private city, with little concern for the welfare of surrounding rural populations. The Mahindra World City was thus an island of exceptional and high-performance infrastructure "unbundled" from its "immediate geographic context."[4] This unbundling is characteristic of the shift from state-regulated capitalism to neoliberalism, which has everywhere "entailed a fundamental break from the universalist, nationalizing model of public infrastructure provision" (Brenner 2004: 244). Whereas "spatial Keynesianism" sought to extend "utilities, communication, and transport grids evenly across the entire national territory," under neoliberalism this aspiration has been abandoned as states offload infrastructure provision to the private sector and focus on building "premium networked spaces" to attract footloose capital (Brenner 2004: 246; Graham 2000). In Chapter 2, I argued that an analogous "spatial Nehruvianism" could be seen in the state-led development that drove dispossession for decades after India's independence. Public-sector industrial townships sought to incorporate surrounding populations into company towns (Sanchez and Strumpell 2014) while parastatals like RIICO built industrial estates in remote rural districts.[5] The main difference between spatial Nehruvianism and spatial Keynesianism is that the former was abandoned at a much lower level of achievement. India's private SEZs—and the broader proliferation of special investment zones, high-tech cities, PPP infrastructure, gated communities, and corporate enclaves of all sorts—represent a retreat from the spatial ambitions of the developmentalist era and thus an abandonment of any effort to check the unevenness of capitalist development. In addition to marginalizing the labor of dispossessed farmers in Rajpura, the Mahindra World City thus also frustrated their expectations that it would bring infrastructure and other markers of "development" to the village.

Second, the Mahindra World City was an enclave economy by virtue of its limited linkage effects. Enclave economies have typically been seen as extensions of "metropolitan" economies within the "periphery" that concentrate income and have limited transformative effect on the larger domestic economy (Cardoso and Falleto 1979: 71; De Janvry 1981; Rodney 1981: 234; Ferguson 2006).[6] While challenging the automatic connection between foreign investment and underdevelopment, Hirschman (1958, 2013) proposed that economic sectors could be ranked according to their "linkage effects"—that is, the extent to which "an ongoing activity gives rise to economic or other pressures that lead to the taking up of a new activity" (2013: 170). Backward linkages arise when an economic activity induces investment into the supply of its inputs, while forward linkages involve the utilization of outputs. In the absence of such productive linkages, Hirschman suggests, enclaves' main chance of contributing to national development lies in the state's ability to tax them. Because India's SEZs are tax-free, this fiscal linkage was not only absent but negative.[7] And because of its sectoral composition—dominated, like two-thirds of India's SEZs, by the IT/ITES industry—the Mahindra World City generated few productive linkages in Rajpura or other surrounding villages.

Together, these features of the Mahindra World City, each driven by broader shifts in Indian capitalism, help to explain why the location of an SEZ in Rajpura did not create broad-based economic transformation.[8] The first process relegated Rajpura's dispossessed farmers to a disinvested urbanizing village on the margins of a "world city," a potential "slum" in the making. The second process ensured that, in the absence of ancillary industries, dispossessed farmers were confined to, and dependent upon, a peripheral informal economy dominated by land rents, petty trade, moneylending, and matrimonial strategies. The third section of the chapter ethnographically examines this non-industrial circulatory economy, which ultimately sustained Rajpura's petty asset managers and neo-rentiers on the periphery of the SEZ. The chapter concludes with a summary assessment of the SEZ's sobering impacts on socio-economic well-being in Rajpura.

Zoning Infrastructure

After lack of jobs, the most unanimous complaint about the SEZ in Rajpura was about the lack of "services" and "facilities" (*suvidayen* or *vyavastha*) provided to the village by the Rajasthan government and Mahindra. Most hoped—and say they were promised by the government—that the SEZ would bring better electricity, water, roads, hospitals, and schools to the village. But while the government provided the SEZ with 24-hour electricity at subsidized prices, villagers suffered from daily—and often day-long—power cuts. While the Rajasthan government supplied the SEZ with guaranteed piped water from the Bisalpur Dam (for which, as Chapter 2 described, many farmers had been dispossessed in the 1990s), villagers were facing an acute shortage of potable water and were forced to purchase tanker water of questionable quality at their own expense. One youth bluntly summed it up: "Water to the rich, and nothing to the poor."

And while the Rajasthan government was building connector roads between the SEZ, the national highway, and the Jaipur International Airport—all of which involved additional land acquisition—village roads were in their same deplorable condition. As one youth pointed out, the only road improvement occurred, "One time [when Chief Minister] Gehlot came. They cemented the road up to the SEZ and not into the village. To show that good development is happening." This lack of investment in village roads may have reflected a larger looming threat: the SEZ's plans called for closing the road connecting Rajpura to the National Highway. When implemented, this would substantially lengthen the commute to Jaipur for workers and choke off Rajpura's petty mercantile economy by rerouting SEZ traffic away from the village market.

Nine years after the initial land dispossession, the compensation plots allotted to farmers next to the SEZ had no roads, electricity, or water. As Hari Mohan Bohra, a Brahmin farmer, put it, they were "getting second-class locations," with narrow roads and no facilities. "If the government gave us a piece of land amongst the capitalists, that would be more beneficial. . . . They have built us a slum (*kacchi basti*)." While Hari Mohan was not alone in using the term "slum" to describe the emerging infrastructural disparity, he was among the minority of better-off villagers who still owned compensation plots. Given that these plots had an astronomical exchange value by 2014, it seemed conceivable that they would eventually form middle class neighborhoods with the necessary amenities. But the village proper was another story: it was becoming a congested and unplanned periphery of a privately planned city.

Education and health facilities had also been little touched by the SEZ's arrival. While the MWC's "Lifestyle Zone" was slated to have elite private educational institutions and "24 × 7 medical care" catering to the middle-class purchasers of the zone's high-end housing, there were no plans for such investments in the surrounding villages. Private, for-profit colleges were setting up on purchased farmland around the SEZ and advertising their proximity to the Mahindra World City, but most people in Rajpura had neither the means nor the qualifications to attend them. Public schools remained as dreadful as ever, forcing many families to send their children to nominally better but more expensive private ones. At least two private clinics opened up in the village, but these were expensive, of questionable quality, and only rarely had doctors.[9] The nearest public emergency room was still in Jaipur. In a pinch, people had to rely on an expensive private hospital 10 km away on the highway. All of this conspired to keep medical expenses a large source of debt in poor households—as we saw with Mahesh and Lada.[10]

This slighting of infrastructural and service investment in Rajpura affected all but the richest non-resident villagers. As one Jat youth summarized, "it's been five years, no development, no roads, water, or electricity." A Balai youth concurred: "They deceived us. They said that they would provide water, schools, hospitals, roads, facilities." Asim Hussein remarked:

> They did a wrong deed (*galat kaam*). If someone is sick, they have to go to SMS [hospital in Jaipur]. They should build a hospital. . . . There are no services. . . . The water here is bad. . . . People are getting sick. . . . They took the land of nine villages to make a Special Economic Zone. . . . They should do something for the village.

In 2014, Rajpura was still a village but "becoming a city." As the preceding quotes suggest, many anticipated the services, amenities, and jobs they associated with the city—and were aggrieved that they were unforthcoming. It would be a simplification, however, to conclude with Dipankar Gupta (2009: 89) that, "Agrarian India, whether relatively rich or poor, holds little attraction for the villager." In Rajpura, most residents valued facets of village life that were receding—the ability to keep cattle and grow food, the "open environment" and tranquility, the absence of crime, and so on. It seemed that what most of them had had in mind was not living in a city like Jaipur, but living in a village with urban amenities: a fact that was connected to their desire to find off-farm jobs but keep their farmland. Most could not imagine themselves living in a Jaipur apartment building—all but the neo-rentiers knew that the more likely scenario was living in a slum. The hybrid character of their aspirations could be observed in how farmers built houses when they obtained money: concrete and (if possible) multi-storey, but with courtyards for animals and often an outdoor *chula* (earthen stove) for cooking with wood or cow dung. Rather than rejecting the rural for the urban, they were trying to preserve elements of the rural while welcoming the material advantages—infrastructure, facilities, and jobs—of the urban. As it was, their land and livestock were mostly gone and other valued qualities of village life were rapidly receding in the face of traffic, pollution, the influx of "outsiders," and crime. The anticipated benefits of the urban, meanwhile, remained conjectural.

Rajpura's residents were thus acutely aware of the spatial disparity emerging between the village and the "world class city" occupying their former land. Some worried, like Hari Mohan, that the village would become a "slum" (*kacchi basti*). One Jat youth predicted that there would be a "border" (*seema*) between the village and city: "There'll be a city, a town (*kasbaa*) over there. But this place will remain a village, there will be no services." This perception that Rajpura was being incorporated, through government commission and omission, into a subordinate niche in the peri-urban fabric seemed accurate. Administratively, the immediate peripheries of the SEZ were a kind of black hole. The MWC's corporate administration extended only to the SEZ boundary walls; the Block Development Officer in Sanganer considered the area to be urbanizing and thus not a priority for rural development programs; and yet the villages were not part of a municipal corporation. Government officials conceded in interviews that neither the SEZ developers nor any government agency was taking responsibility for improving infrastructure in the villages or planning for their growth. When I asked Sanganer's *tehsildar* (head of the sub-district) whether anyone would invest in the villages whose land was taken, he said, "the SEZ people will develop, but *inside* the zone. Outside, no one will develop."

The Mahindra World City, like India's SEZs broadly, represented a retreat from the spatial ambitions of the developmentalist era. For Rajpura, it was premature.

Missing Linkages

In addition to being an exclusionary island of "world class" infrastructure, the Mahindra World City was an enclave in the older political economic sense: an economic installation with minimal productive linkages to the surrounding economy. Transmitting digital symbols through fiber-optic cables to companies in the Western hemisphere—the main business of the IT/ITES firms operating inside the MWC—created no scope for forward linkages in India, much less Rajpura. The primary inputs for these firms were computers and high-end office furniture. And, as a Deutsche Bank manager explained to me, a large benefit of the SEZ policy was that these capital goods could be imported duty free. Aside from the services identified in the previous chapter—security, transportation, landscaping, and housekeeping—and the construction of the office buildings themselves, it was hard to identify any concrete industries spurred by these investments. One Rajpura shopkeeper supplied milk pouches to a canteen operator inside the SEZ for a little over $2 per day in profit; and one village youth started a small canteen in the SEZ, employing three people. Such a paucity of linkages would place the Mahindra World City quite low on Hirschman's index.

Illuminating this absence of linkages is aided by comparison with India's steel towns and industrial estates, the principal forms of industrial land dispossession in pre-liberalization India. Steel and other forms of "intermediate manufacturing" rank high on the linkage scale (Hirschman 1958: 106), and India's public-sector steel towns stimulated significant ancillary industries: the Bhilai Steel Plant, for example, gave rise to a nearby industrial estate with over two hundred manufacturing units, many of them labor-intensive enterprises run by small and medium-size firms (Parry 2003).[11] Industrial estates contributed to the emergence of large industrial clusters, such as in Ghaziabad, where Saxena (1989) describes a complex and geographically concentrated web of linkages: hydrogenated oil, beer, pharmaceutical, corrugated box, and machinery manufacture create demand for tin containers, glass bottles, craft paper, and primary metals; cotton textile, paper, glass, and soap industries give rise to synthetic fiber and chemical industries; pig iron generates units for wrought iron; primary metals give rise to machinery and parts manufacture; machine manufacturing creates demand for casting and forging units; and all of this encourages small units for nuts, bolts, nails, screws, chains, cables, ball bearings, tools, gauges, and so forth (Saxena 1989: 231–232). The Mahindra World City showed no signs of generating such an "economy of concentration" (Saxena 1989: 231). Nor did it resemble the kind of decentralized industrial cluster observed in the South Indian town of Tirrupur, which was transformed by small farmers-turned-capitalists into a global center for knitwear production. As Chari describes it, "the whole town is a decentralized factory," with spinning, knitting, packaging, processing, and accessorizing units that spill out of the public-sector industrial estates into almost every neighborhood (Chari 2004: 9, 59). The MWC can also be contrasted with the labor-intensive manufacturing SEZs of South China, which transformed neighboring villages of the Pearl River Delta into industrial clusters with thousands of factories attracting migrant laborers from across China (cf. Guldin 2001).

No such productive transformation of its environs could be observed outside of the MWC's gates. The SEZ's limited impact on the regional economy was again well-summarized by the *tehsildar* for Sanganer, famous for its block print textiles. When I asked him what the sub-district's main industry was before and after the SEZ, his response was, "It was printing, *and still is printing*. The SEZ hasn't made any difference. . . . Besides the artificial property boom, nothing has changed."

Circulation and Survival

This "artificial property" boom did, as Chapter 5 showed, send huge sums of (largely "black") money circulating through Rajpura. The Mahindra World City generated significant capital gains that could theoretically be invested in productive expansion. But in the absence of productive linkages with the SEZ, farmers invested these capital gains almost entirely into forms of rent, petty trade, and usury. These investments—coupled with house expenditures, vastly ramped-up matrimonial strategies, and the laundering of capital into religious merit—contributed to a burgeoning informal economy in which circulation and rents predominated over production. Although peripheral to the zone's core economic activities, this informal economy fed upon—and rose and fell with—the interlinked real estate and construction market. Marginalized from the formal economy inside the SEZ, Rajpura's non-fully-proletarianized households depended almost entirely on this informal circulatory economy for survival.

My survey asked every family who received any amount of land money—whether through sale of compensation plots, farmland, or brokerage commission—what they reinvested in. Figure 7.2 illustrates the percentage of households who allocated money to different categories of investment, while Table 7.1 disaggregates the same data by caste. While the survey only captures the incidence, not the quantity, of investment in each category, it sufficiently demonstrates the overall pattern.

Upon receiving land money, most farmers first paid off debts, built houses, and paid for weddings. Unsurprisingly, 92% of SC/ST families had to allocate money to debts compared to 56% of General Caste families. My ethnographic observations also strongly indicate that the lower castes were not only more likely to be in debt, but carried far heavier debt loads relative to income and thus had to use a much higher proportion of their (smaller) land earnings to liquidate them. After paying off debt, the second most common use of money was to upgrade earthen huts to concrete houses. This was a consumption expenditure that improved quality of life, but can also be viewed as an investment in two senses. Some built extra rooms—or even added floors, like Mahesh—to

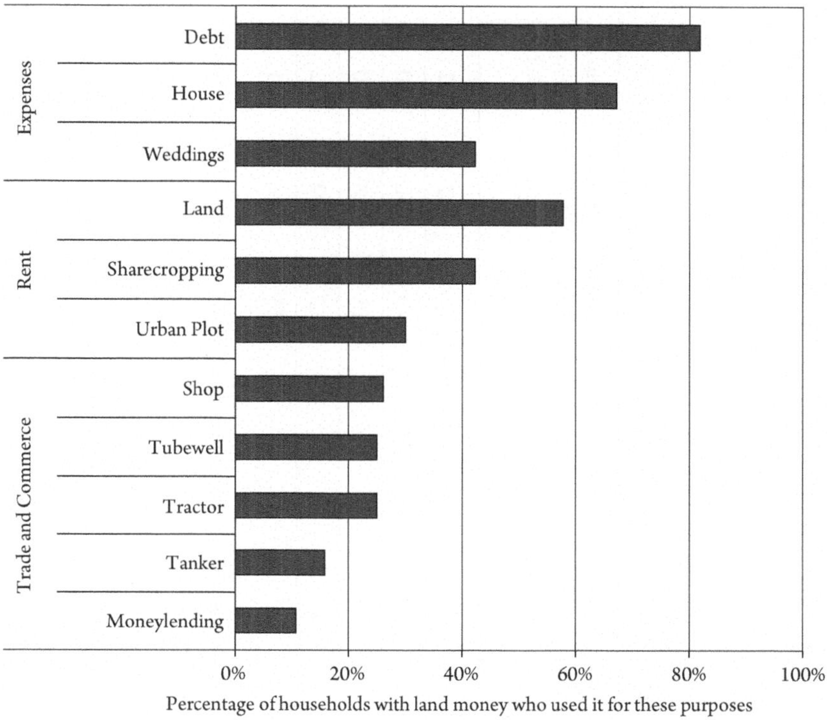

Figure 7.2 Allocation of real estate earnings.

rent to (mostly skilled) migrant workers or to the private college students who started appearing after 2012. But house construction was also more generally an investment in status which could be converted through various routes back into economic capital. Most obviously this conversion worked through marriage, on which 42% of families spent land money (not including the allocations to prior debt, reported previously, that may have accrued from marriages). Concrete houses improved marriage prospects, which not only increased the dowries one could expect (for a son) but bought better in-laws. While villagers once looked for in-laws with farmland, a clear preference was emerging for marriage partners closer to the city with urban employment. An acquaintance of Mahesh's in a more rural village was, for example, passed over for marriage by one of Mahesh's neighbors because he had a *kaccha* house; they settled on a TV repairman with a shop on the highway. Matrimonial strategies, and the "practical kinship" (Bourdieu 1990) networks they generated, were investments in social capital that were becoming only more important. But to buy good in-laws one had to "ante in" by investing in markers of status—a concrete house had become a basic minimum for a "good match"—and the competition only led upward. Marriage expenditures themselves—how many people were invited, how large

Table 7.1 **Allocation of Real Estate Earnings by Caste**

Caste (No. of Households)	*Paid off debt (%)*	*Built house (%)*	*Married children (%)*	*Bought land (%)*	*Became absentee landlord (%)*	*Bought urban plot (%)*	*Started small shop/ business (%)*	*Drilled tube well (%)*	*Bought tractor (%)*	*Bought tanker (%)*	*Gave loans (%)*
General (9)	56	78	78	67	33	22	44	44	33	22	22
Jats (10)	80	60	40	80	40	30	50	70	40	30	10
OBC (13)	85	61	46	54	46	30	23	0	15	8	0
SC/ST (25)	92	68	28	48	44	32	12	12	2	12	12
All (57)	82	67	42	58	42	30	26	25	25	16	11

Note: This table includes all households (n = 57) who received any type of income from land transactions, whether land sales, plot sales, or brokerage commission. An earlier version of this table appeared in Levien (2011). Reprinted with permission from John Wiley and Sons.

the dowry, one or two *sabzis* (vegetable dishes), the poor man's *barfi* or the rich man's *ladoo*—also became points of competition.

Beyond weddings, some successful neo-rentiers invested lavishly in displays of religiosity: Laduram and Mahinder both sponsored *pujas* and feasts; two brokers built a Durga Mata temple in front of their new houses, complete with murals, loudspeakers, and an electronic drum. For neo-rentiers aspiring to office, these investments had a political function that I return to in the next chapter. One can split hairs about whether these expenditures on houses, marriage, and ritual were investments or consumption. At the level of households, investments in status could indirectly yield economic returns; at the same time, increased status competition pressured everyone to divert capital from much more directly profitable avenues, putting a squeeze on poor families who had fallen behind erstwhile peers. At the level of the local economy, these expenditures recycled land money into the construction industry, further land rents (extra rooms and marriage gardens), and petty trade (wedding supplies, tents, and household appliances), thus connecting to our next category of investment.

A majority of farmers put land money back into land—specifically farmland in more remote villages or urban plots. Overall, 58% of families with land earnings bought land, though Jats (80%) and General Castes (67%) were much more successful at it than OBCs (54%) and SC/STs (48%). Since most did not want to—or could not—shift their houses to far-off villages, the majority of those who bought land became absentee landlords expropriating one-third of a monsoon millet crop from tenants. Thus while only 8% of households rented out land before the SEZ's arrival, 42% of households who received land money did so after. Ironically, then, the entry of the most advanced sectors of the Indian economy into rural Rajasthan led to an *expansion* of rent-in-kind sharecropping. For many smallholders, as we saw in the last chapter, this was a net loss—often the land was less productive, they received a one-third share rather than the full crop, it was difficult to supervise tenants, and they had to incur transportation costs. But we also saw that some farmers established themselves as large absentee landlords. Significantly, I found little evidence that any of these landowners were investing in the agricultural productivity of their holdings. For the savvier investors, moreover, rent-in-kind from their tenants was only a short- to medium-term strategy until the land appreciated. Such farmer-speculators bought land looking not for better soils but for capital gains—just beyond the existing urban frontier or in the vicinity of highways. Real estate capital thus reverberated out from SEZ-affected villages to transform the land markets and agrarian relations of more peripheral villages. The search for capitalist ground rent also led 30% of farmers with land money to buy urban plots in some of the many residential colonies that were sprouting up on the outskirts of Jaipur or in expanding small towns near the highway.

Just over a fourth of households used their land money to start small businesses. The market in Rajpura was transformed from a handful of shops run by the "traditional" *banias* and artisanal castes to a bustling profusion of sometimes redundant enterprises run by non-traditional merchants. These shops included general provision stores, mobile phone and photo shops, *chai* and juice stalls, small vegetable carts, tire-puncture stalls, motor-cycle parts and repair shops, home appliance stores, clothing and shoe stores, and two small eateries (*dhabas*). A significant proportion of these shops were owned by farmers from neighboring villages who had not been dispossessed but benefited from real estate appreciation. At first these businesses mostly catered to the newly commercialized needs of dispossessed farmers and the growing consumer demands of those with land money in the bank (or dresser, to avoid taxes). But by the time of my 2014 revisit, outside traffic had increased significantly, and a daily stream of people—truck drivers, chauffeurs, migrant workers and supervisors, students from the new colleges—had substantially expanded the village market.

Calling these small businesses forms of self-employment or informal enterprise would be correct but undiscriminating: there was huge variation in their profitability. For many dispossessed farmers—especially the lower-caste semi-proletariat—these were "strategies of minimal survival" (Burawoy 2001: 47) and a stop-gap measure against proletarianization. Recall Mahesh's erratic foray into the now competitive vegetable vending business, or the potter's shuttered tobacco kiosk. Ismail Khan opened a tire repair business in the market when there were only two, but soon there were six. One Gujjar who opened an electrical supply store reported making only Rs 2,000–4000, explaining, "What to do? The kids have to be fed, we're uneducated. I was doing *mazduri* before." A photo shop owner and a *chai* stall proprietor similarly reported incomes that were less than construction wages, and many referred to their business as a "time pass." Many businesses quickly failed, such as a small eatery opened by several Mali brothers (who play an important role in the next chapter), a shop opened by a lower-caste broker (who wound up renting it to the goldsmith), and even the small shop of a traditional *bania*. Village shops went through significant turnover, and at least a dozen storefronts were shuttered at any given time. These informal enterprises can be seen as disguised wage labor, but it is important to understand that *farmers invested in small enterprises precisely in order to avoid wage labor*. Even at the same level of income, being a small proprietor was immensely preferable to being a footloose proletarian at the mercy of contractors and fickle labor markets.

Yet some of these businesses were far more than survival strategies. Chapter 5 provided several examples of profitable mercantile investments: Mahinder Singh's construction business, Laduram Meena's apparel store, Mahinder Choudhary's juice and cold drink shop, Mohan Nayak's *dhaba* and "sex hotel,"

Kanaram Regar's integrated vegetable stand/supply business, and Ram Bunkar's tire puncture kiosk. Several Brahmins in Shivpura had opened up moderately profitable businesses supplying tents and cooking equipment for weddings, while another nephew of Laduram Meena set up a profitable digital photography business. Increased traffic increased the scope for repair shops—a few young men had learned to service motorbikes, and while there were no car repair shops, there were several shops for fixing flat tires. Success changed over time, with many more businesses struggling during my first round of fieldwork but a growing sense of buoyancy when I returned in 2012 and 2014—corresponding to the resurgence of the real estate and construction market.

This booming real estate and construction market created new small businesses and increased the profitability of some existing ones. Two brothers from the Lakhera (bangle-maker) subcaste had, for example, by 2012 added Coke and Pepsi "chillers" to their adjacent provision store and *chai* stall. One estimated that business was up 20%. Another Lakhera shopkeeper had, prior to the SEZ, run a small shop selling ready-made jewelry, accessories, and various household goods. While noting other losses from the SEZ, he explained that, "After the SEZ came, our business has grown a lot." Pointing to his merchandise: "Before we did not stock so much. . . . Before, profit was Rs 1,000. Now it's 5,000." By 2014, he had opened a second shop for "ladies apparel" run by his wife. Barbers reported having more customers, even though there were now six instead of two. The village goldsmith (Soni) was profiting from increased wedding expenditures, and moved his shop into the main market to capture non-village customers. A young shoe-seller who used to harangue me for hours became, by 2014, too busy hawking shoes on many evenings to talk. And while the three families of *banias*, the traditional merchant caste, no longer had a monopoly on the retail trade, the overall increase in demand compensated for the increased competition. They reported business being up—and the one who shuttered his shop had, by 2014, at least started a small Ayurvedic dispensary of moderate profitability in a small room on his second floor.

While most of these businesses were only indirectly related to the SEZ, the main direct—and most classically "productive"—linkage to the SEZ was in construction. The construction companies building the SEZ were willing to use local suppliers to save on transportation costs. Each company maintained connections with three to four suppliers for each material. I was told that there were as many as ten to fifteen suppliers in the village, though I met fewer than that. They were mostly, though not entirely, from the village elite—Jats, Laduram Meena's nephew, Mahinder Singh. Table 7.1 shows that 25% of households invested their land money in tractors, which typically cost around $8,000. But in Rajpura tractors were no longer primarily an agricultural implement. They had, instead, two main non-agricultural functions. The first was transporting construction supplies with a hitched-on trailer. These trailers could be seen daily moving through the village market. At first, investment in non-tractor methods of transportation appeared so insignificant that I did not think to include it in my survey. But by 2014, I noticed more village men who had invested in lorries of various sizes. Several were from Muslim families who had some prior family experience in the construction business. With his tire repair shop becoming less profitable, Ishmail Khan had, for example, bought a small lorry for transporting supplies. But he explained that there were now ten other such lorries in the market and he was only making $80 to $100 per month. More successfully, Ahmed Mohammad had bought a larger lorry (costing $36,000) and was making $1,000 per month carrying sand from Tonk to the Mahindra World City.[12] Asim Hussein had taken over his father's construction business and financed a newer truck with which he supplied contractors with sand, gravel, and stone. After driving for seven years, he was now employing one to two drivers and making $600 to $800 per month. Laduram Meena's nephew Banshi had bought a similar truck and, with his uncle's contacts, was deploying it profitably with paid drivers.

The other main use for tractors was selling groundwater to Mahindra, other builders, and even fellow villagers. Twenty-five percent of farmers used land money to drill tubewells, but these were almost entirely Jats and Brahmins who still had land. Some bored these wells for home water consumption and minor irrigation, but many did so with the express purpose of selling groundwater. Sixteen percent of dispossessed farming families bought a tanker for this purpose. Although this practice could only expedite the depletion of the village's aquifers, the short-term logic of this investment was clear: the local water supply was entirely inadequate for the Mahindra World City and the surrounding residential colonies. In addition to the MWC's estimated requirement of half a million liters per day, there was the large volume of water necessary for construction (principally for concrete). Although the MWC was promised water from the Bisalpur reservoir, it took several years for this connection to be completed and it still went dry for part of the year—leaving the MWC (and Jaipur) in the lurch. Local farmers responded to the opportunity. Tubewells cost around $2,000 to drill, and could be anywhere from 150 to 550 feet deep. Tankers cost around $1,250. The prevailing price for a 500-liter tanker of water started out at $5, but quickly dropped to around $3 when suppliers multiplied; from this one had to subtract costs (electricity for pumping, fuel for the tractors, and, if one employed a driver, about $3 per day in labor costs). One relatively poor Brahmin in Shivpura bought his tanker and well with loans, and reported selling two to three tankers of water per day in 2010, netting a little over $4 per day before interest payments. He was effectively making just a little more than casual wage labor, and it would take him several years to pay off the debts. "What to do? We need to eat," he explained. Laduram Meena and his nephew, however, reported selling ten tankers per day during the summer, making about $400 to $600 per month. There were probably about ten water-sellers in Rajpura, and more from nearby villages (see Figure 7.3).

But selling water was a risky business. With water tables rapidly receding, some wells quickly went dry. Conversely, when water was more abundant after good monsoons, Mahindra could rely on its pipeline connection from Bisalpur and no longer needed local suppliers. Farmers could still sell to local villagers who were now dependent on tanker water for household use, but this was a much smaller market. The water business did not seem so lucrative in the end, leaving some small investors in the lurch. It was also, of course, a tragically short-term form of asset mining that commodified the village's underground aquifers and accelerated their disappearance.[13]

A final prominent outlet for land money was in good old-fashioned usury. Eleven percent of respondents and 21% of the General Castes reported lending out some of their land money—though there was likely substantial under-reporting both because of its residual stigma, and because some might not have thought to include casual loans to friends and family. Adding to this burgeoning population of new and non-traditional moneylenders were the proliferating small shop owners who provided merchandise on credit. The prevailing

Figure 7.3 Tractors pulling water tankers through the village market. Photo by author.

interest rate was 2% to 3% per month or 24% to 36% annually, which made moneylending a profitable and easy outlet for those with even modest real estate gains. Laduram and his nephew were large moneylenders, and even gave out loans at a higher interest rate for property investments. A number of Jats and Brahmins continued in their roles as landowner-moneylenders but with higher volumes of cash in circulation: in Shivpura I met an old Brahmin who now spent his days driving around the village in his new jeep distributing and collecting loans. But even some Dalits with modest land earnings entered into the moneylending business, leading the always-astute Lada to quip: "Those who before didn't even have grain and one meal per day are now giving loans." Land earnings also attracted requests for help from relatives and in-laws that could be difficult to refuse.

Borrowers were not hard to find, and mostly came from the proletarianized lower castes who, after land loss, were struggling to keep their heads above water. After paying off debts, many had quickly fallen back into it: 25% of dispossessed OBC families and 35% of SC/ST families reported having more debt than before land acquisition (42% and 24%, respectively, reported no change)—and this appeared to be only increasing as people's land money gradually dried up. The infusion of cash through land sales thus expanded the pool of village moneylenders filling the credit gap left by post-liberalization retrenchment in public-sector rural lending (Shah, Rao, and Shankar 2007), and profiting from the poverty of the proletarianized.

Curiously, then, the arrival of the Mahindra World City in Rajpura breathed new life into old forms of profit.[14] While land dispossession decimated agriculture, real estate speculation fueled forms of capital that were historically parasitic upon it: landlordism, petty trade, and usury. While farmers were drawn into this informal economy by high land prices and the desire to avoid complete proletarianization, they were also pushed into it by the limited linkages generated by the SEZ and the lack of stable wage labor it provided. Aside from construction, a rent-heavy industry closely tied to real estate, this economy was largely circulatory; it was fueled by dramatic real estate speculation that injected cash into the local economy; and it was thus now dependent upon the further expansion of the Mahindra World City. This aligned the interests of Rajpura's neo-rentiers and petty asset managers, in important but not all respects, with the SEZ; as the next chapter explores.

As a source of livelihood, this informal economy—reflecting what Davis (2006) calls "urbanization without industrialization"—was both a vibrant micro-capitalism and a purgatory for not-quite-proletarians: profitability within it varied tremendously, from Ranjan Gujjar's $3-per-day *chai* stall to Laduram Meena's numerous and highly profitable enterprises. An avenue of upward mobility for some, a last-ditch survival strategy for more, these informal enterprises did not give rise to a coherent petit bourgeoisie but to a highly differentiated stratum of people living from rent, trade, and interest rather than wage labor. The longer term sustainability of this pattern of growth—how many shopkeepers, moneylenders, and *chai* stalls can India's economy support?—remains beyond the scope of this investigation. The following chapter will turn to the implications of this pattern of non-industrial growth for class formation and politics. For now it seems sufficient to observe with Jan Breman (2010: 34) that the "industrial-urban order, of the sort which vastly improved the lot of former peasants of the Northern hemisphere, has not materialized." Indeed, one might say that the turn from public-sector-led agricultural and manufacturing expansion to enclaves of hi-tech and high-end real estate signals the Indian state's abandonment of its efforts to create such an order.

Reprise: Dispossession without Development

It is a well-worn cliché that India is a country of striking disparities, with islands of extreme wealth surrounded by a sea of poverty. State-directed developmentalism in the mid-20th century built an industrial base that broke the country out of colonial stagnation but failed to substantially redistribute wealth and came woefully short of assuring all of India's citizens a minimum standard of well-being. In rural India, the Nehruvian state bequeathed large pockets of deprivation and generally low levels of human development to its post-liberalization successor. In the 1990s, India's political leaders steered the country toward a neoliberal economic model that, by the 2000s, had accelerated economic growth. But this growth, as many scholars have shown (Bardhan 2010; Kohli 2012; Dreze and Sen 2013; Corbridge and Shah 2013), has come at the expense of even greater inequalities while making a disappointingly modest impact on poverty and human development. India's growth over the past two decades stands out, in comparative terms, as particularly exclusionary. Rajpura is a crucible that allows us to observe some of the mechanisms underlying this exclusionary growth. And an appreciation of these mechanisms will help us to understand, as Chapter 9 will demonstrate, why land dispossession is so contentious in contemporary India.

The historical specificity of the socio-economic changes we observed in Rajpura is brought out by comparison with the well-documented effects of the large public-sector infrastructure and industrial projects of state-led development. These projects, as Chapter 2 demonstrated, were productivist in orientation. Although large dams and public-sector industry contributed to land appreciation in their vicinity, land appreciation was not their main purpose or effect (indeed, government policy often sought to discourage it). Dams, for all their problems, delivered irrigation to hundreds of thousands of farmers, contributing to food output and agricultural accumulation. Although criticized at the time for their capital intensity, India's public-sector industrial towns were far more labor-intensive than today's steel plants—not to mention high-tech parks. They built a manufacturing base from scratch and generated, for at least a few decades, a labor aristocracy that included some dispossessed farmers (Parry and Struempell 2008). Both dams and steel towns had significant economic linkages, whether agro-processing or ancillary industrialization. And public-sector industrial townships sought to absorb rather than exclude surrounding rural populations (Sanchez and Strumpell 2014). Arguing that dispossession during this period was more productivist, labor-absorbing, and geographically even is not to defend it; these projects were only *relatively* more successful on these indices. Because of very poor compensation, they were often more uniformly impoverishing for the dispossessed than today, and their costs were also disproportionately borne by women (Mehta 2009). Although it was structurally easier to include dispossessed farmers in heavy manufacturing and commercial agriculture, there was woefully insufficient effort to do so. This is partly attributable to the fact that the dispossessed belonged disproportionately to politically marginalized indigenous populations (Fernandes 2008: 91–92). Large dams and other large infrastructure projects exhibited, moreover, many of the social, logistical, and ecological failures of "high-modernist" social engineering (Scott 1998). India's period of Nehruvian developmentalism was no golden age for dispossession; it was just dispossession for a very different form of capitalism.

Rajpura's farmers were dispossessed for the financialized and non-labor-intensive rentier capitalism that began in the 1990s and attained ascendency in mid-2000s India. The Mahindra World City was an exclusive enclave of high-end real estate and the "knowledge economy" that had little chance of absorbing dispossessed farmers into a stable, much less prosperous, working class; concentrated public and private investment inside an exclusionary corporate enclave; and generated little ancillary activity except for construction. With their destroyed agrarian assets outweighing the scarce, temporary, and low-paying positions available to them in the "knowledge economy," the fate of Rajpura's residents has come to be determined by their own ability to commodify land and to reinvest their capital gains into an informal non-industrial economy dominated by land rents, petty trade, and usury. This is remarkably different from the state-directed agricultural and industrial capitalism for which the Indian state dispossessed farmers for forty years after Independence. Dispossession in India today is being carried out by states that have abandoned the broad developmentalist aspirations of the past—before those aspirations could be realized.

India's new phase of capitalism is thus compounding the development failures of the past. With land speculation offering the primary avenue for upward mobility in the present, life chances in Rajpura are still strongly shaped by the arbitrary inequalities of pre-capitalist Rajasthan. The failures of land reform, that central promise of postcolonial nation-building (Low 1996), continues to reverberate in the unequal trajectories of Rajpura's residents in speculative land markets. The Nehruvian state's failure to invest in rural education continues to be felt in the vast distance between Rajpura's farmers and the knowledge- and capital-intensive sectors driving India's economy. And the failures of the Nehruvian state to provide twenty-four-hour electricity, piped water, health clinics, and other facilities to rural India helps to justify the current model of privatized and thus enclaved infrastructural provision that leaves a ten-foot boundary wall between Rajpura and a "world class" city.

Six years on, the consequences of this massive project for well-being in Rajpura were sobering. As Figure 7.4 shows, 65% of families and 88% of SC/ST families reported having "less income" after losing land for the SEZ; 50% of families and 75% of SC/ST families reported having "less food"; and 76% of families and 88% of SC/ST families thought they had received more loss than benefit from the SEZ. These findings are not only depressing in the aggregate, but lend support to macro-level studies which suggest that economic inequalities between castes may be growing in post-liberalization India (Desai and Dubey 2011; Deshpande 2011).

I administered the survey in 2011; it is possible that these assessments could change—or have already changed—as the SEZ develops over time. Barring a crash in the real estate market, the well-being of those who still have their compensation plots—disproportionately the landed upper castes—will most likely

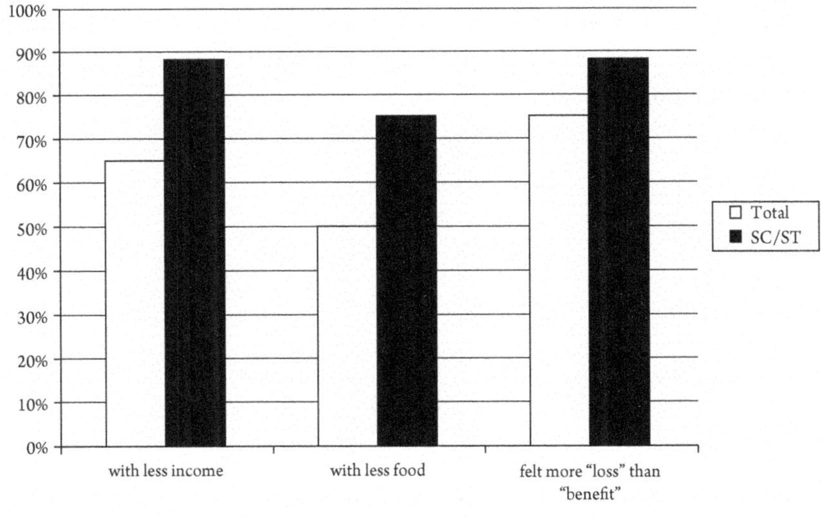

Figure 7.4 Effect of the SEZ on dispossessed households' income, food security, and subjective well-being.

increase once they cash out. Against this, the majority of the lower-caste semiproletariat cashed out long ago; those dependent on the village grazing land had no titled property to begin with; and real estate speculation—coupled with a gender-biased compensation scheme—has only reproduced women's lack of independent land rights and marginalization from the public sphere. For those who lost nothing—the truly assetless—the SEZ has been a very modest boon in the form of additional (but still sparse) low-wage casual work close to home. Short of a massive reorientation of the SEZ from high-end services toward labor-intensive manufacturing and significant investments in local infrastructure—with water being the most pressing—continued growth along existing grooves appears, at best, an extremely indirect way of improving the conditions of the rural poor. But it is a very good way of generating massive inequalities based, in complex but determinate ways, on those of the past.

Yet, the collision between the Mahindra World City and Rajpura is troubling for both "brisk metropolitan progressives" and "rural sentimentalists" (Williams 1985: 299). Neither an exclusionary and unequal process of social change nor a hierarchical rural village warrants idealization. Avoiding both romanticism and modernizing faith, and abstaining from a utilitarian weighing of "costs" and "benefits," this book has examined the empirical consequences of dispossession and put them in comparative perspective. What preceding chapters have demonstrated is that the causes and consequences of land dispossession have changed profoundly in post-liberalization India and that this change is not usefully understood as universal progress or homogenous predation. This is largely a matter of perspective, which varied not only between the dispossessed and the "outside" beneficiaries of their dispossession, but also between different fractions of the dispossessed. In Rajpura, as the next chapter shows, opinion was deeply divided. And this division also illustrates the shortcomings of the classical Marxist theory of dispossession. For dispossession did not plant the seeds of its own redemption.

8

Politics after Dispossession

There is no unity. Everyone builds their own house.

—Rajesh Bunkar

When the Mahindra World City arrived in 2005, Rajpura did not have a strong history of political mobilization. As Chapter 3 observed, I could find no evidence of a peasant rebellion in its past, nor was there significant participation in farmers' or lower-caste movements. Village politics was dominated by the *thakur* for decades after Independence and was only challenged in the 1970s by a Brahmin contender, who alternated with the *thakur* in power thereafter. This political history, declining water, substantial off-farm diversification, and a high level of inequality were all important factors explaining why there was no initial "land war" in Rajpura.

But lack of organized resistance should not be equated with consent (Scott 1985). As Chapter 4 demonstrated, villagers were not informed or consulted, much less given a choice about whether to give their land for the MWC. Their dispossession was decided for them by the Rajasthan government on behalf of a large private corporation. Compliance to dispossession in Rajpura was made easier by its pre-existing socio-economic structure and political history, but was produced by the compensation model that gave farmers stakes in the resulting land appreciation. This market-based compensation did not work simply by offering farmers higher prices. What was crucial, rather, was that the policy individualized farmers' relation to the project and thereby utilized pre-existing inequalities to dissolve any potential for solidarity that may have existed. Inequalities in economic, cultural, and social capital led different individuals to different assessments of how they could benefit from the SEZ and to different strategies for utilizing compensation plots. Some farmers, as the previous three chapters have demonstrated, ultimately benefited; but more insisted that they had suffered a grievous loss. This chapter examines how villagers in Rajpura responded politically to the socio-economic changes that followed their dispossession.

Politics after dispossession is structurally different from politics before dispossession. Once the land is gone, its former occupiers have far less leverage to make demands on the state or on the land's new owner. Although there are cases in which militant post-dispossession resistance—such as blockading factory gates—can halt a project, this typically involves strong organization and, often, support by political parties. Even where these are present, it has proved challenging for dispossessed farmers to re-establish possession of legally acquired land (Oskarsson and Nielsen 2014; Sampat 2015). It is far more likely for post-dispossession politics to be limited to bargaining over compensation and enforcing the promises made before dispossession. Such bargaining with state agencies or company officials is shaped, moreover, by any divisions that have emerged or intensified in the process of dispossession itself.

Politics after dispossession in Rajpura was shaped by the conflicting forces outlined in the previous chapters. On the one hand, there was deep and broad anger about the marginalization of village residents from good jobs and facilities inside the SEZ. Such common interests vis-à-vis jobs and village improvements provided the main objective basis upon which collective mobilization *could* have occurred. And these grievances were understood through an "agrarian populist" framework, such as that implied by predatory theories of dispossession, in which farmers as a whole were seen as the victims of outside urban forces. But this sense of shared victimization was limited and complicated by the sharp inequalities land speculation had generated within Rajpura. Differentiation by speculation divided interests and bulldozed the types of social relations that *would be necessary* for such collective action. The only protest that did emerge in Rajpura was organized by the neo-rentiers with the purpose of maximizing their compensation; a goal that also benefited some petty asset managers, but entirely marginalized the proletarianized and excluded. While relatively powerless and preoccupied with the struggle for existence, the proletarianized turned their anger toward brokers in a largely symbolic everyday "war of words" (Scott 1985). And brokers were only the flashpoint in a more pervasive division of interest and sentiment not just between castes but within castes and families. Differentiation by speculation was experienced as a rapid individualization that eroded the types of solidarity that would be necessary for collective action and channeled resistance into easily containable forms. A few holdouts and distressed grazers pursued individualized tactics, such as legal cases and petty encroachments. But in the absence of collective organization, these could only slightly modify the terms of dispossession. The electoral arena remained a very indirect way for villagers to express their grievances, and this largely took the form of voting for politicians who promised to bring the still elusive "development," which during my fieldwork included BJP candidates at the state and national levels.

In Rajpura, then, there were no signs of a populist village uprising against the SEZ or a radicalization of the proletarianized. In place of resistance or redemption, there was largely adjustment. Should we conclude that Rajpura's farmers largely support the form of neoliberal capitalism that consumed their land? This argument has been made not only by the modernization theorists discussed in Chapter 1 but also by anthropologists who have critiqued anti-dispossession social movements and intellectuals for ignoring how projects like SEZs resonate with the aspirations and "dreams" of villagers (Cross 2014). By looking closely at the aspirations of Rajpura's villagers *and* asking the extent to which they are *realizable*, this chapter reaches a different conclusion. Seen in the context of the pattern of capitalist development that consumed their land, the aspirations of villagers in Rajpura are almost utopian. Rather than the aspirations themselves, it is the structural impossibility of their fulfillment that, I suggest, will likely shape Rajpura's politics into the future. And this mismatch between subjective aspirations and objective possibilities is crucial for understanding the future of India's "land wars."

Aspirations and Objective Possibilities

Anthropologists have urged us to consider the extent to which projects of India's new economy—like SEZs—resonate with the aspirations of rural farmers. In his study of an SEZ in Andhra Pradesh, Cross (2014) argues that we should not think of SEZs as impositions by state and capital on unwilling farmers but as "dream zones" upon which villagers project their aspirations and remake them in the process. "Rather than attempt to evaluate the successes and failures of India's SEZs by subjecting the claims that are made for them to empirical scrutiny," Cross suggests that we should "think of them as generative social and cultural spaces" (2014: 188). The SEZ was, especially for the lower castes, "a space of promise and hope" (Cross 2014: 71). This subjectivist approach dovetails with an increasing focus of business consultants and political analysts on "aspirational India,"[1] now seen as a market segment and voting bloc.

But to understand their political implications, aspirations must be related to the objective possibilities for their realization (Bourdieu 1984). And this requires precisely that we subject the claims made on behalf of projects like SEZs to their actual outcomes. This is important because farmers do this themselves and this shapes their political behavior. And unrealizable aspirations, regardless of their surface alignment with dominant ideologies, can be interpreted as latent critiques of, rather than evidence of consent to, a given structure and trajectory of society. Recognizing this is necessary for understanding the conditions under which such critiques might become manifest and lead to social change.

The aspirations of Rajpura's farmers were undoubtedly concrete, though this has been no less true of *revolutionary* peasants in other times and places (Scott 1979). They were also discursively compatible with the claims made on behalf of the economic model that consumed their land. But if one asks, as one should, whether these aspirations are realizable by that economic model, then serious doubts begin to appear. Indeed, what was so striking about these aspirations was not how closely they resonated with India's neoliberal growth model, but how clearly utopian they were with respect to it.

Although observation was often more revealing than interviews, I asked many farmers about their desires, goals, and conceptions of "development." The latter term had broad purchase in Rajpura—as in much of rural India (Gupta 1998)—and was thus a good condensation of socio-economic aspirations. For most farmers in Rajpura, development meant, first of all, high quality jobs and facilities. The emphasis was on *good* jobs—*naukri* not *mazduri*, as Chapter 6 illustrated—and facilities *in* the village not in a gated enclave *next to* the village. Development, for the Dalit Prakash Bunkar, thus meant "increasing employment, services. Not in the SEZ, where they don't let us enter. In the village." For the young Brahmin *chaiwala* of Shivpura, "The meaning of development is that factories, schools, everything comes here. . . . If we can study here and work, then there is no hassle to go outside." When I asked him what kind of work, he was adamant: "Good work. It should be Rs 10,000 minimum," meaning $200 per month, which at the time was the starting salary of a back-office worker and roughly three times the wage of a casual laborer. In Rajpura, as for the young men described by Cross (2014: 68), "it was the promise of stable, secure, employment that lay at the heart of their hopes for the future." Few aspired to poorly paid and temporary wage labor through contractors. Not only did they want high-paying formal-sector jobs but, as Chapter 6 illustrated, they wanted their families to keep their land while they ventured into the urban labor market, cognizant that it was impossible to support their families otherwise. Finally, they wanted a solution to the pressing water problem. When I asked a group of women at Lada's house what was the most important thing for development, they answered unanimously and without hesitation: "Water. The water is bad here. . . . Second, employment." In other words, they wanted precisely those things which the SEZ had respectively depleted and failed to provide.

Aspirations in Rajpura were not only unrealized by the MWC but were at variance with the broader trajectory of capitalism in India. People in Rajpura aspired to good formal-sector jobs while policies of the Indian and Rajasthan states were advancing casualization and flexibilization.[2] They wanted to be managers and supervisors making at least $200 a month when such salaries were not only scarce but required a good BA and English-speaking abilities. Most simply, they wanted work while India's non-labor intensive growth model was systematically under-absorbing new entrants into the workforce. They also wanted facilities and infrastructure to be delivered to their village at a time when such investments were increasingly left to the profit motive of the private sector and thus confined to elite enclaves. And they wanted to keep their land and livestock while all this happened because they knew that the employment available to them was insufficient in their absence. Their ideal village was thus one in which the young received formal-sector jobs, the family kept farming, and the village had good roads, piped water, twenty-four-hour electricity, good schools, and a nearby hospital. This vision of development may be achievable, but even remotely realizing it would require a radical restructuring of India's political economy.

As the previous chapters have shown, these aspirations were not even approximately fulfilled by the Mahindra World City. Land dispossession imposed real costs, as detailed in Chapter 3, while benefits were slow in coming. Decimation of the agricultural economy at a time of high food price inflation pinched not only the incomes but food consumption of a majority of families. Anger about the enclosure of the village grazing land was almost universal: from the large commercial milk producer to the Dalit family with a few goats, almost everyone in Rajpura was deeply aggrieved at the loss of fodder and thus livestock. And while land dispossession had undermined agricultural means of production and subsistence, the jobs and facilities farmers expected in return had not materialized. There was thus a fairly broad feeling—across class, caste, gender, and post-SEZ household trajectories—that "farmers had received very little."

My survey—taken five years after the initial land acquisition—found that 76% of families and 88% of SC/ST families thought they had received more loss than benefit from the SEZ (see Figure 7.4). What this subjective sense of loss meant was not self-evident, as will become clear. But there was a broad feeling that farmers had gotten a raw deal, and that the SEZ's main benefits had flowed to "outsiders."

Victimized by Outsiders

Anger in Rajpura was at a low simmer for much of my fieldwork. Grievances toward the SEZ were strong and often expressed in an "agrarian populist" idiom. Agrarian populism, as a principle of apprehending the social world, rests on depicting peasant communities as the victims of outside urban forces (Byres 1988; Gupta 1998; Brass 2000). Because "peasant communities" are themselves often characterized by significant inequalities, agrarian populism can be seen as a simplification that can be activated, in certain times and places, to counter external threats. In Rajpura, as previous chapters illustrated, there were ubiquitous complaints that jobs were going to "outsiders" and that all facilities and infrastructural investment were concentrated inside the SEZ. As an OBC man pronounced to the approval of a group of Balai youth:

> Before the SEZ, they told us that we would get water, electricity, employment. . . . The SEZ people said that we will do this. But there hasn't been even one benefit. It is a complete loss. The work that the SEZ does give is through contractors. . . . Outsiders are coming here for work and we have to go outside.

"Rich" and "outsiders" were often used interchangeably. Although this conflation was becoming less accurate as land values increased and poorer migrant laborers arrived in Rajpura, the poor farmer versus rich outsider principle of dividing the social world could be upheld in relation to the large companies, private land investors, and IT professionals who were profiting the most from the Mahindra World City. It was used by the village rich and poor alike. Thus, even Bansilal Sharma, Brahmin ex-*sarpanch* of Shivpura, could claim, "The outsiders are eating the real cream and we are only receiving the fruit of our sweat."[3]

The outside forces victimizing Rajpura were perceived as a nexus between the rich and the state. Farmers were acute critics of the land broker state. Even many who ultimately benefited from their compensation plots refused to grant legitimacy to the process of land dispossession. In place of the legalistic Hindi term for land acquisition,[4] farmers commonly used words like "snatched" (*chhin liya*), "stole" (*chor liya*), "looted" (*luta*), or "seized" (*kabza kiya*) and emphasized that it was done "by force" (*zabardasti se*) rather than consent. Sitting under a tree by his demolished house and bulldozed fields, Haldiram Sharma questioned the unconsensual nature of government land dispossession: "The government should have *asked* us. The government didn't *ask* us anything." Another farmer explained, "People don't want to sell, so they took it *by force*."

Farmers were critical not only of the use of force, but of its use on behalf of the "rich" at the expense of the "farmer," "poor," or "common man." They identified the upward redistribution this involved in much the same terms I used in Chapter 2. As Motilal Sharma put it to me, "The JDA acts like a broker (*dalal*), and gives benefit to the capitalist class. The farmer hasn't received any benefit." Motilal was not alone in identifying capitalists as the main beneficiaries. As I walked away from a heated discussion at his *chai* stall, Kailash Sharma yelled at me, "Write this, Mike: the capitalists are looting the poor." The prevalent use of the Hindi verb *lutna* (to loot) suggests a broad perception that land acquisition amounted to theft. As one farmer observed, "From top to bottom, they are looting us." As a BMW carrying urban property investors drove past us in the village market, a butcher remarked, "They come from outside to loot us, all of them." Since "outside" investors and companies were generally richer than most villagers, the "poor" became expansive in such formulations. Thus, even a well-off Brahmin could observe, "Rich people are getting the benefit. The big builders and the companies are getting most of the benefit. The benefit for farmers is less."

Not only was the government (*sarkaar*) working on behalf of wealthy outsiders but it was lost on no one that its officials were lining their pockets in the process. On one of my first days in the village, a group of farmers quipped, "everyone from the peon to the head of the JDA is getting commission." Even Mahinder Singh observed, "JDA is a moneymaking machine for government and the bureaucracy. . . . And for the bureaucrats. . . . It is the biggest land grab agency." Politicians' role in such land brokering was taken for granted—an assessment that was reinforced by a briefly lived episode of political mobilization, to be discussed shortly.

Dispossession for the Mahindra World City thus generated widespread grievances, which were filtered through an "agrarian populist" frame of a farming community victimized by outside urban forces (Gupta 1998). On one side were the "rich" (*paisewales*), which included the land broker state and its officials, Mahindra and the companies inside the SEZ, private investors that bought up plots and farmland, and the educated IT sector workers who took all the good jobs; and on the other were the "poor" farmers who received comparatively little. Even the village elite who benefited massively from land speculation and brokerage participated in this narrative. Indeed, they had an interest in emphasizing it. For while Rajpura's neo-rentiers sought to portray themselves as part of the "poor farmers" victimized by the nexus of government and capitalists, the proletarianized saw the neo-rentiers—and especially the brokers—as themselves part of this nexus.

And this is where the agrarian populist frame faced its limits and faltered. While marginalization from the SEZ created broad grievances, a shared sense of victimization by "outsiders," and a trenchant critique of the land broker state, differentiation by speculation had divided the village from within. And this proved to be far more powerful. Rajpura's farmers were ultimately more divided among themselves than united against the "outsiders" profiting from their former land.

Differentiated Interests

By promising quick riches without work, real estate speculation incited the aspirations of many in Rajpura. But Chapter 5 demonstrated how these aspirations were differentially realized across social space. And it was this *unequal realization* that most profoundly shaped opinions and political behavior in Rajpura. For those who profited, real estate speculation offered a substitute for otherwise inclusive development. Despite their acute critiques of a land brokering state government and their exclusion from jobs and facilities, a significant enough fraction of the village benefited handsomely from the SEZ-induced land boom. Although many of these still considered the forcible acquisition of their land illegitimate, this was a moot point. Attitudes toward the SEZ boiled down to individual success in real estate.

Rajpura's neo-rentiers were basically on board. Sitaram Meena, farmer and public utility retiree who built a sprawling California-style family compound with his tremendous real estate windfall, told me over tea in his (anomalous) front yard, "The SEZ is excellent, for us. . . . It will be an excellent place. It was just jungle before." As a Brahmin *dalal* put it, "I'm happy that SEZ has come. Land rate has increased." A Brahmin school teacher with rapidly appreciating land remarked, "I think it's a good thing that SEZ has come. If it didn't come, it would take fifty years to see this kind of progress." Another Brahmin explained the benefits of the SEZ in the most precise possible terms: "We had a little land, we sold and doubled our land. We built a shop and now we don't have to work." When I remarked to one Brahmin farmer in 2014 that he was now sitting on land worth tens of millions of rupees, he smiled with satisfaction: "Before we were Bangladesh. Now we are America." Many of the petty asset managers agreed, even if the magnitude of their gains was far less and some still harbored anger at brokers who benefited far more. Their small plots and businesses aligned their interests with the Mahindra World City.

So while the neo-rentiers and petty asset managers shared in the common disappointment with the lack of jobs and facilities, their main concern was getting the maximum exchange value for their land. They were angry about dispossession, but mostly because this deprived them of the land's full market value. Whereas they had received plots one-fourth the size of their land's original acreage, farmers outside the SEZ's footprint could freely sell their land at full market value. "Government ate 75% of the land," went the common complaint. As one Brahmin put it, "They *take* land from us, why did they *take* it? . . . If Mahindra [had] bought it directly from us, we'd get good money and buy [land] elsewhere, and we'd be happy."

The distinction between dispossession and free market sale materially and subjectively divided the nearby village of Premdhani. Farmers on one side of the village road had their land acquired for the SEZ and received compensation plots; on the other side, many sold their land to the private Omaxe City residential colony for very large sums, or were still holding out for more money. Comparing the deal on each side, Haldiram Sharma concluded, "Better if it was Omaxe." Free market exchange provided the basis for the neo-rentier critique of dispossession. Their dissatisfaction boiled down to what I have called the rate of accumulation by dispossession, which they readily estimated by comparing the value of their compensation plots to the present market value of surrounding farmland.

Although private land values would not have gone up so dramatically without the SEZ being located in Rajpura, they still felt comparatively short-changed.

With land dispossession a fait accompli, however, the neo-rentiers' most salient grievance was that the JDA had failed to develop and hand over their compensation plots. Throughout my fieldwork, the actual physical plots were nothing more than white boundary markers on disused agricultural land. As one farmer put it, "They make an effort to seize but not to give."[5] Even a JDA official admitted to me, in private, that there was little political will to develop the "resettlement" colonies—a misleading term since, as we have seen, a majority of the plots were quickly bought by large companies and wealthy investors. To add insult to injury, the JDA was demanding expensive lease fees in order for farmers to take possession: while this was a standard fee for the conversion of agricultural land to urban, it was not one that farmers expected to pay after being involuntarily dispossessed of their land. The JDA's handling of the compensation plots generated extreme anger among those who still retained them. But their demands were modest: the JDA should build the infrastructure and deliver the plots. As Banvarilal Sharma explained: "If we get land, we'll be happy. It's like this: they promised developed land. There should be gutters, electricity, water, roads. They don't even have boundaries. We don't know where it is." A few Brahmins also had non-monetary objections to the plot system: the random assignment of compensation plots by lottery threatened to undermine caste-based residential segregation (although the majority of lower castes had already sold their plots and thus would not be living there). But ultimately, the material motive was foremost. The poor state of the plots, and the fact that their values plateaued for several years after the 2008 financial crisis, helps to explain why even some who had clearly benefited from the land boom were among those who reported, in my 2011 survey, that they had received "more loss than benefit."

And many who were angry at the slow rate of plot development were in a noticeably lighter mood by 2014. By then, the global financial crisis had abated, new companies were coming into the SEZ, and the land boom had returned: the price of compensation plots had multiplied *tenfold* from 2011. This turned even very small plots of land into lottery tickets. Chapter 6 told the story of Prakash Bunkar, the frustrated driver who saw his fortune potentially change as his miniscule plot appreciated massively. While he was one of the most vocal and articulate critics of the SEZ during my initial fieldwork, his tune had changed when I visited again in 2014. He explained, "There hadn't been that much development then. Now the plots are worth *crores*. . . . When you came before [the price per square meter] was Rs 1,200 to Rs 1,500. Now it is Rs 15,000 to Rs 20,000." Among those who had managed to hold onto their plots for the past nine years, there was a palpable giddiness; land prices of this magnitude could substitute for "development," more broadly conceived.

Of course, a majority of lower-caste villagers had *not* managed to hold onto their plots. The happiness of the neo-rentier was inversely related to the unhappiness of those who, through a combination of factors—including economic necessity, lack of information, and *dalal* malfeasance—had already liquidated them at retrospectively low prices. Chapter 5 demonstrated that this included just over half of total households, 82% of Scheduled Caste households, and 58% of OBC households. While a little less than half of SC/ST households were able to buy land elsewhere, this was usually in far more remote villages outside of the SEZ's orbit where land had only agricultural value. A majority of smallholding lower castes were either proletarianized or—like Lada and Mahesh—barely holding onto very small assets. While fellow villagers became fantastically wealthy and built rural mansions, those who sold their land cheaply ruefully watched the value of their former land multiply exponentially. Their complaint thus also boiled down to their share in, not the fact of, land commodification. As one Dalit put it, "Everyone has become wise only after they have been ruined. It came late." They had lost a winning lottery ticket.

Or had it stolen, as many saw it. For while some of the proletarianized blamed themselves, many blamed their fellow villagers-cum-brokers who had made money at their expense *in alliance with outsiders*. I will discuss shortly the anger this generated toward village brokers. But the immediate point is that those who sold their land quickly now had no "stake in the game" of land markets and nothing they could demand from the government or SEZ on that score. The most they could hope for now were jobs in the SEZ, facilities in the village, and some solution to the water problem. These were also the hopes of those—like the sweepers—who had no land but had an interest in expanding employment and village improvement. While a few sweeper families had at least a handful of sanitation jobs to point to, the majority of the landless—including the Bavariyas, herders, and those without clean title—had seen no concrete improvement in their lives.

But while the problems of employment, facilities, and water ostensibly united the village, the neo-rentiers were far more interested in maximizing the value of their compensation plots than seeing to these pressing concerns of the village poor. And this basic division of interests was reflected in the single major instance of collective action in Rajpura.

The Struggle Committee

Before my arrival in 2009, the *sarpanches* of the nine affected villages organized a "struggle committee" (*sangarsh samiti*) that staged several protests against Mahindra and the JDA. Its leaders are by now familiar—Laduram Meena, *sarpanch* and mega-broker of Rajpura; Bansilal Sharma, sweet shop proprietor, broker, and former *sarpanch* of Shivpura; and Mahinder Singh, grandson of Rajpura's *thakur,* real estate mogul, and then soon-to-be *sarpanch.* These village "big men" received support from the local member of the Rajasthan Legislative Assembly (MLA) and head of the sub-district panchayat committee (*pradhan*). Through the *samiti,* they orchestrated two or three protests (*dharna*) in front of the Mahindra World City gates, in which a few hundred villagers blocked the entrance, prevented construction, and at one point even overturned a government vehicle. These protests were ultimately broken up by the police, resulting in several injuries and arrests.

Behind the militant tactics—now part of the generic repertoire of protests of the left and right in India—were modest demands. The *samiti's* organizers had no desire to stop the project; indeed, each of them had substantial interests in its continuation. Their demands focused instead on the compensation plots: they wanted to increase the compensation plot size from 25% to 50% of the original land and, more realistically, to speed up their construction and scrap JDA's lease fees. These demands reflected the interests of the neo-rentiers and petty asset managers who had retained ownership of their plots.

In response to the protests, the JDA agreed to drop its demand for expensive lease fees and promised to expedite plot construction. It did not fulfill the latter promise: for the next several years, construction moved at a snail's pace. But the *samiti* was dissolved and never revived. When I asked Mahinder, who claimed to be the *samiti's* leader, why it was no longer functioning, he explained, "JDA started listening to us." He was now letting things take their course through the system. Other villagers saw more sinister motivations; many believed that Mahinder and the other leaders were "bought off." A Brahmin from Shivpura explained, "We selected four to five people [as leaders] to resist SEZ policies, but the officers gave money to them and allotted them land at proper places. Then they quit and built their own houses. . . . Whether MLA, *sarpanch,* or *pradhan,* they're all builders." A similarly disgruntled Jat remarked caustically that politicians "came and said your land won't go anywhere. They spoke bullshit. They were bought out. After that, the movement broke up. People were angry."

The *samiti* was from the beginning limited in its organization and aims. Far from a grassroots "people's movement" of the kind that pioneered resistance to large dams in India, the *samiti* was a top-down instrument of the *sarpanch-dalals* who organized it, and thus largely continuous with the pre-existing pattern of local politics. Although the *sarpanch-dalals* tapped into local anger and mobilized some villagers to participate—mostly, from what I could tell, those with plots—there was no pretense of democratic structure. Mahinder matter-of-factly explained that "The *samiti* functions since I am coordinator. Most of the things I do. I believe in decentralization. But for this you need groups that have mental capabilities like you. . . . Which is a problem in our area."[6] From the beginning the *samiti's* goals reflected the interests of its elite organizers: maximizing the value of their compensation. These goals also largely corresponded with those of the petty asset managers, though the *samiti's* dissolution left them in the lurch since delays in plot construction imposed a much greater hardship upon them. But the *samiti's* goals were of no use to those most victimized by dispossession: the proletarianized and the excluded. Increased compensation would not help those who had already sold their compensation plots cheaply—through the very brokers organizing the protest. And the concerns of those dispossessed from the village grazing land without compensation, like the Bavariyas and landless pastoralists, were never raised. When I asked Mahinder what would happen to the families still living on the grazing land, he replied indifferently, "Who asked them to build on *panchayat* land in the first place?" There were no protests when they were subsequently evicted.

A fleeting and limited instance of collective action, the *sangarsh samiti* was an expression of village divisions more than solidarities. Discontent continued to brew in the village, but the possibility for collective action only receded further as the inequalities of real estate speculation further divided interests and eroded what village solidarities remained. When I asked angry and distraught farmers why they did not start a *sangathan* (a protest organization) to press for their demands, the common response was that "unity has decreased" (*ekta kam ho gaya*). But many farmers more explicitly mentioned *dalals*. An old farmer named Puranji, for example, attributed the lack of resistance to the fact that there are "lots of *dalals*" and, because of them, "many have sold." Another farmer explained: "There is no unity. The people of this village are *dalals*." *Dalals* were certainly not the only reason why strong collective mobilization failed to emerge in Rajpura; they were themselves an expression of the prior lack of unity in a class- and caste-divided village. But there is no question that *dalals'* alacrity at turning social relations into capital made them solvents of whatever solidarity may have existed. *Dalals* divided the village vis-à-vis "outsiders" and unleashed a bitter, but largely symbolic, struggle *within* Rajpura.

Solvents of Solidarity

Dalals were seen by almost everyone except the *dalals* themselves as having taken advantage of fellow villagers for their own enrichment.[7] Their connections with urban investors gave them privileged access to useful information about land markets, but rather than share this information with fellow villagers, they used it for their own advantage. More than failing to share information, *dalals* actively sowed misinformation and some, as we saw, crudely cheated illiterate lower-caste farmers. That they had done so in connivance with "outsiders" who were now reaping fortunes from the former land of other villagers was particularly galling. Those who felt cheated directed their anger not simply at "outsiders" but at the nexus of outsiders and the village elite: and the latter were far closer at hand.

Phrases such as "the *dalal*s looted us," "sold the village cheaply," "fooled people," "ruined us," "snatched land," and "took advantage of the common man," were *very* common in Rajpura. As one lower-caste man who had sold cheaply put it: "The influential got the highest benefit. . . . The *dalals* sold the poor's land. [The poor] were looted through deals. Because of the *dalals*, the farmers lost greatly." Another: "The ones who wanted to buy the land gave the information, so how was the farmer supposed to know? They said you will get 25%; they didn't say how much the price will go up. The rich took it and got benefit." "Eating" was, as in other agrarian contexts,[8] a popular metaphor for elite exactions in Rajpura, and was the term of choice for *dalals* (as with the labor brokers analyzed in Chapter 6). As Lada put it, "the *dalals* don't give a correct (*sahi*) price, they eat it. They buy low and sell high." Another youth complained, "They sold off the whole village's land [to others] . . . and ate commission." By aligning with outsiders to "eat" income that could have accrued to local villagers, brokers were seen as traitors. And their betrayal was seen as particularly egregious in such a serious matter as people's land.

Particular anger was directed at Laduram Meena, "the biggest *dalal* of them all." *Sarpanch* at the time of the SEZ's arrival and consulted by its developers and government officials, he apparently felt no responsibility for maximizing the welfare of fellow villagers vis-à-vis the SEZ. Instead, he treated his political position as an extension of his brokerage business, minting millions of dollars by encouraging fellow villagers to sell land through him at what he clearly knew to be low prices. Dinesh Regar, an illiterate Dalit who, as we saw in Chapter 5, claimed to have been tricked by Laduram into selling twice as much land as he intended, expressed the common evaluation: "He cuts people's throats after robbing their pockets. He completely takes advantage. The *dalal*s have benefited, not the farmers." One Balai man, in a particularly angry moment after being fired from his driving job, clearly connected the eating of "outsiders" and "insiders": "We will murder Mahindra, and all the people like Laduram Meena who are eating. We'll throw them out; it is our village, isn't it?" Another Regar who had sold cheaply described Laduram's role: "We didn't know how much the land would be worth going forward. . . . Villagers didn't know what would happen, what the scheme was. His job was to tell us. He did not educate the village. He had the information, but he didn't tell the village." Mahesh elaborated on the milk metaphor: "The *sarpanch* took the cream of the buttermilk, and divided the rest among everyone else. . . . He eats the cream and butter, and pours everyone milk. And even milk he doesn't pour."[9]

Such interpretations of broker immorality were predictably not accepted by *dalals* themselves. To begin with, most brokers used the English term "property dealer" to refer to themselves rather than the more stigmatized Hindi term *dalal*. In their eyes, they were not mere middlemen or fixers, but legitimate businessmen.[10] While many of them privately admitted to me that they facilitated land sales at "very low prices," they publicly dismissed the hostility of their fellow villagers as the envy of those who did not work hard, misspent their earnings, and did not know how to get ahead. The licitness of brokerage earnings was thus the subject of a symbolic struggle between brokers, who sought to portray their activities as normatively legitimate, and other villagers (especially the "losers" from land sales) who saw them as self-seeking and exploitative. This low-level and constant symbolic struggle—what Scott (1985) calls the "war of words"—largely played out as back-biting and slander, but occasionally broke into public disagreement in the vigorous public sphere of the village *chai* stall.

On one particular afternoon, I was sitting with a group of mostly OBC and SC farmers in one of the market *chai* stalls. The assembled were unanimously criticizing the government for snatching their land, the SEZ developers for failing to give them employment, and the *dalals* for cheating them out of their compensation plots. The *dalals*, they said, "take advantage of the common man." As we were speaking, a hefty Jat named Kalaram Choudhary got out of a new white Maruti-Suzuki car and walked over. As he approached, the others shot me a sly look. For my benefit, one of them posed to Kalaram the same question I had asked them: "Is there loss or benefit because of the SEZ?"

KC: The SEZ is good. There's excellent work inside it. . . . It's good for everyone.

FARMER 1: It's good for him because he gets rent.

KC: No, it's good for *everyone*.

FARMER 2: He's a rich man. A big man.

FARMER 1: He's a property dealer.

KC [WITH RAISED VOICE]: The SEZ is good for everyone. It's not bad for anyone. Very good work has been gotten. . . . Hard workers get work. The rest are sitting here [gesturing to the *chai* stall benches].

FARMER 3: He got money from being a commission agent and selling people's land. Then he used the money to buy a JCB machine and rent it out to Mahindra.

At this point one of the critical farmers turned to me and, returning to a question I had asked him earlier, said, "*These* people don't let us start a *sangathan*."

This exchange brought to the fore the main normative weapons available in the everyday symbolic struggle between brokers and other villagers. While Kanaram had clearly profited more than others by becoming a broker and reinvesting his earnings in an earth-moving machine, he was keen to emphasize that *everyone* had benefited. If some had benefited more than others, he ultimately conceded, it was because they were "hard workers." The losers—the present company included—were lazy by implication. But Kanaram's interpretation rested on portraying his *rental income,* with its cultural associations of passivity and unearned wealth, as *work.* And the other farmers refused to accept this: Kanaram had become wealthy, they repeatedly insisted, by virtue of "rent" and "commission." Not only was it impossible for Kanaram to convince them that collecting rent was a form of work, but the fact that his rent originated in "selling other people's land" made it especially ill-gotten.

My own presence and modest provocation in this case brought latent disagreements and backstage character assassination into the open. I witnessed many other disagreements about the SEZ's consequences for the village, although rarely between people of very divergent class and caste status. As the final comment suggested, Rajpura's politics were still dominated by "big men," almost all of whom were now brokers. Indeed, I observed in other instances that the arrival of a "big man" could change the tenor of a conversation completely. On my first visit to Rajpura, I was sitting outside of a small mobile phone shop with a group of farmers who had just finished telling me about the "clever" brokers who misled people into selling their land cheaply, when Shiv Choudhary arrived and the tone noticeably shifted. Shiv, to recall from Chapter 5, was from a rich Jat family with over 100 *bighas* of land, was Laduram Meena's real estate partner, and was reportedly the real power behind Laduram's candidacy for *sarpanch.* Although he had not sold his own land, he had made a fortune brokering the land of others.

Shiv began by saying that villagers had not gotten any benefit: only diploma-holders had gotten jobs, and everyone else was unemployed. But as far as the land went, "People made a lot of money selling their land.... The problem is that they misused it.... Those who sold their land lived lavishly for two years, and now they are laborers." In Shiv's view, people drank away their money, squandered it on large houses, and would have been fine if they had "systematically invested their money." This standard-fare blame of the victim is remarkable only because the other farmers remained silent. The enduring power of "big men" in the village pushed much critique of them into the "private transcript" (Scott 1990).

If constrained from expressing it in front of the bigger and politically influential brokers, few villagers actually accepted brokers' normative interpretation of their behavior. Brokers could argue that farmers willingly sold and misused their funds, but their activities remained too far beyond the normative pale to be considered legitimate. As in the Malaysian village studied by Scott (1985: 225), in Rajpura "new opportunities for 'profit-making' have far outpaced the normative means available to justify taking full advantage of them." Brokers' attempts to morally launder their economic gains—through building temples, sponsoring *pujas,* and hosting feasts—largely failed.

But villagers were under no illusion that older norms still had any sanctioning power. As the village economy shifted even further from agriculture, there was anyway little need for economic cooperation across classes, making a peasant "moral economy" (Scott 1976, 1985) economically irrelevant. While brokers might still be sensitive to *chai* stall slander that eroded their symbolic capital, they were now starting to keep different company and had large houses to retreat behind.[11] While norms of fairness, honesty, respect for land, and general village solidarity vis-à-vis outsiders might inevitably have fallen by the wayside as the village urbanized, brokers' alacrity in turning their social relations into capital expedited the process. While the war of words against brokers was the main axis along which the emerging pattern of inequality in Rajpura was politically contested, such contestation was materially ineffective.

"There Is No Unity"

Brokers were lighting rods of discontent because they were seen as behaving unjustly toward fellow villagers. But they were also the cause and effect of a far broader fracturing of not just interest but sentiment in Rajpura. The prior unity of a class-, caste-, and gender-divided village should certainly be questioned; because I initially assumed there to be little, I was struck by the constant complaints of villagers that "unity has decreased," "tensions have increased," and "relations have been ruined." Such complaints can be interpreted as strategic components of the "war of words," in which nostalgic renderings of the past—specifically of a harmonious and moral village order—serve to critique the present (Scott 1985). But they also indicated a real transformation in social relations. While Rajpura was riven by class, caste, and gender inequalities before the SEZ's arrival, what I believe was most responsible for this sentiment was the fact that real estate speculation introduced unprecedented levels of inequality *within* castes and even within families. Such inequalities eroded forms of solidarity that would be necessary to sustain collective action. And they help to explain its absence even among the deeply aggrieved.

While success in real estate speculation corresponded, on average, with preexisting caste inequalities, there were also highly variegated outcomes within castes. This was partly due to the inescapable element of chance inherent to a speculative land market, which introduced some fluidity into social trajectories. But more significantly it was because success in land markets was shaped not only by landholdings but by market savvy and social networks. While landholdings within Dalit castes were unequal—largely because of variations in family size and thus subdivision—subtle variations in cultural and social capital could also translate into vastly different outcomes for those with comparable assets. So, while the Dalit castes with land—the Balais and Regars but not the landless Sangats and Ranas—did worse on average than upper castes, almost all of them had some relative "winners." In each *mohalla,* one could see at least a few ostentatious concrete and marble houses towering over the earthen huts of neighbors and even relatives. Perhaps more significantly, there was gradation between these extremes. The Balai *mohalla* I resided in was a rich site for observing such stratification and the pressure it exerted upon social relations.

Before the SEZ's arrival, the twenty-two households in the Balai *mohalla* consisted almost entirely of semiproletarianized cultivators. Although their holdings were too small—given the lack of irrigation—to entirely support families, they were relatively large compared to Dalit holdings in other parts of India.[12] They were also larger than those of the other Dalit subcastes in Rajpura. In the context of extremely high land values, this left greater scope for divergent gains in the land market. While socio-economic differentiation within the *mohalla* was largely within poverty before the SEZ's arrival, real estate speculation greatly magnified previously small inequalities.

Previous chapters illustrated how Mahesh and Lada, my hosts and landlords, were only tenuously keeping their heads above water, their lack of economic, cultural, and social capital leading them from one less-than-profitable endeavor to another. Down the lane was Prakash, who struggled as a laborer in the block print mills and then as a driver, but was poised for a change of fortune by virtue of his wherewithal to maintain one small plot. The young and entrepreneurial Sanjay, meanwhile, was running a profitable tire-puncture repair kiosk, but more importantly was formulating plans for his family's un-acquired highway-front land—not sold, likely on the advice of his uncle, who was deputy *sarpanch* under Laduram Meena. The houses along the *mohalla's* three perpendicular lanes not only contained many more varied stories, but expressed them.

Immediately adjacent to Mahesh and Lada was the *kaccha* house of Boduram, who had sold his land very early for a pittance—Rs 40,000 per *bigha*. His family was considered to be the poorest in the *mohalla,* his wife and daughters pitied for their "useless" father. The nicest house for most of my fieldwork was perpendicular to Mahesh and Lada's and belonged to the only *dalal* in the *mohalla,* not counting Mahesh and his one deal. Gopalal had previously been working in Jaipur and used a contact to cut a small number of deals and buy two plots. Until then, the most prosperous person in the *mohalla* was his brother, Ram Niwas, who had anomalously for his generation passed the twelfth standard and obtained a government job in an Ayurvedic dispensary in Jaipur. His neat brick house, the nicest in the *mohalla* before the land boom, now seemed modest. But while Gopalal's well-timed foray into land brokerage appeared to have paid off more handsomely than Ram Niwas' government job, Ram Niwas was shrewd enough not to liquidate his compensation plots like most others in the *mohalla*. When I returned in 2014, he had cashed out and completed construction on a towering three-story concrete and marble structure that was now by far the largest in the *mohalla*. Mahesh, whose family had a rather grudging relationship to the family of Ram Niwas, now expressed unhappiness with his own house. And so on. Each time I returned to Rajpura, some modest shift in the *mohalla's* economic and symbolic hierarchy could be discerned. Whereas before the SEZ's arrival, there were only one or two households with their heads slightly above generalized poverty, the *mohalla* was now the site of substantial inequality.

The consequences of these new inequalities for "relations" (*rishte*) in the *mohalla* were much commented upon. The major theme was how *rishte* had given way to greed (*lalach*), arrogance (*ghamand*), and envy (*jalna*: literally to burn). One day I asked Lada whether she thought people in the *mohalla* were happy, and this got her started:

> People are not happy. They are envious. Say you come to have money. If I have money, then I don't think anything of you. I don't talk to you. Here people do not consider each other humans, they consider each other money. They worship those who have money.

Lada acknowledged that there were always feuds and jealousies in the *mohalla,* but insisted that they had increased. Those with money became arrogant while those without money became jealous. Some people in the *mohalla,* including women, no longer talked to each other. Ram Niwas, she thought, became jealous after Mahesh and Lada built their house and no longer spoke to them. "Before they would come here to talk, now they don't. . . . If we're sitting here, he thinks that we must be cutting him." Always reflexive, Lada laughed, "If I get money, I also might not talk to you!" Neighbor Rajesh Bunkar concluded literally and metaphorically, "Everyone builds their own house."[13]

Such observations were hardly unique to the Balai *mohalla.* Villagers commonly complained that people didn't sit or smoke together anymore; that they sold rather than shared milk and buttermilk; and that they generally didn't help each other out. A young Jat farmer explained, "The government has made some tension between the village." His friend Sanjay confirmed, "Relations have become less." An SC farmer described it more starkly as "complete enmity" (*bilkul dushmani*). Mohammed Khan, an elderly Muslim man, complained that "people had sold their faith," "given up their decorum," and even drew on the (Hindu) Bhagavad Gita to suggest that people had lost the path of *karmayog* (roughly: righteous and disciplined action). "So much sin has come. . . . Everything is ruined," he insisted. Another farmer complained, "People don't believe in relations or caste anymore. Unity has become less." By caste, he did not mean the caste hierarchy; but rather the solidarity of one's own caste.

Such laments of a passing moral order, hardly novel in the annals of rural ethnography (cf. Scott 1985; Gupta 1998: 134–136), should be read at more than face value. For one thing, many elements of the old order were clearly oppressive for the poor, lower castes, and women; when such people dipped into the past, they did so selectively for just those elements that contrasted with disagreeable aspects of the present (Moore 1978: 351–352; Scott 1985). No one had nostalgia for crushing rents, forced labor, or caste oppression. For another, as Lada acknowledged, feuds, factions, and jealousies were a pervasive aspect of village life before the SEZ's arrival, as they probably are in most villages.[14] And finally, the village had clearly not been transformed into a Hobbesian war of all versus all. Villagers continued to cooperate with each other for a limited number of purposes on a variety of scales. For these reasons, I draw a careful conclusion from these ubiquitous complaints: many people in Rajpura perceived that social relations they valued were being eroded; and they attributed this erosion to the massive influx of real estate money since the SEZ's arrival. My interpretation is that these complaints had less to do with nostalgia for the old order as a whole than with the introduction of vast new inequalities into units of social life in which they were previously muted, and from which people were most likely to expect solidarity and reciprocity in the past. In addition to one's subcaste, this included one's kin.

The divisions generated by land speculation reached into the publicly sanctified, if always troublesome, domain of the family. What many of my informants found most disturbing was how the land boom created—or magnified—conflicts among kin. Central to kinship relations is, of course, the question of inheritance (Mayer 1960: 246); and an important backdrop to these conflicts was the subdivision of jointly held family property. Under the Hindu Succession Act, ancestral land is divided among heirs upon the death of its owner. In practice, joint families often continue to cultivate the land together; or divide the land in practice but not on record. When land was forcibly acquired for the Mahindra World City, compensation plots were put in the joint name of all the land's legal owners (which was often multiple brothers, but could also include the sons or widows of a pre-deceased brother). But the high and increasing value of these plots encouraged their sale or division. The real estate boom in farmland around the SEZ, moreover, encouraged the rapid subdivision of previously undivided family property. As Figure 8.1 shows, the number of subdivisions per year in Rajpura spiked dramatically during the land boom as families sold out and brothers divided up their shares. This often, but not always, resulted in the dissolution of joint families. Division into separate households is not in itself indicative of increased conflict: land money

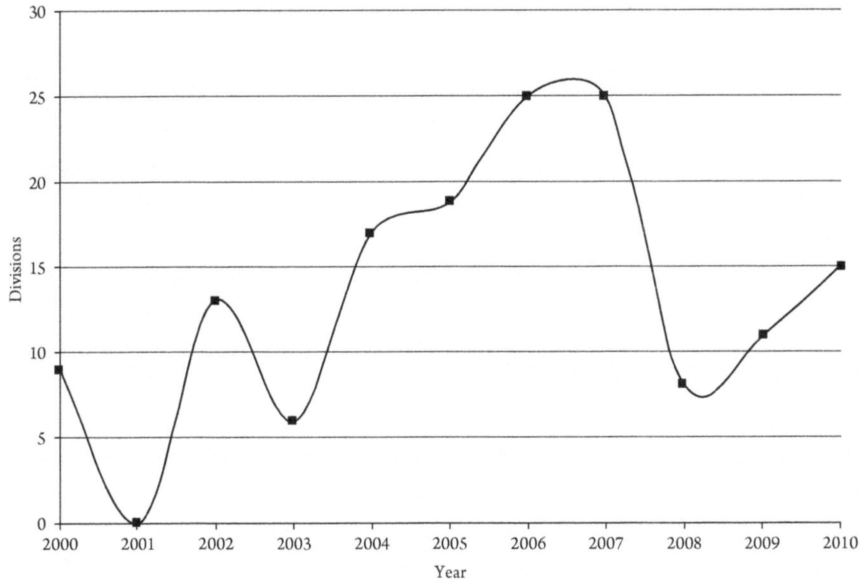

Figure 8.1 Subdivision of land among heirs in Rajpura. Source: Rajpura Land Records.

could simply provide the means for establishing independent households where the desire already existed. But partitions are seldom free of contention (Mayer 1960: 241), and increased land values only increased the stakes. The subdivision of joint property, moreover, expanded the possibility for distinct and unequal trajectories among siblings. And these new intra-family inequalities stoked envy.

In Rajpura, I was repeatedly told stories of land money generating fights between brothers. Although this "closest genealogical relationship" may often be "the site of the greatest tension" (Bourdieu 1990: 170), it is also one of the most sentimentalized. For villagers, calling attention to increasing tensions between brothers was meant to emphasize the degree of moral decline. There were stories of brothers running off with compensation; of disagreeing over whether or not to sell; and even of brokers convincing their own brothers to sell for commission. The Nai (barber) family next door to Lada and Mahesh, for example, did not get its full share of compensation because the ancestral property was registered in the name of the father's older brother.

There were also fights between brothers and sisters, a relationship subjectively infused with expectations of protection and love, but objectively underlain by material inequality. As discussed in Chapter 3, even though women are now legally entitled to an equal share of the family inheritance, in practice they are given dowry upon their marriage as a substitute for land. With land and compensation plot prices increasing dramatically in their natal village, a few married daughters came back to claim their share of the family inheritance, whether of their own volition or, as some suggested, at the behest of their husbands and in-laws. These claims were generally not accepted by brothers and were widely condemned within Rajpura—even by many women, a fact I return to later.[15] But the daughters had a good chance in court if they persisted. That such claims were made on only a minority of households despite their firm legal standing is a testament to the strength of patriarchal norms (see Agarwal 1994: 260–266; Chowdhry 2011).

While family fights were public knowledge in Rajpura, my extended presence in Lada and Mahesh's house gave me detailed insight into precisely how land speculation could fray kinship relations. Mahesh and his two brothers, as seen in Chapter 5, equitably divided their father's land and even jointly invested their compensation money in farmland in a more remote village. But Mahesh and his older brother, Kheemu Ram, quickly fell out over the price of the latter's empty storefront. By 2014, the conflict had proceeded so far that Kheemu Ram was working for Mahesh's main competitor as a vegetable vendor. This fight between older and younger brother was a constant source of tension in Mahesh's household. Although the most painful because the most proximate, it was not the only land-related conflict in the family.

Another ongoing dispute was with Lada's brother Prabhu, an uneducated laborer who drank heavily. One part of the family's small holding in Premdhani, Lada's natal village on the opposite side of the SEZ, was acquired for the SEZ and another part remained outside. Prabhu had already sold a compensation plot and failed to pay back a loan to Mahesh and Lada with the proceeds.[16] For this reason, they were not on speaking terms for much of my fieldwork. On Rakhi, the Hindu festival that celebrates the bond between brother and sister, Lada did not go back to her family's house to bestow blessings on her brothers, even though she would customarily receive *saris* or a few hundred rupees in gifts. The conflict grew much worse and engulfed the whole family when her brother threatened to sell the remaining land that was in possession of their widowed mother. One day, Lada's other brother and elderly mother came to the house to figure out how to stop him. They asked my advice, and I naïvely suggested that they try to approach the *patwari* (land records official) to prevent him from registering the sale. That night they instead went to a *maata devi* (exorcist) to try to expel the ghost (*bhoot*) that they believed to be possessing him. As I should have known, given my experience with the *patwari,* both strategies had approximately the same chance of success. As it turned out, they succeeded in subduing Prabhu, who was at least temporarily rehabilitated within the family and thereafter occasionally came to Lada and Mahesh's for dinner. On one such night, I saw Lada's mother lay on the guilt, recalling that in the old days they "had to make *rotis* with tree bark and *sabzi* from carrot tops. . . . We were so poor but still never sold the land. Now some money comes and they sell all the land." Prabhu looked down sheepishly.

In Rajpura, I believe family tensions were sharpening for several reasons. First, the land boom made the collective patrimony unprecedentedly valuable, which greatly increased the stakes of inheritance and subdivision. Subdivision, in turn, introduced previously unheard-of inequalities between brothers when they made different and differentially successful decisions about their shares and the reinvestment of their money; or when one became a broker. Second, with the dispossession of farmland the household was no longer—or was only minimally—a unit of agricultural production, which rendered unnecessary economic cooperation within joint families. Success in an urbanizing economy depended increasingly on forming ties to potential employers, business partners, merchants, brokers, and anyone who might be able to provide information, introductions, or a favor of some kind. Such "weak ties" (Granovetter 1973) could often be the property of an individual within the extended family; brothers, for example, often kept their own circles of friends and acquaintances.

They also had their own in-laws. While the decline of farming reduced the need for economic cooperation among immediate kin, more complete immersion into an urban economy increased the importance of what Bourdieu calls "practical kinship" (1990: 168, 180): "genealogically ambiguous relationship[s]" (Bourdieu 1990: 172) that are cultivated and maintained for their practical usefulness, although typically disavowed as such. Building practical kinship networks involved constant "maintenance work" (Bourdieu 1990: 170); and it was actually called work. While unemployed, Mahesh would often announce in the morning, "I have some work today." This "work" often involved a visit by motorcycle to a distant relative or connection. Such visits, which I sometimes accompanied him on, involved cups of *chai,* shared *beedis,* and a better-than-usual meal, often without any apparent agenda except reaffirming the connection and all-around good will. But weeks or months later, I would observe the same individual reemerge again in connection to some plan. This kind of "work" was constantly taking place in Rajpura. It was intertwined with matrimonial strategies, which were both a purpose and an outcome of practical kinship. While by no means new, such practical kinship work was greatly facilitated by mobile phones and the motorcycles that many farmers purchased with land money. And it had probably assumed much greater economic significance post–land boom, especially for the petty asset managers and neo-rentiers who had more time for it because they were not doing *mazduri* all day. It was not so much, then, that the importance of kinship was decreasing. Rather, the most proximate genealogical links were becoming more fraught and less useful, while extended ones were becoming more important.

Yet distant kin relations could also be fraught, especially when used in the brokerage economy. Chapter 5 showed how Mahesh entered a land deal with

Lada's cousin, and ultimately felt cheated when the cousin refused to pay him the entirety of the commission Mahesh thought they had agreed upon. Leading up to the deal, I had witnessed many meetings between the two, in which good faith was reaffirmed over cups of *chai* and *beedis.* But in the end, as Lada observed, "The whole relation has been broken because of money." While cousins through marriage is a good example of "practical kinship," the utilization of this relationship to broker land cannibalized the good will that had been so assiduously cultivated.

How these tensions between men in families and subcastes pertained to relations between women was not straightforward. While men strategized how to profit from land markets and increasingly clashed wills in the process, women—as we have seen—bore disproportionate costs of land dispossession and were entirely excluded from the ensuing real estate economy. Many struggled with men's misuse of land money as well as the ongoing prevalence of domestic violence. Women were also most affected by the cuts in NREGA and its poor implementation at the *panchayat* level. And women were the "objects" of the increasingly expensive and city-directed matrimonial strategies that were used to build "practical kinship." Women had many shared interests that cut across the households of which they were a part.

At the same time, women of different castes and classes experienced the SEZ's arrival differently. Previous chapters demonstrated that while many women in upper-caste or upwardly mobile families were confined to *purdah,* many lower-caste women were forced into the most precarious forms of wage labor. Even within lower castes, inequalities made their way into relations between women. In the Balai *mohalla,* where I was most allowed to observe the everyday interactions between women, ties of both solidarity and division complexly co-existed. In Lada's front courtyard, I was often present as several generations of women from different families gathered in conversation during lulls in the day's activities. These conversations often turned toward men's use of compensation money, domestic violence, and mothers-in-law. Sometimes they turned toward non-payment of NREGA wages and critiques of the village *sarpanch.* These discussions were also embedded in forms of everyday cooperation: exchanging dishes of food or missing ingredients, sewing together, and helping out when someone was sick or recovering from an operation. On one occasion, women went together to the *panchayat* office to—unsuccessfully—request work on NREGA. In some instances, solidarity between women prevailed over conflict between brothers: for example, the wife of the abusive Kheemu Ram would often come to Lada's for comfort and meals. But there were also many divisions and jealousies, which could lead to women not talking to other women within the same *mohalla* or even extended family. Although their houses were only 20 feet apart, the women in Ram Niwas' house rarely came over to Mahesh's, and vice versa. Women also shared interests and loyalties with their families, and were thus also caught up in the divisions between them. This explains women's disapproval, which I heard on several occasions, of married sisters coming back to claim shares of family property.

Differentiation by speculation introduced new inequalities at almost every social scale and this only attenuated the kinds of solidarities that *might* enable collective action. Even those who did share common interests and grievances could not rely on the solidarity of those relatively close to them in social space: those in their own castes and families. While differentiation by speculation distributed "winners" and "losers" unevenly across castes, it was experienced as a creeping individualization of life chances that reduced the homogeneity of interests within castes and families. This helps us to understand why collective action did not occur around acute and widely shared grievances. The livelihood strategies examined in previous chapters were the main ways in which most villagers in Rajpura responded to the rapid economic changes unleashed by the SEZ. Aside from cursing the *dalals*, the truly disgruntled were left to pursue individualized strategies of resistance vis-à-vis the SEZ.

Holdouts, Litigants, and Trespassers

There remained some individuals who, in a largely uncoordinated fashion, pursued various responses to the SEZ that might be described as "resistance." These included one family of holdouts, several families who filed court cases, and a number of people who engaged in petty trespass and sabotage. These strategies involved a relatively small number of people and mostly aimed at either negotiating the terms of dispossession or temporarily mitigating its effects. Some succeeded—or were likely to succeed—in increasing compensation or in prolonging previous land uses.

One family in Rajpura appeared determined to defend their land: Goverdhan Saini, his wife Rada, and the families of their six sons. The Sainis, who were of the OBC Mali (gardening) caste, owned 11 *bighas* of partially irrigated land, where they also kept their home and substantial herds of buffalo, cows, and goats. The day before my first trip to Rajpura, the Sainis had clashed with the police and Jaipur Development Authority—the altercation was even reported in the Jaipur edition of a major Hindi paper. The JDA had ostensibly acquired the Saini's land under the Land Acquisition Act and sold it to the Mahindra World City, which had sold it to the State Bank of India (SBI). SBI, India's largest public-sector bank, was planning on building its regional headquarters inside the zone's Domestic Tariff Area. But the Sainis refused to vacate, arguing that they had not received compensation and that their land had not been legally acquired. On December

12, 2009, when Jaipur Development Authority officials arrived with a squadron of police to take possession of the land, the entire Saini family confronted the police with fists and stones. In the ensuing fight, twelve family members were arrested, brought to a jail on the highway, and charged with obstructing government work. By nightfall JDA employees had erected a fence around the property and destroyed standing crops. When I arrived the next morning, the posts had been pulled up and the fence overturned. With much of the family still in jail, the JDA then erected a concrete wall around the Saini land, excluding a small parcel around their house.

For the remainder of my fieldwork, the Saini homestead was thus surrounded by a concrete wall on three sides. Inside their remaining compound were rows of vegetables irrigated by a gushing well, a handful of cows and buffalo tethered by a haystack, and an old house accommodating a large extended family. On the other side of the wall was the remainder of their agricultural land with most of its trees cut down. It was entirely enclosed except for a gated entrance facing the 250 Foot Road on the opposite side where a handful of security guards stood watch. But the Sainis quickly punched a hole in the top of the fence, built a dirt ramp on each side, and resumed grazing their livestock inside. For the next five years, the Saini family single-handedly obstructed the regional headquarters of India's largest domestic bank.

The Sainis were unafraid to scrap with the authorities, but their staying power ultimately rested on their capacity to pursue a legal case. Goverdhan Saini was not literate and his sons were mostly laborers: one ironically was a security guard in the Mahindra World City. But the second-oldest son, Jashpal, worked in the office of a friend who was a small-time builder in Jaipur. Through his contacts, Jashpal hired a lawyer and filed seventeen cases against the MWC in the Jaipur Sessions Court. From what I could tell, their case rested on a discrepancy in the SEZ plans which, it seemed, did not include their farm. Their land was not legally acquired, they argued, and therefore not Mahindra's to sell to SBI. The Jaipur Sessions Court saw enough merit in their argument to issue a stay on construction. This stay was apparently in effect but ignored by the JDA when it came to evict them from their land in December 2009.

Despite the ongoing case, MWC executives seemed determined to press on. In December of 2010, preparations were underway for the inauguration of the SBI office. Rumors circulated through Rajpura that the Chief Minister of Rajasthan would be attending. A stage was erected, a red carpet rolled out, and portable toilets trucked in. Kanaram Choudhary's JCB machine had been rented and used to clear more land near the entrance. I was at the Sainis' house as these preparations unfolded. We had just finished *chai* when several security guards came up to the wall and told the women that they would have to remove their livestock, whose presence on the enclosed land had been de facto tolerated. The guards, from Rajpura, explained that the Chief Minister was coming. But the women refused and there was a back and forth until the guards' boss was adamant that the livestock be removed. The guards started rounding up the livestock with their sticks, and tried to lead them back over the ramp into the Saini compound. One of the Saini daughters-in-law took a bunch of sticks and blocked the opening. The guards then led the cattle out of the main gate on the opposite side and onto the 250 Foot Road. With a cordon of fifty security guards stationed along the Sainis' wall and a bus full of police on hand, the inauguration went ahead, although the Chief Minister never showed.

Signs for SBI subsequently appeared on the concrete wall, which enraged Goverdhan. On one occasion, I overhead him yelling at the guards to the effect that they had beaten him, put him in jail, and now put this sign up: "Whose is it? This is mine. They have seized it." The guards were just there to collect their (low) wages and did not take the bait. They were themselves critical of how fellow villagers had been treated. As one observed to me, "If they got a fair deal, there wouldn't be any confrontations (*takarav*)." It was perhaps suspicions of such disloyalty that subsequently prompted SBI to replace the village security guards with non-local retired soldiers.

The Sainis' legal challenge got traction. The court maintained its stay on construction and by February of 2011, a lock had been put on the gates. The Sainis had painted over the wall: "There is a stay on this land in the Jaipur Sessions Court." According to the Sainis, Mahindra was now trying to negotiate a settlement. And this is when the Sainis' end game became a bit clearer—or perhaps changed. When I first arrived, they insisted that they had no interest in compensation and just wanted to keep their land. The women in the house seemed quite adamant about this, as did Goverdhan. But when I stopped by the homestead in the summer of 2012, their tune seemed to have changed. A small *dhaba* they had opened on the front of their property had closed, the younger brother had been (predictably) fired from his security guard job, and the property office where Jashpal worked had been closed. Goverdhan had also suddenly passed away the preceding year. The Jaipur Sessions Court had given them a favorable decision and Mahindra seemed more inclined to negotiate. I asked the Saini brothers if they were ultimately looking to sell the land. Jashpal responded quickly, "Yes, why not, we'll get a good price. If Mahindra wants to give us a good price, we'll sell it to them too." I observed that they had previously insisted that they did not want to sell. "At the time, the mind was full of the police harassing us." Whether or not it was the plan from the start, they were now just holding out for a better deal. By the summer of 2016, they were still holding out but reportedly coming close to a deal—eleven years after their land had ostensibly been "acquired."

I have zoomed in on the Saini standoff for several reasons. First, its initial suppression was a reminder to the entire village that the government's "acquisition" of land was backed by force. Virendra Sharma concluded from the incident that "When people fight against the government they get thrown in jail. The police are also with them. Whatever the government wants to do, they do." A group of Dalit youth in one of the smaller nearby villages perceptively articulated the government's effective combination of coercive and material compliance: "What can you do against the government? . . . They have guns. . . . And those who got plots are happy." Having effectively divided the village with material inducements, the government could easily repress isolated holdouts. While some may have sympathized, no one in Rajpura came to the Sainis' defense. As one of the Saini brothers remarked, they fought entirely alone because "villagers have sold out." The singularity of the Saini standoff illustrates how *successful* the Rajasthan government's compensation policy was at diffusing opposition.

What is also remarkable, however, is how disruptive even a single and isolated holdout can be. Although the Sainis were the most militant in defending their land, a few other families also filed legal cases against the government for its acquisition of land for the connecting highways. Throughout my fieldwork, the new four-lane 250 Foot Road connecting the SEZ to the Jaipur airport and national highway conspicuously swerved around a single home whose family "had a case going." A new road connecting the SEZ to the national highway long faced a similar obstruction. In China, these holdouts are called "nail households," as in protruding nails that await being hammered (Hsing 2010: 18). India's legal system can allow such nails to stick out for quite a while. Individualized and limited in their goals, such small skirmishes are a way by which farmers, in the absence of collective action, negotiate the terms of their inclusion into the economic growth consuming their land.

As the Sainis and a few individual landowners used the legal system to holdout for more money, others merely sought to continue with previous land uses: a de facto postponement of their dispossession. Even after nine years, Mahindra was utilizing only a small portion of the 3,000 acres acquired for it and had erected only temporary barbed wire fencing around much of it. In several places, grazers had cut open fencing and pushed over supports, allowing livestock to freely graze inside (see Figure 8.2). Some people even continued to cultivate their technically acquired land inside the SEZ fencing where Mahindra had yet to start any construction. I was riding back with Mahesh from the block headquarters one day when I saw several families cultivating land inside the SEZ fence, the Deutsche Bank headquarters rising behind them. Thinking this might be a form of resistance, I quickly asked Mahesh to pull over. To my surprise, the cultivators were actually tenants, sharecropping

Figure 8.2 Grazing inside the SEZ boundary. Source: Rajpura Land Records.

the land of a wealthy landowner. Although he no longer possessed title, the Brahmin landlord was still able to expropriate rent from his tenants. I asked the sharecroppers why they were paying rent on land that their landlord no longer owned. They explained that they did not know anything about the legal technicalities; if they didn't give the landlord his share, he would "create problems." I subsequently learned that a number of big landowners—including Laduram and Mahinder—were still leasing out land inside the SEZ; in fact, Mahinder explained that this temporary arrangement with the MWC was one of the outcomes of the *samiti's* protests. Local relations of domination and exploitation had found their way into what, at a superficial glance, appeared to be anti-enclosure resistance.

Absorption into real estate speculation, in sum, not only divided villagers' interests but channeled opposition into manageable—if still disruptive—forms. Holdouts and legal cases could improve compensation, but they did not challenge dispossession itself. Everyday forms of reoccupation, meanwhile, promised no more than marginal and temporary resumptions of previous land uses. Without political organization to defend them, such reoccupations are an adaptation to defeat, not a recipe for success. I do not think anyone in Rajpura had any illusions about this. As one herder predicted while leading his goats through a hole in the SEZ fence, "Now they'll make one out of iron."

Voting for Development

I have focused thus far on the social underpinnings of informal political (in)action. Electoral politics remained an indirect avenue for expressing political subjectivities that were at least partly shaped by the post-dispossession socio-economic changes in Rajpura. And Rajpura was no exception to growing support for the BJP in Rajasthan during my fieldwork. When I first arrived, the Congress was in power at the state and national level, but growing support for the former BJP Chief Minister Raje was notable. On more than one occasion, a farmer who had just finished telling me about the "complete loss" they had suffered from the SEZ went on to express support for Vasundhara Raje—who as chief minister had initiated the project. And by 2014, Rajpura appeared to have voted heavily for the BJP's Narendra Modi in the national election. How do we explain the paradox of growing support for the party and individual who initiated the dispossession of the village? Although voting behavior is shaped by multiple factors, I believe people's post-SEZ economic trajectories shaped their political preferences in several ways that made them compatible with BJP politics—at least for some time.

The first is that all those who still had land—the neo-rentiers and petty asset managers—had an interest in rising land prices and these were associated with the Raje regime. While Raje had presided over the tremendous land boom, Gehlot had presided over the bust. As one *dalal* put it, "in two years, when Vasundhara Raje was CM, lots of land was sold." A barber-*dalal* who was an ardent BJP supporter explained, "If BJP comes to power, [the village] will become more developed. The land price was good under Raje." Those who did well during this time, as another villager put it, "built houses, drank, and felt like bosses." Because the Mahindra World City was Raje's pet project, there was also a perception that Gehlot's indifference explained the JDA's failure to construct their compensation plots. As one person put it, "If Vasundhara Raje was here, we would get compensation. BJP should come back."

The second was that after losing their land and livestock, the majority of Rajpura's ex-farmers were now net food buyers, and the Congress regime (at both the state and national level) coincided with dramatic food price inflation. This was a major concern for everyone but the neo-rentiers. For the petty asset managers, this squeeze was felt simultaneously with the land price dip: while the real estate slowdown meant that they would have to wait longer for their assets to appreciate, escalating food prices made it more difficult to live in the meantime without a stable *income*—which most did not have. When I asked a group of young men who were angry about the SEZ why they supported Raje, they explained that under her regime, "food prices were lower and land prices were higher." High food prices were, of course, most troubling to Rajpura's proletarianized and excluded who were disproportionately Dalit and traditionally Congress supporters. Among these groups I also found some support for the BJP, albeit more conditional. While a Regar man thought the Congress did "excellent work" with "two-rupee wheat [in the public distribution system], NREGA, and pensions," ultimately he and others voted for Raje "because of inflation. That's the main thing. Petrol, vegetables."

By the time of the 2014 national election, the land boom had returned—mostly, it seemed, due to the MWC's expansion—but the problems of inflation and employment remained foremost in people's minds. I revisited Rajpura two weeks after the 2014 national election that sent Narendra Modi and the BJP to power in Delhi. While notorious for his Hindu nationalist politics and accused of complicity in the 2002 pogrom of Muslims in Gujarat, Modi had emphasized an economic platform promising "development for all." Amid growing disillusionment with the Congress, Modi promised to generalize the "Gujarat model" of development to the rest of India. As the self-styled CEO of Gujarat, Modi had aggressively promoted private investment through deregulation, subsidies, and cheap land (Sud 2012). He was an ardent supporter of Special Economic Zones, high-tech cities, infrastructure corridors, Special Investment Regions, and so on. Many thus interpreted the BJP's landslide victories in rural North India as a mandate for this aggressively pro-business model of growth and a sign that the Congress' populist politics were out of sync with "aspirational India." Modi's resounding victory included a clean BJP sweep of Rajasthan's parliamentary seats.

Rajpura clearly voted heavily for Modi, though not as thoroughly as the Brahmin-heavy Shivpura. From ethnographic evidence, this support appeared to be based on a combination of Congress' failures and Modi's promise to bring the development that had so far proven elusive in Rajpura. A young Meena summed up the common sentiment on the first: "Congress didn't control inflation." Mahesh echoed that it was "because of inflation" while his young son added, "People think he'll make the land prices go up and employ them." A few repeated Modi's campaign slogan: "With Modi, good days are coming." When I asked an older barber whether he thought the village had experienced development, he said, "Development? It hasn't come yet. It will come now that Modi has come." Another explained that people voted for the BJP "because of Modi, so that there will be development."

Others were less convinced. Many were cynical about both parties. As one youth put it, "For us, they are all the same. We don't see them. They don't come here." Another predicted, "Modi will do what he feels. He won't do anything for us." The question for him, as for most youth, was which party would bring jobs. Among a group of mostly pro-Modi youth, one was particularly skeptical that the Gujarat model could accomplish that. Having traveled there once to visit family, he reported: "There is no development in Gujarat, no development at all. . . . I went to Ahmedabad. The poor there are very poor. There is wage labor (*mazduri*) and nothing else. Only *mazduri*." *Mazduri*, as Chapter 6 illustrated, was generally disdained; it was formal-sector employment—*naukri*—that was central to most youth's aspirations. For most young men I spoke with, then, their support for Modi was based on the hope that he would bring the employment that previous politicians had not. Their support was thus contingent. As one youth put it, "We will see what Modi will do. Like Obama, he says he will change the world." A Balai foreman said, "We will see how much development there will be. Congress will come back after five years if not."

We will see. Modi's economic program has been to replicate the form of pro-business economic growth embodied by the Mahindra World City, which has thus far proven so disappointing to many in Rajpura. More of the same seems unlikely to quell that disappointment. But the point is this: even a massive restructuring of Indian capitalism would be unlikely to deliver the high-quality jobs, education, health, and infrastructure to even a fraction of Rajpura's—and India's—expanding population of rural job seekers. So, while support for the BJP in Rajpura is certainly evidence against the hypothesis that dispossessing peasants contributes to their radicalization, it is not evidence that farmers share in an ideological consensus around the capitalist model of development (Nielsen 2010); or that they simply renew their dreams in the face of their lack of fulfillment (Cross 2014). What the preceding does illustrate, I believe, is that Rajpura's dispossessed farmers have concrete economic goals, that they assess the ability of parties to realize those goals, and that they adjust their political behavior in light of past performance. Since their goals are unlikely to be realized within the given trajectory of Indian capitalism, it is a mistake to interpret them as congruent with that trajectory. It is not aspirations per se that will animate politics in Rajpura for the foreseeable future, I suggest, but their lack of realization. Rajpura's farmers are very likely to continue to vote for politicians like Raje or Modi who promise to bring development. But they will vote those politicians out of office when the development does not arrive, as they have done in the past.

Given the adherence of both major parties to a similar set of economic policies, electoral choices are limited. Whether the aspirations of Rajpura's villagers can be articulated to an alternative political project more likely to realize them is an open question; in Rajasthan there are no likely political vehicles. And such a project is far more likely to gain traction in villages where a significant fraction of farmers has *not* been absorbed into and divided by speculative land markets.

Panchayat politics provides the most direct opportunity for expressing political preferences, but has the least capacity to transform the broader economic structures that shape life chances in Rajpura. And it remains constrained by a pattern of patronage politics, shaped by the history of princely rule, and predicated on the ability of relatively educated and connected "big men" to "bring development." A moderately hopeful epilogue to this story—though one entirely congruent with this pattern—is that, in 2015, Rajpura's voters rejected the re-election bid of Laduram Meena, the unscrupulous broker. Instead, they re-elected Banvarilal Sharma, the three-time Brahmin *sarpanch* who had first challenged the *thakur's* dominance in the 1970s and who was widely considered more honest and development-minded. In early 2016, I learned by email that he had succeeded in securing a new drinking water supply for Rajpura.

Conclusion: Waiting for Development

Rajpura was a village full of grievances but largely devoid of solidarity. The SEZ's failure to provide jobs, facilities, and infrastructure created widespread anger. The vast majority of people in Rajpura felt marginalized by the Mahindra World City and they expressed this discontent in the agrarian populist idiom of poor farmers being victimized by urban "outsiders." But this agrarian populism was limited and complicated by the fact that Rajpura's farmers had been absorbed into, and fared radically unequally in, speculative land markets. The Rajasthan government's market-based compensation policy profoundly divided the village by differentiating interests, allowing opportunistic insiders to exploit fellow villagers, and by more broadly individualizing life chances and eroding solidarities even within castes and families. As a political strategy, this was a tremendous success. A briefly lived protest movement was limited to advancing the real estate interests of relatively privileged villagers, while the truly disgruntled were isolated and reduced to individualized strategies of resistance. Such strategies did create disruptions for the SEZ developers. But without broader support and organization, these strategies had no chance of doing more than bettering the terms of inclusion or allowing for marginal land uses to continue until the SEZ was completed.

Whether the simmering anger among a significant section of Rajpura will be channeled into further acts of organized opposition remains an open question. One potentially explosive issue is the SEZ's plan, mentioned in Chapter 7, to eventually block off the main road connecting the national highway to the village market. If carried through, this would mean much longer commutes to Jaipur and much less traffic through the Rajpura market—an issue that could potentially unite the village's workers, petty asset managers, and neo-rentiers. If the *samiti* is resuscitated or reinvented it will most likely be for this, or to push the JDA again to speed up the construction and delivery of the compensation plots to those lucky enough to still own them. But absorption into the game of real estate has effectively kept opposition within the terms of state and capital—that is, receiving a stake in the commodification made possible by their dispossession. Stripped of their land, but now occupying heterogeneous class positions in a largely informal economy, Rajpura's residents have few interests in common except for more high-quality jobs and better village infrastructure and facilities. The inability of the current trajectory of capitalist growth to deliver these will shape their political behavior for the foreseeable future, perhaps in unforeseeable ways. In the meantime, the Mahindra World City expands slowly and Rajpura residents adjust, according to their ability, to the peculiar and rapid transformation of their village.

9

Conclusion

"Land Wars" and Development

> The State shall, in particular, direct its policy towards securing: (a) that the citizens, men and women equally, have the right to an adequate means of livelihood; (b) that the ownership and control of the material resources of the community are so distributed as best to subserve the common good; (c) that the operation of the economic system does not result in the concentration of wealth and means of production to the common detriment.
>
> —The Constitution of India, Article 39 (1949)

> The acquisition of land from the public by the government is proving to be a major transfer of wealth from the rural populace to the corporate world.
>
> —Comptroller Auditor General of India (2014)

This book has argued that the land grabs of post-liberalization India are neither the necessary cost of development nor a stage in the transition to capitalism; they are rather the product of a specifically neoliberal regime of dispossession. While the developmentalist regime redistributed land from farmers to the beneficiaries of public-sector industry and infrastructure, this neoliberal regime redistributes land directly to private—and increasingly financial and non-industrial—capital. While the first was restrained by developmentalist commitments to productivism, labor intensity, and balanced regional development, the latter dispenses with any consideration but growth at all costs. This new regime, synonymous with the genesis of land broker states, emerged in the 1990s and reached scale with India's SEZs of the mid-2000s. Taking one of the largest SEZs in North India as its case, this book has examined the collision between this new regime of dispossession and the agrarian milieu of Rajpura. It demonstrated, first, how the Rajasthan government's compensation policy absorbed a significant fraction of Rajpura's farmers into speculative land markets, utilizing pre-existing inequalities to elicit individualized compliance. The consequent ability of the Rajasthan government to transfer Rajpura's rain-fed farmland and grazing commons to the Mahindra World City facilitated massive real estate arbitrage—maximizing what I have called the rate of accumulation by dispossession—and the establishment of a tax-free enclave for the "knowledge economy." Conversely, dispossession destroyed Rajpura's pre-existing agricultural economy, led to a disaccumulation of agrarian assets (most importantly livestock), and worsened already acute water shortages, the costs of which were disproportionately borne by women. The MWC's main contribution to the local economy was a dramatic real estate boom, which made some farmers incredibly rich but magnified pre-existing inequalities and excluded landless households and women in general. Aside from land rents, this growth had little to offer Rajpura's dispossessed villagers. "Knowledge-intensive" growth mostly marginalized Rajpura's under-educated labor and absorbed a small fraction into informal sub-contracted work that did not compensate for lost livestock, much less land. And while an elite island of "world class" infrastructure emerged inside the SEZ's boundary walls, villagers remained on the outside looking in. Creating minimal linkages to the surrounding economy, moreover, the SEZ left Rajpura's residents to survive in an urbanizing but non-industrial informal economy. Despite significant anger and disappointment at this exclusion, differentiation by speculation divided the village and undercut its capacity to make collective claims on the company or government.

What are the broader implications of these findings? I argued in the introduction that examining the interactions of particular regimes of dispossession with different agrarian milieux can help to explain variation in the politics of dispossession and its socio-economic consequences. I believe this framework can be extended beyond India and used for both within-country and cross-country comparisons. This book has tried to demonstrate a radical shift between two regimes of dispossession in India, and has used labels—developmentalist and neoliberal—that will resonate elsewhere in the Global South. Nevertheless, I also expect regimes of dispossession to look different in other countries, both in content and in periodization. If most countries of the world have been integrated into a global capitalist system for hundreds of years, a defining feature of that system is its uneven development. State-developmentalism exhibited many varieties in the 20th century, as neoliberalism does in the 21st. A cursory glance across the globe reveals that capitalist growth in different national contexts is today characterized by the predominance of different economic sectors tied to distinct national class configurations, and this introduces great heterogeneity into the causes of dispossession. The concept of regimes of dispossession is deliberately flexible so that it can be re-purposed and reconstructed to capture such heterogeneity. Agrarian milieux, moreover, exhibit even more variation globally. While there are few, if any, pockets of the rural Global South untouched by capitalism, this has not generated socio-economic convergence. Agricultural growth is globally even; class differentiation highly complex, variable, and slow; off-farm diversification widespread; and political histories distinct. Perhaps the biggest generalization we can make is that almost nowhere, with the partial exception of East Asia,[1] are dispossessed peasants being absorbed in great numbers into an industrial proletariat. Instead, diversifying rural populations are, as in India, more likely to mix agriculture with various forms of self-employment or casual employment in the construction or service sectors. The widely observed result is the growth of "pluriactive" and complexly differentiated rural households,[2] which themselves must be disaggregated to understand the various permutations of patriarchy organizing their reproduction. When states decide to dispossess land for a variety of 21st-century advanced capitalist purposes, they thus encounter mind-bogglingly complex agrarian milieux that look nothing like 16th-century England. Such interactions are producing a great variety of capitalist trajectories that are not repetitions of the past and promise no redemption. They are also producing a variety of political responses that should not be dismissed as backward-looking obstructions of progress. If the contribution of dispossession to development is a variable, then examining this variation should help us to understand regional and historical differences in the politics of dispossession. Given the contemporary saliency of dispossession politics in many regions of Asia, Africa, and Latin America, there is vast scope for comparative research to greatly advance our understanding of the relationship between dispossession and capitalism; and the role that anti-dispossession movements might play in transforming it.

In this conclusion, however, I focus on the specific implications of this study for our understanding of dispossession politics in India. For as Rajpura's ex-farmers adjusted to their dispossession, farmers elsewhere in India refused to be dispossessed. By the late 2000s, as Chapter 1 outlined, farmer protests against land dispossession were not only widespread but unprecedentedly successful in stopping and stalling large capital projects. Many of the largest private SEZs in India were canceled and many other investments stuck in land acquisition purgatory. Land acquisition became, for the first time in India's history, an electorally salient issue that opposition parties use against incumbents. Afraid to appear "anti-farmer," state governments found it increasingly difficult to remove farmers by gunpoint. Many were increasing their compensation policies while national debates raged over whether and how to revise the central Land Acquisition Act. India's neoliberal regime of dispossession was, by the late 2000s, politically tenuous; yet few major parties contemplated a dramatic change to the growth model itself. A contradiction had thus emerged between the land requirements of neoliberal capitalism and the political weight of farmers in India's electoral democracy. This concluding chapter asks: what insight does this study provide into whether, how, and for whom this contradiction might be resolved? And what are the implications of these possible resolutions for development?

Drawing out these implications involves recognizing that any concrete process of social change, such as what I observed in Rajpura, is the product of determinations operating on a variety of scales. No two SEZs—much less capital projects—are the same. And this is even more true of India's 640,000 or so villages. But the microprocesses of social change analyzed over the preceding chapters were strongly shaped by social forces operating on a far broader scale. India's neoliberal economic policies have national remit; and most of its states have become land brokers for private capital since the early 1990s. As a highly unequal village dependent on dryland agriculture and growing off-farm diversification, Rajpura is not atypical even if it cannot be representative. But I have also argued that my case—of a drought-prone village that received better-than-average compensation for an SEZ that actually got built by a company, moreover, that has a reputation for corporate responsibility—is an analytically useful one. This is because it is a limiting case for the modernization theory of dispossession: a place where the present regime of dispossession is most likely to be developmental. If Rajpura is indeed a best-case scenario, it strengthens my argument that dispossession without development is a broader feature of India's political economy. Placing Rajpura within this larger context while attending to its particularities, I offer four conclusions about India's "land wars" and their implications for development.

First, I argue that India's current trajectory of capitalism is itself the largest obstacle to dispossessing land for it. While much political debate in India focuses on compensation prices to farmers, this misses the underlying trajectory of exclusionary growth that makes holding onto land and livestock—even in a rain-scarce region—look attractive. Non-labor-intensive and rent-heavy growth, which economists have shown to be a broader feature of India's post-liberalization economy, is creating insufficient exit routes from agriculture; and this makes the ever-growing semiproletarian condition far preferable to the fully proletarian. To the extent that farmers are able to perceive these implications of proposed projects in advance or learn from previous cases of dispossession—which I suggest they increasingly are—then the political implication is that promises of development will be decreasingly convincing. This puts all the weight on land prices as an incentive for compliance. And if land prices are the *only* material incentive for relinquishing land, those land prices must be high.

Second, therefore, the political stability of India's neoliberal regime of dispossession now rests on its ability to substitute land prices for inclusive development. Farmer protests have forced both state and central governments to offer greater material concessions, which, because of the larger growth model, can only come from land prices. And the tremendous discrepancies between compensation prices and market prices, the production of which has become the raison d'être of land broker states, does allow significant room for concessions in the rate of accumulation by dispossession. The case of Rajpura illustrates that absorbing farmers into land speculation is a poor substitute for development; but that it can be a powerful mechanism for generating compliance. Nevertheless, India's new land law—the Right to Fair Compensation and Transparency in Land Acquisition, Resettlement and Rehabilitation Act (henceforth LARRA)—and subsequent attempts at its dilution suggest that the Indian state and business classes are yet unwilling to offer concessions of the kind and degree that could generalize the "success" achieved in Rajpura.

My third argument is that it will be far harder to buy off farmers in agrarian milieux that do not resemble Rajpura—a drought-prone and heavily diversified village with steep inequalities and a relatively quiet political history. Where agriculture is more prosperous, where village solidarity is more easily maintained, and where farmers have more experience collectively resisting state or elite depredations, land broker states are likely to encounter significantly more difficulty.

For the preceding reasons, "land wars" are unlikely to subside anytime soon. So long as dispossession without development remains a defining feature of Indian capitalism, "land wars" will be a prominent feature of Indian democracy. My final argument, therefore, is that these anti-dispossession movements should be seen as agents of—rather than obstructions to—development. While these movements are diverse in their class composition, goals, and ideologies, they are not obstructions to generally beneficial growth but powerful checks on dispossession without development. The question is whether they will merely improve the terms of dispossession; help to make capitalism more developmental; or be harnessed by political projects to reverse the direction of redistribution.

Exclusionary Growth and the Semiproletarian Condition

This study of post-dispossession life in Rajpura has, above all, illuminated a trajectory of capitalism that has little to offer rural populations—except land prices. While destroying Rajpura's agricultural and livestock economy, the Mahindra World City was an outlet for real estate speculation and knowledge-intensive growth that marginalized rural labor, concentrated investment in a "world class" enclave for corporate professionals, and left the surrounding populations dependent on a peripheral informal economy. Even with one of the best compensation policies on offer in India, most farmers retrospectively felt that they had lost more than they gained and wished they had their land back. Rajpura, it must be emphasized, was a drought-prone village whose cultivators were already substantially diversified from agriculture. That even there a majority of farmers—and the vast majority of lower castes—felt that their income, food security, and well-being had diminished after losing their land and livestock for the SEZ is not a testament to a thriving agricultural economy, but an indictment of the exclusionary growth embodied in the Mahindra World City.

While no single case can stand in for the entire trajectory of capitalism in India, the social processes observed in Rajpura were the product of social forces operating on a much larger scale. The accumulation taking place inside the MWC reflected, first of all, the economic sectors and logics driving SEZs across India. Two-thirds of India's approved SEZs are in "knowledge-intensive" industries such as IT/ITES and pharmaceuticals (Government of India n.d.). Most are developed by private companies whose profit model is to transform cheaply acquired rural land into high-value real estate—which is why they are concentrated on the periphery of major cities in relatively affluent regions (Mukhopadhyay 2008; Palit and Bhattacharjee 2008: 39–41; CAG 2014: 13). And SEZs are, by design, "premium networked spaces" that attract private capital by offering exceptional infrastructure and global connectivity "whilst bypassing less powerful users and spaces" (Graham 2000: 185; Brenner 2004). Although the Mahindra World City was only a moderate success in these terms—buffeted by the financial crisis, it was slow in attracting investment and, a decade later, still only using a third of the land dispossessed for it—this was true of most of India's SEZs. Indeed, the MWC was one of India's more successful SEZs: most were sitting on large amounts of unutilized land while many failed to attract investors at all, sought "denotification," and lapsed into pure real estate grabs (CAG 2014).

Contrary to popular belief, moreover, India's SEZs are reflective of—rather than exceptions to—the trajectory of capitalism in 21st-century India. While offering an exceptionally liberal tax and tariff regime, their sectoral composition broadly reflects that of India's post-liberalization economy. Growth in this period has been driven, as Chapter 2 illustrated, by non-labor-intensive industries more than manufacturing; and been fueled by a real estate boom of momentous proportions. And SEZs are only one among multiple policy avenues through which the Indian state has sought to attract private investment into infrastructure and otherwise "zone" development. The SEZ model has become politically tarnished by both land acquisition controversy and massive losses to the public exchequer,[3] as well as become less attractive financially due to its export requirements and changes in the tax code,[4] but it is being superseded by New Manufacturing Zones, Special Investment Regions, Infrastructure Corridors, Smart Cities, Hi-Tech Cities, Modern Industrial Townships, and all manner of public-private partnerships, each of which similarly enables the large-scale transfer of agricultural land to private companies (cf. Balakrishnan 2013; Asher 2014; Sampat 2016a). These proliferating spatial strategies appear to be different bottles filled with the same wine. The wine is a regime of dispossession that subsidizes private corporations with cheap land no matter the purpose or how narrow its beneficiaries. And despite important subnational variation, practically all of India's states are drinking it.[5]

There is a tremendous disjuncture, as we saw in Rajpura, between this trajectory of capitalism and rural India, where over 830 million people now live (Census of India 2011). Despite growing urbanization, this is the largest rural population in India's history. And there is little to romanticize about the conditions under which a large part of it struggles to make a livelihood. India's rural poor continue to suffer from the shortcomings of state-led development—to sufficiently redistribute land, invest in agriculture, health, and education (Bardhan 2010; Kohli 2012; Dreze and Sen 2013), and to reverse entrenched caste and gender inequalities—and are now buffeted by the insecurities of a liberalized agricultural sector (Reddy and Mishra 2010; Vasavi 2012). Although one cannot generalize about agricultural profitability across India's diverse regions (Lerche 2013, 2015), the proportion of rural cultivators forced to find a non-agricultural foothold is only growing. Scholars have tracked for decades the increasing off-farm diversification of agriculturalists (Harriss 1991; Harriss-White and Janakarajan 1997; Jeffrey and Lerche 2000; Jeffrey 2001; Lerche 2015: 53–54; Guérin et al. 2015: 122). And anthropologists have highlighted the prevalence of urban aspirations among rural youth (cf. Gooptu 2013; Cross 2014). These aspirations are often used as evidence in support of dispossessing farmland for non-agricultural purposes (cf. Bardhan 2011). But it is crucial to recognize that the pattern of growth driving dispossession in contemporary India could hardly be less promising for satisfying those aspirations.

India's current trajectory of growth has proven woefully incapable of creating sufficient—and sufficiently attractive—exit routes from agriculture. This is not just a matter of insufficient growth; but one of the *character* of growth. Historically, such exit routes have come from manufacturing (Kaldor 1967). But India's manufacturing growth has not only been stagnant as a percentage of India's GDP but also increasingly capital-intensive and "jobless" (Kannan and Raveendran 2009; Mitra 2013). Given India's integration into competitive global markets, this increasing capital intensity is likely irreversible and reflects a broader trend among late-industrializers, which Rodrik (2016) has termed "premature deindustrialization": a peaking of manufacturing growth and employment at a much lower level of GDP than advanced industrial economies. India's particular pattern of "jobless growth" combines this globally increasing capital intensity with a historically peculiar leap into high-skilled services which, as Chapter 6 illustrated, have little potential for absorbing the labor of dispossessed farmers. Further, much land dispossession in contemporary India is, as Chapter 2 documented, driven by real estate speculation pure and simple—a reflection of India's "rent-thick" pattern of growth over the past several decades (Gandhi and Walton 2012). If and when land flipping subsides, and after short-term construction jobs are filled and vacated by footloose migrants, all that is left is a skeletal work force of security guards, gardeners, and housekeepers, almost assuredly fewer in number than the land's previous cultivators. When one adds the Indian state's commitment to labor flexibilization, this pattern of growth appears to be structurally incapable of satisfying what we saw to be the main aspiration of young villagers in Rajpura: salaried formal-sector employment. Dispossessed farmers in contemporary India are, contrary to the historical predictions of both modernization theory and classical Marxism, being pushed into informal self-employment—the "tertiary sector"—far more than they are into factories (Harriss-White 2012). Success in this sector is highly uneven, shaped by prior agricultural assets and, for most, not an effective substitute for stable employment. Each capital project that dispossesses more farmers than it exploits is a net contributor to a growing "surplus population" that can neither support itself from the land nor find a regular buyer of its labor power. Even where projects create more jobs than the farmers they displace, skill-intensity combined with the system of "footloose" migratory labor typically ensures that the dispossessed and employed are different people.

Faced with insufficient and unpromising exit routes from agriculture, holding onto land is an immanently reasonable livelihood strategy: even if it is only moderately profitable *and* one is trying to diversify from agriculture. In Rajpura, this became evident only *retrospectively* as farmers realized that even the small number of jobs available in the SEZ did not replace the income from foregone livestock. But there is good evidence that in many other parts of India, farmers can see this *prospectively* and that this has been an important motivation for resisting dispossession. Scholars have observed that some of the most tenacious "land wars" have occurred in regions where farmers have had previously disappointing experiences with land-consuming industrial projects—whether during the developmentalist or neoliberal period. Farmers in Nandigram had, for example, observed several rounds of land acquisition for industrial projects since the 1970s, for which local people were poorly compensated and left unemployed, causing "much disillusionment among local people concerning industrialization" (Banerjee 2014: 281).[6] Those resisting the POSCO Steel SEZ in Odisha had seen five hundred nearby families dispossessed for an oil refinery in the 1990s: the dispossessed were given low compensation, the promise of one job per family never materialized, and even neighboring villages did not get electricity.[7] "In both cases," Banerjee (2014: 297) concludes, "local people had learned to discount promises of future benefits made by government officials and corporate executives alike." After a land-consuming IT park near Pune created few local jobs and came to a halt after the global financial crisis, Balakrishnan (2013: 808) observes that nearby farmers "refused to give up their lands for future industrial expansion." Farmers have also learned this lesson from prior phases of the same project: seeing what happened to those dispossessed before them, they have resolved to avoid the same fate.[8]

Each time farmers are dispossessed for a project with disappointing results, it multiplies the number of farmers for whom that lesson is available and reduces the number of villages, like Rajpura, for whom it is not. India's social movements have tried to shorten the learning curve by organizing conferences, hearings, and protests; and by connecting farmers facing dispossession from different parts of India. As cases like Rajpura multiply, this suggests, it is only going to become harder for states to convince farmers that they will benefit from the "development" used to justify their dispossession. It may be easier, all things being equal, for manufacturing projects with significant employment-generating potential. But even these, as we have seen, largely employ higher skill migrants; and it is not possible for state governments or even SEZ developers to make companies hire locals. Short of a larger restructuring of India's overall growth pattern, such projects will remain a minority of land-consuming capital projects. So while the Nehruvian state dispossessed land for economic purposes—like irrigated agriculture and public-sector industrialization—which dispossessed farmers could have at least *theoretically* been included in had the effort been made, the neoliberal regime of dispossession does not even offer this possibility. Promises of "development" are, under this regime, likely to fall flat in more locations and earlier in a project's life-cycle, making them easier to resist.

So while economists justify forcible land acquisition by the macro-level efficiency of transferring land from agriculture to "higher value" land uses (Banerjee et al. 2007; Bardhan 2011; Chakravorty 2013), what must be fully appreciated is the micro-level rationality behind farmers' opposition to this transfer, which is itself a response to macro-economic conditions. Dispossession without development makes holding onto land, all things being equal, a prudent livelihood strategy. This is even true, as we saw in Rajpura, among semiproletarianized cultivators of unirrigated land whose small single-cropped holdings and livestock proved more valuable than any job available to them in the SEZ. The vast chasm between India's neoliberal growth trajectory and the majority of India's poor and relatively under-educated rural population—a compounding of historical development failures (cf. Kohli 2012; Dreze and Sen 2013)—is a huge structural obstacle to politically stabilizing the current regime of dispossession. This obstacle will not go away without a major reorientation of Indian capitalism.

India's political leaders are not interested in such a reorientation. Faced with intractable and politically costly protests and unable to offer farmers a significant place in the accumulation generated by dispossession, their response has been to offer one-time payouts as a substitute for development.

The Politics of Payouts

For over a half century, the Indian state dispossessed farmers with pitiful compensation and powerful appeals to national development. Offering farmers low prices for their land, the Indian state exhorted farmers to "sacrifice for the nation"; and brought out police batons when they demurred. Sometimes, especially when faced with farmers with a modicum of political clout, they offered inclusion in the form of irrigated land or public-sector jobs. When the causes of dispossession changed in the 1990s, state methods of producing compliance initially did not. Over the next decade, however, they became decreasingly effective.

Appeals to sacrifice for the nation had already worn thin by the end of the developmentalist era; and it was even harder to convince farmers that they should "sacrifice" for the profits of multinational corporations. Maintaining low compensation to farmers while corporate recipients cashed in on booming real estate was hard to justify as development and could be critiqued with the more expansive developmentalist ethos of the Nehruvian era. Privately built SEZs, which orchestrated this transfer of wealth most transparently and on the largest scale, became the epicenter of these protests. And because most SEZs—and other "new economy" capital projects—were in the peri-urban plains, they encountered more politically influential farmers than had dam projects in remote river valleys. Proliferating farmer protests began to exact economic damage, and forcibly suppressing them proved politically costly. The Nandigram uprising of 2007, and Mamata Banerjee's subsequent victory over the Left Front government in the 2011 West Bengal elections, proved that violently dispossessing farmers could exact an electoral cost. Opposition parties soon picked up on her formula as a way to brand incumbent parties as "anti-farmer." Almost all parties soon voiced reservations about acquiring land for SEZs, which even the BJP (responsible for the initial SEZ policy) called "real estate exploitation" and "a naked land grab for real estate firms and corrupt politicians" and the CPM (responsible for the Nandigram carnage) called "an instrument of reckless real estate development and land speculation."[9] The Land Acquisition Act itself was now widely branded as a draconian colonial-era law, with the longstanding social movement demand for its repeal being taken seriously for the first time.[10] Farmers' movements and a surprising number of mainstream politicians argued, in the ensuing debates, that land should not be acquired for private companies at all—a remarkable critique of land broker states themselves and a testament to the enduring ideological strength of Nehruvian developmentalism. But there was a broader recognition that, at the very least, compensation to farmers would have to be substantially increased.[11] If it was not to be abandoned, India's neoliberal regime of dispossession needed a stronger material basis of compliance.

Several states with politically influential farmers' groups—such as Haryana and Uttar Pradesh—passed compensation and resettlement and rehabilitation policies that were far more generous than under the Land Acquisition Act (Kennedy 2014: 179; Pai and Kumar 2014). Maharashtra, like Rajasthan, already had more generous than average compensation policies on the books. While several pro-business states like Gujarat, Andhra Pradesh, and Tamil Nadu continued to acquire land relatively cheaply, they were also experiencing significant—if less publicized—opposition that was prompting them to introduce more limited reforms (Asher 2014; Srinivasalu 2014; Vijayabaskar 2014). In its waning days, the chastened Left Front adopted a new land acquisition policy in West Bengal.[12] And upon taking power, the TMC brought land acquisition to a (at least temporary) halt. By the end of the 2000s, almost no state's land acquisition policies remained unchanged.

In the immediate aftermath of the 2007 Nandigram carnage, the Congress-led central government announced its intention to amend the Land Acquisition Act. After dragging on for four years, the process was given a political boost by a farmer uprising in Western Uttar Pradesh in 2011. Farmers in the villages of Bhatta and Parsaul were having their land acquired at below-market price for the Yamuna Expressway, a project being built on a PPP basis by the Jaypee Group, to whom the government was also transferring large amounts of adjacent farmland for high-end real estate construction. Enraged at their low compensation, farmers kidnapped three officials of the Uttar Pradesh State Road Transport Corporation who were conducting a survey for the project. When the police tried to rescue them, a gunfight ensued that left two farmers and two policemen dead. Seeing an opportunity, Congress leader Rahul Gandhi snuck into the village on a motorbike and embarked on a *padyatra* (foot march) with farmers. [13] He castigated Uttar Pradesh Chief Minister Mayawati, of the Bahujan Samaj Party (BSP), for her "brutalities" against farmers. Whether Gandhi's support for farmers was sincere or cynical, the uprising presented the Congress with a wedge issue against the BSP in the run-up to the critical 2012 state assembly elections.[14] In the verbal duel that ensued, Gandhi and Mayawati each promised to introduce new land acquisition policies that would be more "pro-farmer" than the other. [15]

With an eye toward upcoming state and national elections, the UPA government thereafter moved relatively swiftly to replace the Land Acquisition Act. Sonia Gandhi appointed Jairam Ramesh, who as a relatively zealous Minister of Environment and Forests had attracted the ire of business, to the portfolio of rural development and tasked him with pushing through the amendments. Ramesh was adamant that the existing LAA had to be replaced by a more progressive bill; he also saw his task as striking a compromise between farmers and business.[16] Almost all farmers' groups wanted to prevent land acquisition for private companies, subject land acquisition for all purposes to the consent of farmers, and dramatically increase compensation levels and resettlement provisions. Business associations, in contrast, wanted to maintain the status quo. Almost all insisted that the state continue to acquire land for private companies, worried that any procedural safeguards would delay projects, and insisted on the need to keep land "affordable" to industry. Representatives of each side made their positions known in several rounds of consultations, parliamentary depositions, and in the media. Opinion was also divided within the government. Prime Minister Manmohan Singh and the pro-business wing of his cabinet were wary of creating obstacles for business. State governments were adamant about maintaining their land brokering prerogatives and argued for state-level flexibility. Preparing to lead their party into national elections, Sonia and Rahul Gandhi wanted a pro-farmer bill that would resonate with farmers.[17]

Ramesh's draft bill, the Right to Fair Compensation and Transparency in Land Acquisition, Rehabilitation and Resettlement Act (LARRA) was, in substance, an attempt to rescue the neoliberal regime of dispossession with land prices. On the crucial issue of what constituted a "public purpose," the bill unambiguously clarified that private projects would be included. The regime of dispossession would stay, but with procedural checks and higher compensation. Eighty percent of affected farmers would have to approve land acquisition for a purely private project, 70% for a public-private partnership. And an independent committee, part of a new multi-tiered resettlement and rehabilitation bureaucracy, would conduct Social Impact Assessments for each project to determine the affected populations and to gauge whether the benefits outweighed the costs. Compensation would be set at six times the land's assessed agricultural value and a range of resettlement and rehabilitation benefits, including for landless populations, would be mandatory. It was reportedly Rahul Gandhi who came up with the idea of changing the bill's name to make it sound like a new right—the right to be dispossessed fairly, as it were.[18]

Social movements and farmers' organizations considered the bill a "sell-out" to corporate interests. They argued that there should be no land acquisition for private companies, that the compensation and R&R benefits were still inadequate, and that there were huge loopholes in the consent procedures, which would also exclude landless populations. Surprisingly, their position was echoed by a number of opposition parties, including not just the TMC, for whom land acquisition had become a defining issue. A chastened CPM, several regional parties, and even many members of the BJP—including its parliamentary speaker—clamored for a more radical bill, the latter pushed forward by farmers' groups within the *Sangh Parivar* (the Hindu nationalist "family of organizations"). In debates over the bill, parliamentarians quoted Tagore and Premchand while offering paeans to the Indian farmer.[19]

India's business classes, however, believed that the bill was so pro-farmer that it would bring economic growth to a grinding halt—and waged a political offensive against it. All the major industry associations—the Confederation of Indian Industries (CII), the Associated Chambers of Commerce and Industry (ASSOCHAM), and the Federation of Indian Chambers of Commerce and Industry (FICCI)—along with regional associations, the builders' lobby, and individual corporate executives united in opposing it.[20] They objected to consent thresholds and any procedural constraints that would delay projects. And, although Ramesh tried to convince them that higher compensation would actually reduce costs by eliminating political uncertainty, most believed that the compensation and R&R benefits were too costly and would make private investments unviable.[21] The dip in India's growth between 2011 and 2013 worked in their favor, as they—and notably Prime Minister Manmohan Singh—identified delayed infrastructure projects as a major factor hampering India's growth. Their lobbying culminated in a media barrage in the weeks leading up to the parliamentary vote in August 2013.

This capitalist class offensive, buttressed by the pro-business arms of the central government and the state governments *en masse*, led to substantial dilutions. Thirteen legislations covering land acquisition for specific purposes—like railways, coal, and highways—would be exempted from consent and social impact assessments, as would dam projects. Significantly, an attempt to exempt SEZs failed—a testament to their relative lack of legitimacy. How to implement many provisions, including the crucial consent requirement, would be left to states, which failed to inspire confidence among farmers' groups. And ultimately the compensation price multiplier was effectively reduced from 6 times the assessed agricultural value to 2 or 3 times that value, depending on distance from the city—the exact distance being left for states to establish.

Despite these substantial dilutions, capitalists and many economists still believed that the law erred on the side of farmers and "would raise the cost of land acquisition to unsustainable levels" (Chakravorty 2015; see also Chakravorty 2013, Panagariya 2014).[22] When the pro-business Narendra Modi and the BJP defeated the Congress in the 2014 national election, business associations quickly seized the opportunity. As Chief Minister of Gujarat, Modi was revered by industry associations for his pro-business administration, which included rapid provision of cheap land to industrialists (Sud 2012). Within days of his coming to office on a platform that included fast-tracking large private investments, industry associations began a lobbying offensive to amend the law. Amid this effort, I asked a CII representative which was more important to industry, reducing compensation costs or minimizing delays and uncertainty: his response was "both," suggesting that industry had not bought Ramesh's argument that higher land prices were a worthwhile tradeoff for avoiding farmer agitations.[23] Business expected Modi to amend the bill in order to overcome the UPA's "policy paralysis," deliver on his mega-infrastructure plans, and restore investor confidence. A real estate consultant I interviewed called the amendments "mission critical."[24]

On December 30, 2014, the government duly issued an ordinance—a temporary executive order that must ultimately be approved by parliament—that overturned key provisions of LARRA, including the consent and social impact assessment requirements. This ordinance, coupled with crackdowns on civil society groups, seemed to indicate a willingness of the new government to revert to coercive methods for dispossessing farmers.

This proved to be a miscalculation. Immediate and widespread opposition—including marches and hunger strikes led by a reinvigorated Congress and even supported by factions of Modi's *Sangh Parivar*[25]—forced the BJP, with an eye toward upcoming state elections, to back down seven months later. After expending a tremendous amount of political capital during his first year in office, Modi was forced to completely withdraw the ordinance. This was Modi's first major reversal, and a remarkable concession. Once again, India's neoliberal regime of dispossession ran up against the political weight of farmers. As a *Tehelka* (2014) editorial summed up the political lesson, "no party can afford to sound non-socialist when it comes to the peasantry." LARRA remains the law of the land, so the question is now: will this usher in a new consensual age of dispossession without land wars?

The case of Rajpura demonstrates that inclusion into real estate speculation is a powerful mechanism of compliance. For some farmers, it suggests, land prices can be an effective substitute—at least politically—for "development," more broadly conceived. However, it also shows that the compensation provisions under LARRA will not even approximately close the gap between compensation and market prices in many settings. We have seen that the rates of accumulation by dispossession facilitated by land broker states are massive: in the case of the MWC, I estimated it to be over 1,700% for the project's residential component. Michael Goldman (2011: 568) has documented discrepancies around peri-urban Bangalore of well over 1,000%,[26] while Manshi Asher found that farmers protesting a DLF-promoted SEZ in Punjab were being offered compensation at a 500% to 800% markdown.[27] The Greater Noida Industrial Development Authority (GNIDA), another target of farmer protests in Western Uttar Pradesh, has been documented acquiring land at Rs 820 per square meter and reselling it to developers at Rs 35,000 (Sood 2011)—a rate of 4,250% just on the public increment.[28] Multiplying compensation by two or three is not going to close these gaps or create a sense of justice. Farmers have repeatedly proven unwilling to accept the agricultural value of land when it is to be turned over to urban or industrial uses. Where urbanization has, unlike in previously rural Rajpura, already driven up market prices relative to assessed agricultural prices, farmers start off with a tacit estimate of this discrepancy in their heads. And when land prices dramatically escalate after the announcement of acquisition, which usually takes over a year to complete, farmers feel entitled to a share—and have demanded it again and again.

Had Rajpura's farmers been compensated under LARRA, they would have received less than half of what the average farmer did receive through the plot system.[29] Other state governments have, before and since, adopted a similar policy—returning anywhere between 5% and 50% of the acquired land back to farmers in the form of developed land.[30] They have no doubt been motivated by the assessment, as in Rajasthan, that such a policy "softens" opposition. Under LARRA, such a concession would have to be on top of—but could not entirely substitute for—the base level of compensation demanded by law. And because the inter-state competition for investment militates toward keeping costs of acquisition low, land broker states are only likely to make such a concession when faced with significant political pressure. Since this pressure varies by state, the extent to which India's various land broker states move beyond LARRA to offer farmers some stake in future land appreciation is likely to vary considerably (Sud 2014b; Bedi and Tillin 2015). The model, one should not forget, rests on the existence of a booming land market and is thus vulnerable to dips in India's globally integrated property markets. This makes it less replicable in remote areas without booming land markets or where there is less privately titled land.[31]

What this study also suggests is that farmers' movements should assess any compensation policy on the scope it gives to brokers. Brokers, this book has shown, are powerful solvents of agrarian solidarity. They are ingenious at finding ways to profit from dispossession. And they are very effective at using the threat of government dispossession to pressure farmers into selling land or compensation rights. They are to dispossession politics what "kulaks" were to agrarian revolution, the difference being that they are not a stable class and can emerge from many different positions in the agrarian class structure. Compensation policies that increase the scope for brokers to operate are more likely to diffuse potential resistance. Rebuffing the operation of brokers, conversely, is a major challenge for anti-dispossession movements.

Nevertheless, there remain many examples in India of villages maintaining cohesion in the face of brokers and of flatly refusing to negotiate with state agencies. The idea of orchestrating a class compromise on the terrain of commodification presumes what needs to be explained: which is why some farmers are more or less willing to treat their land as a commodity. And explaining this requires not simply policy analysis, but the comparative sociology of agrarian milieux.

Agrarian Determinants of (Non-)Compliance

While the Rajasthan government was able to utilize land prices to dissipate opposition in Rajpura, this was greatly facilitated by specific features of its agrarian milieu. I have highlighted three important ones: water scarcity and significant off-farm diversification; a high degree of class and caste inequality; and a political history short on peasant rebellion. But forms of agricultural production, patterns of inequality, and political histories vary tremendously across India's diverse agrarian milieux, which are themselves constantly changing. Although a comparison between Rajpura and other sites of dispossession in India (much less elsewhere) is beyond the scope of this investigation, a cursory examination of India's "land wars" suggests a highly uneven terrain for the Indian state's would-be-material compromise.

Agricultural Profitability and Dependence

Agricultural profitability is a starting—but not ending—point for explaining the willingness of farmers to comply with dispossession. Rajpura's rain-fed agriculture and livestock rearing was not strictly unprofitable or in "crisis," but increasingly unreliable monsoons had forced a majority of Rajpura's residents to partially diversify from agriculture and made them receptive to the SEZ's promise of jobs and urban facilities. Many of my informants bluntly maintained that "if there was water, then there would have been a fight." There is no testing this counterfactual, but there are many examples of "land wars" in fertile agricultural regions—such as in the Green Revolution heartlands of Haryana, Punjab, and Uttar Pradesh where almost all the land is fertile and much of it irrigated (Asher 2014); in Singur, West Bengal, where farmers cultivated three crops and were renowned for their potatoes; in Jagatsinghpur, Odisha, where farmers cultivate lucrative betel vines; in Kakinada, Andhra Pradesh, where farmers were defending relatively rich rice, cashew, coconut, and mango-producing coastal land (Srinivasalu 2014: 93–94); and also in Dholera, Gujarat, where dryland farmers would prefer to wait for the long-promised Narmada water than give their land for a Special Investment Region (Sampat 2016a: 61–63). Conversely, scholars have identified agricultural unprofitability as a factor explaining lack of strong resistance in other locations, such as Tamil Nadu (Vijayabaskar 2014) and parts of coastal Karnataka (Mody 2014). Profitability is, of course, partly a function of holding size, which varies enormously across India but is generally small by global standards. But the effects of land size are not straightforward: while micro-holdings can make agriculture unviable and thus reduce the "cost" of dispossession, they also limit the absolute gains from compensation. Rajpura's landholdings were, in this respect, "ideal" for eliciting compliance—three times larger than the national average but unirrigated, which maximized the discrepancy between the land's value as real estate and as farmland.

Yet, there are also many "land wars" in regions without irrigated or particularly fertile land: Nandigram, with its unirrigated land, is a prime example; Polepally in dry Telangana another. It may be, rather, that it is the *relative* profitability of agriculture vis-à-vis urban opportunities and thus the degree of farmers' dependence on land that is more important. Vijayabaskar (2014: 308) argues that it is the contrast between Tamil Nadu's dynamic urban economy—with the second highest share of manufacturing employment in India—and "the most unremunerative farming in the country" that largely explains the relative "silence" around SEZs there. But the ability to take advantage of non-farm employment is also at least partly shaped by the skill and education levels of farmers. One can imagine a milieu in which high levels of nearby manufacturing growth combine with a relatively educated rural population to make land dispossession less explosive. This does not describe most of India; but relative differences in these factors may help to explain some variation in (non-)compliance to dispossession.

To complicate matters, these factors probably have different effects on different kinds of farmer protests. Farmers engaged in anti-dispossession protests can be divided into two categories: those who are bargaining for more compensation and those who refuse to bargain. Many land acquisition protests, especially in the highly commercialized peri-urban plains, are primarily over prices (Asher 2014; Kennedy 2014). It is possible that every farmer has his or her price; and it is true that farmers who start by flatly refusing may eventually come to the negotiating table. But in practice, there are many examples of farmers absolutely refusing to negotiate. Comparative research into the agrarian-determinants of (non-)compliance must keep this distinction in mind.

But while agricultural profitability, off-farm diversification, and ability to succeed in an urban economy vary in the aggregate across regions or villages, they also clearly vary within them. And this highlights the importance of the next factor.

Local Patterns of Inequality

Rajpura's substantial inequalities, rooted in the failures of postcolonial land reform to fully transform the feudal distribution of property in a former princely state, made it easier for the Rajasthan government to undercut any opposition to dispossession. A deeply unequal and caste-based distribution of land created the foundation for markedly unequal abilities to diversify from agriculture in the post-independence decades. These inequalities were reflected not only in distributions of economic capital but also, by virtue of diversification, in distributions of cultural and social capital. While Chapter 3 demonstrated that each of these species of capital could be traced to the failures of land reform to undermine a comprehensively unequal feudal order, Chapter 5 illustrated that each had an independent effect on farmers' ability to profit from land markets. Economic capital shaped how much land farmers could speculate on and how long they could wait, cultural capital affected farmers' ability to shrewdly navigate land markets, and social capital enabled well-connected villagers to become brokers. In sum, market-based compensation worked so well politically because Rajpura's residents had such unequal capacities to profit from land markets economically. But this raises the question of whether it will be as easy to elicit compliance where such inequalities are muted; for example, where land reform was more successful (e.g., Kerala and West Bengal) and economic inequalities less pronounced; where education or informal business experience is uniformly low; and where extra-village social networks are either more homogenous (because of greater equality in other forms of capital) or simply rarer due to geographic remoteness.

More than degree of inequality, however, the case of Rajpura allows us to see the importance of qualitatively specific patterns of inequality. As a thought experiment, one can imagine a village with the same Gini coefficient of landholdings as Rajpura, but that is relatively polarized between a small class of rich upper-caste landlords—say a handful of Mahinders—and a majority of impoverished lower-caste smallholders. In such a situation, which lacks the complex and graduated stratification of Rajpura, one can more easily imagine the lower-caste poor maintaining solidarity and rebuffing the *dalals* in their midst. If Rajpura's farmers were not so complexly stratified, things may have turned out different politically. Things are also likely to have turned out differently if a larger section of Rajpura was excluded from compensation because they lacked private property rights. The Bavariyas could be so brutally evicted without compensation because they were small in number and politically marginalized. But the excluded—whether tenants or untitled "encroachers" on forest or grazing land—are a much higher proportion of the population in other agrarian milieux. My analysis suggests that while the truly assetless among the excluded may be indifferent to dispossession, the landless who are dependent on non-titled agrarian land for subsistence or habitation have much to lose and little to gain. Whether the more modest provisions for landless populations in LARRA will provide a sufficient inducement to such populations remains to be seen; but the landless cannot be brought into a real estate-based political compromise.

Political Histories

Finally, Rajpura had a relatively muted political history with no living memory of peasant insurgency. In their pioneering studies of the first-wave of anti-dispossession movements in India, Ramachandra Guha (1989), Amita Baviskar (1995), and Nandini Sundar (2007) emphasized the importance of political histories or "popular memories" of resistance to contemporary struggles against dams and extractive industries. Similarly, studies of more recent anti-SEZ protests have found that many of the most militant land wars have arisen in regions with strong histories of political agitation, whether against the colonial state, landlords, or prior attempts by the Indian state to dispossess land. Peasants in Nandigram, for instance, declared their sub-division independent from British rule during the Quit India movement, digging trenches around their villages—the same tactic they would reuse against the proposed SEZ seventy years later. They were also, along with the farmers of Singur, participants in the communist-led Tebhaga rebellion of the 1940s, which demanded two-thirds of the crop for cultivators (Sen 1979: 450). And many were beneficiaries of the Left Front's land reform of the 1970s, which made the same government's usurpation of that land for private capitalists all the more galling. Outside of the particularly combustible conditions of West Bengal, a "hotbed of revolt" since the early colonial period (Gough 1979: 117), many of the movements resisting SEZs and other large land acquisition projects also drew on strong histories of peasant agitation. The villages where farmers successfully stopped Reliance's Maha Mumbai SEZ had participated in the Seven Year Peasant Strike for land reform and the "Forest Satyagraha" against colonial rule in the 1930s (Mujumdar and Menezes 2014: 253). The villages protesting a DLF SEZ in Southern Punjab had, since the Green Revolution, been a "hotbed of peasant activism and militancy" (Asher 2014: 156), while those protesting against SEZs around Chandigarh had a history of resistance to land acquisition dating to the initial construction of the state capital (Asher 2014: 158; Kalia 1999: 35, 127). The bloody land wars of Bhatta-Parsaul during the 2000s were rooted in over a decade of land acquisition struggles (Pai and Kumar 2014) and, along with those of Punjab and Haryana, participation in the "farmers' movements" of the 1980s for remunerative prices, most notably the Bharatiya Kisan Union (BKU). The successful struggle against the Cipla SEZ in Goa drew on memories of the anti-Portuguese independence struggle and more recent opposition in the 1990s to a DuPont nylon factory proposed for the same land (Sampat 2015).[32] And one of the few movements resisting a SEZ in Tamil Nadu arose in villages with "a strong history of communist mobilization" (Vijayabaskar 2014: 324). While not every anti-dispossession protest is rooted in such a history, the preceding strongly suggests that the diverse political histories of India's agrarian milieux contribute to a highly uneven terrain for producing compliance to dispossession. As more farmers acquire such political experience, moreover, they will be harder to dispossess in the future.

The Upshot: A Politically Tenuous Regime of Dispossession

While comparative research will surely illuminate other salient features of agrarian milieux—and combinations of those features—that affect farmer compliance to dispossession, this study suggests that compliance may be more difficult where agriculture is more profitable and/or off-farm opportunities lower; where inequalities are more muted and less graduated; and where experiences of political insurgency are stronger. India's diverse agrarian milieux vary tremendously on each score. The scholarly implication is that comparative research into the agrarian determinants of (non-) compliance to dispossession is a wide open and rich field for social science. The political implication is that India's neoliberal regime of dispossession is very likely to have mixed success for the foreseeable future. This study suggests that there is a possibility, where state governments offer adequate concessions, to orchestrate a material compromise in agrarian milieux resembling Rajpura. But land broker states are going to have a hard time in many other places, especially if they do not go beyond LARRA. Yet, as this book goes to press, five BJP-ruled states (including Rajasthan) have passed laws that actually dilute LARRA (Menon, Kohli, and Gupta 2017), which suggests that the tide may once again be moving in the opposite direction.

With inadequate concessions and a long-gone ability to make farmers "sacrifice for the nation," there remains, of course, the time-honored route of coercion and violence. Initially, the BJP government of Narendra Modi seemed ready to embark on such a route. But, as Modi quickly realized, dispossessing farmers is not as easy as it used to be. India's neoliberal regime of dispossession is far more politically explosive than the developmentalist regime, even during the latter's waning days. And in India's competitive "post-Congress polity" (Palshikar, Suri, and Yadav 2014), there is no shortage of opposition parties willing to take up the issue as a cudgel against incumbents—even if they do so cynically and forget the lesson once in power. This is not to say that violence against resisting farmers will stop, particularly against politically marginalized populations like Dalits and *adivasis* in relatively remote locations, not to speak of those in proximity to the Maoist insurgency (Sundar 2016: 45–47). And if LARRA is further diluted, it is not clear how else state governments will be able to elicit farmer compliance. But it does seem decreasingly likely that violent repression will be effective; and more likely that it will unleash a new wave of "land wars."

If one can wager one prediction with confidence, it is that India's "land question" remains far from resolution. It may, in fact, be irresolvable under the conditions of neoliberal capitalism in India's electoral democracy. The question, then, is what kind of politics do anti-dispossession movements represent; and what are their prospects for transforming neoliberal capitalism?

Land Wars and Development

The politics of dispossession has seldom been taken seriously. It has been over two decades since anti-dam movements began to shift attention from "conflict in the factory and the field" to "conflict around forests and rivers" (Baviskar

1995: 40). Since then, dispossession politics has become even more explosive and has spread from the hills into the plains. Yet, while modernizers consider these protests to be obstacles to development, some on the left still consider them "populist" diversions from "real" class struggle. I have argued that both dismissals are based on false assumptions. The economic growth driving much dispossession in contemporary India has exceedingly narrow beneficiaries, raising the question of why its obstruction deserves any more condemnation than its promotion. The classical Marxist dismissal, for its part, is based on the counterfactual that dispossessed peasants are revolutionary industrial workers in the making: an assumption that has little basis in current historical trends. In contrast to both positions, scholars associated with what I have called the predatory theory of dispossession have taken anti-dispossession movements seriously but sometimes romantically, seeing them as heroic defenses of the "commons" by presumably egalitarian and sustainable "peasant communities."[33] But India's anti-dispossession movements are, in most instances, defending private property, the distribution of which is almost everywhere unequal and intertwined with caste and patriarchal domination. Agriculture is in many of these places commercialized, resource-intensive, and of declining profitability. None of these are reasons for redistributing land upward to multinational corporations for projects with few claims to "public purpose" aside from their contribution to GDP. But they are reasons for a more nuanced assessment of what dispossession politics is, and what it can accomplish.

Anti-dispossession movements are by nature "defensive" (Tilly 1978) or "state-resisting" (Hung 2011). They arise when villagers come to know that plans are afoot to take their land for some or other purpose. Often, this knowledge comes shrouded in misinformation.[34] But the threat of dispossession, once perceived, is usually quite alarming. In contrast to the ongoing exploitation of landlords or employers, dispossession constitutes a total and one-time threat to means of production, subsistence, and associated ways of life. This threat is felt by all those who find their means of production or subsistence in the cross-hairs of a project. This means that anti-dispossession movements, when they emerge, are inherently cross-class but take their precise social composition from local agrarian social structures. In some cases, this means bringing together relatively more egalitarian small cultivators; in others, large farmers who brutally exploit their lower-caste laborers or tenants. Different factions within the village, moreover, are more or less likely to join an anti-dispossession movement: sometimes upper-caste large farmers take the lead while ignoring marginal farmers and tenants; in other cases, it is the opposite.[35] While the village rich have much to lose absolutely, they are also usually more diversified and better positioned to gain from new economic activities. Purely landless workers are least likely to oppose the dispossession of the landed; but I have suggested that the landless who depend on untitled agrarian property have, along with the semiproletariat, much to lose and little to gain by compensation. The challenge facing anti-dispossession movements is to create an instrumental solidarity among villagers who may otherwise occupy disparate or even antagonistic social positions; and sometimes these antagonisms are too sharp to be bridged. But to defend land against its upward redistribution to capitalists usually means bracketing—at least temporarily—its existing distribution within the village.

Even if local differences can be bridged and commonality found among a critical mass of villagers, there are seldom suitable organizations on hand for resisting it. Aside from the fact that mainstream political parties have historically ignored the issue, dispossession often cuts across political affiliations; and there are often few other formal organizations present in rural areas. While political parties are increasingly entering the fray of anti-dispossession politics in India, this usually occurs at a late stage. Anti-dispossession movements almost always emerge as independent entities, with ad hoc organizations of varying formality put together specifically for the purpose. This is reflected in movement names, which often follow the modular form of "Save the (Place Name) Movement" or "Anti-(Project Name) Struggle Committee." Such organizations usually dissolve once dispossession is stopped or carried through.

The basic strategy of anti-dispossession politics is to keep possession of the land and to create legal and political obstacles to forcible removal. Possession and time are the crucial sources of leverage: projects cannot proceed without land and delays are costly to capitalists. While anti-dispossession movements utilize the generic repertoire of popular protest in India—the sit-in (*dharna*), road block (*rasta roko*), or encirclement (*gherao*) of officials—these are supplemented by more specific counter-enclosure tactics adapted to local geographies. This might begin with the obstruction of preliminary land surveys and the refusal of entry to government or company officials. While dam builders could flood villages from afar once the dam site itself was secured, other projects must remove people before starting construction. Politics at the point of enclosure then becomes a pitched battle to prevent removal, whether through trenches, barricades, or human chains. Such physical obstruction is often combined with legal challenges, which can increase compensation and generate significant delays—as the Saini standoff illustrated in miniature—but seldom stop a project. Legal cases can, however, create time for political strategies to work. Political strategies involve drawing outside attention to the cause by involving media, NGOs, prominent social activists, or even celebrities. In some places, it has involved allying with the National Alliance of People's Movements, farmers' movements or, in certain pockets of central India, the Maoists. Increasingly, it can involve gaining the support of opposition parties which, though opportunistic, can help to amplify one's message in the state capital and thus increase the political costs of violent removal. A major challenge throughout is to rebuff the dissipating effect of brokers and selective state inducements. It is a war of attrition; but if state force can be kept at bay, time is on the side of farmers, especially where sunk costs and borrowed money make delays costly to capitalists. There are now many cases in rural India of companies throwing up their hands and walking away.

That is not always what farmers want. I have suggested that while some anti-dispossession movements want to stop their dispossession entirely, others simply want better compensation. While both kinds of movements might use the same tactics with equal militancy, the first presents a challenge to the regime of dispossession itself while the second seeks to reduce the rate of accumulation by dispossession. These different goals can sometimes be found in the same movement; the goals of a movement change over time due to inducements or despair; and perhaps everyone has their price. But if so, we have not seen it. Although many farmers' protests in the peri-urban plains take the second form, there are many examples of farmers who have steadfastly refused to bargain: Nandigram farmers began protesting before compensation amounts were even discussed; farmers fighting the POSCO steel plant staged a public burning of their compensation packages; those fighting SEZs and mining projects in many other locations have proven unresponsive to enhanced compensation packages. This outright refusal to give land for projects was pioneered by the Narmada Bachao Andolan, which adopted a firm anti-dam stance captured in the slogan, "No one will be moved, the dam will not be built." By refusing to bargain over the land's exchange value, these farmers cannot be brought into a compromise on the terrain of commodification.

No matter which goal they are fighting for, anti-dispossession movements can be expressed through very different political ideologies. Most farmers have no more than concrete material motivations for resisting dispossession; if the project can be shifted onto someone else's land, many may not object (Nielsen 2010; Majumdar 2012). It is not clear why we should expect them to. As Scott (1979) has pointed out of even revolutionary movements, overlaying concrete motivations with ideology has often been left to activists and intellectuals. The explicit political ideologies these movements do articulate are shaped by local agrarian social structures, political histories, and contingent ties to outside activists. Some movements evince various hues of Indian socialism or Gandhianism (Guha 1988; Baviskar 1995); others the type of agrarian populism pioneered by the landed and upper-caste farmers' movements of the 1980s (Byres 1988); some regional chauvinism (Da Silva 2014) or identity-based claims to territory; and, in some pockets, revolutionary Maoism.[36] Anti-dispossession movements have by now attracted support—temporary or opportunistic as it may be—from every single party in India, from Communists to pro-business Hindu nationalists. As Karl Polanyi (2001) observed, "countermovements" can point in very different political directions. Whether these movements can "push beyond contingent alliances against dispossession" (Sampat 2016b: 41) to achieve more offensive redistributive gains will depend on how and by whom they are organized. Given the material stake of large farmers in the existing distribution of land and their dependence on the exploitation of typically low-caste laborers, it is those movements originating in the lower end of the agrarian social structure that will be most amenable to such a project (Lerche 2013). But, in general, the only thing India's "land wars" share is a refusal to be dispossessed, at least on the terms offered.

The case of Rajpura suggests, however, that we should take this refusal seriously. While anti-dispossession protests exhibit almost every single "weakness" attributed to social movements—they are defensive and single-issue, localized in scale, ephemeral and ad-hoc in organization, ambiguous in class, and promiscuous in ideology—they are also, collectively, the single largest obstacle to neoliberal capitalism in India. And this particular historical phase of capitalism is a highly unpromising one for dispossessed farmers, especially the poorest among them. It is generating nothing like the industrial modernity which inspired both technocrats and revolutionaries in the 20th century. And there is little in its trajectory that suggests a path to socialist redemption. India's "land wars" are the symptom of a regime of dispossession that has lost legitimacy, cannot provide inclusion and offers, at best, one-time payouts. Proliferating farmer protests have obstructed its scale of operations and, at the very least, bettered the terms of dispossession. They have checked further upward redistribution in an already massively unequal society. And they have ignited a debate about how, as a long-forgotten commitment once put it, "ownership and control of the material resources of the community" can best "subserve the common good." They reflect aspirations that may be superficially moderate, but whose fulfillment would require a radical reorientation of Indian capitalism. These include, as in Rajpura, good salaried employment, broad access to infrastructure and services, and, until these are satisfied, land.

EPILOGUE

I conducted most of the fieldwork for this book between 2009 and 2011, but have revisited Rajpura every year or two since. In addition to the personal relationships I have built there, my curiosity keeps drawing me back. Would the real estate boom continue? Would the SEZ eventually give people more employment? How will the next generation of youth navigate this new economy? Will urbanization ultimately change gender and caste relations? Would there be some dramatic political uprising? Would time refute my arguments? Each time I boarded the bus in Jaipur, I anxiously anticipated the answers I might find in Rajpura. And each revisit did reveal new twists to individual stories and the overall process of change recorded in this book—which had to be cut off somewhere. For the most part, the book ends in June 2014, when I spent a week in Rajpura shortly after India's national elections. However, two short revisits in the summers of 2016 and 2017—after the book had been written and submitted—revealed notable changes that demanded an epilogue.

First of all, the MWC has continued to expand—albeit slowly. Because MWC officials stopped returning my calls back in 2011, my data on this expansion is limited to public information and what I could observe from Rajpura. But by 2016, a handful of new IT/ITES companies had set up offices, a textile and knitwear tool producer had set up in the handicrafts zone, and a JCB plant had begun to produce construction machines in the Domestic Tariff Area. As far as SEZ development went, this made the MWC comparatively successful—India's Comptroller Auditor General had, in 2014, released a scathing report documenting the failure of many SEZs to attract *any* industry. It was still a relative success. Twelve years after its initiation, MWC was barely using one-third of the land allotted to it, its only major manufacturing unit was producing for the domestic market (the point of SEZs had been to boost exports), and the zone was still not large enough to support the residential Lifestyle Zone, which was to generate most of MWC's profits. In Jaipur, the common impression among government officials was of a less-than-successful project. There were even murmurs in the Rajasthan Assembly about making the company return the unutilized land to farmers.

In Rajpura, the employment situation was not much changed. The few handicrafts units were small, the JCB plant was capital-intensive, and all the companies seemed committed to hiring outside laborers. Although more workers appeared to be commuting daily from Jaipur, people in Rajpura still complained vociferously about not getting work. A small minority still worked as security guards and there was perhaps a slight uptick in the number of drivers, though several complained of being fired because their cars were now too old—even before they could be paid off. So while I could not conduct another survey, I did not see any major change on the employment front—and neither could people in Rajpura.

As of 2016, it did seem like village commerce was growing. A few more shops had come up here and there, several *chai* stalls had added TVs, a liquor store had emerged behind the JCB plant, there was an ATM in Laduram Meena's multistorey complex, and traffic through the market was brisk.

It was, therefore, a tremendous shock when I returned a year later to find the village road barricaded and the village market barely holding onto life. The original MWC plan had called for closing the old village road, which connected Rajpura to the SEZ and the national highway, in order to make the various sector-specific zones contiguous. But this had hovered over the village as a very abstract possibility. In January, it became less abstract as villagers learned that the closure was imminent. The village "big men" organized several protests over the ensuing month. By several counts, three hundred to four hundred people participated. A delegation met with high-level government officials, but to no avail. A month before I arrived, several platoons of police oversaw the barricading of the old village road, as well as two lateral roads that connected the village to nearby towns. The road to Jaipur would now be lengthened by approximately 5 km, a huge nuisance for all those who commuted there for work. Most visibly, this was the death knell for the village market. Closed in on three sides, there was no reason for anyone but village residents to pass through it. Many shops were shuttered, there were few people milling about, and the traffic was so sparse that, as one farmer put it, "you can play cricket." Once jubilant shopkeepers were morose, reporting that their business was down by at least half. While only a fraction of villagers had a stake in this petty mercantile economy, it too was now decimated. It would be hard to imagine a more definitive expression of the uneven and enclaved growth described in Chapter 7.

To top it off, by 2017 the real estate boom had finally gone bust. Over the preceding year, the real estate market had cooled both regionally and nationally. Land prices had actually gone down in Rajpura for the first time—villagers estimated that the prices of compensation plots had halved, but there were simply no buyers. Some quipped that brokers were now studying for government exams. All of this meant little to those who had lost their land long ago or had never had any. But those still resting their hopes on the appreciation of their plots would now have to wait indefinitely, or settle for far less than they expected. Rajpura's get-rich-quick days appeared to be over.

All of the mechanisms of exclusionary growth highlighted in the book, then, appeared to still be operating if not intensifying. Non-labor-intensive growth coupled with a footloose migratory system continued to under-employ Rajpura's dispossessed farmers, the closing of the village market exemplified the spatial unevenness of zoned infrastructural investment, and the speculative land bubble—by far the main contribution of the SEZ to the local economy—had burst. Of the various compensatory schemes, moreover, NREGA was no longer running in the village and the self-help group in the Balai *mohalla* had folded (having never received its sewing machine).

Amid this rather bleak scene was one real gain—which came not from the SEZ but from the efforts of Banvarilal Sharma, the muckraking *sarpanch* elected over Laduram Meena in 2015. Although a Congress *neta* dealing with a BJP government, Banvarilal's relentless pulling of strings in the state administration succeeded in getting a small reverse osmosis water filtration plant, part of a pilot public-private partnership scheme, established in Rajpura. Although the contract with the private company appeared fraught, and the machine periodically broke down, when it worked the plant delivered clean drinking water to villagers at Rs 5 per 20-liter bottle. This was a concrete achievement, even if villagers still complained about not getting the cheaper and more abundant Bisalpur Dam water that was being piped into the Mahindra World City.

The individual lives I detailed in the book continued on their divergent and often precarious trajectories. Laduram Meena was facing possible indictment based on his illegal allocation of *panchayat* land to himself, and his big apartment complex was emptying out with the closing of the village road. But he still had a lot of land and many businesses, including a petrol pump that he had just opened near the SEZ. Mahinder did not come to the village much, though I heard that after the old *thakur's* death the heirs were fighting over the massive inheritance. Mohan Nayak was briefly arrested and his sex hotel closed, then reopened. Mahesh Bunkar was still trying to make a go at the vegetable business, but because of the closing of the village road, he lost his renters and the value of his empty storefront (the source of dispute with his brother) had plunged. The family of his neighbor, the Balai *dalal*, had returned to sharecropping. Prakash Bunkar was still driving, and had not sold his plot—whose value had now halved. The silver lining was that his son had received a scholarship from the Delhi Public School, established on the national highway before the SEZ arrived, and seemed to be genuinely learning English. The Saini standoff continued, though it seemed to be moving toward a resolution that would leave them many times richer. The Sharmas were still living in their temple, and their son was still unemployed. The Gujjar *chai* stall owner had lost his home on the *panchayat* land, his business was hurting with the closing of the village road, and there was "a case going" over his questionably allocated plot. The Bavariyas were long gone, while the Regars and Ranas had still seen little improvement—though one youth was grooming himself to be a Congress politician. The proletarianized continued their search for precarious work, and often had to travel an extra 5 km to find it.

After two booms and two busts, the mood in Rajpura was somber. The expectation that "good days are coming" had largely been dashed. Most now regarded that slogan of the 2014 national election with derision. When I reminded them of it, I got responses like: "Where are the good days? Bad days have come." "Good days have run away." "Development? It hasn't come." All the incumbent politicians, from whom they expected so much three years earlier, were unpopular once again. Aspirations still far outpaced objective possibilities, and that villagers took this out on politicians was a good thing. But I also got the sense that, twelve years after losing their land for the SEZ, those aspirations were deflating. As one lower-caste laborer remarked, as he showed me the barricaded village road, they had been sold a story. The story was "that jobs will come, services will be provided, business will grow." Gesturing toward the concrete wall, he concluded, "The story is over."

NOTES

Chapter 1

1. For Southeast Asia, see Li (2007); Hall, Hirsch, and Li (2011); Hall (2011); Kenney-Lazar (2012); and Dwyer (2013). For China, see Sargeson (2008), Sargeson and Song (2010), Hsing (2010), Chuang (2014), Chuang (2015), and Andreas and Zhan (2016).
2. See the collection of articles in the 2011 special issue on "Land: A New Wave of Accumulation by Dispossession in Africa?" *Review of African Political Economy* 38(128). See also Amanor (2012); Woodhouse (2012); Lavers (2012); R. Hall (2012); Burnod, Gingembre, and Ratsialonana (2013); Buckley (2013); and Fairbairn (2013).
3. For an overview, see the 2012 special issue on "Land Grabbing in Latin America," *Canadian Journal of Development Studies* 33(4); and also Borras et al. (2012), Grandia (2013), Grajales (2013), Oliveira (2013), Graef (2013), and Sullivan (2013).
4. Cognizant of the long and complicated debates over how to categorize rural producers (cf. Wolf 1966; Shanin 1987; Bernstein 2010), I use "farmer" as a convenient shorthand for "cultivator" throughout the text; as will become clear, however, I do not see farmers as a homogenous class but, rather, as comprising differentiated agrarian classes. I use the term "peasants" only to refer to cultivators in previous historical epochs, but largely avoid its use in relation to contemporary farmers in India, who mostly produce for the market and are often otherwise incorporated into capitalist wage labor (Bernstein 2010).
5. This is a twist on Varshney's (1995: 3) observation that, in India, "democracy *preceding* an industrial revolution . . . has led to the empowerment of the rural sector in the polity." Varshney was referring to the farmers' movements for remunerative prices in the 1980s, though one can see a similar logic at work in India's land wars. The twist is that it is not industrialization per se (for which the Nehruvian state very effectively dispossessed land for forty years), but the increasingly non-industrial demands for land under neoliberalism that have sharpened this contradiction.
6. For a useful synthesis of this literature, see Bernstein (2010).
7. For excellent recent assessments of this variation, see the special issue of *Journal of Agrarian Change* edited by Lerche, Shah, and Harriss-White (2013) and Pattenden (2016).
8. This begins with the classical treatments of the "agrarian question" (Kautsky 1988; Lenin 1964). See Byres (1991) and Bernstein (2010) for synoptic overviews of the subsequent literature, and Li (2014) for a more recent empirical illustration.
9. For foundational works on the political economy of "natural" disasters, see Watts (1983) and Davis (2001).
10. While the line between voluntary sale and coercion can be blurry, state expropriation and uncoordinated market alienation are in most cases distinct and distinguishable social processes. While both may result in people being separated from means of production and

subsistence, they are the outcomes of different social forces, are experienced differently, and generate distinct politics.

11. This conflation runs through much of the recent "land grab" literature, including attempts to quantify them (cf. Land Matrix n.d.).
12. Further, while dispossession conveys redistribution, displacement focuses on physical uprooting. While some forms of dispossession—such as for large dams—involve wholesale uprooting and relocation *en masse* to distant locations, others do not. And while dispossession—wholesale uprooting or not—is often devastating in socio-cultural as well as economic terms (Baviskar 1995), displacement puts the emphasis on *en*placement, or the prior place-based attachments to land that can be overstated in essentialized conceptions of rural people, indigenous or otherwise (Baviskar 1995; Li 2010a; Shah 2010).
13. See Midnight Notes Collective (1990), De Angelis (2001, 2007), Linebaugh (2008), and Caffentzis and Federici (2014).
14. Since its invention on the American prairie in 1874, barbed wire has been the most economical technology for enclosing space (see Razac 2002).
15. Those fighting dispossession are, consequently, just as likely to be defending small private property as "commons." Reducing struggles over dispossession to defense of the commons overlooks the unequal class relations and multiple property forms that characterize agrarian milieu in most of the world; and the implications of this for anti-dispossession politics. I return to this in Chapter 9.
16. Reynolds' fascinating history of "expropriation for the common good" in pre–eminent domain Europe is, however, marred by the way in which it internalizes justifications for dispossession into the definition of its object. Largely assuming castles and fortifications to be for the "common good," Reynolds (2010: 20, 23, 43) constantly hedges about who considered them to be so and then struggles to characterize the clearly class-driven enclosures—on which it is best to consult Neeson (1993).
17. The replacement of this act will be discussed in Chapter 9.
18. Perhaps more so than in China (cf. Walker 2006).
19. The direct expropriation of land that is the focus of this book is also distinct from the slow chipping away of customary rights (Thompson 1975), the gradual destruction of a natural resource base through pollution (Kirsch 2014), or gradual encroachment onto the territories and resources of non-sedentary populations (cf. Fratkin and Roth 2005; Galvin 2009). For a remarkable ethnographic account of the latter, see Clastres (1998).
20. For a re-assertion of the significance of the village, see Mines and Yazgi (2010).
21. While I cannot do justice to this literature here, see Rodney (1981) on the role of colonial dispossession in "underdeveloping" Africa. There is also a large literature, referenced in the next chapter, on colonial forestry in India; for Indonesia, see Peluso (1991). On settler colonialism in the Americas, see Banner (2005), Bowes (2014), and Coulthard (2014). On the history of the plantation form, see Mintz (2011). Studies of postcolonial dispossession often have a historical chapter on the colonial legacy (cf. Guha 1989; Baviskar 1995).
22. In India, this literature is particularly vast; important early contributions include Fernandes and Thukral (1989), Thukral (1992), Fernandes and Paranjpye (1997), Mathur (1995a), and Parasuraman (1999). Another large and related literature emerged critiquing the cost-benefit analyses of large dams (cf. Goldsmith and Hildyard 1984; Paranjpye 1988; Singh 1997; Banerji et al. 2000; WCD 2000; McCully 2001; Dharmadhikary 2005).
23. See, for example, Guha (1989), Carney and Watts (1990), Peluso (1991), Peters (1994), Baviskar (1995), Moore (2005), and several of the contributions to Peet and Watts (2004) and Peluso and Watts (2001).
24. Sociologists have observed more generally that neoliberal economic policies are accompanied by the extension of state coercion (cf. Wacquant 2008, 2010).
25. See, for example, several *Journal of Peasant Studies* special issues edited by Peluso and Lund (2011); White et al. (2012); Hall et al. (2015); the *Development and Change* special issue edited by Wolford et al. (2013); the *Third World Quarterly* special issue edited by Edelman, Oya, and Borras (2013); and the *Feminist Economics* special issue edited by Doss, Summerfield, and Tsikata (2014).

26. For a reading of Locke as theorist of agrarian capitalism, see Wood (1984) and Wood (2002). Perhaps the most forthright of the political economists on the connection between propertylessness and the division of labor, Steurt bluntly called for the "separation between parent earth and her industrious child" (quoted in Perelman 2000: 148).
27. Smith (1999: 331–332), quoted in Perelman (2000: 184).
28. On the contradictory relationship between liberalism and empire, see Guha (1997) and Mehta (1999).
29. See also Peters (1994) and Li (2007) for analyses of how the colonial logic of improvement carried over into postcolonial projects involving enclosure.
30. Concerned with Communist-inspired peasant insurgencies, modernization theorists saw peasant protest as irrational behavior that should be controlled by a strong political order (Huntington 1968: Smelser 1968: 127; Eisenstadt 1966: 24; Shils 1965).
31. While rejecting the idea that the dispossession of direct producers inaugurated capitalism (Wallerstein 2011), necessarily generated development (Arrighi and Piselli 1987; Arrighi, Aschoff, and Scully 2010) or was necessary for development (Arrighi 2007), dependency and world systems theorists have largely approached the issue of dispossession through the lens of inter-state transfers. While the plunder of natural resources featured in their accounts of colonialism (Frank 1979: esp. 10, 23, 146, 160–161; Arrighi 1994: 54; and especially Rodney 1981), this mechanism of transferring wealth from periphery to core was attributed less significance than—or not differentiated from—"unequal exchange" (Baran 1957; Frank 1966; Emmanuel 1972; Amin 1974; Mandel 1978). Perhaps because theorists like Frank and Wallerstein assumed that transformations of property relations flowed from the "needs" of the world economy (Brenner 1977: 87), they paid little attention to the actual political processes of dispossessing land for plantations, mines, and the infrastructure of colonial capitalism. But, curiously, dispossession was almost entirely absent from their analyses of postcolonial capitalism. Rodney (1981), who is the most explicit about colonial land dispossession for plantations and mines, directs his critique at the foreign ownership of land rather than the dispossession of land per se. This overriding focus on between-country inequalities leaves open the question of how such theorists would analyze dispossession for national industries that reduce global inequalities while expanding domestic ones.
32. Indeed, we will see shortly that promotion of social development appears, to its most prominent exponent, consistent with the large-scale dispossession of rural people.
33. Central to Hayek's argument about the superiority of the market as a coordinating mechanism is that state intervention—such as redistributing property—creates an ad hoc and arbitrary environment for individual action. If, on the contrary, state activity is restricted to maintaining the rule of law, "the individual can foresee the action of the state and make use of this knowledge as a datum in forming his own plans" and "knows precisely how far he will be protected against interference by others, or whether the state is in a position to frustrate individual efforts" (Hayek 1944: 89). While clearly concerned with warding off demands for progressive redistribution, the principle also stands in tension with the upward redistribution entailed by the dispossession of farmers for private companies.
34. On the distinction between neoliberalism as ideology and as political project, see Harvey (2005), Peck (2010), and Evans and Sewell (2013).
35. Chakravorty (2013: 173).
36. Amartya Sen, interviewed in *The Telegraph* (2007) after the protests in Singur and Nandigram.
37. Bardhan (2011: 56); on the necessity of land acquisition, see also Banerjee et al. (2007).
38. *The Telegraph* (2007).
39. Advocating for a pro-business dilution of India's 2013 land acquisition law (see Chapter 9), Arvind Panagariya (n.d.) argues that, "To build rural roads, highways, affordable housing, industrial corridors, educational institutions and hospitals, public capital must often be combined with private capital, management skills and entrepreneurship." On this basis, he argues that public and private projects should not be treated differently under India's land acquisition laws. Panagariya curiously omits from his list private investments in *unaffordable* housing, SEZs, private factories, and so on, which are more likely to be facilitated by the removal of this distinction. Sanjoy Chakravorty sees the distinction between public and private sector projects as "an unfortunate distraction" in debates over land acquisition since the public sector has

historically been the largest source of displacement—which was certainly true two decades ago, but overlooks the dramatic shift toward land acquisition for the private sector since the early 1990s (Chapter 2) and still leaves unanswered the question of why private corporations should receive similar assistance to state projects. Strangely, Chakravorty (2013: 188–189) argues that "rather than banning the private sector, the state should limit its own power"—but the question at stake is precisely the state's significant power to assist the private sector, which Chakravorty's proposals would expand.

40. As Nozick (2013) observes, utilitarianism is logically consistent with the existence of "utility monsters": individuals or entities that hoard utility at the expense of others so long as aggregate utility is maximized.
41. Of a society of small independent producers, Marx (1977: 928) approvingly quotes Pecueur that to "perpetuate it would be . . . 'to decree universal mediocrity.' At a certain stage of development, it brings into the world the material means of its own destruction. . . . It has to be annihilated; it is annihilated." Aside from such quotes in *Capital,* there are several well-known lines of the *Communist Manifesto* and the 1959 Preface that lend themselves to such a stagist and deterministic reading. Marx's *New York Tribune* writings on colonialism in India are also often taken as strong evidence for this position (Avineri 1969), which Warren (1980) embraces. Ahmad (1992) provides a nuanced reading while Anderson (2010) sees evolution.
42. Marx argues that "as soon as this metamorphosis has sufficiently decomposed the old society . . . what is now to be expropriated is not the self-employed worker, but the capitalist who exploits a larger number of workers. . . . In the former case, it was a matter of the expropriation of the mass of the people by a few usurpers; but in this case, we have the expropriation of a few usurpers by the mass of the people" (Marx 1977: 928, 930). To actually think you could halt the first historical round of expropriation was a form of what Marx, in the *Communist Manifesto,* called *petit bourgeois* socialism and what Leninists call populism. For an orthodox adherence to this view, see Brass (2015). While I am convinced that Marx's views became *less* stagist over time (Shanin 1983; Anderson 2010), I am not convinced that his corpus can be cleansed of this shortcoming. The point, at any rate, should be to reconstruct the theory.
43. See Smith (1999: 371–372).
44. After posing this question about previous accumulation, *Wealth of Nations* quickly trails off into a discussion of its further accumulation and division, never returning to the question.
45. He also discussed "bloody legislation" to make the dispossessed submit to wage labor and the public debt, which "endows unproductive money with the power of creation and thus turns it into capital" (Marx 1977: 919). While Foucault (1995) built on the former, Arrighi (1994, 2010: 373–374) extended the latter, arguing that it was a mechanism by which declining hegemonic states try to stave off crisis by investing in rising capitalist states.
46. Marx clearly thought that both were important—hence his devotion of entire chapters to each—but was contradictory about their relative importance. While stating that "so-called primitive accumulation, therefore, is nothing else than the historical process of divorcing the producer from the means of production" (1977: 875), he also calls processes of colonization "the chief moments of primitive accumulation" (1977: 915).
47. Marx (1977: 873) called it "an accumulation which is not the result of the capitalist mode of production but its point of departure." He further clarified, "It appears as 'primitive' because it forms the *pre-history* of capital, and the mode of production corresponding to capital" (Marx 1977: 875, emphasis added). In the more Hegelian idiom of the *Grundrisse,* Marx (1973: 459) states, "The conditions and presuppositions of the *becoming,* of the *rising,* of capital presuppose precisely that it is not yet in being but merely in *becoming*; they therefore disappear as real capital arises, capital which itself, on the basis of its own reality, posits the conditions for its realization."
48. To the extent that primitive accumulation temporally continues, it does so *serially* as different societies transition to capitalism (I thank Michael Watts for this formulation). Thus Marx (1977: 931) observes that, "In Western Europe, the homeland of political economy, the process of primitive accumulation has more or less been accomplished. . . . It is otherwise in the colonies." He also provides the suggestion that "the history of this expropriation assumes different aspects in different countries, and runs through its various phases in different orders of succession, and at different historical epochs" (Marx 1977: 876). But he provides no

suggestion that dispossession has an ongoing relation to capitalism once developed in any particular context. I thus remain unconvinced that one can derive a theory of "ongoing" primitive accumulation from Marx's own writings (Perelman 2000; De Angelis 2007). Marx's historical delimitation of primitive accumulation is puzzling, especially when one considers that he wrote extensively about colonialism (Avineri 1969; Anderson 2010) and recognized that capitalism would increase demands on land and natural resources (Foster 1999). Perelman (2000: 29–33) argues that Marx sought to downplay the ongoing significance of primitive accumulation to maintain his political focus on exploitation as the main evil of capitalism. Whatever the reason, Marx did not leave a theory of the ongoing relationship between dispossession and capitalism.

49. In Chapter 25 of *Capital,* Marx (1977) calls this "The General Law of Capitalist Accumulation."
50. In his late letters to the Russian revolutionary Vera Zasulich, Marx wrote that his "so-called theory" of primitive accumulation was confined to the "genesis of capitalist production" in Europe and had limited applicability to other contexts. Marx thus advised that Russia did not need to pass through capitalism to get to socialism, and even suggested that, under certain conditions, the peasant commune (*mir*) could be "the fulcrum for social regeneration in Russia" (Shanin 1983: 124). I believe it is a stretch to argue that Marx held this view all along, and more likely that his view became less unilinear over time (Anderson 2010). The important point is that Marx himself saw the problem with turning his account of "primitive accumulation" into a universal theory.
51. As Sewell (2005: 84) defines it, "A teleological explanation is the attribution of the cause of a historical happening neither to the actions and reactions that constitute the happening nor to concrete and specifiable conditions that shape or constrain the actions and reactions but rather to abstract transhistorical processes leading to some future historical state. Events in some historical present, in other words, are explained by events in the future."
52. Large debates in the second half of the 20th century focused upon whether capitalism, in fact, originated in rural England; and whether the enclosures were central to this process. These empirical questions fueled a larger theoretical debate about what defined capitalism, and how one could determine where one mode of production gave way to another. Interest in these questions was motivated, in the 1960s and 1970s, by the communist and anti-colonial "peasant wars" raging across Asia, Africa, and Latin America. The question of whether and how capitalism was developing in the agrarian societies of the Third World was seen as central to their prospects for revolutionary change and, failing that, economic development. Debates in various national contexts over "the extent to which capitalism has developed in the countryside, the forms that it takes, [and] the barriers which may impede its development" (Byres 1991: 9) became the bread and butter of a reinvigorated peasant studies for several decades. For a collection of the so-called "modes of production" debate in India, see Patnaik (1990).
53. On the first, see Bhaduri (1983), who stressed the importance of debt to primitive accumulation; and on the latter, see Preobrazhensky (1965), Byres (1991: 11), De Janvry (1981: 37), Ka and Seldon (1986), and Hung (2016: Ch. 2). My argument is not that these applications are wrong, but that they illustrate why primitive accumulation is an ambiguous term of uncertain applicability to land dispossession specifically (see also Hall 2013a).
54. Gerschenkron (1962) provided an early critique of that argument. In a more recent analysis, Arrighi, Aschoff, and Scully (2010) build on the work of Hart (2002) to argue that excessive proletarianization has inhibited capital accumulation in South Africa.
55. Those who opposed this deterministic framework were denounced as "populists." See, for example, Brass (1995, 2000, 2015). I also believe the "agrarian transition" framework advanced so brilliantly by Byres (1991, 1996) ultimately fell into this trap. While critiques of peasant essentialism are well taken, the presumed counterfactual that dispossessing peasants creates the material and political foundations for socialism has proven unconvincing—as this book underscores.
56. Indeed, when we correct for the consequential mistranslation, it leaves us with the oxymoron of "ongoing original accumulation."
57. It is impossible to cite all the scholarship applying this term to land grabs alone, attesting to the concept's enduring popularity.

58. However, the problematic of transition faced its own difficulties and its relevance may anyway be declining along with the importance of agriculture to national industrialization (Bernstein 2012; Lerche 2013).
59. For the best analysis of how financialization has contributed to the recent "farmland rush," see Fairbairn (2014).
60. On growing surplus populations and complex patterns of class formation in the "developing" world, see Bernstein (2006), Davis (2006), Standing (2011), Li (2010b), and Endnotes (2015).
61. While Harvey never addresses the class positions of those targeted by accumulation by dispossession, after making the case for dispossession politics he worries—in older Marxist fashion—that they may be backward-looking and obstruct "more positive changes" (Harvey 2003: 163–164).
62. Luxemburg was alone among the early Marxist theorists of imperialism to stress the importance of land dispossession. "Classical" Marxist theories of imperialism were less interested in the consequences of colonialism for colonized people than with whether it served to offset capitalist crises in the West (Lenin 1939; Bukharin 1973; Hilferding 1981). While theorists of imperialism disagreed on the precise economic significance of colonialism (Arrighi 1978), the need for access to foreign markets was given more importance than the dispossession of natural resources. It was *political control over territories rather than the dispossession of land* that animated classical Marxist theories of imperialism (on the distinction, see Elden [2013]).
63. Of Polanyi's fictitious commodities, land receives the shortest and least coherent treatment. After a brief discussion of the English enclosures, Polanyi's chapter on land swiftly moves into a discussion of free trade in agricultural products rather than the commodification of land itself.
64. In addition to the expropriation and privatization of land, Harvey includes the extraction of rents from intellectual property rights; the privatization of collective social assets (such as pensions, healthcare, and other social entitlements); and the various predations of finance capital.
65. Harvey states, "What accumulation by dispossession does is release a set of assets (including labor power) at very low (and in some instances zero) cost. Over-accumulated capital can seize hold of such assets and immediately turn them to profitable use" (Harvey 2003: 149).
66. Confusingly, however, Harvey continually oscillates between using primitive accumulation and accumulation by dispossession. The distinction, for Harvey (2003: 164), seems to rest on whether the process "opens up a path to expanded reproduction" or "disrupts and destroys a path already open." Harvey seems to be thinking about the contrast between industrialization and financial devaluations, but this certainly makes the concept even more confusing when applied to land dispossession. Land dispossession for projects like SEZs—which Harvey gives as an example—choke off forms of agrarian accumulation (of varying profitability) but might very well open up paths for capitalist accumulation.
67. See also Ashman and Callinicos (2006: 119–120).
68. Brenner (1977) made this point persuasively in his account of the early development of capitalism, though does not appear to believe that dispossession has ongoing significance under capitalism (Brenner 2006). De Angelis (2007), on the other hand, advances a conception of "ongoing primitive accumulation" that is differentiated from "expanded reproduction" and that emphasizes class struggle as the animating force of, and limit to, primitive accumulation. What prevents me from embracing his theoretical framework is, first, its prolongation of "primitive accumulation," which I believe cannot capture the ongoing role of land dispossession under capitalism and its variation over time and space. And second, De Angelis equates primitive accumulation with "enclosure," whose referent is "the commons," defended by "commoners." The problem, as already argued, is that dispossession targets multiple property forms, including private property. Recognizing this leads to a less romantic but more accurate understanding of dispossession politics.
69. While Harvey sees over-accumulation as an inherent tendency of capitalism, he sees crises of over-accumulation as emerging from "core regions" where declining rates of profit lead them to export capital to "new dynamic spaces of capital accumulation" (see Harvey 2003: 67,

120–121). At some point, over-accumulation crises also afflict these new spaces. But, given India's robust growth rates, it would be hard to yet characterize its economy in this way.

70. McMichael (2012a) sees land grabs as "illusory solutions to a fundamental accumulation crisis precipitated by the neoliberal globalization project" and an "expression of food regime restructuring." Both he and Araghi (2009a, 2009b), who advances the concept of "accumulation by displacement," specifically locate contemporary land grabs as a response to "the end of cheap food" (see also Moore 2015). In addition to sharing the same shortcomings as Harvey's theory, they are narrowly focused on transnational farmland investments with unclear relevance to land grabs for non-agricultural purposes.
71. These include mafias, drug cartels, paramilitaries, individual landlords or even small farmers (cf. Li 2014; Hall, Hirsch, and Li 2011; Hall 2011; Grajales 2013). Such decentralized dispossession may be too unsystematic and uncoordinated to have a regime-like quality.
72. While scholars have questioned the coherence of "the state" (cf. Abrams 1988; Mitchell 1991; Gupta 1995; Gupta 2012), dispossession is one of the more coherent ways in which state power can be experienced.
73. Chapter 9 discusses subnational variation in the politics of dispossession.
74. Such periodizations are typically constructed around the "core" or "hegemonic" countries of global capitalism (Arrighi 1994), leaving open the question of how peripheral states fit into them.
75. For this reason, I suggest that hegemony is a misleading rubric for dispossession politics (cf. Nielsen and Nilsen 2015).
76. Even authoritarian states, as we see in China today, often feel compelled to justify dispossession as serving the public interest.
77. This is clearly the story of urban renewal in the United States (cf. Denton and Massey 1993). The literature on racialized dispossession in Southern Africa is large, but see Moore (2005). On the role of race in urban evictions in Brazil, see Perry (2013). Rural land dispossession in India is not systematically targeted at particular caste groups, though, as the next chapter discusses, *adivasis* (indigenous groups) have been disproportionately affected by large dams and mining (Fernandes 2008). Caste is, however, a major structuring principle of most agrarian milieux and powerfully shapes the ability of dispossessed farmers to benefit from the resulting economic changes.
78. Here I build on Weber's analysis of domination as "the probability that certain specific commands (or all commands) will be obeyed by a given group of persons" (Weber 1978: 212). While there are severe data challenges to quantifying this probability, potential indicators include the percentage of capital projects stalled or canceled due to land acquisition problems or, more indirectly, their average time-to-completion.
79. Hart (2009: 199) refers to this as "big-D Development," in contrast to the "little-d development," which refers to "tendencies inherent in the workings of global capitalism." I use "development" here without the capitalization to refer to the 20th century historical project and the discursive legitimations attached to it; I will use trajectories of capitalism to talk about the latter.
80. Many scholars have noted the ambiguity of the term "neoliberalism." As Evans and Sewell (2013) observe, the term can refer to an economic theory, a political ideology, a policy paradigm and a social imaginary. Its implementation has varied significantly and is everywhere marked by large gaps between theory and practice (Harvey 2005; Peck 2010). The resulting difficulty in precisely defining neoliberalism has led some critics to suggest that we abandon the term (cf. Parnell and Robinson 2012). The problem with this suggestion is that we have no better one to describe the dramatic economic restructuring of global capitalism since the 1980s, in which almost every country abandoned versions of Keynesianism or developmentalist planning in favor of a far greater role for markets. While India's neoliberal reforms have some particularities, they also share a family resemblance with this broader trend. As the following chapter illustrates, I follow Peck (2010: 33) in approaching "neoliberalization not as some automatic system, but as an earthly process, realized through political action and institutional reinvention."
81. For those operating with the binary between enclosure by capital and defense of the "commons," see Midnight Notes Collective (1990), De Angelis (2001, 2007), Linebaugh (2008),

and Caffentzis and Federici (2014). In India, Vandana Shiva and colleagues set up a binary between "corporate capital" and "small peasants" defending land, food and seed sovereignty and thus an "earth democracy" (Shiva, Jani, and Fontana 2011).

82. See, for instance, Low (1996), De Janvry (1981), and Frankel (2005).
83. See Carney and Watts (1990); Thukral (1996); Humphries (1990); Mehta and Srinivasan (2000); Federici (2004); Dewan (2008); Sargeson (2008); Mehta (2009); Sargeson and Song (2010); Julia and White (2012); Doss, Summerfield, and Tsikata (2014); Li (2015); and Levien (2016). For an excellent illustration of these intersections in the context of urban dispossession, see Perry (2013).
84. Since then, one ethnographic monograph on an SEZ has been published (Cross 2014). While the book is partly focused on labor inside an old public sector EPZ in Andhra Pradesh that was converted to an SEZ, it also discusses land acquisition for a newer private SEZ. Given the book's predominant focus on villagers' aspirations, I most directly address its findings in my discussion of unrealized aspirations in Chapter 8.
85. I personally conducted each survey in Hindi, sometimes accompanied by a paid local research assistant/motorcycle driver. In addition to helping me find informants, using a research assistant was particularly useful for building trust (which was particularly important in the neighboring villages where I had spent less time), and for occasionally translating vernacular Rajasthani into Hindi (which was particularly necessary with older informants). While generating a sample of households from a list of individual voters introduces the slight bias of over-sampling large families, I could not obtain complete household lists for the villages, and there is no reason to think that this biased the outcomes of interest in any particular direction. The proportion of Scheduled Castes to General Castes in my sample closely matched that recorded by the 2001 Census, suggesting that the sample was representative of the villages in terms of basic caste composition. When making arguments about the dispossessed specifically, I use only the subset of households in my sample who had their land acquired ($n = 49$). Data from the remaining households illustrate how the non-dispossessed benefited—or not—from the SEZ.
86. On the value of revisits, see Burawoy (2009: Ch. 2).

Chapter 2

1. See Stern (1988: 86). The exception was Ajmer, which was directly ruled by the British from 1818 onward.
2. Eesvan Krishnan (2014: 8) demonstrates that "to a remarkable degree, land acquisition law was shaped in the interests of the British-controlled ('sterling') railway companies operating in India."
3. Citing a colonial government source, Stern writes, "Until the 1920s when it became politically expedient for the government to concern itself with the chiefs' tenants, it was only worth a note in passing that 'in nine cases out of ten' cultivators who were dispossessed by their *durbars* to make way for railways were not compensated" (1988: 191). The cultivators would have had only customary tenure; whether they would have been allotted alternative land is unknown. But the British themselves demanded "the gratuitous surrender of land" from the princely states for the imperial railways passing through Rajputana; while many balked, Jaipur's ruler, Sawai Ramsingh, saw an opportunity for centralizing *durbar* revenue by steering the railway through Jaipur (Stern 1988: 131–140). Later, Jaipur State, along with the princely state of Baroda, pressured the colonial Government of India to compensate it for revenue land lost to imperial railways, a demand to which it acceded in 1909 (Krishnan 2014: 88). Jaipur State's own railway lines, built with financing from London, ultimately earned 10%–12% returns for the *durbar* (Stern 1988: 191–192).
4. As the Rudolphs note, "Institutional changes which had taken place over more than one hundred years [elsewhere in India] were brought into being in Rajasthan in less than five" (Rudolph and Rudolph 1984: 3). One result, the Rudolphs observe, was that, "the princely state civil servants selected for the post-independence services of Rajasthan showed the marks of patrimonial service and court relations in their manners and style" (Rudolph and Rudolph 1984: 13). A former top bureaucrat of the state bluntly argued that a "feudal

mindset" predominated in which the rulers looked down upon merchants (*banias*), "power [still] flows from the land," and the "administration did not encourage and facilitate industry" (Interview, 8/19/10, Jaipur).

5. This includes: 2,452 families for the Rana Pratap Sagar Dam on the Chambal River (Mathur 1997: 7); 6,979 families for the Mahi Bajaj Sagar Dam and 5,940 families for the Kadana Dam, both on the Mahi River bordering Gujarat (Mathur 1997: 11, 14); 898 families for the Son Kama Ambla Dam (Mathur 1997: 19); 3,000 families for the Mansi Wakil Dam in Udaipur (G. Srivastava 1995: 19); and 6,230 families for the Bisalpur Dam on the Banas, which would ultimately provide drinking water to Jaipur (Mathur 1997: 19; I. C. Srivastava 1995: 80).
6. Originating in late 19th century Manchester and Chicago, industrial estates were utilized to reconstruct war-torn Europe and, in the 1950s, were promoted by the United Nations and the United States International Cooperation Administration as a tool to industrialize Third World countries (United Nations 1961: 1; Bredo 1960). Beginning with the First Five Year Plan, the Indian government promoted industrial estates with the purpose of catalyzing small-scale, labor-intensive industrialization. By the late 1960s, industrial estates lost their association with the Small Scale Industries (SSI) program and, renamed "industrial areas," became the primary means by which state governments promoted medium- and large-scale industry.
7. There is almost no information about the numbers dispossessed for these estates. One study suggests that 2,500 families lost land to the 2,500-acre Bhiwadi Industrial Estate (P. Srivastava 1995: 112).
8. For an overview of this vast literature, see Mahapatra (1999), Cernea (2000), and Fernandes (2004, 2008).
9. On the distinction between resettlement and rehabilitation, see Cernea (1999).
10. Those displaced for the Mahi Bajaj Dam, for example, were "mechanically" allotted government land that was encroached by other people. Twenty years after the project was initiated, only 40% had gotten possession of their land, and almost all of it was bad. The sites had no water and the schools had no teachers (Sekhar 1995; Mathur 1997). Resettlement for the Kadana Dam was similarly bad (Vyas 1995).
11. These points come out very clearly in the two main volumes on displacement in Rajasthan (Mathur 1995c, 1997), and are also common findings elsewhere in India.
12. Goldman (1994: 155, n. 9) reports that many took one look at the desert land and sold it for a return bus ticket.
13. For example, the non-tribal oustees of the Mahi Bajaj Sagar Dam fared far better than the tribal oustees, who constituted a majority of the displaced (Mathur 1997: 12). While the *adivasis* were given bad land—or no land at all—and terrible resettlement sites, a model resettlement site was erected for those displaced from the home village of the Chief Minister. Similarly, in the case of Bisalpur Dam a large corruption scandal was unearthed that involved the local rich getting "huge" compensation in collusion with officials, who manipulated land classifications in their favor (Mathur 1997: 21). Vyas (1995: 61) similarly reports a similar outcome for the Kadana Dam. This resonates with research elsewhere in India showing that politically connected groups among the dispossessed sometimes received irrigated land or public sector jobs (Parasuraman 1999).
14. See R. L. Arora v. State of U.P. (1961).
15. Goldman calls the Command Area Development Agency for the Indira Gandhi Canal, "a highly bureaucratized central authority to control all aspects of everyday life in the canal command area," which was responsible for a massive extension of state authority into Northwest Rajasthan (Goldman 1994: 111, 168, n. 33).
16. Interview, 2/17/11, Jaipur.
17. This rationale was set out by a committee appointed in 1959 by the Government of India to investigate how to control land prices in Delhi. The committee's recommendations were put into practice by the Delhi Development Authority, which had been founded in 1957 (Jain 2009: 63–69). The Delhi Development Authority Act, as Ghertner writes, "defined land in Delhi as public and was arguably the largest land nationalization program in the history of India." The first Delhi Master Plan called for 25% of residential units in the city to be reserved for the poor (Ghertner 2015: 25–26).

18. A high-ranking former RIICO official explained that while there were restrictions on selling and penalties for not producing on industrial estate plots, it was too difficult to prevent land sales altogether. RIICO consequently adopted the policy that it would collect 17.5% to 20% of the sale price on vacant plots. The official explained that he "cancelled many lands that people didn't do anything on," which made him unpopular. Most of the phone calls he received were requests for extension. The implication was that RIICO had not always been as fastidious in adhering to these rules. (Interview, Jaipur, 6/24/14).
19. "Working the system" was, as Chibber (2003: 188–192) observes, a more general outcome of an interventionist planning apparatus that subsidized private capital but was too weak to discipline it. While Chibber documents how large firms manipulated the central industrial licensing system, the aforementioned methods of working state-level parastatal agencies appear to have been widely exploited by small- and medium-sized regional firms. Compared to industrial licensing, however, land acquisition was a form of state support for private capital that was arguably more conditional on compliance with minimum planning priorities. The state's reserve in using the power of eminent domain directly for private and speculative activities contrasts sharply with its enthusiasm in the neoliberal era.
20. Goswami (2004: 130) observes, "The postcolonial developmentalist regime, particularly its Nehruvian avatar, sought to overcome the inherited colonial geography of uneven development by extending infrastructures and capital investment to so-called backward regions understood to have temporally lagged behind the nation as a whole."
21. Interview, 12/24/10, Jaipur.
22. Until the early 1990s, RIICO's newsletters also routinely advertised rebates of up to 50% on industrial land for Scheduled Castes and Tribes, the handicapped, ex-servicemen, war widows, women, and small industries.
23. In 1967, the Government of India issued a directive that all public sector industries should provide one job to each family that lost land for them (Parasuraman 1999: 55). Some state governments passed policy circulars enshrining this practice (Ramanathan 2008), though such promises were often only kept after farmer agitation and court cases that lasted decades (Ramanathan 2008: 30–33; Burman 1968). Parasuraman (1999: 110) found that two-thirds of the households displaced for the Durgapur Steel Plant (DSP) in West Bengal received one permanent job in the plant, making them part of the public sector "labor aristocracy" for at least one generation. These jobs were high-paying, secure, and came with substantial perks like housing, healthcare, education, transportation allowances, and access to subsidized consumer items. Another 24% were employed by informal sector industries or services. This inclusion appears partly due to the efforts of the Communist Party of India (Marxist), which advocated for the displaced to receive employment. The CPI(M) also convinced the DSP to redistribute 2,500 acres of unused acquired land to landless families (Parasuraman 1999: 112–114).
24. Interview, 6/24/14, Jaipur.
25. Khagram (2004: 34), for example, speaks of the "overwhelming political consensus behind big dam building." Klingensmith (2007) shows the central place of large dams in the nationalist imaginary of political leaders, administrators, engineers, and intellectuals.
26. A question Srirupa Roy (2007) similarly poses in her analysis of India's steel towns. It is plausible, as Sharma (1992) suggests happened in Madhya Pradesh, that a combination of nationalism and the promise of development persuaded some villagers to leave their land voluntarily. On the other hand, there was local resistance to some of the most prestigious showpieces of post-independence development: the Hirakud Dam (Hart 1956; Viegas 1992), the dams of the Damodar Valley Corporation (Hart 1956), the Rourkela Steel Plant (Burman 1968; Parry and Struempell 2008; Struempell 2014), and the construction of Chandigarh (Kalia 1999). What seems crucial, however, is that these agitations were largely unsuccessful or were quickly reduced to modest demands over the terms of compensation.
27. This seems to be supported by the limited evidence available. Perhaps the most detailed account of the interaction between the Nehruvian state and dispossessed villagers in the immediate post-independence period comes from Henry Hart, an American political scientist funded by the Ford Foundation to tour India's dams in the early 1950s (and quite sympathetic to India's dam-building project). Hart paints a picture of reluctant villagers, laborious

attempts of government officials to persuade villagers, and ultimately resignation that shifting was inevitable. He observes, "If occasionally a family or a village refused to pull up roots so deep before the dams are built, it is not extraordinary. What is remarkable is the resignation with which thousands of families in hundreds of villages have moved. . . . Perhaps the most valuable of the lessons will turn out to be the willingness of the Indian villager to make way for a nation-building project, provided he [*sic*] is convinced that the sacrifice he [*sic*] is called upon to make is unavoidable" (Hart 1956: 189).

28. Even Gandhi—from whom the dispossessed might have expected sympathy—disapproved of the agitation by oustees of the Hirakud Dam, prompting Congress members to withdraw their support (Dwivedi 2006: 147). In many subsequent instances, Gandhian NGOs have played the role of encouraging people to accept compensation (Mankodi 1992: 95; Dwivedi 2006: 158).
29. While it probably occurred in Rajasthan, there is more evidence of violent repression in other states. Protests against the Hirakud Dam in the 1950s were violently suppressed, with police forcing villagers out of their homes and onto trucks with batons (Viegas 1992: 45–46). The Andhra Pradesh government called in the army to make villagers vacate their land for the Nagarjunasagar Dam (Singh and Samantray 1992: 66). When anti-dam movements started to emerge in the 1970s and 1980s, many were met with brutal beatings, shootings, rapes, arson, and the pillaging of homes (Khagram 2004: 51; Sangvai 2002).
30. Quoted in Bhanot and Singh (1992: 101). This turned out to be no idle threat: many of the displaced were forced to quickly abandon their homes and possessions when the reservoir was impounded without warning, quickly flooding their villages (Bhanot and Singh 1992: 110). Those dispossessed for the Koyna and Rihand dams were similarly caught unprepared by rising water (Thukral 1992: 15).
31. Contributing to these cost overruns were shortages of capital goods and foreign exchange which, Chibber (2003: 208) argues, resulted from the inability of India's planning apparatus to effectively control private investments.
32. These figures are from CMIE's CapEX database; analysis by Smriti Upadhyay. The data does not tell us how much, if any, land was acquired for various capital projects.
33. During this period, infrastructure's share of GDP increased from 4.8% to 7.97% (Gulati 2011: 380).
34. The Indian government has been eagerly looking for ways to attract more investment into infrastructure. In 2010, the Reserve Bank of India created a new category of Non-Banking Financial Companies called Infrastructure Finance Companies (Gulati 2011: 394). Prime Minister Manmohan Singh made attracting infrastructure investments a large priority (*Hindustan Times* 2011). Prime Minister Narendra Modi has, if anything, been a more aggressive proponent of private investment in infrastructure.
35. Pro-liberalization critiques of ULCRA have focused on its presumably inherent "distortionary" effects on land markets; Siddiqui's (2013) research in Mumbai shows that it was never implemented as intended.
36. This is first considered in the Eighth Five Year Plan (1992–1997) and actively promoted in the Ninth (1997–2002) and subsequent plans.
37. By 2011, flats in central Mumbai and Delhi were selling for the equivalent of 180 and 580 years of average income, respectively (Chakravorty 2013: Table A13).
38. EPZs were born out of US Cold War policy toward Latin America in the 1950s and subsequently spread throughout Asia (Moore and Schrank 2004; Kranakis 2008). According to the ILO, by 2006 there were 3,500 EPZs (or derivatives thereof) in 130 countries (ILO 2007).
39. The only privatized one (in Surat, Gujarat) was built in 1994 and thus reflects the transition I have documented for industrial areas.
40. India's EPZs were small in size (93–700 acres), attracted more domestic than foreign investment, and contributed only marginally to exports, employment, and foreign exchange (Kundra 2000; Banumathi 2010).
41. Interview, 1/17/10, New Delhi. Although some private SEZ developers do enter into PPPs with state governments (to help secure land and regulatory approvals), the SEZ Act does not require it. If we count foregone revenue from tax and tariff concessions and the subsidization of supporting infrastructure, of course, the statement does not hold.

42. An official overseeing the SEZ unit of a major Indian industry association explained that real estate developers lobbied for SEZs because they would be "very low cost" as the government would "provide some benefits like basic infrastructure facilities . . . as well as [the] cheapest land" (Interview, 1/19/11, New Delhi).
43. While it is beyond the scope of this chapter, economic liberalization also unleashed a mineral rush across central and eastern India. Beginning in 1993, India began to liberalize its predominantly state-controlled mining industry (see Singh and Kalirajan 2003). By the 2000s, mineral prices were increasing with the Indian and Chinese construction booms driving up demand. While the mining sector has not grown exceptionally quickly, several states (such as Jharkhand, Chattisgarh, and Odisha) have been particularly pro-active in handing over large mining concessions to private and foreign investors (Kale 2013; Kale and Mazaheri 2014).
44. This Tier I/II/III classification of cities originates with international real estate consultancies and, as Searle (2016: 112) observes, "is not based entirely on population, but on the size of the real estate market and the presence of the IT industry in a particular city."
45. The barriers to capitalist development posed by these specific qualities of land have long been recognized within agrarian political economy; however, they were seen as constraints on capitalist agriculture that were not applicable to industry (Kautsky 1988: 147; Adnan 1985: 58). On the distinction between alienability and valuation in the process of commodification, see Castree (2003).
46. Rajpura land records 2004.
47. The average holding in Rajasthan, according to the 2010-11 Agricultural Census, was 3.07 hectares compared to a national average of 0.8 hectares. The only states with larger average holdings were Punjab and Nagaland (Ministry of Agriculture 2014: 79–81). In West Bengal, by contrast, the average holding was 0.63 hectares. The 1,000 acres of land acquired for the Tata car factory in Singur was reportedly divided between 12,000 owners (Ghatak and Ghosh 2011: 71).
48. It is for these reasons that the World Bank has been a vociferous proponent of modernizing land titling systems, which would "make available a huge amount of high-value peri-urban land for productive investment and development" (World Bank 2007: 2; see also De Soto 2000). Benjamin et al. (2007) provide reason to doubt that such programs actually do reduce transaction costs. But land title modernization would not resolve the other obstacles, enumerated earlier, to consolidating large contiguous tracts of rural land for capital investment.
49. Interview, 7/14/10, MWC Jaipur.
50. With one notable exception: the industrial development official installed in West Bengal after the TMC's Mamata Banerjee defeated the Left Front government in 2013 after campaigning heavily against forcible land acquisition. While his Left Front predecessor adamantly insisted that industrialization could not take place without land acquisition (Interview, 2/28/11, Kolkata), the TMC-appointed official bluntly told me that "We're not acquiring land" and that they were instead looking for under-utilized non-agricultural land. When I pressed him on whether they would be able to find sufficient land for industry without rural land acquisition, he admitted "We have to take hard decisions. But we are postponing. The political leadership is postponing it." Interview, 3/3/14, Kolkata.
51. A RIICO newsletter at the time advertised that "NRIs shall be serviced particularly in a versatile manner to facilitate their investments in the service sector and whatever they are interested in as per the objectives of the state plan" (RIICO 1988c).
52. On the broader modalities of land liberalization and new forms of urban governance, see Sud (2012) and Goldman (2011).
53. Interview, 2/17/11, Jaipur
54. Interview, 1/19/11, New Delhi.
55. Interview, 6/23/14, Jaipur.
56. Interview, 10/21/09, Jaipur. An official with the Maharashtra Industrial Development Corporation (MIDC) similarly (but less bluntly) explained, "[MIDC] has to ensure that the cost of acquisition and the cost of providing infrastructure thereon, is reasonable enough to attract industrialists" (Email interview, 9/25/10).
57. The Greater Noida Industrial Development Authority (GNIDA) started as an industrial promotion agency, but as residential demand began spilling over from Delhi in the 1990s, it

morphed into an urban planner and began acquiring massive amounts of land on Delhi's peri-urban fringe and reselling it to real estate developers at a tremendous mark-up (Sood 2011).

58. While conflating rent with corruption and unable to theoretically reconcile the increase in both with its pro-market orientation, the *Economist* (2014a, 2014b) has called attention to the "crony capitalist" character of India's growth during the 2000s. In 2007, it ranked India sixth in its "Crony-Capitalism Index," a relatively crude measure based on the proportion of billionaire wealth from "rent-heavy" economic sectors as a percentage of GDP. Rent-heavy sectors are defined as those "vulnerable to monopoly or that involve licensing or heavy state involvement," and they include real estate and construction; mining and commodities; infrastructure; banking; defense; utilities and telecom; and casinos. See also Gandhi and Walton (2012).
59. While difficult to prove, it is often alleged that chief ministers and politicians are silent partners in such companies. As one JDA official himself explained to me, "all politicians and bureaucrats buy *benami* land" (Interview, 2/19/11, Jaipur).
60. There is, of course, some uncertainty in this process. As one real estate developer explained, "Sometimes rumors make the price go up. Sometimes bureaucrats have good information. Sometimes a government project changes and the price goes down" (Interview, 3/22/10, Jaipur). This puts a premium on information obtained from high-level sources.
61. In Karnataka, for instance, the alleged shifting of the Bangalore–Mysore Industrial Corridor project to favor connected politicians, along with other irregularities in land allocation, has resulted in a special court probe against the last three chief ministers (Mondal 2012). My conversations with farmers in villages on the outskirts of Greater Noida (near Delhi) revealed that there was a retail market for having one's land exempted from acquisition by the Greater Noida Development Authority, though the rates were out of reach for most farmers (Fieldnotes, 1/16/10, Sadhopur, U.P.).
62. As one Haryana official explained to *The Hindu* (2012), such Changes in Land Use (CLU) are the "mother source of all land scams" as "CLU permission granted on agricultural land escalates its value manifold, resulting in a premium for a nexus of realtors, politicians and bureaucrats."
63. After a spate of several high-profile land-related scams rocked the Congress in the 2000s, party president Sonia Gandhi urged members to rein it in: "We have ample evidence that all discretionary powers, particularly in land allocation, breed corruption. I would like all Congress CMs [chief ministers] and ministers, at both Centre and states, to set an example by reviewing and relinquishing such powers" (*Times of India* 2010). This was not heeded. Shortly afterward, Gandhi's own son-in-law became mired in allegations of corrupt land dealings in Haryana (Dogra 2012). Land-related corruption scandals—along with a major scandal over the allocation of the 2G spectrum—became potent issues that helped to sink Congress in the 2014 national election.
64. This is how, for example, the India Against Corruption campaign presented the matter.
65. From RIICO newsletters and annual reports, I have been able to reconstruct yearly land acquisition totals from 1974 to 2010. While land acquisition actually slowed in the 2000s to 11,863 acres due to the industrial stagnation that ensued in India between 1997 and 2003 following the East Asian crisis (and the backlog of land that RIICO had acquired before the recession in anticipation of continued growth), RIICO was planning to acquire 50,000 acres over the following five years—which, if successful, would be four-fifths of the total land acquired in its forty-year history (Interviews, RIICO officials, 12/15/10 and 12/24/10, Jaipur).
66. These zones were—like the later SEZs—given status as "public utilities," which limits strike activity and gives a government administrator wide discretion to arbitrate labor disputes.
67. RIICO (1994a, 2006, 2009).
68. RIICO's July 2002 newsletter listed forty-nine such simplifications, which included removing the ban against transferring or subdividing a plot before the commencement of production, reducing the charge for transferring vacant plots (from 10% to 5%) and allowing plots to be mortgaged for non-industrial purposes. Plots in RIICO's residential colonies could also now be allotted and transferred to non-entrepreneurs and subdivided (RIICO 2002).
69. Interview, 12/15/10, Jaipur.
70. RIICO officials have been charged with demanding kickbacks for contracts, for preferential allocation of plots in its industrial areas, and for disbursement of loans (see *Times of India*

2011; Jenkins 1999: 100). All of these are likely dwarfed by illicit gains derived from advance knowledge of projects.

71. Interview, 12/15/10, Jaipur.
72. One of the JDA's largest projects was an expansion of the city called Prithviraj Nagar. Land acquisition proceedings against twenty-three villages began in 1988 and continued until 1996. A legal challenge by an oustee held up the project for years, though a Supreme Court Decision in 1997 allowed the project to proceed. The dispossessed families were offered plots of land in a distant colony with no infrastructure, and records indicate that many did not receive that. In the meantime, many private colonizers encroached on the land; and, in a move clearly beneficial to such real estate interests, the government subsequently regularized their encroachments. In 2012, it was reported that the JDA had allotted more plots in Prithviraj Nagar than its entire area, leaving no space for infrastructure like roads and electricity. In sum, the project prefigured the ineptitude that JDA would show in providing compensation plots to those ousted for the Mahindra World City. Many of these details can be found in the Rajasthan High Court judgment in the case Hemant Priyadarshi v. State (2013). See also *Times of India* (2012) and *DNA* (2013).
73. In 1985, a probe was launched into illegal housing plot allocation by the JDA in favor of senior government officials (*Times of India* 1985). In 1987, the JDA was roundly criticized in the press for corruption, inefficiency, and unaccountable governance (Sawhney 1987).
74. As the JDA commissioner explained to me, "The only resource the JDA has is land. We need to use that land for revenue and to plan for the city." Interview, 3/23/10, Jaipur.
75. The JDA's (2011) Master Plan 2025 calls for further expansion: from encompassing 478 villages and a total urban area of 1,959 sq. km to 725 villages and 2,939 sq. km.
76. Interview, former revenue official, 6/24/14, Jaipur.
77. Interview, 2/19/11, Jaipur.
78. Interview, former revenue official, 6/24/14, Jaipur.
79. Interview, 2/19/11, Jaipur.
80. Interview, 6/24/14, Jaipur.
81. Interview, 10/13/2009, Jaipur.
82. Interview, 10/21/2009, Jaipur.
83. This high-level official was posted in the Rajasthan Housing Board when the policy was formulated. Interview, 8/19/10, Jaipur.
84. Interview, 12/15/10, Jaipur.

Chapter 3

1. In present-day Madhya Pradesh, under circumstances that are still debated. By some accounts, Dhola Rai was deprived of his throne by a conniving uncle; in others he left to marry the Chief of Dausa's daughter (Tod 1997[1829], Vol. 2: 281; Chakravarti 1975: 22–23).
2. Tod recorded that it was Dhola Rai who established Amber in the 13th century.
3. Such as slowly differentiating privy purses from the public treasury and transforming retainers into professional advisers (Rudolph and Rudolph 1984).
4. Beginning in the 1860s, the Jaipur *durbar* began to undertake irrigation works, with the assistant of British engineers, on crown (*khalsa*) land. These public works allowed the cultivation of cash crops such as opium, cotton, and sugar and increased *durbar* revenue (Stern 1988: 144, 189). These investments did not extend into *jagir* lands, to be discussed more shortly, where approximately 70% of the state's peasantry resided (Stern 1988: 242).
5. Davis (2001: 167–168) observes that while nearly a million villagers died in Rajputana during this famine, grain traders earned immense profits while British officials deported starving refugees fleeing from the princely states.
6. Whether Rajasthan's princely states should be classified as feudal has been the subject of a long and complex debate. James Tod (1997[1829]), the early British official and chronicler, used the term based on the similarities he saw between contemporary Rajasthan and medieval Europe. The colonial government's acceptance of Tod's analysis led them to several miscalculations, such as overestimating their ability to transform Rajasthan's "clannish" nobility into a cohesive counterweight to princely power—they wound up, instead, reinforcing princely

absolutism (Stern 1988). The postcolonial Indian government's major enquiry into agrarian conditions in Rajputana argued that the resemblance between Rajput rule and feudalism was "superficial," primarily because of the former's strong clan system (Government of India 1950: 14). Thorner (1956), in contrast, accepted the feudal designation while Stern (1988) called princely rule in Jaipur "something very like feudalism." Among contemporary anthropologists of Rajasthan, Brara (2006) uses the term extensively while Gold calls the entire debate "Eurocentric" before admitting that she is unable to avoid it to describe "not so much an economic structure as the ambiance of rank and tribute" (Gold and Gujar 2002: 74–75). But rank and tribute were very real attributes of Rajasthan's socio-economic structure and not simply an "ambiance." Feudalism, narrowly defined, reasonably captures this structure.

7. Stern (1988: 242) estimates that 70% of Jaipur State's peasants were in *jagirs*.
8. Although technically intermediaries, "So far as the tenant was concerned, the Jagirdar behaved in all respects as the 'owner' of the land; and the tribute paid by the Jagirdar to the State did not bear any direct relation to the rents he actually realised from his tenants" (Singh 1964: 33). Tribute was typically based on the assumed income at the time of the grant (ibid.).
9. Singh (1964: 33) remarks, "The ingenuity of the man (Jagirdar) did not leave any of the forms of exploiting the cultivator untouched."
10. Worried about potential unrest, one British agent warned in the 1920s that "The condition of the peasantry in Jaipur is as bad as the very worst in the Rajputana" (cited in Stern 1988: 231).
11. Mahinder, Jagat Singh's grandson, told me that they received their *jagir* sometime in the early 19th century. Despite persistent efforts, I was unable to discover any official documents on the founding, size, or tribute burden of the Rajpura *jagir*. My inquiries with Mahinder were consistently deflected. Singh (1964: 9) ran into a similar problem.
12. Quoted in Guha (2007: 72).
13. We can consider this a lower-bound estimate. Because they put their land in the names of extended family and even trusted non-family members in multiple villages, it was impossible to verify their exact holdings.
14. This is based on the census data and land records for the three villages (Rajpura, Shivpura, and Neempura) for which complete data were available to the author. In Rajpura alone, SC/STs were 41.4% of the population and owned 20% of the land.
15. Although Jats are classified as OBCs in Rajasthan, given their status as a dominant landowning caste I separate them here and throughout the book for analytical purposes.
16. Kautsky (1988: 175) spoke of a class of "dwarf-holders" who "are dependent on wage-labour or another supplementary occupation, and which no longer produce for the market," while Lenin (1964: 177) described in Russia "a class of allotment-holding wage-workers" who were characterized by "insignificant farming on a patch of land," "inability to exist without the sale of labour-power," and "an extremely low standard of living." Rajpura's semiproletariat produce for the market and the "significance" of their farming is a matter of perspective. Despite both Kautsky's and Lenin's assumption of their imminent demise, such small-holding wage workers show no signs of disappearing in India.
17. It should be clear that I follow Bourdieu (1986, 1990) in seeing social capital as an unequally distributed private good and not, following Putnam (1993, 1995), as a collective "stock" of networks, norms and trust adhering in larger social units like a village or region. See Levien (2015) for a detailed discussion.
18. Stern (1988: 196) notes that while Jaipur was first among Rajput states in educational expenditures, 85% of its schools were in Jaipur city, where approximately 6% of the population lived.
19. I was told that because of the widow's devotion, "the blind were able to see, the crippled able to walk, and water came back into dry wells."
20. While there are different (and also gender-unequal) inheritance laws for Muslims in India (see Agarwal 1994), the Hindu Succession Act applies to the vast majority of households in Rajpura. On the promise of the 2005 Hindu Succession (Amendment) Act, see Agarwal (2005). On its lack of implementation, see Landesa Rural Development Institute (2013).
21. Rajasthan is almost entirely absent, for example, from Guha's (1999) classic *Elementary Aspects of Peasant Insurgency* and Desai's (1979) compendium *Peasant Struggles in India*.
22. The major one being the 1938 Sikar rebellion (Stern 1988).

23. A certain number of seats each year are reserved for Scheduled Castes, Scheduled Tribes, or women.

Chapter 4

1. As of the time of writing, the company was worth $16 billion.
2. According to an MWC executive, about 15%–20% of Mahindra Lifespaces portfolio is in SEZs.
3. Rising from the rice paddies of rural Tamil Nadu, MWC Chennai is a self-contained private city with over thirty-three companies as tenants, including most of India's IT giants. Its centerpiece is a 13,000 employee campus for Infosys, which has helped to populate its high-end residential colonies, malls, and private schools (Interview, Mahindra World City Chennai, 12/1/10).
4. Mahindra executives explained that "in day-to-day operations, RIICO has no role. Its role is to ensure government support. . . . Assure that government commitments move at right speed" (Interview, 10/26/09).
5. This is all detailed in the 2005 Memorandum of Understanding between the Government of Rajasthan and Mahindra and Mahindra, which was obtained through a Right to Information Act request filed by a civil society organization in Jaipur (Government of Rajasthan and Mahindra and Mahindra Ltd. 2005).
6. After the SEZ was announced, however, there was a delay of about one year before this was accomplished, which allowed speculation on to-be-acquired farmland to continue. Once registration was frozen, power of attorney contracts allowed for a seamless progression of real estate speculation.
7. That was the estimate consistently given to me by land brokers.
8. Because this is generally how SEZs are implemented, it is misleading to suggest that they are "*equally* shaped . . . by the hopes of farmers and the rural poor" (Cross 2014: 90, emphasis added).
9. Interview, MWC manager, 10/29/10.
10. Interview, MWC manager, 7/14/10.
11. I cannot compute the public rate because Rajasthan's compensation policy gave farmers small plots of land instead of a uniform price. As a value for P1 (see Figure 2.3), one could substitute the Jaipur Development Authority's per acre development cost of the compensation plots; however, I was unable to obtain that information (the sorry state of those plots suggest that it was small). Nevertheless, because we are concerned here with the profits of Mahindra as private SEZ developer, we only need P2 (the price at which they received it from the government) and P3 (its resale cost).
12. The price at which the government sold the land to the company is taken from correspondence between the Rajasthan State Industrial Development and Investment Corporation (RIICO) and the Jaipur Development Authority (RIICO 2006b) and between Mahindra World City and the Government of Rajasthan (MWC 2007), obtained through Right to Information petitions. This per-acre price is an average of the price of the acquired private farmland (Rs 245 *crore* for 2,000 acres) and the public (grazing) land (Rs 61.17 *crore* for 1,000 acres). (A *crore* in India, refers to 10,000,000). Thus, the total cost for the 3,000 acres was Rs 306.17 *crore* or Rs 1,020,567 per acre. While I combine the public and private land here for simplicity, it is worth noting that the rate of ABD is steeper on public land. Here and elsewhere I use the exchange rate of Rs 50 per $1.
13. Email correspondence with author, 7/29/10.
14. Interview, MWC manager, 7/14/10.
15. Mahindra Gesco Developers (later Mahindra Lifespaces) was, like its parent company Mahindra and Mahindra, listed on the National Stock Exchange (NSE) and Bombay Stock Exchange (BSE): in 2006, approximately 26% of its shares were held by Foreign Institutional Investors (Mahindra Gesco Developers 2006: 14).
16. Almost all of the private SEZ developers are Indian companies. While a high-level Department of Commerce official admitted to me that, "honestly, we don't know where the finance is coming from," he said that the level of FDI had been disappointing (Interview, 1/17/11),

and the relatively incomplete DoC data given to the author showed very little—only 11 of 42 "notified" SEZs for which there were data list any FDI at all, in either their development or in their productive units. Another top official in charge of regulating SEZs in nine states told me that there had been "very little" FDI and that most of the SEZs were, like the MWC, being financed by internal accruals and domestic bank loans. Of the 100 approved SEZs in his region, he added that perhaps only three or four had FDI in their development, with maybe 20% of units in the IT sector having some FDI and very little in other sectors (Interview, 1/25/11).

17. The commission's head and several of its members refused to be interviewed.
18. Mahindra Gesco Developers' 2005–2006 Annual Report noted, "IT and IT Enabled Services, which are the major drivers of growth for the real estate industry continue to experience buoyancy and as such the demand for commercial and housing space is unlikely to abate in the near future" (Mahindra Gesco Developers 2006: 5).
19. Interview, Infosys manager, 4/2/10.
20. Interview, Deutsche Bank manager, 10/24/09.
21. Interview, Commerce Ministry, 1/17/11.
22. Interview, MWC manager, 7/14/10.
23. Interview, Infosys manager, 4/2/10.
24. Interview, MWC manager, 7/14/10.
25. Interview, MWC managers, 10/26/09.
26. See www.mahindraworldcity.com/jaipur.aspx (Accessed March 25, 2014).
27. Interview, MWC manager, 2/23/10.
28. For deconstructions of "waste" and "barren" land, see Robbins (1998), Mehta (2001), Gidwani (2008), and Baka (2013).
29. Government of Rajasthan (2009: 162).
30. Prices for vegetables like *tindi* ("apple gourd") and *guar-ki-phalli* were increasing—the latter because of its use in natural gas fracking in the United States (Harris 2012; Rowley 2012).
31. Calculating precise farm incomes is notoriously difficult, and I did not have much luck trying to establish reliable figures through interviews or surveys.
32. To provide some historical perspective, the 1899–1900 famine that struck Rajasthan decimated 40% of the livestock in Jaipur district (Kachhawaha 1992).
33. For similar findings, see Mehta (2009: 24).

Chapter 5

1. For the debate in India, see the collection edited by Patnaik (1990).
2. Albeit more for rural livelihoods than economic development or revolutionary politics (Bernstein 2012; Lerche 2013).
3. Many companies—some founded in 2004 or 2005 and with little or no web presence—show up on JDA's list of people whose land was acquired for the SEZ. In Rajpura alone, there are twenty-six such companies—and many individuals not from the village—that clearly bought land from farmers before land acquisition proceedings began.
4. Except in direct quotes, I have converted rupees into dollars based on an exchange rate of Rs 50 per dollar.
5. In Rajasthan, 1 *bigha* = .25 hectares or .62 acres. A *lakh* = 100,000.
6. As noted in Chapter 3, while Jats are (after successful lobbying) classified as OBCs in Rajasthan, I separate them from other OBCs for analytical purposes.
7. These disparities were even more pronounced in the sale of un-acquired farmland, though I do not include these figures because government restrictions on SC/ST land alienation artificially depress prices for SC/ST farmland (but not urban plots). While the Rajasthan Tenancy Act of 1955 prevents the alienation of SC/ST agricultural land to non-SC/ST people, brokers and investors have evolved ingenious methods for evading them. An old method was to form a trust with nominal SC/ST board members, but the more common practice now is to sign a private right-to-purchase contract with the SC/ST landholder, get the urban development authority to convert the land to "urban" on their behalf (which requires substantial bribes), and then formally conclude the now-legal purchase.

8. I adopt the first term from Adduci (2009: 492) who uses "neo-rentier class" to identify a caste of traditional landlords who now appropriate rent through control over the state apparatus (2009: 492). In this case, the neo-rentiers arise from multiple castes on the basis of their ability to tap into speculative land markets. Given the complexity and diversity of their class positions, neo-rentier *stratum* might be a better term. Petty asset managers might be seen as a particularly "non-productive" and rent-dependent variation on what Marxists have historically called petty commodity producers. I avoid the formulation of "intermediate classes" advanced by Kalecki (1972), applied to India most prominently by Jha (1980), and reconstructed by Harriss-White (2003). The focus of these analyses were those classes—principally rich peasants and (agricultural) traders—who profited from stagnation and state controls under state-led development, whereas my focus is on new strata of rentiers formed by post-liberalization growth. Distinctions within this highly differentiated stratum—such as that between neo-rentiers and petty asset managers—may be politically significant on some issues, as I suggest in Chapter 8.
9. We can consider this a lower-bound estimate. Because they put their land in the names of extended family and trusted non-family members, and because the land is spread over multiple villages covering several contemporary *panchayats*, I was unable to confirm the exact size of their holdings through village land records.
10. As discussed in Chapter 3, his family evaded land reforms by putting their land in the names of extended family and trusted retainers.
11. For a more complete analysis of the brokerage economy, see Sud (2014a) and Levien (2015).
12. While the average holding in Rajpura and the three other villages surveyed was 4 hectares, the national average in 2005–2006 was 1.23 hectares (Ministry of Agriculture 2014: 12).
13. The scholarship here is vast, but for North India see Jeffrey and Lerche (2000); Jeffrey (2001); and Jeffrey, Jeffery, and Jeffery (2008). For South India, see Harriss-White, Janakarajan, and Colatei (2004).
14. This observation is clearly in tension with the "perfect information" assumption of neoclassical economics and Chakravorty's (2013: 18) generalization that India's "land losers are now better informed and know that they can say 'no.'"
15. While Dalits have often been seen as disproportionately hurt by land dispossession (cf. Fernandes 2008), in his study of an SEZ in Andhra Pradesh Cross argues that for Dalits the zone was "a space of promise and hope" (2014: 70) and "a great leveller" (2014: 91) and that the resettlement site for the dispossessed was experienced by young Dalit men as "socially liberating" (2014: 70, 91, 82). Curiously, he elsewhere documents extremely low compensation prices (far lower than in Rajpura), widespread disappointment about the resettlement sites, and the failure of the SEZ to deliver the hoped-for employment. As one of his own Dalit informants concludes about caste inequality, "The situation hasn't changed" (Cross 2014: 82). Aside from the tenor of interpretation, this analysis suggests the need to differentiate Dalits by livelihood and landownership; and finds not "levelling" but statistically rare examples of Dalit upward mobility in the context of expanding inter-caste inequalities. Chapter 8 further explores the political and social implications of expanding economic inequalities among landed Dalits.
16. Sobering assessments of India's development achievements over the last few decades include Bardhan (2010), Kohli (2012), and Dreze and Sen (2013).
17. Current evidence for this in India includes very low rental yields, large inventories, slowing growth, and a highly indebted infrastructure sector (cf. Ambit Capital 2015; Sender 2015).

Chapter 6

1. Upadhyay and Vasavi (2008: 32) note the need for such research.
2. As discussed earlier, both Bardhan and Sen have defended the Indian state's practice of acquiring land for the private sector. This chapter suggests that India's exclusionary growth, which these scholars have done much to document, has unsettling implications for their positions on land acquisition.
3. The first figure comes from the 2001 Census, the second from my survey.

4. In the wake of central government initiatives to privatize higher education, the number of higher education institutions in Rajasthan more than doubled between 2003–2004 and 2007–2008 (Government of Rajasthan 2009: 85a). For an insightful analysis of educational privatization in rural India, see Kumar (2014).
5. Bourdieu (2004) observes how the corporeal bearing—or bodily *hexis*—of peasants reflects and reinforces the domination of the urban over the rural in the field of cultural capital.
6. For similar findings on this distinction, see Dipankar Gupta (2009: 134–136).
7. For a useful and largely congruent reading of this concept, see Endnotes (2015).
8. Elsewhere, they are also referred to as jobbers, *sardars, mukadams,* or *kanganies.*
9. The more likely possibility is to demand welfare benefits from the state, as informal construction worker unions have done in some parts of India (Agarwala 2013). Such organizing has remained weak in Rajasthan.
10. In a report on India's private security industry sponsored by FICCI, Ernst & Young (2013: 15) note that "The demand for manned guarding is expected to increase rapidly in the future, with the burgeoning of shopping malls, SEZs, townships, IT parks and other private infrastructure facilities."
11. Private security firms are paid on a per-guard basis, making them a "labor-cost plus mark-up business" (Ernst & Young 2013: 11).
12. See McCallum (2013) for an account of the campaign to implement a global agreement over wages and conditions in India's security industry. McCallum argues that the campaign had "partial success" in bringing "market-leader" and UK-based G4S into compliance with national law (McCallum 2013: 143). But India's private security industry remains highly fragmented: the top ten firms are estimated to account for only 10% of India's six million guards—of which, only 35% are in the organized sector (Ernst & Young 2013: 14).
13. There was a higher echelon of security guards that acted as supervisors; these were mainly ex-soldiers recruited from outside the village.
14. *Koi matlab ki baat nahin hai.*
15. This is a huge literature, but see Nash and Fernandes-Kelly (1983), Ong (1987), and Kabeer and Mahmud (2004). On rural industrialization more broadly, see Wolf (1992) and Lynch (2007).
16. Although I met two young Brahmin women in Rajpura with BA degrees who expressed a desire to work on computers in the SEZ—and whose relatively liberal parents might have let them—they were subject to the same exclusion as the village's young men.
17. For a comprehensive analysis of this political struggle over NREGA in Rajasthan, see Pande (2014).
18. For an excellent comparative analysis of dominant class efforts to obstruct NREGA, see Pattenden (2016: 113–131).
19. As with many corporations, Mahindra advertises its CSR initiatives prominently on its website: http://www.mahindra.com/about-us/social-responsibility.
20. http://www.nstedb.com.
21. I borrow this concept from Chayanov (1986) without accepting his conclusion that it defines a non-capitalist peasant economy.
22. This is a perfect illustration of how, as Bourdieu (1984: 413) writes, "In forcing on everyone, uniformly, problems which only arise for a few, by a procedure as irreproachable as the administration of a questionnaire with pre-formed answers to a representative sample, there is every likelihood of creating a pure artefact out of thin air. Opinions are made to exist which did not pre-exist the questions, and which otherwise would not have been expressed. . . ."

Chapter 7

1. This securitized separation between the SEZ and what is called the Domestic Tariff Area was required by India's Special Economic Zones Act in order to maintain the integrity of the zone's "bonded" duty-free status. However, the security was not limited to the zone's processing area.
2. As Adnan (2015: 34) puts it, "The proposition that there are self-employed units in the contemporary Indian economy that are entirely 'excluded' from the circuit of capital is extremely difficult to substantiate."

3. Cross (2010) powerfully critiques Ong's classification by demonstrating the "unexceptional" nature of the precarious work available to informal laborers in an SEZ in Andhra Pradesh.
4. This formulation is Neil Brenner's (2004: 247), building on Graham (2000).
5. It is also reflected in the still incomplete attempt to create a universal national electrical grid (Kale 2014).
6. Whether plantation agriculture or extractive industries, enclave sectors are seen to have these detrimental attributes because their demand comes from abroad or a small section of domestic elites, and because their profits are repatriated rather than reinvested domestically. Moreover, because they typically form political coalitions between foreign capital, agrarian elites (in the case of plantations), and a "comprador" domestic bourgeoisie, they are also seen as product and cause of neocolonial domination (Cardoso and Falleto 1979). On the governance of extractive enclaves, see Watts (2004).
7. Sahoo (2015: 26) estimates that India's SEZs have cost the central government over $35 billion in foregone revenue between 2004 and 2010.
8. Although neither a foreign investment nor an extractive one, there is some resonance here with Ferguson's (2006) distinction between economic investments that are "thick" or "thin" on the ground.
9. Remarkably, one was opened by a twenty-five-year-old Dalit (Beirwa) from a nearby village who was reinvesting land money. The doctor came on Sundays, and for the rest of the week the young BA graduate treated patients himself at a small storefront clinic. Seeing about 150 patients per week—mostly poor villagers and migrant laborers—he was making Rs 8,000 per month, though he referred to it as "social service." The second was a for-profit Ayurvedic clinic that had been opened behind the Balai *mohalla* by a Jat from Neempura, also with recycled land money.
10. The SEZ's plan calls for a new private hospital in the "Lifestyle Zone," which will likely be even more expensive.
11. See McCartney (2009: 101–103) on the success of India's industrial planning regime in generating forward linkages.
12. Construction supply is a highly informal sector that often depends on illegal mining undertaken by so-called sand mafias, which are active in the region (cf. Gupta 2013).
13. This is a non-agricultural extension of what Dubash (2002) calls "tubewell capitalism." See also Brara (2006: 232).
14. Scholars of rural India have long noted the persistence of what Marx (1981: 728) called "antediluvian" or "pre-capitalist" forms of capital and worried that their relative profitability obstructed or distorted capitalist development (see Harriss [1982] and the debates in Patnaik [1990]). My findings suggest that they are being fueled by advanced capitalism and, as Harriss-White (2012) argues, there is no reason to assume they are transitory.

Chapter 8

1. For the consulting literature, see McKinsey and Co. (2007: 12), which categorizes India's population/consumer market into "global strivers," "seekers," "aspirers," and "deprived," with the latter projected to shrink from 54% in 2005 to 22% in 2025 (see Ghertner 2015 for a critique). For analyses of the role of "aspirational India" in electing Narendra Modi, see Barry (2014) and Sardesai (2014). Appadurai (2004) is a major point of reference for anthropologists; see also the contributions to Gooptu (2013). The observation of changing aspirations in rural India is not, however, new. In his 1950s fieldwork in "Rampura," Srinivas (1976: 268) observed that "Independence and adult franchise also brought new ideas and aspirations to the villagers."
2. A policy direction reinforced by Rajasthan's 2014 amendments to central labor laws, which collectively make it easier to fire workers, harder to form unions, easier to use contract labor, and reduce the number of firms subject to health and safety inspection. The reforms were greeted enthusiastically in the national and international business press (Iyer 2014; Mallet 2015) where many argued they would lead to job creation in the state. None asked: if labor deregulation was the key to stimulating manufacturing employment, why hasn't it emerged in the state's largest SEZ?

3. *Asli malaai to baaharwale khaa rahe hain or hamen paseene ka paisa mil rahaa hai.*
4. *Bhoomi adhigrahan.*
5. *Kabza karne ki koshish karte hain lekin dene ki koshish nahin karte.*
6. Interview, 2/16/11.
7. Whether it is "fixing" bureaucratic problems for commission (Reddy and Haragopal 1985; Srivastava and Chaturvedi 1986), peddling influence and patronage (Plunkett 1984), or acting as market intermediaries (Bayly 1983: 371, 412), few doubt that such well-connected mediators use their positions for financial or political gain. For these reasons, brokers and middlemen have long attracted moral opprobrium (Bayly 1983: 412; Bailey 1960: 185; Srinivas 1976: 266, 306). Krishna's (2002) more positive interpretation of brokers as "new leaders" is a major exception; for critiques, see Levien (2015) and Pattenden (2016: Chapter 5).
8. See Scott (1985: 187).
9. *Chaach ki malaai sarpanch ne le li baaki sab ko chaach baant diyaa. . . . Maalai-makkhan khaate hain, or sab ko dudh pilaate hain. Dudh bhi nahin pilaate.*
10. Searle (2016: 155) finds similar "boundary work" among urban brokers.
11. Scott (1976: 61) notes how the intrusion of capitalist agriculture in colonial Southeast Asia made the village elite "no longer so dependent on local validation and support for their position" as "new outside backing allowed them to incur local disapproval at less risk." This risk is even more attenuated when agriculture itself gives way to an urban economy.
12. The average size of an SC holding in India was 0.8 hectares in 2010–2011; in Rajasthan as a whole it was 2.58 hectares (Ministry of Agriculture 2011: 82–84).
13. *Sab apne ghar banaate hain.*
14. Srinivas (1976: 28, 245) suggests: "Factions are an integral part of rural life. . . . A faction-free village was difficult to come across or even contemplate."
15. In patrilocal rural India, women's inheritance rights are often feared on the grounds that they "mean more chance for the land to leave agnatic hands" (Mayer 1960: 242). In his study of a village in rural Madhya Pradesh, Mayer found "no evidence of very distant agnates claiming land" but speculated that "if pressure on land and other occupations becomes very intense this might start—for men would seize any opportunity to claim from distant intestate kin. Such a strengthening of extended agnatic ties would come just at a time when the rights of women (and through them affines) are being reinforced. And these rights may create rivalry between brothers and sisters, in contrast to the close and emotionally binding tie I have noted" (Mayer 1960: 246). While allowing for the possibility that women were themselves agents in these demands, and although I would not call it a strengthening of ties, this is otherwise a highly prescient observation.
16. Since a brother is expected to lend assistance to his sister rather than vice versa, that Prabhu had taken a loan from his sister's husband already indicated his failure to fulfill brotherly obligations.

Chapter 9

1. Even in China, Julia Chuang (2015) finds a disconnect between those who are dispossessed for urbanization projects and those absorbed into migrant labor circuits.
2. Growing dependence on off-farm income in many rural areas of the Global South and North has led to growing literatures on "pluriactivity," "multi-functionality," and "multiple livelihoods," and has led some scholars to speak of "new ruralities." See Kay (2008) for a critical survey and Vasavi (2012) for an application to India.
3. The CAG (2014) estimated that tax concessions alone represented a revenue loss of Rs 83,000 *crore*: roughly $14 billion.
4. Beginning in April 2012, SEZ developers and units became subject to the Minimum Alternative Tax, which made them less tax-free than their investors had hoped. Adding to SEZs' difficulties were the effects of the post-financial crisis recession on India's IT/ITES and real estate sectors.
5. My interviews with industrial development corporation officials in six other major states (Haryana, Maharashtra, West Bengal, Odisha, Andhra Pradesh, Tamil Nadu) revealed differences in sectoral emphasis, compensation policies, and overall "success," but all had moved

toward acquiring land for a similar set of economic purposes beginning in the 1990s; all had moved into SEZs in the 2000s. All reported acquiring more land in the post-liberalization period.

6. See also People's Tribunal on Nandigram (2007: 6).
7. Banerjee (2014: 293); Fieldnotes, 11/14/10.
8. This occurred in the case of the Mangalore SEZ in Karnataka (Mody 2014) and the Tata Steel project in Kalinga Nagar, Odisha.
9. On the BJP quotes, see Parliament of India (2007: Annexure III) and BJP (2009). For the CPM quote, see Parliament of India (2007: Annexure II).
10. Even Supreme Court justices were observing that the Act had become an "engine of oppression for the common man" (Venkatesan 2011).
11. See the remarkably "pro-farmer" testimonies before the Parliamentary Standing Committee on the proposed amendments to the LAA (Government of India 2012) and the subsequent parliamentary debate (Parliament of India 2013).
12. Interviews, West Bengal Industries Minister and West Bengal Industrial Development Corporation (WBIDCO) Managing Director, 2/28/11, Kolkata.
13. BJP President Rajnath Singh also tried to enter the village, but was turned away and held a 24-hour fast in Ghaziabad to protest "the atrocities of the UP government and growing lawlessness in the state" (*NDTV* 2011).
14. The BSP ultimately lost, but the Congress failed to capitalize and even lost the Bhatta-Parsaul seat. Whatever the reason for this loss, Gandhi was criticized for lack of follow-through in helping farmers (cf. Polanki 2012).
15. On Mayawati's response, see Khan (2011). In interviews, high-level Congress officials emphasized the importance of the Bhatta-Parsaul agitation and Rahul Gandhi's role in pushing the new bill forward. Gandhi had taken up the land acquisition issue once before, supporting the Dongria Kondh indigenous group in their fight against a Vedanta bauxite mine in the Niyamgiri Hills of Odisha. On a visit in 2008, Gandhi told the local people, "Kalahandi [the district of Odisha] and the tribals have one soldier in Delhi, and his name is Rahul Gandhi" (quoted in Sardesai 2014: 62). In August of 2010, the environment ministry refused to grant the project environmental clearance.
16. Ramesh was vocal about this in the press and in the interview I conducted with him, and has since written a book on the subject defending the bill's more progressive components (Ramesh and Khan 2015).
17. See, for instance, Ghildiyal (2012).
18. Interview, Congress politician, 7/9/14, New Delhi.
19. See Government of India (2012) and Parliament of India (2013).
20. FICCI briefly took the position that the government should not have a role in acquiring land for private companies. This anomalous difference of opinion with CII vanished (and was perhaps explained) when FICCI's Secretary General ran for the West Bengal State assembly in 2011 on the TMC ticket, and, upon victory, became Mamata Banerjee's Finance, Commerce and Industries Minister. FICCI's position on the issue promptly took a 180-degree turn and aligned with that of the other industry associations.
21. Ramesh's perception was that "industry was so used to getting land acquired for them, on pretty much the terms that they wanted" that most wanted "to just tweak the Act, increase the compensation, and be done with it" (Interview, 7/5/14). See Pande (2013) for an articulation of the case by one of his deputies.
22. Chakravorty predicts that "The political problem of resistance to land acquisition will go away . . . but an even bigger economic problem will be created" (2013: 184). But the bill did not raise prices even to market levels and is unlikely to make the political problem of resistance go away. Whether the price levels are "unsustainable" is surely debatable given the large discrepancies between compensation prices and the price of the same land once handed to private companies for urban-industrial purposes. But the question is ultimately political: the goal of higher compensation is precisely to reduce corporate profitability for the benefit of farmers.
23. Interview, New Delhi, 6/12/14.
24. Interview, Gurgaon, 6/10/14

25. See Sreedathan (2014).
26. He notes acquisition prices of Rs 3.5 to 6 *lakh* per acre against land prices of Rs 40 *lakh* to 1.5 *crore* per acre; the Karnataka parastatal offered land to Infosys at Rs 9 *lakh* per acre, making for a hefty private increment (Goldman 2011: 568).
27. Farmers here were offered Rs 800,000 to Rs 1.3 million per acre for land whose market price was already between Rs 4 million and Rs 10 million (Asher 2014: 156).
28. The price of the high-end flats would ultimately be far more.
29. The assessed agricultural value of land in Rajpura was approximately $4,000 per *bigha* before the SEZ's arrival. Since Rajpura was within Jaipur's urbanizable limits, LARRA would most likely have doubled that to $8,000 per *bigha*. While we have seen how unequally farmers benefited from their compensation plots, the average farmer in Rajpura received $18,000 per *bigha*, more than quadruple the assessed value.
30. This includes Punjab (Asher 2014: 159), Haryana (Kennedy 2014: 178), Uttar Pradesh (Pai and Kumar 2014: 343), Maharashtra (Interview, MIDCO official, 9/25/10), and Karnataka (Balakrishnan 2013: 797). Parastatals in Maharashtra and Uttar Pradesh each appear to have started the practice (in pockets) as early as the 1990s, while Punjab and Haryana followed in the 2000s.
31. For example, in forest and some coastal areas.
32. This history also came out in the Goa People's Audit of SEZs (Fieldnotes, 12/19/10, Kerim, Goa).
33. See Midnight Notes Collective (1990), De Angelis (2001, 2007), Linebaugh (2008), Caffentzis and Federici (2014), Shiva, Jani, and Fontana (2011).
34. This can be due to both deliberate opacity and negligent government outreach. The vacuum is filled with rumors, which can cut both ways: while inadequate information can help to disable collective action as it did in Rajpura, it can also incite it based on fears of the worst, as it did in Nandigram. See also Oskarsson's (2013) account of "dispossession by confusion."
35. Seethalakshmi (2009) documents the former in the case of the Sri City SEZ in Andhra Pradesh; Banerjee (2006) and Nielsen (2010) document the latter in the case of Singur, West Bengal.
36. The precise relationship between mining and Maoism remains a complex question, which is nestled within a charged debate over why people join the Maoists generally (cf. Sundar 2006, 2013, 2016; Shah 2013a, 2013b, 2013c). Without wading into this debate, I believe it is relatively uncontroversial that the Maoists have supported anti-dispossession struggles in some places.

REFERENCES

Abrams, Philip. 1988. "Notes on the Difficulty of Studying the State." *Journal of Historical Sociology* 1(1): 58–89.

Adduci, Matilde. 2009. "Neoliberal Wave Rocks Chilika Lake, India: Conflict over Intensive Aquaculture from a Class Perspective." *Journal of Agrarian Change* 9(4): 484–511.

Adnan, Shapan. 1985. "Classical and Contemporary Approaches to Agrarian Capitalism." *Economic and Political Weekly* 20(30): PE53–PE64.

———. 2013. "Land Grabs and Primitive Accumulation in Deltaic Bangladesh: Interactions between Neoliberal Globalization, State Interventions, Power Relations and Peasant Resistance." *Journal of Peasant Studies* 40(1): 87–128.

———. 2015. "Primitive Accumulation and the 'Transition to Capitalism' in Neoliberal India: Mechanisms, Resistance, and the Persistence of Self-Employed Labour." In *Indian Capitalism in Development*, edited by Barbara Harriss-White and Judith Heyer, 23–45. London: Routledge.

Agarwal, Bina. 1988. "Who Sows? Who Reaps?: Women and Land Rights in India." *Journal of Peasant Studies* 15(4): 532–581.

———. 1994. *A Field of One's Own: Gender and Land Rights in South Asia*. Cambridge: Cambridge University Press.

———. 2005. "Landmark Step to Gender Equality." *The Hindu*, September 25.

Agarwala, Rina. 2013. *Informal Labor, Formal Politics, and Dignified Discontent in India*. Cambridge: Cambridge University Press.

Ahluwalia, Isher Judge. 1998. "The Contribution of Planning to Indian Industrialisation." In *The State, Development Planning and Liberalisation in India*, edited by Terence J. Byres, 254–297. New Delhi: Oxford University Press.

Ahmad, Aijaz. 1992. *In Theory: Classes, Nations, Literatures*. New Delhi: Oxford University Press.

Amanor, Kojo Sebastian. 2012. "Global Resource Grabs, Agribusiness Concentration and the Smallholder: Two West African Case Studies." *Journal of Peasant Studies* 39(3–4): 731–750.

Ambit Capital. 2015. *Real Estate: The Unwind and Its Side Effects*. Mumbai: Ambit Capital.

Amsden, Alice H. 1989. *Asia's Next Giant: South Korea and Late Industrialization*. New York: Oxford University Press.

Anderson, Kevin B. 2010. *Marx at the Margins: On Nationalism, Ethnicity, and Non-Western Societies*. Chicago: The University of Chicago Press.

Anderson, Perry. 1974. *Lineages of the Absolutist State*. London: New Left Books.

Andreas, Joel, and Shaohua Zhan. 2016. "Hukou and Land: Market Reform and Rural Displacement in China." *Journal of Peasant Studies* 43(4): 798–827.

Appadurai, A. 2004. "The Capacity to Aspire: Culture and the Terms of Recognition." In *Culture and Public Action*, edited by V. Rao and M. Walton, 59–84. Stanford: Stanford University Press.

Araghi, Farshad. 2009a. "The Invisible Hand and the Visible Foot: Peasants, Dispossession and Globalization." In *Peasants and Globalization: Political Economy, Rural Transformation, and the Agrarian Question*, edited by A. Haroon Akram-Lodhi and Cristobal Kay, 111–147. London: Routledge.

———. 2009b. "Accumulation by Displacement: Global Enclosures, Food Crisis, and the Ecological Contradictions of Capitalism." *Review (Fernand Braudel Center)* 32(1): 113–146.

Arora, Amit. 2009. "Land Crunch Threatens Gujarat Industrial Projects." *DNA*, October 5.

Arora, Ashish, V. S. Aruncahalam, Jai Asundi, and Ronald Fernandes. 2001. "The Indian Software Services Industry." *Research Policy* 30: 1267–1287.

Arrighi, Giovanni. 1978. *The Geometry of Imperialism: The Limits of Hobson's Paradigm*. London: New Left Books.

———. 1994. *The Long Twentieth Century: Money, Power and the Origin of our Time*. London: Verso.

———. 2007. *Adam Smith in Beijing: Lineages of the Twenty-First Century*. London: Verso.

———. 2010. *The Long Twentieth Century: Money, Power and the Origin of our Time, 2nd ed.* New York: Verso.

Arrighi, Giovanni, Nicole Aschoff, and Ben Scully. 2010. "Accumulation by Dispossession and Its Limits: The Southern Africa Paradigm Revisited." *Studies in Comparative International Development* 45: 410–438.

Arrighi, Giovanni, and Fortunata Piselli. 1987. "Capitalist Development in Hostile Environments: Feuds, Class Struggles, and Migrations in a Peripheral Region of Southern Italy." *Review* 10(4): 649–751.

Asher, Manshi. 2014. "Gujarat and Punjab: The Entrepreneur's Paradise and the Land of the Farmer." In *Power, Policy and Protest: The Politics of India's Special Economic Zones*, edited by Rob Jenkins, Lorraine Kennedy, and Partha Mukhopadhyay, 137–170. New Delhi: Oxford University Press.

Ashman, Sam, and Alex Callinicos. 2006. "Capital Accumulation and the State System: Assessing David Harvey's *The New Imperialism*." *Historical Materialism* 14(4): 107–131.

Avineri, Shlomo, ed. 1969. *Karl Marx on Colonialism and Modernization*. New York: Anchor Books.

Bag, Kheya. 2011. "Red Bengal's Rise and Fall." *New Left Review* 70(69): 98.

Bailey, F. G. 1957. *Caste and the Economic Frontier*. Manchester: Manchester University Press.

———. 1960. *Caste, Tribe, and Nation: A Study of Political Activity and Political Change in Highland Orissa*. Manchester: Manchester University Press.

Baka, Jennifer. 2013. "The Political Construction of Wasteland: Governmentality, Land Acquisition and Social Inequality in South India." *Development and Change* 44(2): 409–428.

Balakrishnan, Sai. 2013. "Highway Urbanization and Land Conflicts: The Challenges to Decentralization in India." *Pacific Affairs* 86(4): 785–811.

Banerjee, Abhijit Vinayak, Pranab Bardhan, Kaushik Basu, Mrinal Datta Chaudhury, Maitreesh Ghatak, Ashok Sanjay Guha, Mukul Majumdar, Dilip Mookherjee, and Debraj Ray. 2007. "Beyond Nandigram: Industrialisation in West Bengal." *Economic and Political Weekly* 42(17): 1487–1489.

Banerjee, Parthasarathi. 2006. "Land Acquisition and Peasant Resistance at Singur." *Economic and Political Weekly* 18: 4718–4720.

———. 2014. "Orissa and West Bengal: The SEZ Imbroglio." In *Power, Policy, and Protest: The Politics of India's Special Economic Zones*, edited by Rob Jenkins, Lorraine Kennedy, and Partha Mukhopadhyay, 272–303. New Delhi: Oxford University Press.

Banerji, Pranab, Ramaswamy R. Iyer, R. Rangachari, Nirmal Sengupta, and Shekhar Singh. 2000. *India Country Study Prepared for the World Commission on Dams*. Cape Town: World Commission on Dams.

Banner, Stuart. 2005. *How the Indians Lost Their Land: Law and Power on the Frontier*. Cambridge: The Belknap Press of Harvard University Press.

Banumathi, M. 2010. "Special Economic Zones: An Instrument of Economic Development." In *Special Economic Zones in India*, edited by P. Arunachalam, 65–76. New Delhi: Serials Publications.

Baran, Paul. 1957. *The Political Economy of Growth*. New York: Monthly Review Press.

Bardhan, Pranab. 1984. *The Political Economy of Development in India*. Delhi: Oxford University Press.

———. 2010. *Awakening Giants, Feet of Clay: Assessing the Economic Rise of China and India*. Princeton: Princeton University Press.

———. 2011. "Industrialization and the Land Acquisition Conundrum." *Development Outreach*, April: 54–57.

Barry, Ellen. 2014. "Hopes of a Generation Ride on Indian Vote." *New York Times*, May 15.

Baviskar, Amita. 1995. *In the Belly of the River: Tribal Conflicts over Development in the Narmada Valley*. Oxford: Oxford University Press.

Baviskar, Amita, and Nandini Sundar. 2008. "Democracy versus Economic Transformation?" *Economic and Political Weekly* 43(46): 87–89.

Bayly, Christopher A. 1983. *Rulers, Townsmen and Bazaars: North Indian Society in the Age of British Expansion, 1770–1870*. Cambridge: Cambridge University Press.

BBC. 2008. "India's Divisive Economic Zones." *BBC News*, September 24.

Bedi, Heather Plumridge, and Louise Tillin. 2015. "Inter-State Competition, Land Conflicts and Resistance in India." *Oxford Development Studies* 43(2): 194–211.

Bendix, Reinhard. 1947. "Bureaucracy: The Problem and Its Setting." *American Sociological Review* 12: 493–507.

Benjamin, Solomon, R. Bhuvaneswari, P. Rajan, and Manjunatha. 2007. *Bhoomi: "E-Governance," Or, An Anti-Politics Machine Necessary to Globalize Bangalore?* A CASUM-M Working Paper.

Bernstein, Henry. 2006. "Is there an Agrarian Question in the 21st Century?" *Canadian Journal of Development Studies* 27(4): 449–460.

———. 2010. *Class Dynamics of Agrarian Change*. Halifax: Fernwood Publishing.

———. 2012. "Agrarian Questions from Transition to Globalization." In *Peasants and Globalization: Political Economy, Rural Transformation, and the Agrarian Question*, edited by A. Haroon Akram-Lodhi and Cristobal Kay, 239–261. London: Routledge.

Bhaduri, Amit. 1983. *The Economic Structure of Backward Agriculture*. London: Academic Press.

Bhagwati, Jagdish N. 1982. "Directly Unproductive, Profit-Seeking (DUP) Activities." *Journal of Political Economy* 90(5): 988–1002.

Bhanot, Renu, and Mridula Singh. 1992. "The Oustees of Pong Dam: Their Search for a Home." In *Big Dams, Displaced People*, edited by Enakshi Ganguly Thukral, 101–142. New Delhi: Sage Publications.

Bhargava, Sandeep. 1995. "Industrial Liberalisation: Policy Issues at State Level." *Economic and Political Weekly* 30(34): M117–M123.

Birkenholtz, Trevor. 2008. "Contesting Expertise: The Politics of Environmental Knowledge in Northern Indian Groundwater Practices." *Geoforum* 39(1): 466–482.

BJP (Bharatiya Janata Party). 2001. "Economic Resolution Passed at the BJP National Council Meeting in Nagpur." September 9.

Block, Fred. 2001. "Introduction." In *The Great Transformation: The Political and Economic Origins of Our Time*, by Karl Polanyi, xviii–xxxviii. Boston: Beacon Press.

Borras, Saturnino M., Jennifer C. Franco, Sergio Gomez, Cristobal Kay, and Max Spoor. 2012. "Land Grabbing in Latin America and the Caribbean." *Journal of Peasant Studies* 39(3–4): 845–872.

Bourdieu, Pierre. 1984. *Distinction: A Social Critique of the Judgment of Taste*. Cambridge: Harvard University Press.

———. 1986. "The Forms of Capital." In *Handbook of Theory and Research for the Sociology of Education*, edited by J. E. Richardson, 46–58. New York: Greenwood Press.

———. 1990. *The Logic of Practice*. Stanford: Stanford University Press.

———. 2004. "The Peasant and His Body." *Ethnography* 5(4): 579–599.

———. 2014. *On the State: Lectures at the Collège de France, 1989–1992*. Cambridge, MA: Polity Press.

Bowes, John. 2016. *Land Too Good for Indians: Northern Indian Removal*. Norman: University of Oklahoma Press.

Brara, Rita. 2006. *Shifting Landscapes: The Making and Remaking of Village Commons in India*. New Delhi: Oxford University Press.

Brass, Tom, ed. 1995. *New Farmers' Movements in India*. Ilford: Frank Cass.

———. 2000. *Peasants, Populism and Postmodernism: The Return of the Agrarian Myth*. London: Frank Cass.

———. 2015. "Peasants, Academics, Populists: Forward to the Past?" *Critique of Anthropology* 35(2): 187–204.

Bredo, William. 1960. *Industrial Estates: Tool for Industrialization*. Bombay: Asia Publishing House.

Breman, Jan. 1990. *Labour Migration and Rural Transformation in Colonial Asia*. Amsterdam: Free University Press.

———. 1994. *Wage Hunters and Gatherers: Search for Work in the Urban and Rural Economy of South Gujarat*. Oxford: Oxford University Press.

———. 1996. *Footloose Labour: Working in India's Informal Economy*. Cambridge: Cambridge University Press.

———. 2007. *The Poverty Regime in Village India: Half a Century of Work and Life at the Bottom of the Rural Economy in South Gujarat*. New Delhi: Oxford University Press.

———. 2010. *Outcast Labour in Asia: Circulation and Informalization of the Workforce at the Bottom of the Economy*. New Delhi: Oxford University Press.

Brenner, Neil. 2004. *New State Spaces: Urban Governance and the Rescaling of Statehood*. Oxford: Oxford University Press.

———. 2013. "Theses on Urbanization." *Public Culture* 25(1): 85–114.

———, ed. 2014. *Implosions/explosions: Towards a Study of Planetary Urbanization*. Berlin: Jovis.

Brenner, Neil, and Nik Theodore. 2002. "Cities and the Geographies of 'Actually Existing Neoliberalism.'" *Antipode* 34(3): 349–379.

Brenner, Robert. 1976. "Agrarian Class Structure and Economic Development in Pre- Industrial Europe." *Past and Present* 70: 30–75.

———. 1977. "The Origins of Capitalist Development: A Critique of Neo-Smithian Marxism." *New Left Review* 104: 25–92.

———. 2006. "What Is, and What Is Not, Imperialism?" *Historical Materialism* 14(4): 79–105.

Buckley, Lila. 2013. "Chinese Land-Based Interventions in Senegal." *Development and Change* 44(2): 429–450.

Bukharin, Nikolai. 1973. *Imperialism and World Economy*. New York: Monthly Review Press.

Burawoy, Michael. 1976. "The Functions and Reproduction of Migrant Labor: Comparative Material from Southern Africa and the United States." *American Journal of Sociology* 81(5): 1050–1087.

———. 1979. *Manufacturing Consent: Changes in the Labor Process under Monopoly Capitalism*. Chicago: University of Chicago Press.

———. 1985. *The Politics of Production: Factory Regimes under Capitalism and Socialism*. London: Verso.

———. 1989. "Marxism without Micro-Foundations." *Socialist Review* 89(2): 53–86.

———. 1998. "The Extended Case Method." *Sociological Theory* 16(1): 4–33.

———. 2001. "Transition without Transformation: Russia's Involutionary Road to Capitalism." *East European Politics and Societies* 15(2): 269–290.

———. 2009. *The Extended Case Method: Four Countries, Four Decades, Four Great Transformations, and One Theoretical Tradition*. Berkeley: University of California.

Burman, Roy. 1968. *Social Processes in the Industrialisation of Rourkela (with Reference to Displacement and Rehabilitation of Tribal and Other Backward People)*. New Delhi: Office of the Registrar General, Ministry of Home Affairs.

Burnod, Perrine, Mathilde Gingembre, and Rivo Andrianirina Ratsialonana. 2013. "Competition over Authority and Access: International Land Deals in Madagascar." *Development and Change* 44(2): 357–379.

Byres, Terence J. 1988. "Charan Singh, 1902–87: An Assessment." *Journal of Peasant Studies* 15(2): 139–189.

———. 1991. "The Agrarian Question and Differing Forms of Capitalist Agrarian Transition: An Essay with Reference to Asia." In *Rural Transformation in Asia*, edited by Jan Breman, 3–76. Oxford University Press: New Delhi.

———. 1996. *Capitalism from Above and Capitalism from Below: An Essay in Comparative Political Economy*. London: Macmillan.

Caffentzis, George, and Silvia Federici. 2014. "Commons Against and Beyond Capitalism." *Community Development Journal* 49(Suppl. 1): i92–i105.

CAG (Comptroller and Auditor General). 2014. *Performance of Special Economic Zones*. New Delhi: Department of Revenue, Government of India.

Cardoso, Fernando Henrique, and Enzo Faletto. 1979. *Dependency and Development in Latin America*. Berkeley: University of California Press.

Carney, Judith, and Michael Watts. 1990. "Manufacturing Dissent: Work, Gender and the Politics of Meaning in a Peasant Society." *Africa* 60(2): 207–241.

Castree, Noel. 2003. "Commodifying What Nature?" *Progress in Human Geography* 27(3): 273–297.

Census of India. 2001. *Census of India*. New Delhi: Government of India, Ministry of Home Affairs.

———. 2011. *Census of India*. New Delhi: Government of India, Ministry of Home Affairs.

Cernea, Michael. 1999. *The Economics of Involuntary Resettlement: Questions and Challenges*. Washington, D.C.: World Bank.

———. 2000. "Risks, Safeguards, and Reconstruction: A Model for Population Displacement and Resettlement." *Economic and Political Weekly* 35(41): 3659–3678.

Chakravarti, Anand. 1975. *Contradiction and Change: Emerging Patterns of Authority in a Rajasthan Village*. New Delhi: Oxford University Press.

Chakravarty, Sukhamoy. 1987. *Development Planning: The Indian Experience*. Oxford: Oxford University Press.

Chakravorty, Sanjoy. 2013. *The Price of Land: Acquisition, Conflict, Consequence*. New Delhi: Oxford University Press.

———. 2015. "Improving an Unworkable Law." *The Hindu*, January 7.

Chandavarkar, Rajnarayan. 1994. *The Origins of Industrial Capitalism in India: Business Strategies and the Working Classes in Bombay, 1900–1940*. Cambridge: Cambridge University Press.

Chandra, Kanchan. 2015. "The New Indian State." *Economic and Political Weekly* 50(41): 47.

Chandrasekhar, C. P., and Jayati Gosh. 2002. *The Market that Failed: Neoliberal Economic Reforms in India*. New Delhi: LeftWord Books.

Chari, Sharad. 2004. *Fraternal Capital: Peasant-Workers, Self-made Men, and Globalization in Provincial India*. Stanford: Stanford University Press.

Chatterjee, Partha. 2008. "Democracy and Economic Transformation in India." *Economic and Political Weekly* 43(16): 53–62.

Chayanov, A. V. 1986. *The Theory of Peasant Economy*. Madison: University of Wisconsin Press.

Chibber, Vivek. 2003. *Locked in Place: State-Building and Late Industrialization in India*. Princeton: Princeton University Press.

———. 2013. *Postcolonial Theory and the Specter of Capital*. London: Verso.

Chopra, Anuj. 2008. "India's Biggest Industrial Barrier? Farmers?" *The Globe and Mail*, October 7.

Chowdhry, Prem. 2011. *Political Economy of Production and Reproduction: Caste, Custom, and Community in North India*. New Delhi: Oxford University Press.

Chuang, Julia. 2014. "China's Rural Land Politics: Bureaucratic Absorption and the Muting of Rightful Resistance." *China Quarterly* 219: 649–669.

———. 2015. "Urbanization through Dispossession: Survival and Stratification in China's New Townships." *Journal of Peasant Studies* 42(2): 275–294.

CII (Confederation of Indian Industries). 2011. "CII Recommends Government's Proactive Role in Land Acquisition." June 6.

Clastres, Pierre. 1998. *Chronicle of the Guayaki Indians*. New York: Zone Books.

CMIE (Center for Monitoring Indian Economy). 2012. "Sharp Increase in Projects Getting Shelved." August 15.

Colson, Elizabeth. 1999. "Gendering Those Uprooted by 'Development.'" In *Engendering Forced Migration: Theory and Practice*, edited by Doreen Indra, 22–39. New York: Berghahn Books.

Corbridge, Stuart, and Alpah Shah. 2013. "Introduction: The Underbelly of the Indian Boom." *Economy and Society* 42(3): 335–347.

Coronil, Fernando. 1997. *The Magical State: Nature, Money, and Modernity in Venezuela*. Chicago: University of Chicago Press.

Coulthard, Glen Sean. 2014. *Red Skin, White Masks: Rejecting the Colonial Politics of Recognition*. Minneapolis: University of Minnesota Press.

Cross, Jamie. 2010. "Neoliberalism as Unexceptional: Economic Zones and the Everyday Precariousness of Working Life in South India." *Critique of Anthropology* 30(4): 355–373.

———. 2014. *Dream Zones: Anticipating Capitalism and Development in India*. London: Pluto.

Da Silva, Solano Jose Savio. 2014. "Goa: The Dynamics of Reversal." In *Power, Policy and Protest: The Politics of India's Special Economic Zones*, edited by Rob Jenkins, Lorraine Kennedy, and Partha Mukhopadhyay, 108–136. New Delhi: Oxford University Press.

Das, Gurcharan. 2002. *India Unbound: The Social and Economic Revolution from Independence to the Global Information Age*. New York: Anchor Books.

Davis, Mike. 2001. *Late Victorian Holocausts: El Niño Famines and the Making of the Third World*. London: Verso.

———. 2006. *Planet of Slums*. London: Verso.

De Angelis, Massimo. 2001. "Marx and Primitive Accumulation: The Continuous Character of Capital's Enclosures." *The Commoner* 2: 1–22.

———. 2007. *The Beginning of History: Value Struggles and Global Capital*. London: Pluto Press.

De Janvry, Alain. 1981. *The Agrarian Question and Reformism in Latin America*. Baltimore: Johns Hopkins University Press.

De Neve, Geert. 2014. "Entrapped Entrepreneurship: Labour Contractors in the South Indian Garment Industry." *Modern Asian Studies* 48(5): 1302–1333.

De Soto, Hernando. 2000. *The Mystery of Capitalism: Why Capitalism Triumphs in the West and Fails Everywhere Else*. New York: Basic Books.

Denning, Michael. 2010. "Wageless Life." *New Left Review* 66: 79–97.

Denyer, Simon. 2011. "In India, Fresh Clashes over Rural Land as Farmers Stand Up to Government." *Washington Post*, May 21.

Desai, Sonalde, and Amaresh Dubey. 2011. "Caste in 21st Century India: Competing Narratives." *Economic and Political Weekly* 46(11): 40–49.

Deshpande, Ashwini. 2011. *The Grammar of Caste: Economic Discrimination in Contemporary India*. New Delhi: Oxford University Press.

Dewan, Ritu. 2008. "Development Projects and Displaced Women." In *India Social Development Report 2008: Development and Displacement*, edited by Hari Mohan Mathur, 127–140. New Delhi: Oxford University Press.

Dharmadhikary, Shripad. 2005. *Unravelling Bhakra: Assessing the Temple of Resurgent India*. Badwani: Manthan Adhyayan Kendra.

DNA. 2010. "Gujarat SEZs Fail to Live Up to Promise." *DNA*, October 15.

———. 2011. "Need to Think Afresh on Land Acquisition Issue: Manmohan Singh." *DNA*, May 28.

———. 2013. "No Regularisation Camps for PRN Plots this Month." *DNA*, August 22.

Dobb, Maurice. 1947. *Studies in the Development of Capitalism*. New York: International Publishers.

Dogra, Chander Suta. 2012. "Web of Political Links Helped Vadra's Land Deals." *The Hindu*, November 2.

Doss, Cheryl, Gale Summerfield, and Dzodzi Tsikata. 2014. "Land, Gender, and Food Security." *Feminist Economics* 20(1): 1–23.

Dossani, Rafiq, and Martin Kenney. 2007. "The Next Wave of Globalization: Relocating Service Provision to India." *World Development* 35(5): 772–791.

Dreze, Jean, and Amartya Sen. 2013. *An Uncertain Glory: India and Its Contradictions*. Princeton: Princeton University Press.

Dubash, Navroz K. 2002. *Tubewell Capitalism: Groundwater Development and Agrarian Change in Gujarat*. New Delhi: Oxford University Press.

Dwivedi, Ranjit. 2006. *Conflict and Collective Action: The Sardar Sarovar Project in India*. London: Routledge.

Dwyer, Michael B. 2013. "Building the Politics Machine: Tools for 'Resolving' the Global Land Grab." *Development and Change* 44(2): 309–333.

Economic Times. 2011. "Economic Survey: Infrastructure Projects' Timely Execution a Top Priority." *Economic Times*, February 25.

Edelman, Marc, Carlos Oya, and Saturnino M. Borras, Jr. 2013. "Global Land Grabs: Historical Processes, Theoretical and Methodological Implications and Current Trajectories." *Third World Quarterly* 34(9): 1517–1531.

Eisenstadt, S. N. 1966. *Modernization: Protest and Change*. Englewood Cliffs: Prentice Hall.

Elden, Stuart. 2013. *The Birth of Territory*. Chicago: University of Chicago Press.

Emmanuel, Arghiri. 1972. *Unequal Exchange: A Study of the Imperialism of Trade*. New York: Monthly Review Press.

Endnotes. 2015. "An Identical Abject-Subject?" *Endnotes* 4.

Ernst & Young. 2013. *Private Security Services Industry: Securing Future Growth*. Kolkata: Ernst & Young LLP.

Etzioni, Amitai. 1961. *A Comparative Analysis of Complex Organizations*. London: The Free Press.

Evans, Peter. 1995. *Embedded Autonomy: States and Industrial Transformation*. Princeton: Princeton University Press.

Evans, Peter B., and William H. Sewell, Jr. 2013. "Neoliberalism: Policy Regimes, International Regimes, and Social Effects." In *Social Resilience in the Neoliberal Era*, edited by Peter A. Hall and Michele Lamont, 35–68. Cambridge: Cambridge University Press.

Evans, Peter, and John D. Stephens. 1988. "Studying Development since the Sixties: The Emergence of a New Comparative Political Economy." *Theory and Society* 17(5): 713–745.

Fairbairn, Madeleine. 2013. "Indirect Dispossession: Domestic Power Imbalances and Foreign Access to Land in Mozambique." *Development and Change* 44(2): 335–356.

———. 2014. "'Like Gold with Yield': Evolving Intersections between Farmland and Finance." *Journal of Peasant Studies* 41(5): 777.

Federici, Silvia. 2004. *Caliban and the Witch: Women, the Body and Primitive Accumulation*. Brooklyn: Autonomedia.

Ferguson, James. 2006. *Global Shadows: Africa in the Neoliberal World Order*. Durham: Duke University Press.

Fernandes, Walter. 2004. "Rehabilitation for the Displaced." *Economic and Political Weekly* 39(12): 1191–1193.

———. 2008. "Sixty Years of Development-Induced Displacement in India." In *India Social Development Report 2008: Development and Displacement*, edited by Hari Mohan Mathur, 89–102. New Delhi: Oxford University Press.

Fernandes, Walter, and Vijay Paranjpye, eds. 1997. *Rehabilitation Policy and Law in India: A Right to Livelihood*. New Delhi: Indian Social Institute.

Fernandes, Walter, and Enakshi Ganguly Thukral, eds. 1989. *Development, Displacement, and Rehabilitation: Issues for a National Debate*. New Delhi: Indian Social Institute.

Foster, John Bellamy. 1999. *Marx's Ecology: Materialism and Nature*. New York: Monthly Review Press.

Foucault, Michel. 1995. *Discipline and Punish: The Birth of the Prison*. New York: Vintage Books.

Fourcade-Gourinchas, Marion, and Sarah L. Babb. 2002. "The Rebirth of the Liberal Creed: Paths to Neoliberalism in Four Countries." *American Journal of Sociology* 108(3): 533–579.

Frank, Andre Gunder. 1966. *The Development of Underdevelopment*. Boston: New England Free Press.

———. 1979. *Dependent Accumulation and Underdevelopment*. New York: Monthly Review Press.

Frankel, Francine. 2005. *India's Political Economy: 1947–2004*. Delhi: Oxford University Press.

Fratkin, Elliot M., and Eric Abella Roth. 2005. *As Pastoralists Settle: Studies in Human Ecology and Adaptation*. New York: Kluwer Academic Publishers.

Friedman, Thomas L. 2006. *The World Is Flat: A Brief History of the Twenty-First Century*, updated and expanded. New York: Farrar, Straus and Giroux.

Fuller, Chris, and Haripriya Narasimhan. 2008. "Empowerment and Constraint: Women, Work and the Family in Chennai's Software Industry." In *In an Outpost of the Global Economy: Work and Workers in India's Information Technology Industry*, edited by Carol Upadhya and A. R. Vasavi, 190–210. London: Routledge.

Gadgil, Madhav, and Ramachandra Guha. 1993. *This Fissured Land: An Ecological History of India*. Berkeley: University of California Press.

Galvin, Kathleen A. 2009. "Transitions: Pastoralists Living with Change." *Annual Review of Anthropology* 38: 185.

Gandhi, Aditi, and Michael Walton. 2012. "Where Do India's Billionaires Get Their Wealth?" *Economic and Political Weekly* 47(40): 10–14.

Gerschenkron, Alexander. 1962. *Economic Backwardness in Historical Perspective: A Book of Essays*. Cambridge: Harvard University Press.

Ghatak, Maitreesh, and Parikshit Ghosh. 2011. "The Land Acquisition Bill: A Critique and a Proposal." *Economic and Political Weekly* 46(41): 65–72.

Ghertner, D. Asher. 2015. *Rule by Aesthetics: World-Class City Making in Delhi*. New York: Oxford University Press.

Ghildiyal, Subodh. 2012. "Sonia Gandhi Vetoes Dilution of Land Acquisition Bill." *Times of India*, October 20, 2012.

Ghosh, Jayati. 2015. "Growth, Industrialisation and Inequality in India." *Journal of the Asia Pacific Economy* 20(1): 42–56.

Gidwani, Vinay. 2008. *Capital, Interrupted: Agrarian Development and the Politics of Work in India*. Minnesota: University of Minnesota Press.

Gold, Ann Grodzins, and Bhoju Ram Gujar. 2002. *In the Time of Trees and Sorrows: Nature, Power and Memory in Rajasthan*. Durham: Duke University Press.

Goldman, Michael. 1994. "'There's a Snake on Our Chests': State and Development Crisis in India's Desert." PhD Dissertation, University of California, Santa Cruz.

———. 2011. "Speculative Urbanism and the Making of the Next World City." *International Journal of Urban and Regional Research* 35(3): 555–581.

Goldman, Michael, and Rachel A. Schurman. 2000. "Closing the 'Great Divide': New Social Theory on Society and Nature." *Annual Review of Sociology* 26: 563–584.

Goldsmith, Edward, and Nicholas Hildyard. 1984. *The Social and Environmental Effects of Large Dams*. San Francisco: Sierra Club Books.

Gooptu, Nandini. 2013. *Enterprise Culture in Neoliberal India: Studies in Youth, Class, Work, and Media*. London: Routledge.

Goswami, Manu. 2004. *Producing India: From Colonial Economy to National Space*. Chicago: University of Chicago Press.

Gough, Kathleen. 1979. "Indian Peasant Uprisings." In *Peasant Struggles in India*, edited by A. R. Desai, 85–126. Bombay: Oxford University Press.

Government of India. 1950. *The Rajasthan-Madhya Bharat Jagir Enquiry Committee*. New Delhi: Government of India Press.

———. 1992. *Eighth Five Year Plan*. New Delhi: Planning Commission.

———. 1994. *National Policy for Development-Induced Displacement and Rehabilitation of Persons Displaced as a Consequence of Acquisition of Land*. New Delhi: Ministry of Rural Development.

———. 2008. *Development Challenges in Extremist Affected Areas: Report of an Expert Group to Planning Commission*. New Delhi: Planning Commission.

———. 2012. *The Land Acquisition, Rehabilitation and Resettlement Bill, 2011: Report of the Standing Committee on Rural Development*. New Delhi: Lok Sabha Secretariat.

———. n.d. "Special Economic Zones in India, Ministry of Commerce and Industries." Available at: http://sezindia.nic.in [accessed February 1, 2011].

Government of Rajasthan. 1959. *Report of the State Land Commission for Rajasthan*. Jaipur: Government of Rajasthan.

———. 1994. *Investment Policy*. Jaipur: Government of Rajasthan.

———. 2003. *Policy on Special Economic Zones*. Jaipur: Government of Rajasthan.

———. 2009. *Rajasthan Statistical Abstract*. Jaipur: Directorate of Economics and Statistics.

Government of Rajasthan and Mahindra and Mahindra Ltd. 2005. *Memorandum of Understanding between the Government of Rajasthan and Mahindra and Mahindra Ltd.*

Graef, Dana J. 2013. "Negotiating Environmental Sovereignty in Costa Rica." *Development and Change* 44(2): 285–307.

Graham, Stephen. 2000. "Constructing Premium Network Spaces: Reflections on Infrastructure Networks and Contemporary Urban Development." *International Journal of Urban and Regional Research* 24(1): 183–200.

Grajales, Jacobo. 2013. "State Involvement, Land Grabbing and Counter-Insurgency in Colombia." *Development and Change* 44(2): 211–232.

Gramsci, Antonio. 1977. *Selections from the Prison Notebooks*. New York: International Publishers.

Grandia, Liza. 2013. "Road Mapping: Megaprojects and Land Grabs in the Northern Guatemalan Lowlands." *Development and Change* 44(2): 233–259.

Granovetter, Mark. 1973. "The Strength of Weak Ties." *American Journal of Sociology*: 1360–1380.

———.1985. "Economic Action and Social Structure: The Problem of Embeddedness." *American Journal of Sociology* 91: 481–510.

Guérin, I., G. Venkatasubramanian, and S. Michiels. 2015. "Labour in Contemporary South India." In *Indian Capitalism in Development*, edited by B. Harries-White and J. Heyer, 118–135. London: Routledge.

Guha, Ramachandra. 1988. "Ideological Trends in Indian Environmentalism." *Economic and Political Weekly* 23(49): 2578–2581.

———. 1989. *The Unquiet Woods: Ecological Change and Peasant Resistance in the Himalaya*. New Delhi: Oxford University Press.

———. 2007. *India after Gandhi: The History of the World's Largest Democracy*. London: Macmillan.

Guha, Ranajit. 1996. *A Rule of Property for Bengal: An Essay on the Idea of Permanent Settlement*. Durham: Duke University Press.

———. 1997. *Dominance without Hegemony: History and Power in Colonial India*. Cambridge: Harvard University Press.

———. 1999. *Elementary Aspects of Peasant Insurgency in Colonial India*. Durham: Duke University Press.

Gulati, Ashok, and Shweta Saini. 2013. "Taming Food Inflation in India." Discussion Paper no. 4. New Delhi: Commission for Agricultural Costs and Prices, Government of India.

Gulati, Manisha. 2011. "The Infrastructure Sector in India 2010–2011." In *India Infrastructure Report 2011: Water: Policy and Performance for Sustainable Development*, 379–396. New Delhi: Oxford University Press.

Guldin, Gregory Eliyu. 2001. *What's a Peasant to Do? Village Becoming Town in Southern China*. Boulder: Westview Press.

Gupta, Akhil. 1995. "Blurred Boundaries: The Discourse of Corruption, the Culture of Politics, and the Imagined State." *American Ethnologist* 22(2): 375–402.

———. 1998. *Postcolonial Developments: Agriculture in the Making of Modern India*. Durham: Duke University Press.

———. 2012. *Red Tape: Bureaucracy, Structural Violence, and Poverty in India*. Durham: Duke University Press.

Gupta, Dipankar. 2009. *The Caged Phoenix: Can India Fly?* New Delhi: Penguin.

Gupta, Poonam, and Utsav Kumar. 2012. "Performance of Indian Manufacturing in the Post-Reform Period." In *Oxford Handbook of the Indian Economy*, edited by Chetan Ghate, 225–252. Oxford: Oxford University Press.

Gupta, Surojit. 2013. "High Stakes, Mega-Bucks Fuel Illegal 'Dig-Load-Sell' Sand Business." *Times of India*, August 11.

Habib, Irfan. 2002. *Essays in Indian History: Towards a Marxist Perception*. London: Anthem Press.

Hall, Derek. 2011. "Land Grabs, Land Control, and Southeast Asian Crop Booms." *Journal of Peasant Studies* 38(4): 837–857.

———. 2013a. "Primitive Accumulation, Accumulation by Dispossession and the Global Land Grab." *Third World Quarterly* 34(9): 1582–1604.

———. 2013b. *Land*. Cambridge: Polity Press.

Hall, Derek, Philip Hirsch, and Tania Li. 2011. *Powers of Exclusion: Land Dilemmas in Southeast Asia*. Singapore: Nus Press.

Hall, Ruth. 2012. "The Next Great Trek? South African Commercial Farmers Move North." *Journal of Peasant Studies* 39(3–4): 823–844.

Hall, Ruth, Marc Edelman, Saturnino M. Borras, Jr., Ian Scoones, Ben White, and Wendy Wolford. 2015. "Resistance, Acquiescence or Incorporation? An Introduction to Land Grabbing and Political Reactions 'From Below.'" *Journal of Peasant Studies* 42(3–4): 467–488.

Harris, Gardiner. 2012. "In Tiny Bean, India's Dirt-Poor Farmers Strike Gas-Drilling Gold." *New York Times*, July 16.

Harriss, John. 1982. *Capitalism and Peasant Farming: Agrarian Structure and Ideology in Northern Tamil Nadu*. Bombay: Oxford University Press.

———. 1991. "Agriculture/non-Agricultural Linkages and the Diversification of Rural Economic Activity: A South Indian Case Study." In *Rural Transformation in Asia*, edited by Jan Breman, 429–457. Delhi: Oxford University Press.

Harriss-White, Barbara. 2003. *India Working: Essays on Society and Economy*. Cambridge: Cambridge University Press.

———. 2012. "Capitalism and the Common Man: Peasants and Petty Production in Africa and South Asia." *Agrarian South: Journal of Political Economy* 1(2): 109–160.

Harriss-White, Barbara, and S. Janakarajan. 1997. "From Green Revolution to Rural Industrial Revolution in South India." *Economic and Political Weekly* 32(25): 1469–1477.

Harris-White, Barbara, S. Janakarajan, and Diego Colatei. 2004. "Introduction: Heavy Agriculture and Light Industry in South Indian Villages." In *Rural India Facing the 21st Century: Essays on Long Term Village Change and Recent Development Policy*, edited by Barbara Harriss-White and S. Janakarajan, 3–45. London: Anthem.

Hart, Gillian. 2001. "Development Critiques in the 1990s: *Culs de Sac* and Promising Paths." *Progress in Human Geography* 25(4): 649–658.

———. 2002. *Disabling Globalization: Places of Power in Post-Apartheid South Africa*. Berkeley: University of California Press.

———. 2009. "D/developments after the Meltdown." *Antipode* 41(S1): 117–141.

Hart, Henry C. 1956. *New India's Rivers*. Bombay: Orient Longman.

Harvey, David. 1989. *The Urban Experience*. Baltimore: Johns Hopkins University Press.

———. 2003. *The New Imperialism*. Oxford: Oxford University Press.

———. 2005. *A Brief History of Neoliberalism*. Oxford: Oxford University Press.

———. 2006. *The Limits to Capital*. London: Verso.

Hayek, F. A. 1944. *The Road to Serfdom*. Chicago: University of Chicago Press.

Hemadri, Ravi. 1995. "The Resettlement of Bisalpur Dam Oustees: An NGO View." In *The Resettlement of Project-Affected People: Proceedings of a Training Seminar Held at the HCM Rajasthan State Institute of Public Administration*, edited by Hari Mohan Mathur, 93–107. Jaipur: The HCM Rajasthan State Institute of Public Administration.

Hemant Priyadarshi v. State. 2013. High Court of Rajasthan. Civil Writ Petition No. 2740/2006.

Herring, Ronald J. 1983. *Land to the Tiller: The Political Economy of Agrarian Reform in South Asia*. New Haven: Yale University Press.

Hildferding, Rudolf. 1981. *Finance Capital: A Study of the Latest Phase of Capitalist Development*. London: Routledge.

Hilton, Rodney, ed. 1978. *The Transition from Feudalism to Capitalism*. London: Verso.

Hindustan Times. 2011. "PM Sets Investment Target of Rs 2 Lakh Crore for 9% Growth." *Hindustan Times*, June 6.

Hirschman, Albert O. 1958. *The Strategy of Economic Development*. New Haven: Yale University Press.

———. 1967. *Development Projects Observed*. Washington, D.C.: The Brookings Institute.

———. 2013. *The Essential Hirschman*, edited by Jeremy Adelman. Princeton: Princeton University Press.

Hsing, You-Tien. 2010. *The Great Urban Transformation: The Politics of Land and Property in China*. Oxford: Oxford University Press.

Humphries, Jane. 1990. "Enclosures, Common Rights, and Women: The Proletarianization of Families in the Late Eighteenth and Early Nineteenth Centuries." *Journal of Economic History* 50(1): 17–42.

Hung, Ho-fung. 2011. *Protest with Chinese Characteristics: Demonstrations, Riots, and Petitions in the Mid-Qing Dynasty*. New York: Columbia University Press.

———. 2016. *The China Boom: Why China Will Not Rule the World*. New York: Columbia University Press.

Huntington, Samuel. 1968. *Political Order in Changing Societies*. New Haven: Yale University Press.

IDFC (Infrastructure Development Finance Corporation). 2008. *India Infrastructure Report 2008: Business Models of the Future*. New Delhi: Oxford University Press.

———. 2009. *India Infrastructure Report 2009: Land—A Critical Resource for Infrastructure*. New Delhi: Oxford University Press.

ILO (International Labor Office). 2007. *ILO Database on Export Processing Zones*.

Iyer, Vaidhyanathan. 2014. "Rajasthan Shows Way in Labour Reform." *The Indian Express*, June 18.

Jaffrelot, Christophe. 2003. *India's Silent Revolution: The Rise of the Low Castes in North Indian Politics*. Delhi: Permanent Black.

Jaffrelot, Christophe, and Cyril Robins. 2009. "Towards Jat Empowerment in Rajasthan." In *The Rise of the Plebeians: The Changing Face of the Indian Legislative Assemblies*, edited by Christophe Jaffrelot, 164–187. New Delhi: Routledge.

Jain, A. K. 2009. *Urban Land Policy and Public-Private Partnership for Real Estate and Infrastructure Projects*. New Delhi: Readworthy Publications.

JDA (Jaipur Development Authority). 2011. *Master Plan 2025*.

Jeffrey, Craig. 2001. "'A Fist Is Stronger than Five Fingers': Caste and Dominance in Rural North India." *Transactions of the Institute of British Geographers* 26(2): 217–236.

———. 2010. *Timepass: Youth, Class and the Politics of Waiting in India*. Stanford: Stanford University Press.

Jeffrey, Craig, Patricia Jeffery, and Roger Jeffery. 2008. *Degrees without Freedom? Education, Masculinities, and Unemployment in North India*. Stanford: Stanford University Press.

Jeffrey, Craig, and Jens Lerche. 2000. "Stating the Difference: State, Discourse and Class Reproduction in Uttar Pradesh, India." *Development and Change* 31(4): 857–878.

Jenkins, Rob. 1999. *Democratic Politics and Economic Reform in India*. Cambridge: Cambridge University Press.

———. 2014. "India's SEZ Policy: The Implications of 'Permanent Reform'." In *Power, Policy and Protest: The Politics of India's Special Economic Zones*, edited by Rob Jenkins, Lorraine Kennedy, and Partha Mukhopadhyay, 39–71. New Delhi: Oxford University Press.

Jenkins, Rob, Lorraine Kennedy, and Partha Mukhopadhyay. 2014. "Power, Protest, and India's Special Economic Zones." In *Power, Policy and Protest: The Politics of India's Special Economic Zones*, edited by Rob Jenkins, Lorraine Kennedy, and Partha Mukhopadhyay, 1–38. New Delhi: Oxford University Press.

Jha, P. S. 1980. *The Political Economy of Stagnation*. Delhi: Oxford University Press.

Jodha, N. S. 1985. "Population Growth and the Decline of Common Property Resources in Rajasthan, India." *Population and Development Review* 11(2): 247–264.

Johnson, Chalmers. 1982. *MITI and the Japanese Miracle: The Growth of Industrial Policy, 1925–1975*. Stanford: Stanford University Press.

Joshi, Nidhi, and Ashwani Kumar. 2011. "Physico-Chemical Analysis of Soil and Industrial Effluents of Sanganer Region of Jaipur Rajasthan." *Research Journal of Agricultural Sciences* 2(2): 354–356.

Joshi, Seema. 2009. "IT and ITES as an Engine of Growth: An Exploration into the Indian Experience." Working Paper Series No. E/294/2009. Institute of Economic Growth, New Delhi.

Joshi, Vijay, and I. M. D. Little. 1996. *India's Economic Reforms 1991–2001*. New Delhi: Oxford University Press.

Julia, and Ben White. 2012. "Gendered Experiences of Dispossession: Oil Palm Expansion in a Dayak Hibun Community in West Kalimantan." *Journal of Peasant Studies* 39(3–4): 995–1016.

Ka, Chih-Ming, and Mark Selden. 1986. "Original Accumulation, Equity and Late Industrialization: The Cases of Socialist China and Capitalist Taiwan." *World Development* 14(10): 1293–1310.

Kabeer, Naila, and Simeen Mahmud. 2004. "Globalization, Gender and Poverty: Bangladeshi Women Workers in Export and Local Markets." *Journal of International Development* 16(1): 93–109.

Kachhawaha, O. P. 1992. *History of Famines in Rajasthan, 1900 A.D.–1990 A.D.* Jodhpur: Research Publishers.

Kaldor, Nicholas. 1967. *Strategic Factors in Economic Development*. Ithaca: New York State School of Industrial and Labor Relations, Cornell University.

Kale, Sunila S. 2013. "Democracy and the State in Globalizing India: Case Study of Odisha." *India Review* 12(4): 245–259.

———. 2014. *Electrifying India: Regional Political Economies of Development*. Stanford: Stanford University Press.

Kale, Sunila S., and Nimah Mazaheri. 2014. "Natural Resources, Development Strategies, and Lower Caste Empowerment in India's Mineral Belt: Bihar and Odisha during the 1990s." *Studies in Comparative International Development* 49: 343–369.

Kalecki, M. 1972. *Selected Essays on the Economic Growth of the Socialist and the Mixed Economy*. London: Unwin.

Kalia, Ravi. 1999. *Chandigarh: The Making of an Indian City*. New Delhi: Oxford University Press.

Kannan, K. P., and G. Raveendran. 2009. "Growth Sans Employment: A Quarter Century of Jobless Growth in India's Organised Manufacturing." *Economic and Political Weekly* 44(10): 80–91.

Kapur, Devesh. 2002. "The Causes and Consequences of India's IT Boom." *India Review* 1(2): 91–110.

Kapur, Devesh, D. Shyam Babu, and Chandra Bhan Prasad. 2014. *Defying the Odds: The Rise of Dalit Entrepreneurs*. Gurgaon: Random House India.

Kashwan, Prakash. 2017. *Democracy in the Woods: Environmental Conservation and Social Justice in India, Tanzania, and Mexico*. London: Oxford University Press.

Kautsky, Karl. 1988. *The Agrarian Question*. London: Zwan Publications.

Kay, Cristobal. 2008. "Reflections on Latin American Rural Studies in the Neoliberal Globalization Period: A New Rurality." *Development and Change* 30(6): 915–943.

Kennedy, Lorraine. 2014. "Haryana: Beyond the Rural-Urban Divide." In *Power, Policy and Protest: The Politics of India's Special Economic Zones*, edited by Rob Jenkins, Lorraine Kennedy, and Partha Mukhopadhyay, 170–202. New Delhi: Oxford University Press.

Kenney-Lazar, Miles. 2012. "Plantation Rubber, Land Grabbing and Social-Property Transformation in Southern Laos." *Journal of Peasant Studies* 39(3–4): 1017–1038.

Khagram, Sanjeev. 2004. *Dams and Development: Transnational Struggles for Water and Power*. Ithaca: Cornell University Press.

Khan, Atiq. 2011. "Mayawati Announces New Land Acquisition Policy." *The Hindu*, June 2.

Kindleberger, Charles P., and Robert Z. Aliber. 2011. *Manias, Panics and Crashes: A History of Financial Crises, 6th ed.* London: Palgrave Macmillan.

Kirsch, Stuart. 2014. *Mining Capitalism: The Relationship between Corporations and Their Critics*. Berkeley: University of California Press.

Klingensmith, Daniel. 2007. *"One Valley and a Thousand": Dams, Nationalism, and Development*. New Delhi: Oxford University Press.
Kohli, Atul. 2004. *State-Directed Development: Political Power and Industrialization in the Global Periphery*. Cambridge: Cambridge University Press.
———. 2012. *Poverty amid Plenty in the New India*. Cambridge: Cambridge University Press.
Kothari, Rajni. 1984. "The Non-Party Political Process." *Economic and Political Weekly* 19(5): 216–224.
Kranakis, Eda. 2008. *Moving Companies: How U.S. Engineering Consulting Firms Created the Global Assembly Line, 1949–1969*. Lisbon: INES workshop. Unpublished Manuscript.
Krippner, Greta R., and Anthony S. Alvarez. 2007. "Embeddedness and the Intellectual Projects of Economic Sociology." *Annual Review of Sociology* 33: 219–240.
Krishna, Anirudh. 2002. *Active Social Capital: Tracing the Roots of Development and Democracy*. New York: Columbia University Press.
Krishnan, Eesvan. 2014. "Land Acquisition in British India, c. 1894–1927." DPhil Dissertation, University of Oxford.
Krueger, Anne O. 1974. "The Political Economy of the Rent-Seeking Society." *American Economic Review* 64(3): 291–303.
Kumar, Arun. 2002. *The Black Economy in India*. New Delhi: Penguin.
Kumar, Satendra. 2014. "Privatisation of Higher Education in India: Hopes and Despairs." *Social Change* 44(3): 451–458.
Kumat, R. S. 1995. "Private Lands for Development Projects: Note on Amended Property Acquisition Law." In *The Resettlement of Project-Affected People: Proceedings of a Training Seminar Held at the HCM Rajasthan State Institute of Public Administration*, edited by Hari Mohan Mathur, 36–41. Jaipur: The HCM Rajasthan Institute of Public Administration.
Kundra, A. 2000. *The Performance of India's Export Zones: A Comparison with the Chinese Approach*. New Delhi: Sage Publications.
Land Matrix. n.d. Available at: http://www.landmatrix.org/en/ [accessed June 16, 2016].
Landesa Rural Development Institute. 2013. "Report on Formal and Informal Barriers in the Implementation of the Hindu Succession (Amendment) Act." Available at: http://www.landesa.org/wp-content/uploads/hsaa-study-report.pdf [accessed November 1, 2017].
Lavers, Tom. 2012. "Patterns of Agrarian Transformation in Ethiopia: State-Mediated Commercialisation and the 'Land Grab.'" *Journal of Peasant Studies* 39(3–4): 795–822.
Le Mons Walker, Kathy. 2006. "'Gangster Capitalism' and Peasant Protest in China: The Last Twenty Years." *The Journal of Peasant Studies* 33(1): 1–33.
Lefebvre, Henri. 1991. *The Production of Space*. Oxford: Blackwell Publishers.
Lenin, V. I. 1939. *Imperialism: The Highest Stage of Capitalism*. New York: International Publishers.
———. 1964. *The Development of Capitalism in Russia*. Moscow: Progress Publishers.
Lerche, Jens. 2013. "The Agrarian Question in Neoliberal India: Agrarian Transition Bypassed?" *Journal of Agrarian Change* 13(3): 382–404.
———. 2015. "Regional Patterns of Agrarian Accumulation in India." In *Indian Capitalism in Development*, edited by Barbara Harriss-White and Judith Heyer, 46–65. London: Routledge.
Lerche, Jens, Alpa Shah, and Barbara Harriss-White. 2013. "Introduction: Agrarian Questions and Left Politics in India." *Journal of Agrarian Change* 13(3): 337–350.
Levien, Michael. 2011. "Special Economic Zones and Accumulation by Dispossession in India." *Journal of Agrarian Change* 11(4): 454–483.
———. 2013. "The Politics of Dispossession: Theorizing India's 'Land Wars.'" *Politics and Society* 41(3): 351–394.
———. 2015. "Social Capital as Obstacle to Development: Brokering Land, Norms, and Trust in Rural India." *World Development* 74: 77–92.
———. 2016. "Gender and Land Grabs in Comparative Perspective." In *Gender Equality and Sustainable Development*, edited by Melissa Leach, 105–132. London: Earthscan.
Li, Tania Murray. 2007. *The Will to Improve: Governmentality, Development, and the Practice of Politics*. Durham: Duke University Press.

———. 2010a. "Indigeneity, Capitalism, and the Management of Dispossession." *Current Anthropology* 51(3): 385–414.
———. 2010b. "To Make Live or Let Die? Rural Dispossession and the Protection of Surplus Populations." *Antipode* 41(S1): 66–93.
———. 2014. *Land's End: Capitalist Relations on an Indigenous Frontier*. Durham: Duke University Press.
———. 2015. "Social Impacts of Oil Palm in Indonesia: A Gendered Perspective from West Kalimantan." *Cifor Occasional Paper* 124.
Linebaugh, Peter. 2008. *The Magna Carta Manifesto: Liberties and Commons for All*. Berkeley: University of California Press.
Locke, John. 1980. *Second Treatise of Government*, edited by C. B. Macpherson. Indianapolis: Hackett Publishing Company.
Low, D. A. 1996. *The Egalitarian Moment: Asia and Africa, 1950–1960*. Cambridge: Cambridge University Press.
Luxemburg, Rosa. 2003. *The Accumulation of Capital*. London: Routledge.
Lynch, Caitrin. 2007. *Juki Girls, Good Girls: Gender and Cultural Politics in Sri Lanka's Global Garment Industry*. Ithaca: Cornell University Press.
Magdoff, Fred. 2013. "Twenty-First-Century Land Grabs: Accumulation by Agricultural Dispossession." *Monthly Review* 65(6): 1.
Mahapatra, L. K. 1999. "Testing the Risks and Reconstruction Model on India's Resettlement Experiences." In *The Economics of Involuntary Resettlement: Questions and Challenges*, edited by Michael Cernea, 189–230. Washington, D.C.: World Bank.
Mahindra Gesco Developers. 2006. *Seventh Annual Report 2005–2006*.
Majumdar, Sarasij. 2012. "'Who Wants to Marry a Farmer?' Neoliberal Industrialization and the Politics of Land and Work in Rural West Bengal." *Focaal—Journal of Global and Historical Anthropology* 64: 84–98.
Mallet, Victor. 2015. "Rajasthan Spearheads India's Reform Drive." *Financial Times*, January 21.
Mandel, Ernest. 1978. *Late Capitalism*. London: Verso.
Mankodi, Kashyap. 1992. "Resettlement and Rehabilitation of Dam Oustees: A Case Study of Ukai Dam." In *Big Dams, Displaced People*, edited by Enakshi Ganguly Thukral, 77–100. New Delhi: Sage Publications.
Margulis, Matias E., and Tony Porter. 2013. "Governing the Global Land Grab: Multipolarity, Ideas, and Complexity in Transnational Governance." *Globalizations* 10(1): 65–86.
Marx, Karl. 1973. *Grundrisse*. London: Penguin.
———. 1977. *Capital, Vol. I*. New York: Vintage.
———. 1981. *Capital, Vol. III*. New York: Vintage.
Massey, Douglas S., and Nancy A. Denton. 1993. *American Apartheid: Segregation and the Making of the Underclass*. Cambridge: Harvard University Press.
Mathur, Hari Mohan, ed. 1995a. *Development, Displacement, and Resettlement: Focus on Asian Experiences*. New Delhi: Vikas Publication House.
———. 1995b. "Struggling to Regain Lost Livelihood: The Case of the People Displaced by the Pong Dam in India." Unpublished paper.
———. 1995c. *The Resettlement of Project-Affected People: Proceedings of a Training Seminar Held at the HCM Rajasthan State Institute of Public Administration*. Jaipur: The HCM Rajasthan State Institute of Public Administration.
———. 1997. *Managing Projects that Involve Resettlement: Case Studies from Rajasthan, India*. Washington, D.C.: Economic Development Institute of the World Bank.
Mayer, Adrian C. 1960. *Caste and Kinship in Central India: A Village and its Region*. Berkeley: University of California Press.
McCallum, Jamie K. 2013. *Global Unions, Local Power: The New Spirit of Transnational Labor Organizing*. Ithaca: Cornell University Press.
McCartney, Matthew. 2009. *India: The Political Economy of Growth, Stagnation and the State, 1951–2007*. London: Routledge.
McCully, Patrick. 2001. *Silenced Rivers: The Ecology and Politics of Large Dams*. London: Zed Books.

McKinsey and Co. 2007. *"The Bird of Gold": The Rise of India's Consumer Market.* McKinsey Global Institute.

McMichael, Philip. 2012a. "The Land Grab and Corporate Food Regime Restructuring." *Journal of Peasant Studies* 39(3–4): 681–701.

———. 2012b. *Development and Social Change: A Global Perspective.* Los Angeles: Sage.

———. 2013. "Land Grabbing as Security Mercantilism in International Relations." *Globalizations* 10(1): 47–64.

Mehta, Lyla, 2001. "The Manufacture of Popular Perceptions of Scarcity: Dams and Water-Related Narratives in Gujarat, India." *World Development* 29(12): 2025–2041.

———, ed. 2009. *Displaced by Development: Confronting Marginalisation and Gender Injustice.* New Delhi: Sage Publications.

Mehta, Lyla, and Bina Srinivasan. 2000. "Balancing Pains and Gains: A Perspective Paper on Gender and Large Dams." World Commission on Dams Secretariat, Cape Town.

Mehta, Uday Singh. 1999. *Liberalism and Empire: A Study of Nineteenth-Century British Liberal Thought.* Chicago: University of Chicago Press.

Menon, Manju, Kanchi Kohli, and Debayan Gupta. 2017. "In State-Level Changes to Land Laws, a Return to Land Grabbing in Development's Name." *The Wire*, September 28.

Merillat, H. C. L. 1970. *Land and the Constitution in India.* New York: Columbia University Press.

Midnight Notes Collective. 1990. "Introduction to the New Enclosures." *Midnight Notes* 10: 1–9.

Mines, Diane P., and Nicolas Yazgi, eds. 2010. *Village Matters: Relocating Villages in the Contemporary Anthropology of India.* New Delhi: Oxford University Press.

Ministry of Agriculture. 2014. *Agricultural Census, 2010–11.* New Delhi: Ministry of Agriculture, Government of India.

Mintz, Sidney. 2011. "Plantations and the Rise of a World Food Economy: Some Preliminary Ideas." *Review* 34(1/2): 3–14.

Mitchell, Timothy. 1991. "The Limits of the State: Beyond Statist Approaches and their Critics." *American Political Science Review* 85(1): 77–96.

Mitra, Arup. 2013. *Insights into Inclusive Growth, Employment and Wellbeing in India.* New Delhi: Springer.

Mody, Anjali. 2014. "Karnataka: The Primacy of the Local." In *Power, Policy and Protest: The Politics of India's Special Economic Zones*, edited by Rob Jenkins, Lorraine Kennedy, and Partha Mukhopadhyay, 203–238. New Delhi: Oxford University Press.

Mondal, Sudipto. 2012. "Lokayukta to Probe Krishna, Gowda, Yeddyurappa." *The Hindu*, October 25.

Moore, Barrington. 1966. *Social Origins of Dictatorship and Democracy: Lord and Peasant in the Making of the Modern World.* Boston: Beacon Press.

———. 1978. *Injustice: The Social Bases of Obedience and Revolt.* White Plains, N.Y.: M. E. Sharpe.

Moore, Donald S. 2005. *Suffering for Territory: Race, Place, and Power in Zimbabwe.* Durham: Duke University Press.

Moore, Jason. 2015. *Capitalism in the Web of Life: Ecology and the Accumulation of Capital.* London: Verso.

Moore, Pete W., and Andrew Schrank. 2004. "Overstretch and Underdevelopment: Export Processing Zones, US Hegemony, and the Limits of Soft Power in the Third World." Paper presented at the annual meeting of the International Studies Association, Montreal, Quebec, Canada, 17 March 2004.

Mujumdar, Rohit, and Benita Menezes. 2014. "Maharashtra: Institutional Politics and the Framing of Resistance." In *Power, Policy and Protest: The Politics of India's Special Economic Zones*, edited by Rob Jenkins, Lorraine Kennedy, and Partha Mukhopadhyay, 239–271. New Delhi: Oxford University Press.

Mukherjee, Sanjukta. 2008. "Producing the Knowledge Professional: Gendered Geographies of Alienation in India's New High-Tech Workplace." In *In an Outpost of the Global Economy: Work and Workers in India's Information Technology Industry*, edited by Carol Upadhya and A. R. Vasavi, 50–75. London: Routledge.

Mukhopadhyay, Partha. 2008. "The Promised Land of SEZs." *Seminar* 581, January.

MWC (Mahindra World City). 2007. *Letter to the Principal Secretary of Industries, Government of Rajasthan.*

Nash, June C., and Maria Patricia Fernandez-Kelly. 1983. *Women, Men, and the International Division of Labor.* Albany: State University of New York Press.

NASSCOM (National Association of Software and Service Companies). 2010. *The IT-BPO Sector in India: Strategic Review 2010.* New Delhi: NASSCOM.

———. 2012. *Indian IT-BPO Industry: Key Highlights during FY2012.* New Delhi: NASSCOM.

NASSCOM and A. T. Kearney. 2008. *Location Roadmap for IT-BPO Growth: Assessment of 50 Leading Cities.* New Delhi: NASSCOM.

NDTV. 2008. "Mahindra's SEZ Style in Jaipur." *NDTV,* August 26. Available at: https://www.youtube.com/watch?v=7gRu_IMjZok [accessed November 1, 2017].

———. 2011. "Land Wars: Are They India's Biggest Crisis?" *NDTV,* June 22. Available at: https://www.youtube.com/watch?v=Hv-JIZ354Bo [accessed November 1, 2017].

———. 2011. "Prime Minister Announces Compensation for Bhatta-Parsaul Victims." *NDTV,* May 22.

Neeson, J. M. 1993. *Commoners: Common Right, Enclosure and Social Change in England, 1700–1820.* Cambridge: Cambridge University Press.

Nielsen, Kenneth Bo. 2010. "Contesting India's Development? Industrialisation, Land Acquisition and Protest in West Bengal." *Forum for Development Studies* 37(2): 145–170.

Nielsen, Kenneth Bo, and Alf Gunvald Nilsen. 2015. "Law Struggles and Hegemonic Processes in Neoliberal India: Gramscian Reflections on Land Acquisition Legislation." *Globalizations* 12(2): 203–216.

Nilsen, Alf Gunvald. 2010. *Dispossession and Resistance in India: The River and the Rage.* London: Routledge.

Nisbett, Nicholas. 2013. "Youth and the Practice of IT Enterprise." In *Enterprise Culture in Neoliberal India: Studies in Youth, Class, Work, and Media,* edited by Nandini Gooptu, 175–189. London: Routledge.

Nozick, Robert. 2013. *Anarchy, State, and Utopia.* New York: Basic Books.

Oliveira, Gustavo de L. T. 2013. "Land Regularization in Brazil and the Global Land Grab." *Development and Change* 44(2): 261–283.

Omvedt, Gail. 1993. *Reinventing Revolution: New Social Movements and the Socialist Tradition in India.* Armonk, N.Y.: M. E. Sharpe.

Ong, Aihwa. 1987. *Spirits of Resistance and Capitalist Discipline: Factory Women in Malaysia.* Albany: State University of New York Press.

———. 2006. *Neoliberalism as Exception: Mutations in Citizenship and Sovereignty.* Durham: Duke University Press.

Oskarsson, Patrik. 2013. "Dispossession by Confusion from Mineral-Rich Lands in Central India." *South Asia: Journal of South Asian Studies* 36(2): 199–212.

Oskarsson, Patrik, and Kenneth Bo Nielsen. 2014. "Development Deadlocked: Aborted Industrialization and Blocked Land Restitution in West Bengal and Andhra Pradesh, India." *Development Studies Research* 1(1): 267–278.

Oya, Carlos. 2013. "Methodological Reflections on 'Land Grab' Databases and the 'Land Grab' Literature 'Rush.'" *Journal of Peasant Studies* 40(3): 503–520.

Pai, Sudha, and Avinash Kumar. 2014. "Uttar Pradesh: Contrasting Cases from the National Capital Region." In *Power, Policy and Protest: The Politics of India's Special Economic Zones,* edited by Rob Jenkins, Lorraine Kennedy, and Partha Mukhopadhyay, 332–361. New Delhi: Oxford University Press.

Paige, Jeffrey. 1975. *Agrarian Revolution.* New York: Free Press.

Palit, A., and S. Bhattacharjee. 2008. *Special Economic Zones in India: Myths and Realities.* New Delhi: Anthem.

Palshikar, Suhas, K. C. Suri, and Yogendra Yadav. 2014. *Party Competition in Indian States: Electoral Politics in Post-Congress Polity.* New Delhi: Oxford University Press.

Panagariya, Arvind. 2014. "UPA Hurts India as It Exits." *Times of India,* March 11.

———. n.d. "Land Acquisition: Rationale and the Way Forward." *NITI Ayog Blog.* Available at: http://niti.gov.in/content/land-acquisition-rationale-and-way-forward [accessed November 1, 2017].

Pande, Suchi. 2014. "The Right to Know, the Right to Live: Grassroots Struggle for Information and Work in India." Doctoral Thesis, Institute of Development Studies, University of Sussex.

Pande, Varad. 2013. "A Business Case for the New Land Acquisition Law." *Mint*, September 9.

Pandey, B., and B. K. Rout. 2004. *Development-Induced Displacement in India: Impact on Women.* New Delhi: National Commission for Women.

Paranjpye, Vijay. 1988. *Evaluating the Tehri Dam: An Extended Cost Benefit Appraisal.* New Delhi: Indian National Trust for Art and Cultural Heritage.

Parasuraman, S. 1999. *The Development Dilemma: Displacement in India.* New York: St. Martin's Press.

Parliament of India. 2007. *Parliamentary Standing Committee on Commerce Eighty-Third Report on: The Functioning of Special Economic Zones.* New Delhi: Parliament of India.

———. 2013. "Transcript of Lok Sabha Debate, April 9, 2013." New Delhi: Parliament of India.

Parnell, Susan, and Jennifer Robinson. 2012. "(Re)Theorizing Cities from the Global South: Looking Beyond Neoliberalism." *Urban Geography* 33(4): 593–617.

Parry, Jonathan P. 2003. "Nehru's Dream and the Village 'Waiting Room': Long-Distance Labour Migrants to a Central Indian Steel Town." *Contributions to Indian Sociology* 27: 217–249.

Parry, Jonathan P., and Christian Struempell. 2008. "On the Desecration of Nehru's 'Temples': Bhilai and Rourkela Compared." *Economic and Political Weekly* 43(19): 47–57.

Patnaik, Utsa, ed. 1990. *Agrarian Relations and Accumulation: The "Mode of Production" Debate in India.* Bombay: Oxford University Press.

Pattenden, Jonathan. 2016. *Labour, State and Society in Rural India: A Class-Relational Approach.* Manchester: Manchester University Press.

Peck, Jamie. 2010. *Constructions of Neoliberal Reason.* Oxford: Oxford University Press.

Peet, Richard, and Michael Watts, eds. 2004. *Liberation Ecologies: Environment, Development, Social Movements.* London: Routledge.

Peluso, Nancy Lee. 1991. *Rich Forests, Poor People: Resource Control and Resistance in Java.* Berkeley: University of California Press.

Peluso, Nancy Lee, and Christian Lund. 2011. "New Frontiers of Land Control: Introduction." *Journal of Peasant Studies* 38(4): 667–681.

Peluso, Nancy Lee, and Michael Watts, eds. 2001. *Violent Environments.* Ithaca: Cornell University Press.

People's Tribunal on Nandigram. 2007. *Nandigram: What Really Happened?* Delhi: Daanish Books.

Perelman, Michael. 2000. *The Invention of Capitalism: Classical Political Economy and the Secret History of Primitive Accumulation.* Durham: Duke University Press.

Perry, Keisha-Khan Y. 2013. *Black Women against the Land Grab: The Fight for Racial Justice in Brazil.* Minneapolis: University of Minnesota Press.

Peters, Pauline. 1994. *Dividing the Commons: Politics, Policy and Culture in Botswana.* Charlottesville: University Press of Virginia.

Plunkett, Hugh S. 1984. *Weaving the Web of Power: Middlemen and Social Change in Rajasthan.* New Delhi: Bahri Publications.

Polanki, Pallavi. 2012. "Bhatta-Parsaul Debacle: Rahul Entered Late, Left Early." *Firstpost.* March 9.

Polanyi, Karl. 2001. *The Great Transformation: The Political and Economic Origins of Our Time.* Boston: Beacon Press.

Preobrazhensky, E. 1965. *The New Economics.* Oxford: Clarendon Press.

Putnam, Robert. 1993. *Making Democracy Work: Civic Traditions in Modern Italy.* Princeton: Princeton University Press.

Putnam, Robert. 1995. "Bowling Alone: America's Declining Social Capital." *Journal of Democracy*, January: 65–78.

PWC-ASSOCHAM. 2009. *SEZs More Lucrative for South.* New Delhi: PWC-ASSOCHAM.

Radhakrishna, Meena. 2001. *Dishonoured by History: "Criminal Tribes" and British Colonial Policy*. Hyderabad: Orient Longman.

Radhakrishnan, Smitha. 2011. *Appropriately Indian: Gender and Culture in a New Transnational Class*. Durham: Duke University Press.

Ramanathan, Usha. 2008. "The Land Acquisition Act 1894: Displacement and State Power." In *India Social Development Report 2008: Development and Displacement*, edited by Hari Mohan Mathur, 27–38. New Delhi: Oxford University Press.

Ramesh, Jairam, and Muhammad Ali Khan. 2015. *Legislating for Justice: The Making of the 2013 Land Acquisition Law*. New Delhi: Oxford University Press.

Rastogi, Anupam. 2008. "The Infrastructure Sector in India, 2007." In *India Infrastructure Report 2008: Business Models of the Future*, 1–36. New Delhi: Oxford University Press.

Razac, Olivier. 2002. *Barbed Wire: A Political History*. New York: The New Press.

Reddy, G. Ram, and G. Haragopal. 1985. "The Pyraveekar: The 'Fixer' in Rural India." *Asian Survey* 25(11): 1148–1162.

Reddy, D. Narasimha, and Srijit Mishra, eds. 2009. *Agrarian Crisis in India*. New Delhi: Oxford University Press.

Reynolds, Susan. 2010. *Before Eminent Domain: Toward a History of Expropriation of Land for the Common Good*. Chapel Hill: University of North Carolina Press.

RIICO. 1988a. *Newsletter of the Rajasthan Industrial Development and Investment Corporation*, February.

———. 1988b. *Newsletter of the Rajasthan Industrial Development and Investment Corporation*, April.

———. 1988c. *Newsletter of the Rajasthan Industrial Development and Investment Corporation*, September.

———. 1990. *Newsletter of the Rajasthan Industrial Development and Investment Corporation*, June.

———. 1992. *Newsletter of the Rajasthan Industrial Development and Investment Corporation*, August.

———. 1993. *Newsletter of the Rajasthan Industrial Development and Investment Corporation*, July.

———. 1994a. *Newsletter of the Rajasthan Industrial Development and Investment Corporation*, July.

———. 1994b. *Newsletter of the Rajasthan Industrial Development and Investment Corporation*, December.

———. 1994c. *Newsletter of the Rajasthan Industrial Development and Investment Corporation*, March.

———. 1994d. *Newsletter of the Rajasthan Industrial Development and Investment Corporation*, May.

———. 1995a. *Newsletter of the Rajasthan Industrial Development and Investment Corporation*, October.

———. 1995b. *Newsletter of the Rajasthan Industrial Development and Investment Corporation*, January.

———. 1995c. *Newsletter of the Rajasthan Industrial Development and Investment Corporation*, December.

———. 1996. *Newsletter of the Rajasthan Industrial Development and Investment Corporation*, January.

———. 1998. *Newsletter of the Rajasthan Industrial Development and Investment Corporation*, March.

———. 2002. *Newsletter of the Rajasthan State Industrial Development and Investment Corporation*, July.

———. 2006a. *Rajasthan: The Perfect Infotech Destination*. Jaipur: RIICO.

———. 2006b. *Letter from the Financial Advisor of RIICO to the Secretary of the Jaipur Development Authority*.

———. 2009. *Industrial Land in Rajasthan*. Jaipur: RIICO.

———. 2010. *42nd Annual Report 2010–2011*. Jaipur: RIICO.

R. L. Arora v. State of U.P. 1961. Supreme Court of India. Available at: https://indiankanoon.org/doc/1981888/ [accessed July 25, 2017].

Robbins, Paul. 1998. "Nomadization in Rajasthan, India: Migration, Institutions, and Economy." *Human Ecology* 26(1): 87–112.

Robinson, Joan. 1962. *Economic Philosophy*. Harmondsworth: Penguin Books.
Rodney, Walter. 1981. *How Europe Underdeveloped Africa*. Washington D.C.: Howard University Press.
Rodrik, Dani. 2016. "Premature Deindustrialization." *Journal of Economic Growth* 21: 1–33.
Rosin, R. Thomas. 1978. "Peasant Adaptation as Process in Land Reform." In *American Studies in the Anthropology of India*, edited by Sylvia Vatuk, 460–495. New Delhi: Manohar and American Institute of Indian Studies.
———. 1987. *Land Reform and Agrarian Change: Study of a Marwar Village from Raj to Swaraj*. Jaipur: Rawat Press.
Rostow, Walter. 1959. "The Stages of Economic Growth." *Economic History Review* 12(1): 1–16.
Routledge, Paul. 1993. *Terrains of Resistance: Nonviolent Social Movements and the Contestation of Place in India*. Westport: Praeger.
Rowley, Emma. 2012. "Growing Fracking Industry Boosts Appetite for Guar Gum." *The Telegraph*, June 10.
Roy, Srirupa. 2007. *Beyond Belief: India and the Politics of Postcolonial Nationalism*. Durham: Duke University Press.
Rudolph, Lloyd I., and Susanne Hoeber Rudolph. 1984. *Essays on Rajputana*. New Delhi: Concept Publishing.
———. 2001. "Iconisation of Chandrababu: Sharing Sovereignty in India's Federal Market Economy." *Economic and Political Weekly* 36(18): 1541–1552.
Sahoo, Pravakar. 2015. "Time to Review the Special Economic Zones Act." *Economic and Political Weekly* 50(14): 23–26.
Sampat, Preeti. 2015. "The 'Goan Impasse': Land Rights and Resistance to SEZs in Goa, India." *Journal of Peasant Studies* 42(3–4): 765–790.
———. 2016a. "Dholera: The Emperor's New City." *Economic and Political Weekly* 51(17): 59–67.
———. 2016b. "India's Land Impasse." *Seminar* 682: 48–52.
Sanchez, Andrew, and Christian Strumpell. 2014. "Sons of Soil, Sons of Steel: Autochthony, Descent and the Class Concept in Industrial India." *Modern Asian Studies* 48(5): 1276–1301.
Sangvai, Sanjay. 2002. *The River and Life: People's Struggle in the Narmada Valley*. Mumbai: Earthcare Books.
Sanyal, Kalyan. 2007. *Rethinking Capitalist Development: Primitive Accumulation, Govermentality, and Post-Colonial Capitalism*. New Delhi: Routledge.
Sardesai, Rajdeep. 2014. *2014: The Election that Changed India*. Gurgaon: Penguin.
Sargeson, Sally. 2008. "Women's Property, Women's Agency in China's 'New Enclosure Movement': Evidence from Zhejiang." *Development and Change* 39(4): 641–665.
Sargeson, Sally, and Yu Song. 2010. "Land Expropriation and the Gender Politics of Citizenship in the Urban Frontier." *The China Journal* 64: 19–45.
Sarkar, Ranju. 2008. "Mahindras Cash in on Early SEZ Appeal." *Business Standard*, July 28.
Sassen, Saskia. 2010. "A Savage Sorting of Winners and Losers: Contemporary Versions of Primitive Accumulation." *Globalizations* 7(1): 23–50.
———. 2013. "Land Grabs Today: Feeding the Disassembling of National Territory." *Globalizations* 10(1): 25–46.
———. 2014. *Expulsions: Brutality and Complexity in the Global Economy*. Cambridge, MA: The Belknap Press of Harvard University Press.
Sawhney, Inder. 1987. "Jaipur Urgently Needs Civic Corporation: Rajasthan Newsletter." *Times of India*, May 25.
Saxena, Aruna. 1989. *Perspectives in Industrial Geography: A Case Study of an Industrial City of Uttar Pradesh*. New Delhi: Concept Publishers.
Scott, James C. 1976. *The Moral Economy of the Peasant: Rebellion and Subsistence in Southeast Asia*. New Haven: Yale University Press.
———. 1979. "Revolution in the Revolution." *Theory and Society* 7(1–2): 97–134.
———. 1985. *Weapons of the Weak: Everyday Forms of Peasant Resistance*. New Haven: Yale University Press.

———. 1990. *Domination and the Arts of Resistance: Hidden Transcripts*. New Haven: Yale University Press.
———. 1998. *Seeing Like a State: How Certain Schemes to Improve the Human Condition Have Failed*. New Haven: Yale University Press.
Searle, Llerena Guiu. 2016. *Landscapes of Accumulation: Real Estate and the Neoliberal Imagination in Contemporary India*. Chicago: University of Chicago Press.
Seethalakshmi, S. 2009. *Special Economic Zones in Andhra Pradesh: Policy Claims and People's Experiences*. Hyderabad: ActionAid.
Sekhar, B. 1995. "The Oustees of the Mahi Bajaj Sagar Project: Twenty Years After." In *The Resettlement of Project-Affected People: Proceedings of a Training Seminar Held at the HCM Rajasthan State Institute of Public Administration*, edited by Hari Mohan Mathur, 45–56. Jaipur: The HCM Rajasthan State Institute of Public Administration.
Sen, Amartya. 1984. *Resources, Values, and Development*. Cambridge: Harvard University Press.
———. 2000. *Development as Freedom*. New York: Oxford University Press.
Sen, Sunil. 1979. "Tebhaga Chai." In *Peasant Struggles in India*, edited by A. R. Desai, 442–452. Bombay: Oxford University Press.
Sender, Henny. 2015. "India Infrastructure: Built on Debt." *Financial Times*, June 22.
Sengupta, Somini. 2008. "India Grapples with How to Convert Its Farmland into Factories." *New York Times*, September 17.
Sewell, William H. 2005. *Logics of History: Social Theory and Social Transformation*. Chicago Studies in Practices of Meaning. Chicago: University of Chicago Press.
Shah, Alpa. 2010. *In the Shadows of the State: Indigenous Politics, Environmentalism, and Insurgency in Jharkhand, India*. New Delhi: Oxford University Press.
———. 2013a. "The Intimacy of Insurgency: Beyond Coercion, Greed or Grievance in Maoist India. *Economy and Society* 42(3): 480–506.
———. 2013b. "Tensions over Liberal Citizenship in a Marxist Revolutionary Situation: The Maoists in India." *Critique of Anthropology* 33(1): 91–109.
———. 2013c. "Response to Nandini Sundar's Response to 'Tensions Over Liberal Citizenship in a Marxist Revolutionary Situation: The Maoists in India.'" *Critique of Anthropology* 33(4): 476–479.
Shah, M., R. Rao, and P. S. Vijay Shankar. 2007. "Rural Credit in 20th Century India: An Overview of History and Perspectives." *Economic and Political Weekly* 42(15): 1351–1364.
Shanin, Teodor, ed. 1983. *Late Marx and the Russian Road: Marx and the "Peripheries of Capitalism."* New York: Monthly Review Press.
———. 1987. *Peasants and Peasant Societies*. Oxford: Basil Blackwell.
Sharma, Suresh. 1992. "The Vanquished Tribal World of Shifting Cultivation." In *Images of Rural India in the 20th Century*, edited by Alok Bhalla, 69–85. New Delhi: Sterling Publishers.
Sharma, V. D. 1995. "Problems of Resettlement in Sariska Wildlife Sanctuary." In *The Resettlement of Project-Affected People: Proceedings of a Training Seminar Held at the HCM Rajasthan State Institute of Public Administration*, edited by Hari Mohan Mathur, 140–146. Jaipur: The HCM Rajasthan State Institute of Public Administration.
Shils, Edward. 1965. *Political Development in the New States*. The Hague: Mouton & Co.
Shiva, Vandana, Shreya Jani, and Sulakshana M. Fontana. 2011. *The Great Indian Land Grab*. New Delhi: Navdanya.
Siddiqui, Faizan Jawed. 2013. "Governing Urban Land: The Political Economy of the ULCRA in Mumbai." MA Thesis, Massachusetts Institute of Technology.
Singh, Dool. 1964. *Land Reform in Rajasthan: A Study of Evasion, Implementation, and Socio-Economic Effects*. New Delhi: Planning Commission, Government of India.
Singh, Kanhaiya, and Kaliappa Kalirajan. 2003. "A Decade of Economic Reforms in India: The Mining Sector." *Resources Policy* 29(3–4): 139–151.
Singh, Mridula, and Ranjan Kumar Samantray. 1992. "Whatever Happened to Muddavat Chenna? The Tale of Nagarjunasagar." In *Big Dams, Displaced People*, edited by Enakshi Ganguly Thukral, 54–76. New Delhi: Sage Publications.

Singh, Satyajit. 1997. *Taming the Waters: The Political Economy of Large Dams in India*. Delhi: Oxford University Press.

Sinha, Aseema. 2005. *The Regional Roots of Developmental Politics in India: A Divided Leviathan*. Bloomington: Indiana University Press.

Sisson, Richard. 1969. "Peasant Movements and Political Mobilization: The Jats of Rajasthan." *Asian Survey* 9(12): 946–963.

———. 1972. *The Congress Party in Rajasthan: Political Integration and Institution-Building in an Indian State*. Berkeley: University of California Press.

Sivaramakrishnan, K. 1999. *Modern Forests: Statemaking and Environmental Change in Colonial Eastern India*. Stanford: Stanford University Press.

Smelser, Neil. 1968. *Essays in Sociological Explanation*. Englewood Cliffs: Prentice Hall.

Smith, Adam. 1999. *The Wealth of Nations, Books I–III*. London: Penguin Books.

Sood, Jyotika. 2011. "Road to Disaster." *Down to Earth*, June 15.

Sreedathan, G. 2014. "RSS Outfit Ups the Ante on Land Acquisition Act." *Business Standard*, July 31.

Sridhar, Kala Seetharam, Shuzhong Gu, and Shujie Yao. 2013. "Land Sales as Public Financing Tool in China and India." In *China's Development and Harmonization: Towards a Balance with Nature, Society and the International Community*, edited by Bin Wu, Shujie Yao, and Jian Chen, 132–151. London: Routledge.

Srinivas, M. N. 1966. *Social Change in Modern India*. Berkeley: University of California Press.

———. 1976. *The Remembered Village*. New Delhi: Oxford University Press.

Srinivasalu, Karli. 2014. "Andhra Pradesh: Land Acquisition and Popular Resistance." In *Power, Policy and Protest: The Politics of India's Special Economic Zones*, edited by Rob Jenkins, Lorraine Kennedy, and Partha Mukhopadhyay, 72–107. New Delhi: Oxford University Press.

Srivastava, Ginny. 1995. "'Is "Bigger" Better, or Is "Small" Beautiful?' Displacement and Resettlement." In *The Resettlement of Project-Affected People: Proceedings of a Training Seminar Held at the HCM Rajasthan State Institute of Public Administration*, edited by Hari Mohan Mathur, 17–35. Jaipur: The HCM Rajasthan State Institute of Public Administration.

Srivastava, H. C., and M. K. Chaturvedi. 1986. *Rural Middlemen: Network of Patronage*. New Delhi: Ashish Publishing House.

Srivastava, I. C. 1995. "People Displaced by the Bisalpur Drinking Water-cum-Irrigation Project: Some Emerging Issues in Resettlement." In *The Resettlement of Project-Affected People: Proceedings of a Training Seminar Held at the HCM Rajasthan State Institute of Public Administration*, edited by Hari Mohan Mathur, 79–88. Jaipur: The HCM Rajasthan State Institute of Public Administration.

Srivastava, Punya S. 1995. "Population Displacement Associated with Industrial Development: The Case of Bhiwadi." In *The Resettlement of Project-Affected People: Proceedings of a Training Seminar Held at the HCM Rajasthan State Institute of Public Administration*, edited by Hari Mohan Mathur, 112–119. Jaipur: The HCM Rajasthan State Institute of Public Administration.

Srivastava, Sanjay. 2015. *Entangled Urbanism: Slum, Gated Community, and Shopping Mall in Delhi and Gurgaon*. Oxford University Press: New Delhi.

Standing, Guy. 2011. *The Precariat: The New Dangerous Class*. London: Bloomsbury.

Stern, Robert. 1988. *The Cat and the Lion: Jaipur State in the British Raj*. Leiden: E. J. Brill.

Struempell, Christian. 2014. "The Politics of Dispossession in an Odisha Steel Town." *Contributions to Indian Sociology* 48(1): 45–72.

Sud, Nikita. 2009. "The Indian State in a Liberalizing Landscape." *Development and Change* 40(4): 645–665.

———. 2012. *Liberalization, Hindu Nationalism and the State: A Biography of Gujarat*. New Delhi: Oxford University Press.

———. 2014a. "The Men in the Middle: A Missing Dimension in Global Land Deals." *Journal of Peasant Studies* 41(4): 593–612.

———. 2014b. "Governing India's Land." *World Development* 60: 43–56.

Sullivan, LaShandra. 2013. "Identity, Territory and Land Conflict in Brazil." *Development and Change* 44(2): 451–471.

Sundar, Nandini. 2006. "Bastar, Maoism and Salwa Judum." *Economic and Political Weekly* 41(29): 3187–3192.

———. 2007. *Subalterns and Sovereigns: An Anthropological History of Bastar, 1954–2006*. New Delhi: Oxford University Press.

———. 2013. "Reflections on Civil Liberties, Citizenship, Adivasi Agency and Maoism: A Response to Alpa Shah." *Critique of Anthropology* 33(3): 361–368.

———. 2016. *The Burning Forest: India's War in Bastar*. New Delhi: Juggernaut Press.

Tehelka. 2014. "Land Ahoy!" *Tehelka*, July 26.

The Economist. 2014a. "A Bad Boom: Fighting Corruption in India." *The Economist*, March 14.

———. 2014b. "Planet Plutocrat: Our Crony-Capitalism Index." *The Economist*, May 15.

The Hindu. 2012. "Senior Official Probing Vadra-DLF Land Deal Shunted Out." *The Hindu*, October 16.

The Telegraph. 2007. "'Prohibiting the use of Agricultural Land for Industries is Ultimately Self-Defeating.'" *The Telegraph*, July 23.

Thompson, E. P. 1966. *The Making of the English Working Class*. New York: Vintage Books.

———. 1975. *Whigs and Hunters: The Origin of the Black Act*. New York: Pantheon.

Thorner, Daniel. 1956. "Feudalism in India." In *Feudalism in History*, edited by Rushton Coulborn, 133–150. Princeton: Princeton University Press.

Thukral, Enakshi Ganguly, ed. 1992. *Big Dams, Displaced People*. New Delhi: Sage Publications.

———. 1996. "Development, Displacement and Rehabilitation: Locating Gender." *Economic and Political Weekly* 31(24): 1500–1503.

Tilly, Charles. 1978. *From Mobilization to Revolution*. Reading: Addison-Wesley Pub. Co.

———. 1993. "Contentious Repertoires in Great Britain, 1758–1834." *Social Science History* 17(2): 253–280.

Times of India. 2010. "Sonia Launches Five-Fold Attack on Corruption." *Times of India*, December 20.

———. 2011. "Five RIICO Officials Land in ACB Trap for Graft." *Times of India*, August 3.

———. 2012. "'Prithviraj Nagar Scheme Will Be Like a Slum.'" *Times of India*, April 13.

Tod, James. 1997[1829]. *Annals and Antiquities of Rajasthan, Vols. 1 and 2*. New Delhi: Rupa Publications.

United Nations. 1961. *Establishment of Industrial Estates in Under-Developed Countries*. New York: United Nations Department of Economic and Social Affairs.

Upadhya, Carol. 2007. "Employment, Exclusion, and 'Merit' in the Indian IT Industry." *Economic and Political Weekly* 42(20): 1863–1868.

———. 2011. "Software and the 'New' Middle Class in the 'New India.'" In *Elite and Everyman: The Cultural Politics of the Indian Middle Classes*, edited by Amita Baviskar and Raka Ray, 167–192. New Delhi: Routledge.

———. 2016. *Reengineering India: Work, Capital, and Class in an Offshore Economy*. New Delhi: Oxford University Press.

Upadhya, Carol, and A. R. Vasavi, eds. 2008. *In an Outpost of the Global Economy: Work and Workers in India's Information Technology Industry*. London: Routledge.

———. 2008. "Outposts of the Global Information Economy: Work and Workers in India's Outsourcing Industry." In *Outposts of the Global Information Economy: Work and Workers in India's Outsourcing Industry*, edited by Carol Upadhya and A. R. Vasavi, 9–49. London: Routledge.

Varshney, Ashutosh. 1995. *Democracy, Development, and the Countryside: Urban-Rural Struggles in India*. Cambridge: Cambridge University Press.

Vasavi, A. R. 2012. *Shadow Space: Suicide and the Predicament of Rural India*. Gurgaon: Three Essays Collective.

Venkatesan, J. 2011. "Land Acquisition Act Has Become an Engine of Oppression: Court." *The Hindu*, July 6.

Verghese, Ajay. 2015. "British Rule and Tribal Revolts in India: The Curious Case of Bastar." *Modern Asian Studies* 5(50): 1619–1644.

Verma, Rubina. 2012. "Structural Transformation and Jobless Growth in the Indian Economy." In *Oxford Handbook of the Indian Economy*, edited by Chetan Ghate, 276–310. Oxford: Oxford University Press.

Viegas, Philip. 1992. "The Hirakud Oustees: Thirty Years After." In *Big Dams, Displaced People*, edited by Enakshi Ganguly Thukral, 29–53. New Delhi: Sage Publications.

Vijayabaskar, M. 2014. "Tamil Nadu: The Politics of Silence." In *Power, Policy and Protest: The Politics of India's Special Economic Zones*, edited by Rob Jenkins, Lorraine Kennedy, and Partha Mukhopadhyay, 304–331. New Delhi: Oxford University Press.

Vyas, N. N. 1995. "The Social Consequences of Resettlement on Tribals of Southern Rajasthan: A Case Study of Kadana Project." In *The Resettlement of Project-Affected People: Proceedings of a Training Seminar Held at the HCM Rajasthan State Institute of Public Administration*, edited by Hari Mohan Mathur, 45–56. Jaipur: The HCM Rajasthan State Institute of Public Administration.

Wacquant, Loïc. 2008. "The Militarization of Urban Marginality: Lessons from the Brazilian Metropolis." *International Political Sociology* 2(1): 56–74.

———. 2010. "Crafting the Neoliberal State: Workfare, Prisonfare, and Social Insecurity." *Sociological Forum* 25(2): 197–220.

Wallerstein, Emmanuel. 2011. *The Modern World System III: The Second Era of Great Expansion of the Capitalist World Economy, 1730s–1840s*. Berkeley: University of California Press.

Warren, Bill. 1980. *Imperialism: Pioneer of Capitalism*. London: New Left Books.

Watts, Michael. 1983. *Silent Violence: Food, Famine, and Peasantry in Northern Nigeria*. Berkeley: University of California Press.

———. 2004. "Resource Curse?: Governmentality, Oil and Power in the Niger Delta, Nigeria." *Geopolitics* 9(1): 50–80.

WCD (World Commission on Dams). 2000. *Dams and Development: A New Framework for Decision-Making*. London: Earthscan.

Weber, Max. 1958. *The Protestant Ethic and the Spirit of Capitalism*. New York: Charles Scribner's Sons.

———. 1978. *Economy and Society*, edited by Guenther Roth and Claus Wittich. Berkeley: University of California Press.

White, Ben, Saturnino M. Borras Jr., Ruth Hall, Ian Scoones, and Wendy Wolford. 2012. "The New Enclosures: Critical Perspectives on Corporate Land Deals." *Journal of Peasant Studies* 39(3–4): 619–647.

Whitehead, Judy. 2010. "John Locke and the Governance of India's Landscape: The Category of Wasteland in Colonial Revenue and Forest Legislation." *Economic and Political Weekly* 45(50): 83–93.

Williams, Raymond. 1976. *Keywords: A Vocabulary of Culture and Society*. New York: Oxford University Press.

———. 1985. *The Country and the City*. London: The Hogarth Press.

Willis, Paul. 1977. *Learning to Labor: How Working Class Kids Get Working Class Jobs*. New York: Columbia University Press.

Witsoe, Jeffrey. 2013. *Democracy Against Development: Lower-Caste Politics and Political Modernity in Postcolonial India*. Chicago: University of Chicago Press.

Wolf, Eric R. 1966. *Peasants*. Englewood Cliffs: Prentice Hall.

———. 1999[1969]. *Peasant Wars of the Twentieth Century*. Norman: University of Oklahoma Press.

Wolf, Diane Lauren. 1992. *Factory Daughters: Gender, Household Dynamics, and Rural Industrialization in Java*. Berkeley: University of California Press.

Wolford, Wendy, Saturnino M. Borras, Ruth Hall, Ian Scoones, and Ben White. 2013. "Governing Global Land Deals: The Role of the State in the Rush for Land." *Development and Change* 44(2): 189–210.

Wood, Ellen Meiksins. 2002. *The Origin of Capitalism: A Longer View*. London: Verso.

Wood, Neal. 1984. *John Locke and Agrarian Capitalism*. Berkeley: University of California Press.

Woodhouse, Philip. 2012. "New Investment, Old Challenges: Land Deals and the Water Constraint in African Agriculture." *Journal of Peasant Studies* 39(3–4): 777–794.

World Bank. 2004. *Sustaining India's Service Revolution: Access to Foreign Markets, Domestic Reform and International Negotiations.* Washington D.C.: World Bank.

———. 2006. *Rajasthan: Closing the Development Gap.* Washington, D.C.: World Bank.

———. 2007. *India: Land Policies for Growth and Poverty Reduction.* New Delhi: Oxford University Press.

———. 2014. "Agricultural Irrigated Land (% of Total Agricultural Land)." Available at: https://data.worldbank.org/indicator/AG.LND.IRIG.AG.ZS?view=chart [accessed November 1, 2017].

Zachariah, Benjamin. 2005. *Developing India: An Intellectual History, c. 1930–50.* Delhi: Oxford University Press.

Zoomers, Anneleis. 2010. "Globalisation and the Foreignisation of Space: Seven Processes Driving the Current Global Land Grab." *Journal of Peasant Studies* 37(2): 429–447.

INDEX

The manufacturer's authorised representative in the EU for product safety is Oxford University Press España S.A. of El Parque Empresarial San Fernando de Henares, Avenida de Castilla, 2 - 28830 Madrid (www.oup.es/en or product.safety@oup.com). OUP España S.A. also acts as importer into Spain of products made by the manufacturer.
Printed and bound by CPI Group (UK) Ltd, Croydon, CR0 4YY
14/09/2026
02216286-0012